Cadillacs

OF THE FORTIES

BY
ROY A. SCHNEIDER

CADILLACS OF THE FORTIES

Copyright © 1976 by Roy A. Schneider. This book was manufactured in the United States of America and published simultaneously in the United Kingdom. Copyrighted under International and Pan-American Copyright Conventions. All rights reserved. No part of this work may be reproduced or copied in any form or by any means — graphic, electronic, or mechanical, including photocopying, recording, taping, or information and retrieval systems — without written permission of the publisher, except in the case of brief quotations embodied in critical articles and reviews.

LIBRARY OF CONGRESS CATALOG CARD NUMBER: 76-7120
I.S.B.N. 0-917104-01-3

PRINTED IN THE
UNITED STATES OF AMERICA

FIRST EDITION 1976
SECOND EDITION 1988

Published by
CADILLAC MOTORBOOKS
A Division of Royco
POST OFFICE BOX 7
TEMPLE CITY, CALIFORNIA 91780

THE DE WAR TROPHY, WON IN A FAMOUS STANDARDIZATION TEST—AND THE BASIS FOR CADILLAC'S RANKING, "STANDARD OF THE WORLD."

★

To the Repositories of the Sacred Heritage

the Members of the:

Cadillac—LaSalle Clubs of America and Australia

Contemporary Historical Vehicle Association

Antique Automobile Club of America

Classic Car Club of America

Copyright © 1976 by Roy A. Schneider. All rights reserved.
Illustrative materials are fully covered by copyright
either at the source or by the author and/or publisher.

CONTENTS

		Page
	Publisher's Foreword	6
	Prologue	8
1940	The End of an Era	15
1941	A Timeless Masterpiece	39
1942	A Prelude to War	71
1946-1947	From Reconversion to Full Production	93
1948	Tail-Fins	123
1949	The Overhead Eight	143
	Appendix I: Production, Prices and Accessories	176
	Appendix II: Special Features	184
	Appendix III: Service Man Excerpts	193
	Appendix IV: Clubs for the Enthusiast	236
	Index	238

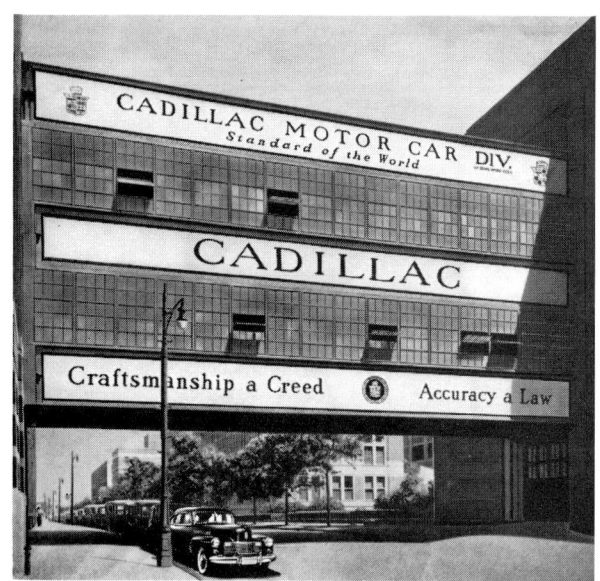

PUBLISHER'S FOREWORD

Perennial leadership in the world's largest manufacturing business does not come easily, yet for generations of Americans one word has conveyed meticulous quality in the manufacture of automobiles. That word is Cadillac, the personification of unsurpassed luxury, rugged dependability, imperious craftsmanship, fine styling, and meritorious engineering. Cadillac, the oldest of Detroit's automakers, maintained its position into the 1970s because nearly every employee sensed and sought to preserve that charactertistic, incisive heritage that alone belonged to the *Standard of the World*.

Cadillac is a name that comes often to the lips of vintage automobile connissuers and sophisticated collectors. There isn't another American luxury marque that, for generation after generation, has had such significant impact on the psyche of the nation's motoring masses. Cadillac's historic contributions during the quarter century preceeding World War II can be matched only by its own technical and styling triumphs in the 25 years that followed. The subject at hand, the 1940s, is rooted of both of these periods of unparalleled progress.

Of the three hundred and forty-five thousand Cadillac motorcars manufactured during the Forties literally thousands survive today. They form a conspicuous part of the magnificent automobiles of the past that command so much respect and interest today. Accordingly, this book is intended for both those who remember and loved these machines when they were the ultimate in contemporary transportation, and those of a later generation who now share this common enthusiasm.

Inasmuch as a wealth of technical information exists in the form of service and body manuals (out of print but widely available) originally published by the Cadillac Motor Car and Fisher Body Divisions of General Motors, this book is not an exhaustive technical work. It is rather a record that traces the year-by-year progression of models with the emphasis on photographs. To the fullest extent possible original factory photographs have been used since they transcend the years providing a graphic account of the original vehicles against backgrounds contemporary to the period. The majority of photographs presented here have never been published before. The primarily sources for these photographs are the combined collections of David R. Holls, Strother C. MacMinn and the author. The author's file of photographic materials was supplemented by contributions from the Cadillac Motor Car Division and the Detroit and Philadelphia Public Libraries. A complete listing of photographic credits and acknowledgments appears below.

Jack Ashcraft—pages 15, 39, 71, 93, 123, 136, 137, 143. Gene Babow—page 79, Rodney Brewer—pages 110 center and bottom, 111. Charles Coleman—page 36 center, 119 top. Larry Fournier—page 173. Frank Hershey—pages 124, 135 bottom. Dave Holls—pages 9, 10, 12 top, 13 top, 16, 17, 19, 20 top, 21, 31, 34, 36 top, 38, 40, 42, 43, 48 top, 50, 51, 53 top, 56, 58 center, 59, 63 top, 64 top and center, 65 top, 68 top, 73, 74, 80, 81, 82, 83, 91 top, 127, 134 top, 165. Cliff Houser—pages 147, 158, 159. Ralph Liebendorfer—page 65 bottom, Strother MacMinn—pages 36 bottom, 37, 120, 121, 140, 172, 173, 175. John Meyer III— 61 center, 88, 89 bottom, 237. George Moffitt—118, 119 bottom. Grayson Nichols—85 top, 86 top, 109, 110 top, 125, 139 top, 160 bottom, 236. Joseph Regan—161 top. Bolton Smith—page 164 top. Carl Steig—page 139. Ron VanGelderen—54 top, 163 top, center. Malcolm Willits—pages 48, 49. Calvin Wright—page 117. Uncredited photographs are from the author's files. SERVICEMAN excerpts on pages 193 through 235 were provided by the Harry Schulman and Carl L. Steig private collections.

Among individuals who are gratefully remembered for providing suggestions and information are: Charlotte Anderson, Robert G. Anderson, Jack Ashcraft, Rodney Brewer, Norbert B. Bartos, Allan R. Bartz, Jere Clark, Thomas N. Clarke, Larry Fournier, Grayson Nichols, Frank Q. Hershey, David R. Holls, Ralph Liebendorfer, Strother C. MacMinn, Joan Maki, John C. Meyer III, William L. Mitchell, George A. Moffitt, B. W. Reese, Bobbie'dine Rodda, Harry Schulman, Carl L. Steig, Ron VanGelderen, and Robert A. Zecher.

Many photographs appearing in this book originally came from the files of the Cadillac Motor Car Division and GM Styling. Photographers working with these entities made frequent use of rooftops for reasons of convenience and security.

PROLOGUE

Anyone interested in the history of automobile progress must necessarily devote most of his time to Cadillac. For not only has Cadillac manufactured motor cars almost since the industry's beginning, but from Cadillac has come nearly every basic advancement of permanent worth.

This brief quotation from the 1942 Cadillac sales brochure is an appropriate preamble to any discussion of the marque's compelling heritage. The epochal engineering triumphs of those first 40 years ran the gamut from the self-starter to the first practical completely automatic transmission.

There was nothing, *circa* 1940, smoother and quieter than the Cadillac V-8. It was an engine that never betrayed the slightest hint of roughness or strain. When it idled only the position of the ammeter was evidence that the motor was running. The L-head V-8 of the 1940s was essentially the design introduced in 1936 and modified in 1937. This proven powerplant in a time-honored chassis represented the heart of a Cadillac, for in its chassis Cadillac engineering and craftsmanship perpetuated the traditions of unparalleled leadership.

Body styling also played an important role in Cadillac history from 1927 to the onset of the 1940s. Although rapid evolution swept the industry during those years, there was a certain continuity in Cadillac designs.

General Motors' senior marque displayed a consistent willingness to carry the automaker's art beyond utilitarian function, and beyond stylistic plateaus, to constitute new levels of motoring fashion. The year-to-year changes were sometimes subtle, and other times dramatic, but they were always determined by an intensive esthetic evaluation of function and appropriateness. Harmony, balance and symmetry, the inalienable requisites of beauty, were consistently fused with such clarity that a tangible school of Cadillac design emerged.

Many who read this book will already have refined their powers of perception and discrimination to the point of recognizing Cadillac character. There were other approaches within the industry, including a few of substantial merit, but when full consideration and study is made of the state of the art, prevailing economics and relative esthetic values, Cadillac, then as now, inevitably emerges as the style leader.

New concepts of appearance are rare in the business of automobile styling. In Cadillac's case the automobiles of the 1930s and most of the 1940s received their formal proportions from three basic conceptual forms.

The first came in 1927 with the marketing of the LaSalle, an American production car endowed with the lean, low, gently curving horizontal lines that had theretofore been equated with the costly products of Europe's finest coachbuilders. The LaSalle's instant popularity signaled a significant change in the industry, and served as the primary insight which established style as a pre-eminent factor in the mass production and distribution of American automobiles. Clamshell fenders, massive chrome radiator shells, deep-drawn headlights, wire wheels, fine detailing and classical utilitarian shapes became the hallmarks of the 1927-through-1933 era.

The second major influence came in 1934. Julio Andrade's proposal for the LaSalle of that year combined esthetic principles of elegance with the precepts of aerodynamics. The result was pivotal not only for Cadillac-LaSalle, but provided the initial design approach General Motors adopted in the primal age of streamlining. Pontoon fenders, shrouded radiators, bullet-shaped lamp housings and air-foil body shapes produced a dramatic evolution in form.

The third phase of development evolved from yet another LaSalle proposal. A team led by a prodigious young stylist named William L. Mitchell re-evaluated and scrutinized every element of contemporary automobile design. They discarded convention, questioned tradition; when they finished, every component, line and shadow of their 1938 LaSalle prototype revealed a fresh, vigorous, new approach.

Familiar items such as running boards, belt mouldings, exposed spare tires, separate headlights and free-standing tail lights were either eliminated or integrated into the architecture of the new body. A distinctive upper structure had thinner roof lines, narrower windshield pillars, thin chrome upper door frames and solid rear quarters. Fenders in a modified pontoon motif terminated with vertical trailing edges. There was a one-piece hood that hinged at the back, and a rear deck that projected generously to enclose a large luggage compartment. Most importantly, every body panel, glass area, trim item and sheetmetal component blended with striking appeal.

Cadillac accepted the low and attractive design and placed it in production as the 1938 Sixty-Special. The entry of this revolutionary new car into the market brought favorable and wide acclaim from both private and industry quarters.

Above, the design proposal from William "Bill" Mitchell's studio which became the Cadillac Sixty-Special of 1938. It served as the basis of GM styling in the early 1940s and marked a milestone in automotive design that would influence the shape of American cars for decades. In its original mock-up form, seen here, it bore LaSalle insignias, grill and hood side panels.

Two views of the first Sixty-Special, the 1938 Style 38-60196S. Its distinctive grill, low sweeping fenders, trim body lines and extended trunk gave it an enduring identity. Structural innovations lowered the floor in relation to ground level and facilitated entrance and exit without running boards.

A new double-drop frame with a large kickup over the rear axle, and the use of an exceptionally sturdy X member in conjunction with side rails of reduced depth, allowed the floor level to be three inches lower than on previous models. In 1938 and 1939 the all-steel bodies with steel floors and one-piece roofs were mounted and trimmed at Cadillac's facilities on Clark Avenue in Detroit, hence these first two editions of the Sixty-Special carried Fisher body tags.

The horizontally-finned grill of 1938 imparted a front end boldness that was discomposed by the unique fine-ribbed deviation of 1939. In both years headlight mountings, license plate brackets, hood side panels, bumpers, wheel discs, instrumentation and dash paralleled companion Cadillacs of the same model years. A wide range of optional special features were offered including leather or fabric coverings on the roof and quarters, special quality upholstery fabrics (including leather), Fleetwood-type trimming motifs, and, in 1939, a sun roof.

Mr. Mitchell's prototype and the subsequent Sixty-Specials are relative to the history of Cadillac in the Forties because all 1940-through-1947 models are a direct extension of the design philosophy developed in the earlier period. William "Bill" Mitchell became supervisor of the Cadillac Studio in 1937 and his group subsequently experimented with broadening the Sixty-Special line. During 1938 two convertible sedans were actually built and a full-size mockup of a two-passenger coupe was completed. Although these handsome proposals never reached production, together with the Sixty-Specials they laid the styling cornerstones for the *torpedo* bodies introduced on 1940 Cadillacs, LaSalles, Buicks and Oldsmobiles.

Below, one of two Sixty-Special convertible sedans built and driven by Cadillac officials during 1938. When one was involved in an accident the other was recalled and evaluated by body engineers preparing the 1940 C-Series convertible sedans. Neither of these prototypes is known to have survived.

Above, a mock-up 1938 Sixty-Special coupe. Although never produced, excercises like this were evolutionary steps in formulating the proportions of the 1940 C-Series bodies. Below, GM's styling chief Harley Earl with the "Y-job," an experimental Buick which featured design innovations that influenced all GM cars in the 1940s.

Above, the 1939 Sixty-Special with its fine-ribbed grill and hood side-panel ports presented a more conservative appearance. Two-color paint combinations were $20 extra, and any color(s) other than standard could be specified for a charge of $25. Fenders finished in a color other than that of the body ran $12.50. Below, Bill Mitchell standing beside a full-size blackboard rendering of the 1939 Sixty-Special. This photograph of Mr. Mitchell, who succeeded Harley Earl as GM's styling chief, was taken in early 1938.

1940

The style-leading 1940 Sixty-Special.

THE END OF AN ERA

    Styles tend to reflect the mood of the times and at Cadillac during 1940 there was a sense of immediacy and impending change. The decade's first year was a pivotal one: The eleven-year reign of the V-16 supercars would be ended, the legendary LaSalle — a consistent favorite with style-conscious buyers since 1927 — would have its last season, and the time-honored Fleetwood custom program — providing large luxury cars in limitless variety from convertibles to towncars — would be curtailed. It was the end of one age and the beginning of another. Revered traditions were bowing to the realities of an evolving social and economic order.

    The drop-out grill featured on 1939 models (called that because at a distance it was indistinguishable from the rest of the car) was given a completely different texture in 1940. The die-cast radiator grill with a sharply V-ed center was carefully restructured with fewer and more-prominent horizontal bars. The harmonizing bumpers were imprinted with the first modern script lettering of the Cadillac name. Long narrow parking lamps incorporating turn signals crowned the front fenders, and sealed beam headlamps were moulded into the hood side panels. The vertical cooling grills on the catwalks flanking the grill were revamped in what was called the *mail-slot* motif. These elements combined to form a distinctive new front ensemble.

    In every era the advertising and sales literature published by Cadillac was lavish and represented the finest in contemporary lithographic art. The magnificent Cadillac-Fleetwood catalog for 1940 was no exception. Its 14'' by 16'' pages provided graphic evidence of the pre-eminence Fleetwood represented in the field of coachcraft. It declared the Sixty-Special and the 75-Series to be *General Motors' masterpieces*.

    Nineteen-forty was the first model year during which the Sixty-Special was built and trimmed at Fleetwood. The standard interior for the third edition of Mr. Mitchell's masterpiece was enhanced by a revised upholstery motif and use of leather trim on seat back, door panels and piping for upholstery. In addition to the standard selections,

Fleetwood cataloged a host of interior options ranging from special finishes on the instrument panel to an electrically operated division glass between compartments ($140 extra). As could be expected, the Fleetwood shops worked their magic on the Sixty-Special stampings and created a towncar which was added to the regular line.

The standard Sixty-Special again carried a base price of $2,090 as it had during 1938 and 1939. The *Sunshine Turret-Top,* a sliding steel panel inset in the roof which when opened exposed the front compartment to the sky, and welled fenders were reoffered extra-cost options.

Several custom Sixty-Specials were also completed during 1940 for important members of GM's corporate hierarchy. The executive models were usually lengthened five inches via frame graft and wider doors, and lowered two inches by reducing window height. These extremely attractive Sixty-Specials had padded leather tops, landau bars on the quarters, special wheel discs, V-16 fender spears, metal stone guards and lavishly appointed interiors.

Long, low and traditionally proportioned, the 75-Series cars had an outward beauty and distinction peculiarly their own. They were impressively large, yet outstandingly graceful. Staunchly built steel bodies had wide seats, generous floor space and abundant conveniences. Beautifully fashioned interiors could be described only as regal. To the Cadillac and Fleetwood union, fifteen years old by 1940, this first year of the new decade marked the final complete edition of luxury motorcars on long wheelbases. Two coupes, two formal sedans, a convertible coupe, a convertible sedan, a town sedan, a towncar and four conventional three-window sedans comprised the last full 75-Series. In 1940 they accounted for merely two-and-one-half percent of the production total.

Rarest of all 1940 Cadillacs were, of course, the Sixteens. Only 61 units were built in this, their last year. The bold styling established in 1938 was retained through 1940, although bumpers, running boards, parking lights, tail lights, license mounting, dash, door panel motif and certain interior fitments were updated each year to parallel the corresponding 75-Series cars. The V-16's massive vertical grill with its commanding pattern of cross-hatched bars played a decisive role in determining the texture of the 1941 grill. The Sixteens are more thoroughly discussed in SIXTEEN CYLINDER MOTORCARS (Heritage House 1974).

Alongside the LaSalle and luxurious Fleetwood-built V-8s and V-16s, Cadillac dealers unveiled two new series of cars in the Fall of 1939. The first was the 62-Series,

Left, a variation on the prow look which was the front end theme for GM cars in 1939 and 1940. Many proposals such as this were studied in the search for a suitable grill for the 1940 Cadillac.

Opposite, a 1940 Cadillac B-body proposal with two borrowed ideas; V-16 hood ports and a vertical eggcrate grill. Cadillac dropped the B-bodied 61-Series in 1940; LaSalles, however, were offered with both B and C type bodies throughout the model year. (A-type bodies were used on smaller GM cars like Chevrolet. The B-type bodies went on intermediate size cars and C-type bodies were designed for luxury models.)

dubbed *The Newest Car in the World* by the advertising department. The organizational word for the new 62s was the *projectile* or *torpedo* design. They were longer, sleeker and more streamlined than cars of the preceding year. Windshields had an increased rake, rear windows were curved, door hinges were concealed, running boards were optional and sidemounts were available only upon special order. The tapering lines of the rear deck, the convex body curve below the windows and the absence of a belt moulding were indicative of the close relationship to the Sixty-Specials. The 62-Series consisted of a five-passenger sedan and a four-passenger coupe when introduced in late 1939; mid-year augmentations to the line included a convertible coupe and a convertible sedan.

With the Sixty-Special and the 62-Series the vista into the new decade was established for the conventional passenger car business. Now Cadillac and GM Styling turned their attention toward the minority but ever-profitable seven-passenger vehicle. Nicholas Dreystadt, General Manager of Cadillac since 1934, made it clear that spreading 2,000 75-Series sales over more than a dozen body styles placed an economic burden on the balance of the line. Now that the custom body era had all but faded away, the Cadillac-Fleetwood of the future would have to consolidate in terms of body types.

Thus the second new series for 1940 was the 72, an ultra-modern, limousine-sized, Fleetwood-built Cadillac with dignified styling which would last a decade. It had a 138-inch wheelbase and was offered in eight variations — all using the same basic body shell — ranging from formal limousine to five-passenger sedan. Its body panels were carefully contoured so that the roof line, quarter windows, trunk and rear fenders had trailing edges that followed a common curve. Chrome reveals encircled the windows constituting a pleasing departure for cars of such size. A broad belt moulding, which had door handles inset, added a balancing touch. The 45-degree sloping windshield, the 100 percent steel body and the recirculating-ball-type steering gear were major engineering advances introduced on the 72.

Under the hood there were minor modifications in manifolding and carburetion which provided vapor-lock protection, additional fuel economy and improved performance in the V-8 engine. Cadillac essentially eliminated the percolating problem that affected many cars during the 1930s. Percolating — gasoline boiling in the fuel pump, fuel lines or carburetor — occurred on unusually warm days when the engine was being operated at low speeds. The fuel pump and fuel lines would fail to receive a sufficient flow of cool air; thus, the combination of atmospheric and engine heat induced a potential vapor-lock condition. The enlarged frontal ram (air-intake) area introduced on 1939 Cadillacs alleviated the problem to a great degree and in 1940 the capacity of the fuel pump was increased by 25 percent as further insurance against vapor-locks.

Occasionally one will hear that Cadillac L-head engines were hard-starting when new. This myth developed when second, third and fourth owners acquired cars with worn or poorly-maintained engines. The major factor affecting starting was — and still is — poor compression caused by improperly seated or warped valves, and/or worn piston rings.

A condition almost certain to be present was an impaired cooling system. Cadillac Service recommended periodic flushing of the block with water and air pressure. Failure to perform this procedure allowed rust and scale deposits to combine into a mud-like substance that blocked water passages and clogged the radiator. Malfunctioning radiator shutters and water pump failure also caused heating problems that precipitated hard starting.

Worn starters, dirty carburetors, slack in the timing chain, ignition failure — even weak batteries — contributed to this myth. Any one of these conditions could cause hard starting, especially when the car was hot, but in many instances veteran engines had a combination of problems. Considering the obstacles it is surprising that many of the older engines started at all. A well-tuned flathead in good repair should start immediately on 6 volts under any conditions including the warmest of weather.

A brief discussion of overheating would be in order at this point. According to Cadillac owners' manuals printed during this period: *The needle (temperature indicator) should register within the NORMAL range except on long, hard drives (especially grades) in summer weather, when it may register HOT. This condition need not cause alarm, as the pressure-operated overflow will normally prevent water losses at temperatures up to 245 degrees Fahrenheit. When the engine does run hot on long drives it is important to check the oil and water levels frequently. If the indicator should show HOT during short runs under normal driving conditions, the cause should be investigated.*

This investigation should begin with a determination of whether the temperature gauge is transmitting accurate information. If indeed the cooling fluid is hot and the shutters (on pre-1942 cars) are completely open the problem can sometimes be traced to the failure of either the radiator pressure cap or the water pump. A new radiator cap rated for five or six pounds is normally sufficient to prevent fluid loss.

Some commercial parts-rebuilding firms are now installing improved seals, stainless steel shafts and bronze impellers in older type water pumps. This is a positive step in the Cadillac L-head engine since the water pump seal must be leak-proof, not only to avoid the loss of cooling liquid, but to prevent air from being drawn into the cooling system. In years past many of these cars were allowed to operate for extended periods with faulty water pumps and serious corrosion developed in the block as a result of aeration of the cooling fluid which caused foaming and promoted oxidation.

A loose water pump drive belt, a restricted exhaust system, sludge in the engine lubricating system, improper ignition timing, or faulty carburetion can also cause symptomatic overheating.

If all of the systems and components mentioned above are deemed to be operating properly and the overheating persists, the problem is in the radiator and block. Occasionally a leaking head gasket or cracked valve seat can be the cause, but in the vast majority of cases the water passages within the block itself, and the tubes in the radiator, are in need of a thorough cleaning. A reputable radiator shop can "rod-out" the radiator; however it should not be installed until the block has been flushed using the water-air procedure outlined in the appendix.

For engines with more serious problems the answer has always been professional quality rebuilding. Considering the availability of parts, the L-head powerplants of the 1940s are inexpensive to restore, and once properly rebuilt they will last indefinitely in a vehicle used mainly for hobby activities.

This stunning wood-metal mock-up was the sight-model for the 1940 62-Series sedan. Rear fenders on this model have no wheel openings; it was crafted in this manner to illustrate with maximum effect the visual aspects and obvious allure of skirted rear fenders.

Below, the attractively balanced dash for 1940 was highlighted with chrome and plastic. Fleetwood used the burled walnut finish for the 75 and 90-Series instrument panels and as seen in this photograph; wood grain was used in some custom Sixty-Specials. Standard instrument panels in 60 and 62-Series cars were painted. Another interesting feature to be noted in this 40-6019SA is 1941-type walnut garnish panels on the doors.

Fleetwood BODIES

Fleetwood's 75-Series employed the same body shells from 1938 through 1940. Opposite page, a three-window sedan proposal with a modified 1938 Sixty-Special-type grill.

Right and below, this 75-Series styling model was, with minor change, okayed for production in March of 1939. This coachwork was typical on Styles 7519, 7519F, 7533 and 7523.

1940 SERIES SEVENTY-FIVE

Illustrations on this and the facing page are from the DeLuxe Cadillac-Fleetwood catalog for 1940. Opposite page, five of the seven basic body types which comprised the 75-Series in 1940. The three-window sedan on the preceding page and the formal sedans (similar in appearance to the towncar but without an open front compartment) were the other models in the line.

Above, the jump seats and division partition featured in Styles 7533 and 7533F. High-back jump seats were typical in seven-passenger models through 1947. Center, the division partition and opera seats used in Style 7559. Below left, the well appointed rear compartments of 75-Series cars were accessible through exceptionally wide doors. Below right, the interior of Style 7557B, a five-passenger coupe. Wood paneling around 75-Series windows was walnut inlaid with sycamore.

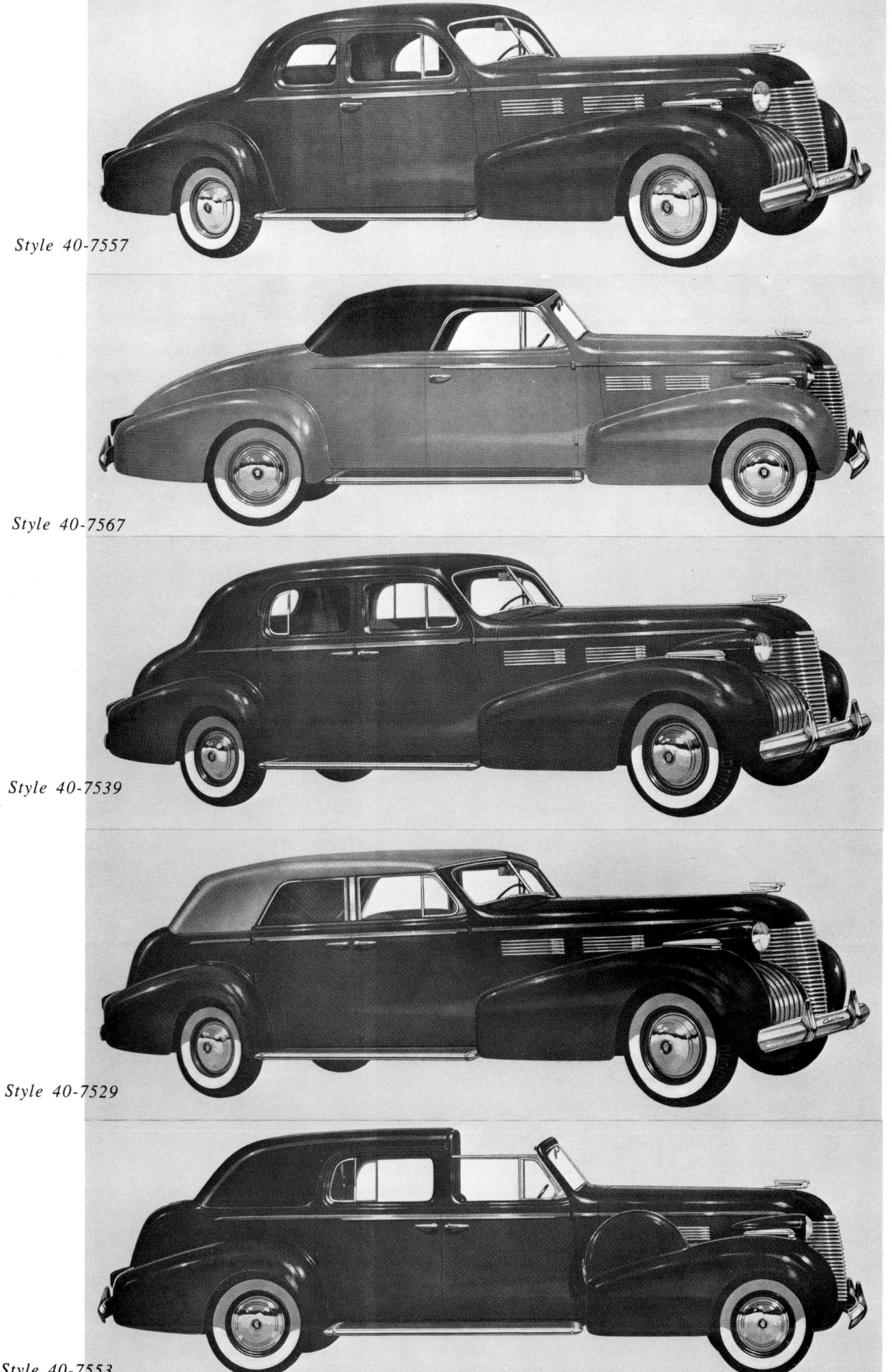

Style 40-7557

Style 40-7567

Style 40-7539

Style 40-7529

Style 40-7553

In many ways the custom Sixty-Specials built for GM's top executives were the ultimate in vehicular elegance during the early Forties. This lengthened and lowered example was crafted for William S. Knudsen who had become President of GM in 1937. The combination of leather and fabric on seat cushions and backs was a portent of the future. Electric windows were controlled by rocker located on the garnish panel of each door.

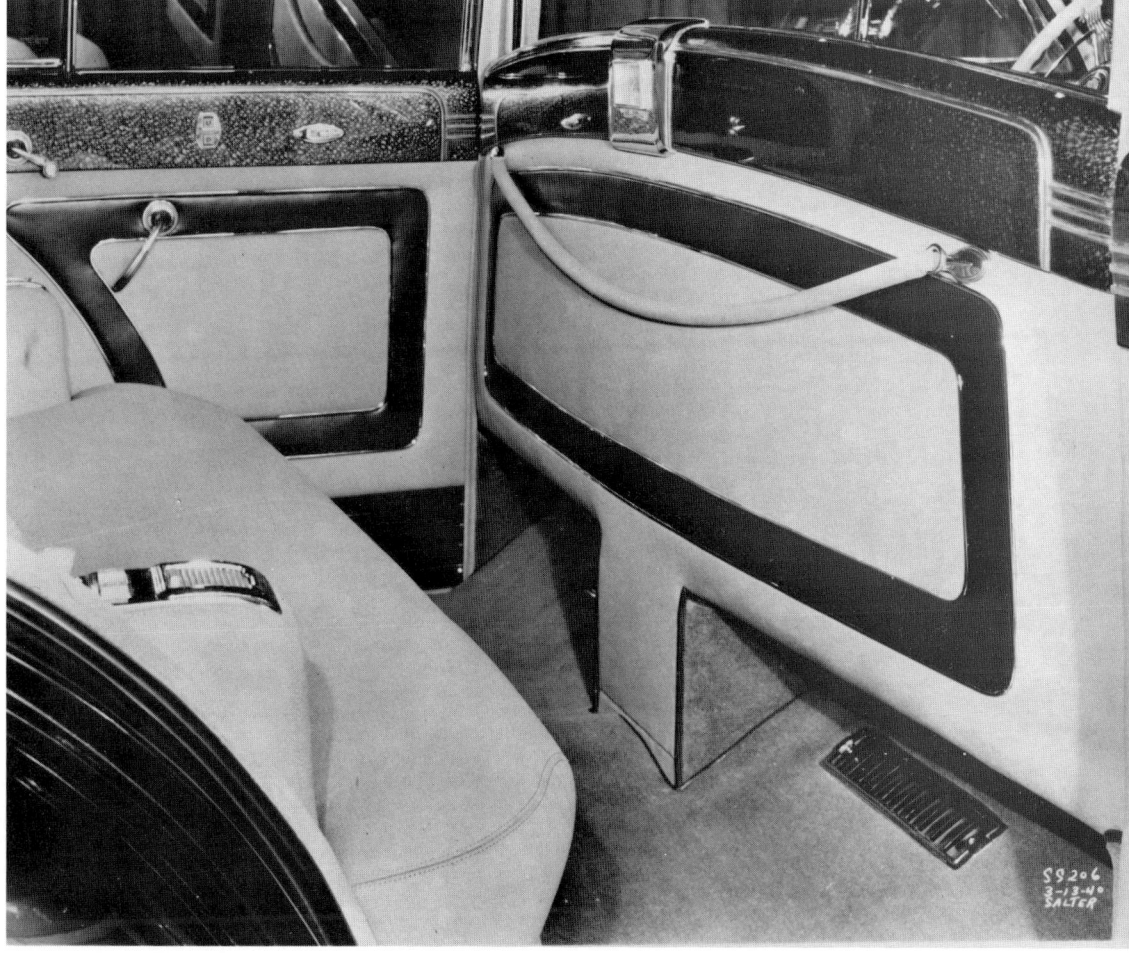

1940 SERIES SIXTY-TWO

Left, two views of the 62-Series coupe for four passengers — style 40-6227. The two lower photographs on this page illustrate the graphic effectiveness of two-tone paint plans.

Below, 1940 was the last model year in which sidemounts were available on a Cadillac. The 40-6219 sedan is also equipped with accessory grill guard, fog lamps, wheel discs and mirrors.

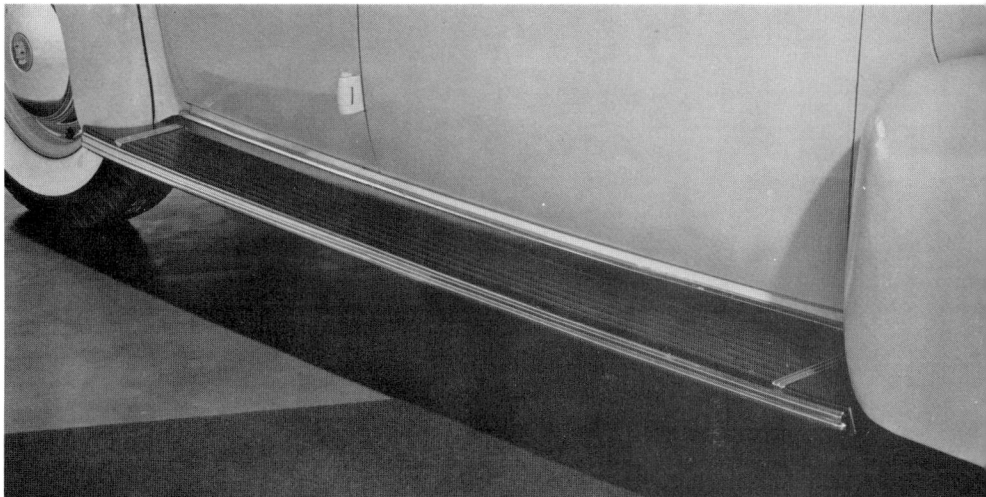

Above, the rear compartment of the 40-6219 sedan. The *torpedo* body had a six-inch wider front seat and a floor one-and-a-half-inches lower than comparable 1939 offerings. Instrument panel, garnish mouldings and plastic trim were finished in either gray or brown to blend with standard upholstery fabric selections.

Center, the optional running board available at no additional cost on the 62-Series in 1940. It was re-offered in 1941; external appearances were the same for both years.

Below, the attractive 1940 front ensemble is admired by many enthusiasts with an appreciation of design in this period. Optional wheel discs were $4 each installed. *Button* hubcaps were standard equipment and wheel trim rings were available for $1.50 each.

A restored 40-6267 convertible coupe. The sharply V'ed center radiator grill was a massive single die-cast component. Cooling grills on the catwalks were also large intricate castings. Parking lights doubled as directional signals, controlled — as they still are today — from a switching lever on the left side of the steering column. Accessory fog lamps were available with amber or clear lenses.

C-body convertible sedans didn't reach dealers until mid-March. A mere 75 were built; added to the Fleetwood bodied 75 and 90-Series four-door convertibles, a total of only 137 Cadillac convertible sedans were manufactured in 1940. Interior leather was plain paneled (no pleats, tucks or buttons) on seat backs and cushions, a long-standing Cadillac tradition in cars of this type and a tradition that ended in 1940.

Above, flush-mounting tail lights and revised bumpers accented the 1940 Sixty-Special's low-to-the-road rear quarter. Trunk lid emblem was also new. Below, a handsome (40-6019S) restoration; sidemounts were optionally available on the Sixty-Special from 1938 through 1940. The attractive sidemount cover was latched at the rear and hinged at the front, following the 1938 and 1939 practice.

Another of the ten custom Sixty-Specials built for GM executives from 1938 through 1941. Many features found on this example were shared with the other nine: Fender spears, special wheel covers, metal stone guards, Fleetwood script on the deck, landau bars and padded top. There were, however, no duplicates in terms of body color, upholstery or interior fitments.

Above, a 1940 V-16 limousine, Style 9033, on display in a Los Angeles showroom. The 90-Series was available in the full range of Fleetwood body types offered in the 75 line. It came equipped with the same dashboard, bumpers, and detailing of companion 1940 Fleetwoods, but its sheetmetal, grill, hubcaps and so forth retained the original sixteen design of 1938.

CADILLAC
V 16

Left, V-16 engines were individually assembled at the factory. During the three-year run, 498 Cadillacs were equipped with the 431 CID flathead sixteen engine; 61 in 1940. This powerplant was a radical departure from the OHV versions of 1930-1937. Improved casting techniques, which allowed a unitized crankcase and blocks and a 135 degree Vee, provided ample room for top-side manifolding and downdraft carburetors. Each bank had its own fuel pump, coil, distributor and water pump. Compared to contemporary eights, the sixteens delivered substantially improved smoothness and power.

1940 SERIES SEVENTY-TWO

Right, 72-Series formal sedans were production rarities. Eighteen were built with the "X" division (no header bar) and fabric front seat — Style 7259 — and 20 with imperial division and leather front compartment — Style 7233F. These models had special rear doors with curved upper rear corners and integral vent windows. Below, Fleetwood's three-window sedan offerings on the 72-chassis included six various interior configurations: Three with division and three without. The special taillight assembly was unique to the 72s.

THE SIXTY-SPECIAL TOWNCAR

At its debut, enthroned in the lobby of the Waldorf-Astoria, the Sixty-Special towncar must have impressed New Yorkers as a novel answer to Manhattan's worsening traffic. This 40-6053LB was one of six leather-topped models built; its metal-topped twin, Style 40-6053MB, accounted for nine sales.

Right, the chauffeur's compartment in the towncar displayed a conventional method of Fleetwood trimming. The leather front compartment's driver's curtain (top) and its supporting framework were stored in the trunk when not in use. Below, a striking view of the Sixty-Special towncar.

CUSTOM BODIES

Left, two recent views of a sporty Brunn-bodied 75-Series towncar. It was commissioned by steel executive E. J. Kulas of Chagrin Falls, Ohio. During the War the car was stored at Sanderson Cadillac in Lakewood, Ohio, then reactivated and used by the Kulas family through 1958.

Below and opposite, one of several custom coachbuilders active in California in the Thirties and early Forties was Bohman and Schwartz of Pasadena. This exotic creation on the 62 chassis had an elongated cowl, abbreviated deck, lowered body and intricate sweep panels that carried through the rear fenders and skirts. This car was one of two such models built on speculation by Bohman and Schwartz; it was first purchased by William Doheny, President of Sinclair Oil.

BOHMAN &
SCHWARTZ

·37·

1941

The intrinsic character of the 1941 front ensemble
is as forceful today as it was during the 1940s.

·38·

A TIMELESS MASTERPIECE

Esthetically, Cadillac was to 1941 what Cord was to 1937, what Duesenberg was to 1929 and what LaSalle was to 1927. So great was the fame of the 1941 Cadillac in its own time, so remarkably crisp and original its force of style, it has remained through the years one of the most cherished of American motorcars. It was a design demonstrating amazing technical virtuosity and considerable imagination, yet its lines were not radical, unnatural or out of touch with the time. More than any of its contemporaries it testified to the state of the art in 1941, and in so doing exerted an influence of incalculable magnitude on the future appearance of the American automobile.

GM stylist Arthur Ross is credited with making the first sketches using the horizontal grill with an egg-crate texture. Bill Mitchell tells of Harley Earl's introduction to the concept: *Earl always liked to come into the studio at night to look around on his own. I had taken one of Art's sketches of this front treatment and left it out on the boards overnight. The following morning I removed it. Earl came down to the studio later that morning and wanted to know what had happened to Ross' sketch. We got it out for him, he took one look and said, "I can make a front end out of this." The interesting thing about Earl was his great faculty for change. Overnight we literally switched from the prow or pointed look to the flat front.*

From any frontal position the broad, heavily chromed grill and the high crowned hood dominated the 1941 look. New features embodied in the front ensemble included the flying lady, fog lamp provisions, hood louvers, parking and turn lights, and the familiar crest with raised wings. Bumpers were heavier, broader, and curved in at the ends to protect the fenders. The grill guard extending between bumper guards was standard on all series. The horizontal valance between bumpers and body was a new concept as was the front fender windsplit extending horizontally rearward from the headlamp; both of these details remained on Cadillacs throughout the Forties.

Developmental design work on the 1941 cars was well advanced before the ventilator panels in the hood were added. The prototype in this photo reveals the need for breaking up the hood sides when combined with 1941-type fenders and the absented belt moulding. Replacement hoods for 1941 models supplied after 1946 had no openings for side ventilators although the shape and size remained the same.

On October 1, 1940, Cadillac introduced the six separate series that comprised the 1941 offerings. Series 61, 62, 75 and Sixty-Special reappeared in addition to two brand new series, the 63 and 67. There were a total of nineteen different body styles including the most ambitious diversification of models priced under $2,000 that any luxury car maker had ever fielded.

The 61-Series, which replaced the LaSalle line, had a base price of $1,345 making it the lowest priced Cadillac V-8 ever produced. The 61s utilized two all new fastback designs. They were handsome aerodynamic Fisher B-bodies that constituted a considerable styling advance over the previous versions of 1939 and 1940 (Cadillac originally introduced the 61-Series in 1939 then dropped it for the 1940 model year). Concealed running boards, chrome mouldings outlining windows, and many of the refinements found on the more expensive models made the 61 an outstanding value.

Essentially the 62-Series was an extension of the four well-balanced torpedo styles developed for the 1940 C-body program: A two-window club-type sedan, a notchback coupe, the Division's last production convertible sedan, and a convertible that proved statistically to be the most popular open Cadillac built until after World War II. Both of the open types have become extremely desirable collectors' cars in recent years with the convertible sedan commanding prices approaching those of open classics five years its senior. As in 1940, the convertible top was raised and lowered by vacuum assisted cylinders (previous models had hand-operated tops). Both convertible coupe and convertible sedan interiors were fashioned by Fleetwood in a choice of eight trim options. In three of these options, red, blue, or green leather could be combined with buff leather. Those three colors as well as tan and black were also available in single-tone interiors.

A little-known fact about 1941 Cadillacs is that running boards were offered as optional equipment on all 62-Series body styles at no additional charge. They were completely rubber covered and, except for mounting braces, were the same as those provided on the 1940 62-Series. Three of every seven 62 buyers had specified running boards in 1940; thus Cadillac kept them available through 1941.

Series 61 and 62 coupes and sedans were available in two styles: The standard specification models and the DeLuxe models. DeLuxe styles had a "D" suffix on the four-digit body-style number embossed on the firewall body tag. For example, a standard specification 62-Series sedan would be a 6219, while the same car with the DeLuxe package would be a 6219D. The special features prescribed for the DeLuxe models included an exclusive pattern in upholstery and door panels, special trim and monogram on the finish mouldings below the window garnish, fluted chrome scuff plates on the lower portions of doors and seat cushions, a special two-spoke ivory steering wheel, rear fender shields (skirts) and rear seat center arm rest (not provided on the 61 standard coupes).

The 63-Series consisted of one body type, an attractive four-door notchback three-window sedan with the highest base price of any closed model on the short wheelbase except the Sixty-Special (Series 61, 62, 63 and Sixty-Special all used the 126-inch wheelbase). Its entry into the crowded line filled a void created by the absence of a traditional Cadillac three-window sedan in 1940 when both the 60-S and 62 sedans were two-window types with solid quarters. With the 61 fastback sedan and the 63 notchback there were two three-window types on the short-wheelbase in 1941 and together they garnered nearly 30 percent of the year's production total.

The 63 had unique chrome mouldings which encircled the side windows then merged with the belt moulding. (The 63 was the only model on the 126-inch wheelbase with a belt moulding.) It was a strikingly attractive car with extensive brightwork and a DeLuxe interior as standard.

There has been speculation about why Cadillac bothered to introduce the 63-Series in 1941. One probable explanation is linked with the phased-out LaSalle. There are photographs of a 1941 LaSalle proposal which show a mockup body which may have been used for die-making patterns. It is even possible that Fisher Body had already made these body dies prior to Cadillac's decision to drop the LaSalle. Since the Division would be charged for a pro-rata share of the die costs in any event, management apparently decided to go ahead with the project under Cadillac identification.

All 1941 Cadillacs have become collectors' items over the years, but the model mentioned more frequently than any other is the Sixty-Special. Fleetwood endowed this, the last edition of the original design, with the sophisticated distinctive quality that had been previously associated with 75-Series V-8s and the 90-Series V-16s. Its walnut mouldings, leather trim and exquisite upholstery imparted a new distinction to the spacious interior.

The splash pan between bumper and body, and the windsplit moulded into the headlight bezels and front fenders typified the innovative detailing that pervaded 1941 styling.

Subsequent changes to this Sixty-Special styling model were minimal. The script Fleetwood name ultimately used on front fenders evolved from the gravel shields on this model; the louvers on the rear quarter panels were adopted in 1942, and the vertically winged hood ornament turned up in the 1950s.

THE
Fleetwood
SIXTY-SPECIAL

Below, note special color on steering column, hand brake and so forth (optionally available on most 1941 models). Fleetwood would quote upon request, and execute if approved, any special interior designs relative to finish and upholstery. This policy resulted in many highly personalized cars.

The sweeping seven-foot long fender that flowed over the front door was a seemingly spontaneous feature that admirably conformed to the fundamental body architecture. The continuous chrome moulding along the base of the body and the massive specially-contoured rear fender skirt created side views of exceptional beauty. Optional features included a division glass — which was cataloged as a *formal division* rather than an *imperial division* to emphasize the owner-driver character of the Sixty-Special — a sun roof, and an almost limitless selection of interiors.

Between 1938 and 1941 the Sixty-Special remained an exclusive Cadillac body. It shared no sheetmetal with other models, not even fenders. In this four year period the only major body component that was interchangeable with other Cadillacs was the grill (1939 through 1941). Restorers are often amazed to find that wood was still being used in 1941. The Sixty-Special was the last Cadillac built with wood main sills; seat frames also contained wood.

The 67-Series evolved as the second all-new long-wheelbase luxury sedan in as many years. Compared to the 75, it was 2½ inches lower to the ground and 1½ inches lower in overall height. Its concealed running boards and generous legroom and head-room were factors Cadillac management considered progressive.

In terms of styling it was more compatible with the contemporary Cadillac than the 75-Series cars, yet, the 75 outsold the less costly 67 — $405 separated the two — by a margin of two to one. That statistical demonstration was not forgotten when production resumed after the War (in 1946 the 67 was dropped in favor of the 75).

It has been said that Buick's General Manager, Harlow H. Curtice, was more instrumental in the creation of the 67-type body than anyone at Cadillac. Mr. Curtice, whose tenure at Buick almost paralleled Nicholas Dreystadt's years at Cadillac, had a flair for promotion and marketing that made Buick one of the really exciting cars of the late 1930s and 1940s. His close personal relationship with Harley Earl resulted in a string of styling successes that peaked in 1938 and again in 1941.

Many Detroit insiders believe the design of the 1941 Buick Limited, which used the same body shell as the Cadillac Series-67, was done expressly for Buick and then given to Cadillac when GM's top brass thought Buick was becoming too involved in the luxury field. A comparison of what the two Divisions did with the body does not necessarily support this theory, however. Cadillac's fenders complement the body better, and the Limited's belt moulding seems incongruous with the design concept.

Be that as it may, the streamlined Fisher-bodied 67s (there is evidence that some 67s were built in the Fleetwood plant) were impeccably detailed, gracefully proportioned big cars with all the fitments and comforts of pedigreed classics.

The new issue of the 75 was a comprehensive demonstration of the fine art of automobile styling. The new frontal format was blended to the 72 body shell of 1940 with stylistic idealism — classical in form, elaborate in detail and exquisite in appointment. There was — and still is — something about a 1941 75 that has the aura of *old money*. It *looks* like a very expensive motorcar. Nevertheless, Cadillac's wealthier patrons were lamenting the fact that they could no longer purchase a Cadillac convertible, convertible sedan, town sedan, coupe or towncar of 75-Series size and stature. A gracious era had passed; an era that could never again return.

The 1941 Book of Special Features listed a host of external variations in paint and trim for the new 75 models. The three-window sedans were offered in a rainbow of colors including two-tone combinations. Since there was no satisfactory color break between front fenders and body, two-color lacquer plans used the body crease just above the belt moulding as the point of separation. For a mere $8 Fleetwood would finish 75-Series body and hood mouldings in color rather than chrome. Striping, above and below body and hood mouldings or on mouldings when painted, was $14 extra.

Series 61 and 62 cars with DeLuxe interiors, along with the Sixty-Specials and Series 63 and 67 cars, enjoyed a wide latitude in optional interior finish and upholstery. For $10 additional all garnish and finishing panels could be painted in one special color; $12.50 for two-tone combinations. This did not include the windshield garnish which was normally chromed, but it could be obtained in wood grain at no extra charge or painted for $4. The cost of having the instrument panel, steering column and hand brake lever painted a special color was $12.50.

Special upholstery fabrics started at $90. The most exotic varieties were $245. Prices included a special quality carpet to match. For $265 extra any DeLuxe interior could be trimmed entirely in leather, headliner and all. Variations employing part leather and part fabric started at $30 and ran up to $200 for genuine leather on everything below the beltline.

The engine used in the 1941 cars had a higher compression ratio — 7.25 to 1 — resulting in a corresponding increase to 150 horsepower. Other changes included new babbitt-lined bearings, new cast iron camshaft, exhaust valves made of a new steel alloy, redesigned valve silencers, and lighter timing chain and sprockets.

Below, the three-spoke steering wheel, wood-grain windshield garnish, thin band of bright metal on door garnish panel, five vertical tucks in door panels and imitation leather scuff pads typify the 61 and 62-Series standard interiors.

Above, a sampling of new models assembled on the roof at the factory for promotional photographs.

The big news in Cadillac's mechanical program for 1941 was Hydra-Matic Drive. In the public's eye Cadillac gained the upper hand over Packard, Lincoln and Chrysler by completely eliminating the third pedal (competitive semi-automatic transmissions continued to require use of the clutch under certain conditions). The self-shifting principle had been used by Oldsmobile for a number of years starting with 1937. By 1940 the fully automatic transmission optionally available in Oldsmobiles was relatively dependable and responsive. Cadillac re-engineered the Olds transmission, which used a fluid coupling, and came up with a beefed-up version with additional clutch plates to accommodate the 150 horsepower V-8.

Early Hydra-Matics seem harsh by modern standards. Bronze-lined rather than composition-faced clutch plates made shifting more severe, and the lubricant fluid then available was not totally effective in silencing the front pump, thus the characteristic *sing*. But the first-generation Cadillac automatic transmission performed well, normally providing many years of trouble-free driving.

An interesting change in the chassis was the adoption of an optional *economy* rear axle for 61, 62, 63 and Sixty-Special cars. The ratio was 3.36 to 1 whereas the standard ratio was 3.77 to 1. The 67 and 75 cars had a standard ratio of 4.27 to 1 with an optional 3.77 to 1 alternate. The *economy* ratio was normally provided on cars with Hydra-Matic Drive. In view of the gathering war clouds an interest in fuel economy was important, but a Cadillac was still a heavy machine. Even the 61 coupe weighing 4,000 pounds and cruising at 50 MPH got only 15.8 miles to the gallon with the 3.77 axle and 17.3 with the 3.36; at 70 MPH it dropped to 11.9 and 12.7 respectively.

In November of 1940 Cadillac instituted the heaviest mid-winter production schedule that had been required since the introduction of the new models had been advanced from the first of the year (1936). Thirty days after the 1941 models were announced unshipped orders for new cars stood at 11,774 units, an all-time Cadillac high.

Through the Spring and Summer months every previous production and sales record fell. The factory was operating at maximum capacity and still there was no way to keep pace with new orders. Cadillac closed out the 1941 model year with 66,130 units, 20,000 more than had been built in 1937 when Cadillac-LaSalle registered its theretofore greatest quantitative success.

Above, the proposed design for the 75 as envisioned February 17, 1940. Center, the finalized car with chrome headlight bezels, flying lady, fender skirt crests and production bumper guards. Evidence that the factory may have considered retaining the 72-Series designation for this body group is indicated by the license plate. Bottom, a catalog illustration of the 75-Series formal sedan (Styles 7533F and 7559).

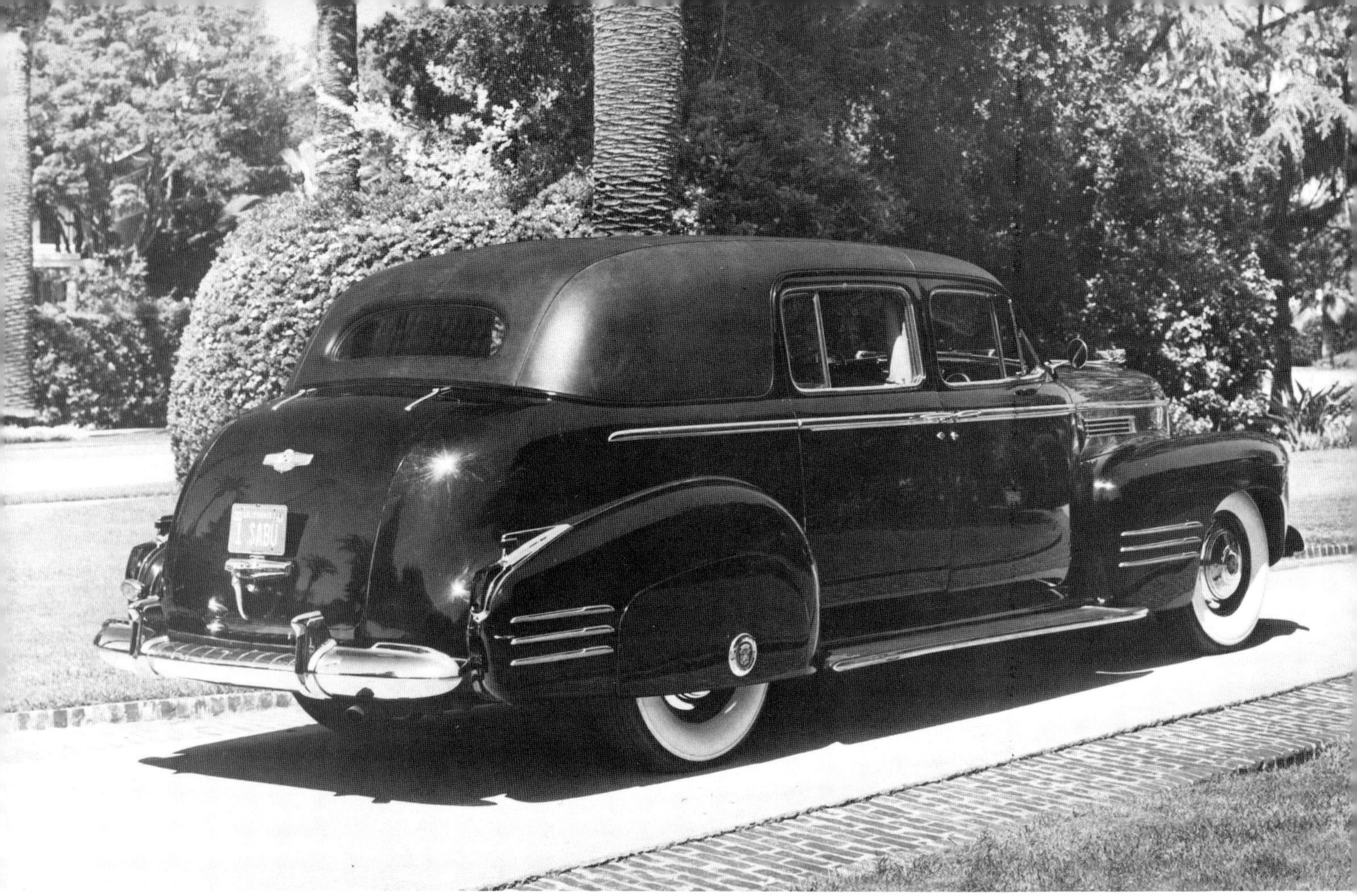
1 SABU

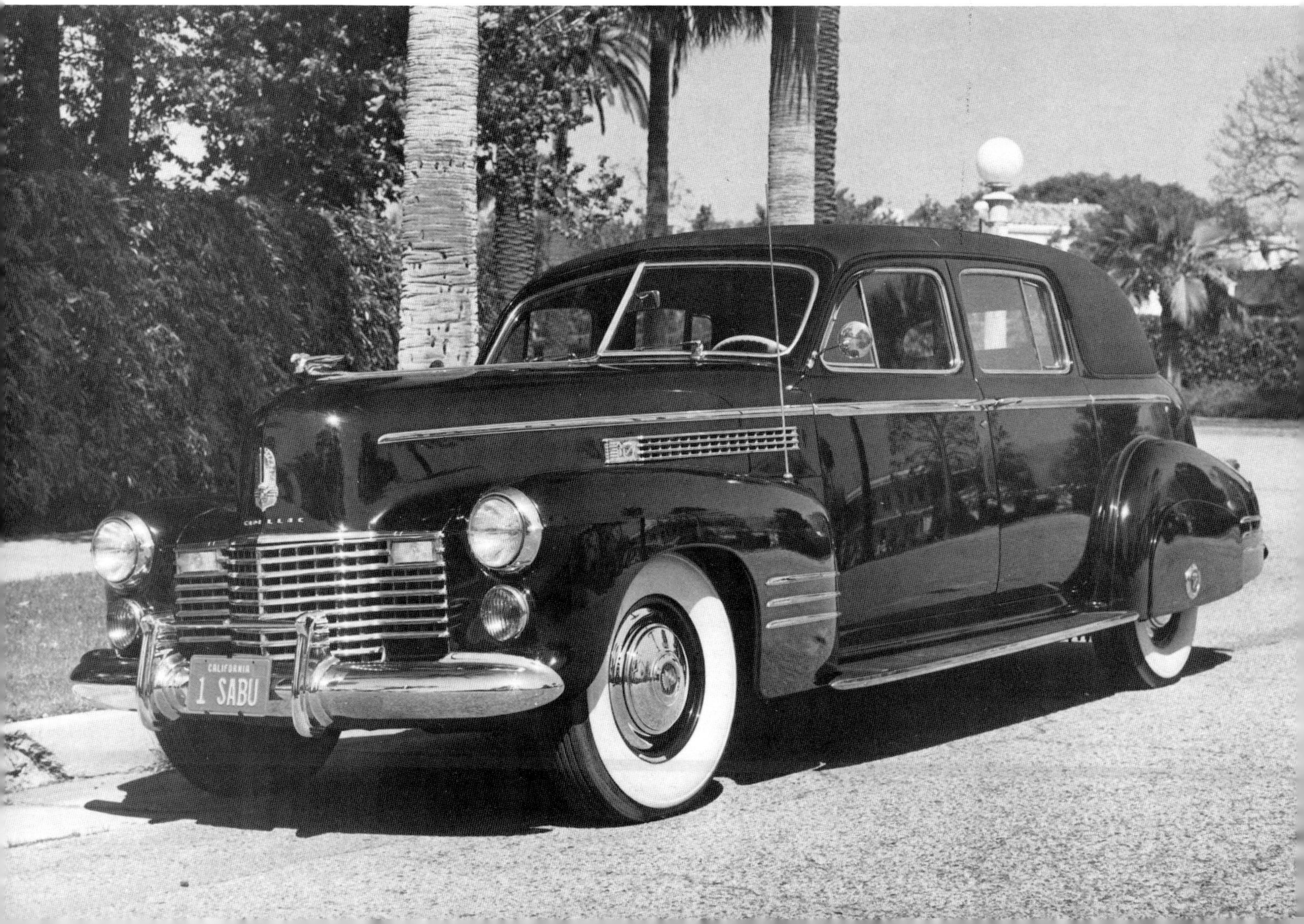
CALIFORNIA
1 SABU

At the pinnacle of the GM line for 1941, in both price and prestigue, was the Cadillac-Fleetwood formal sedan. The strongly traditional lines of the 75-Series blended perfectly with the proportional dictates of this legendary body type. Opposite and below, views of an outstanding, and original, 41-7559. Above, a view that few could afford in 1941, the outlook from the opulent rear compartment of a chauffeured 75.

1941 SERIES SIXTY-SEVEN

Cadillac's secondary line of long-wheelbase offerings was the 67-Series. The subject of these photographs is a pre-production prototype; in finalized form the rear bumper, deck lid hinges and rocker moldings were modified. The seven-passenger rear compartment, shown at the left, was typical of the 67s Fleetwood interiors. Through the utilization of a reduced ground to floor step-up (2½-inches lower than the 75) these Fisher-assembled body shells eliminated the need for traditional running boards. The rakish 67s are relatively rare as only 900 were produced in 1941 and 700 in 1942.

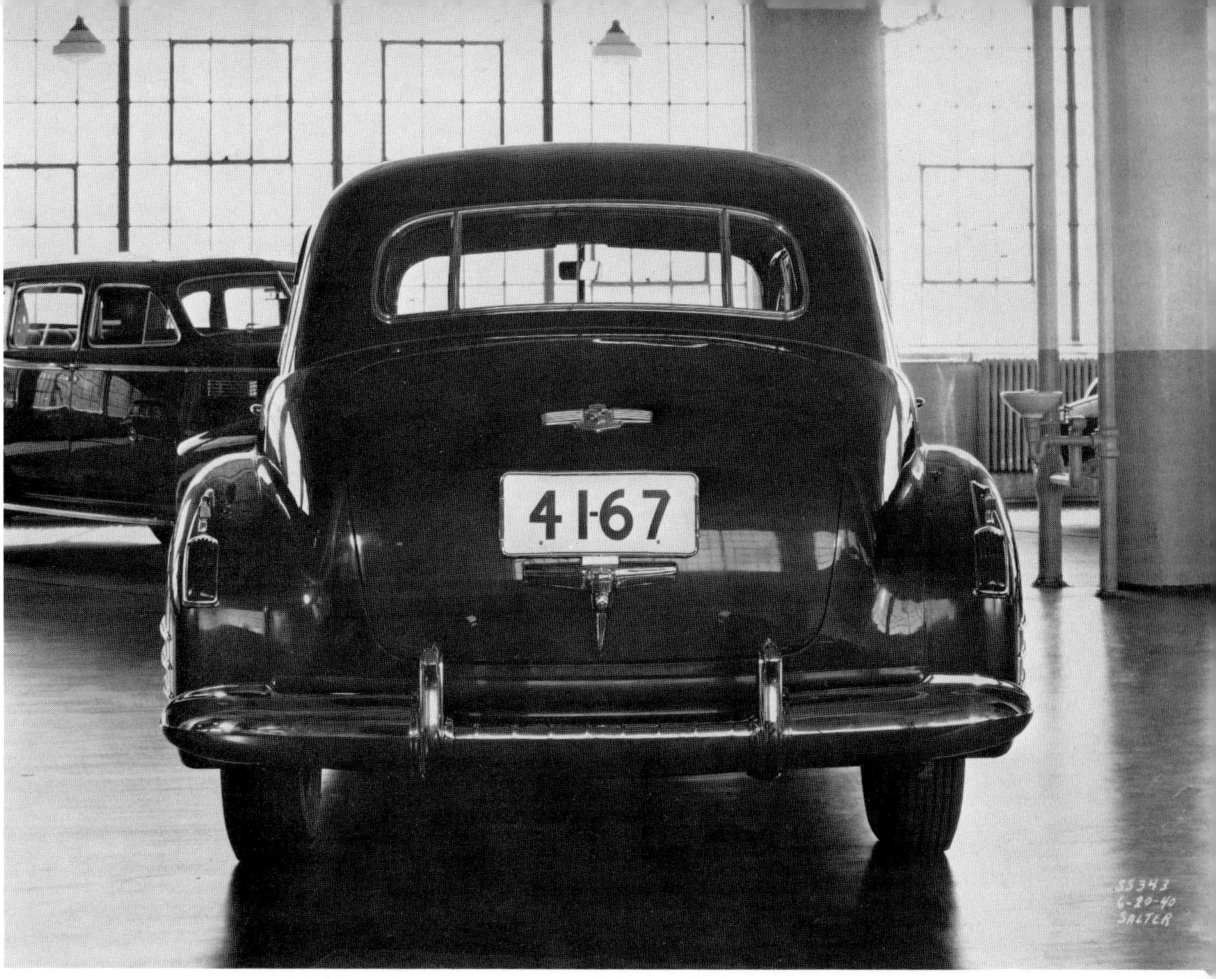
41-67
55343
6-20-40
SALTER

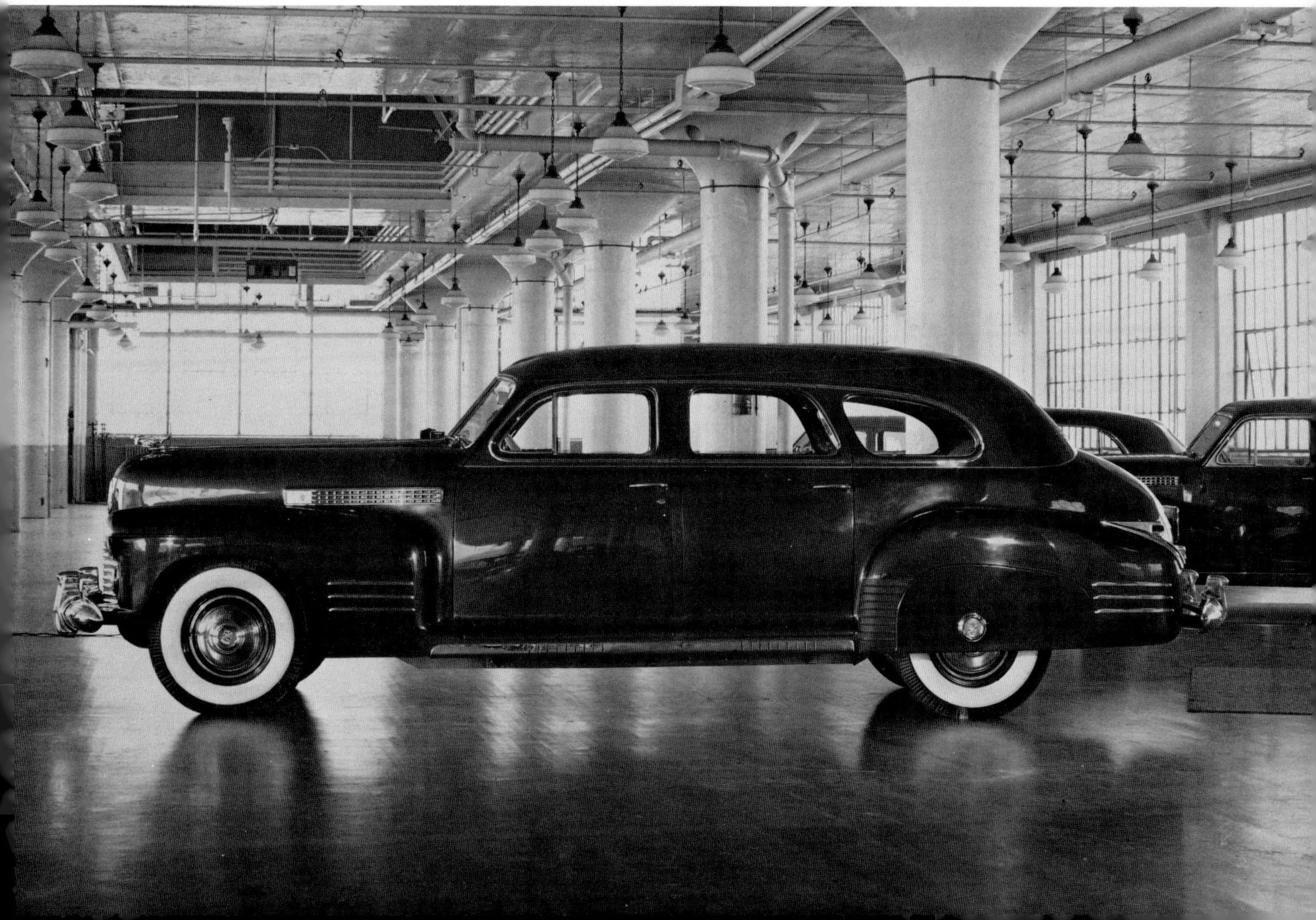

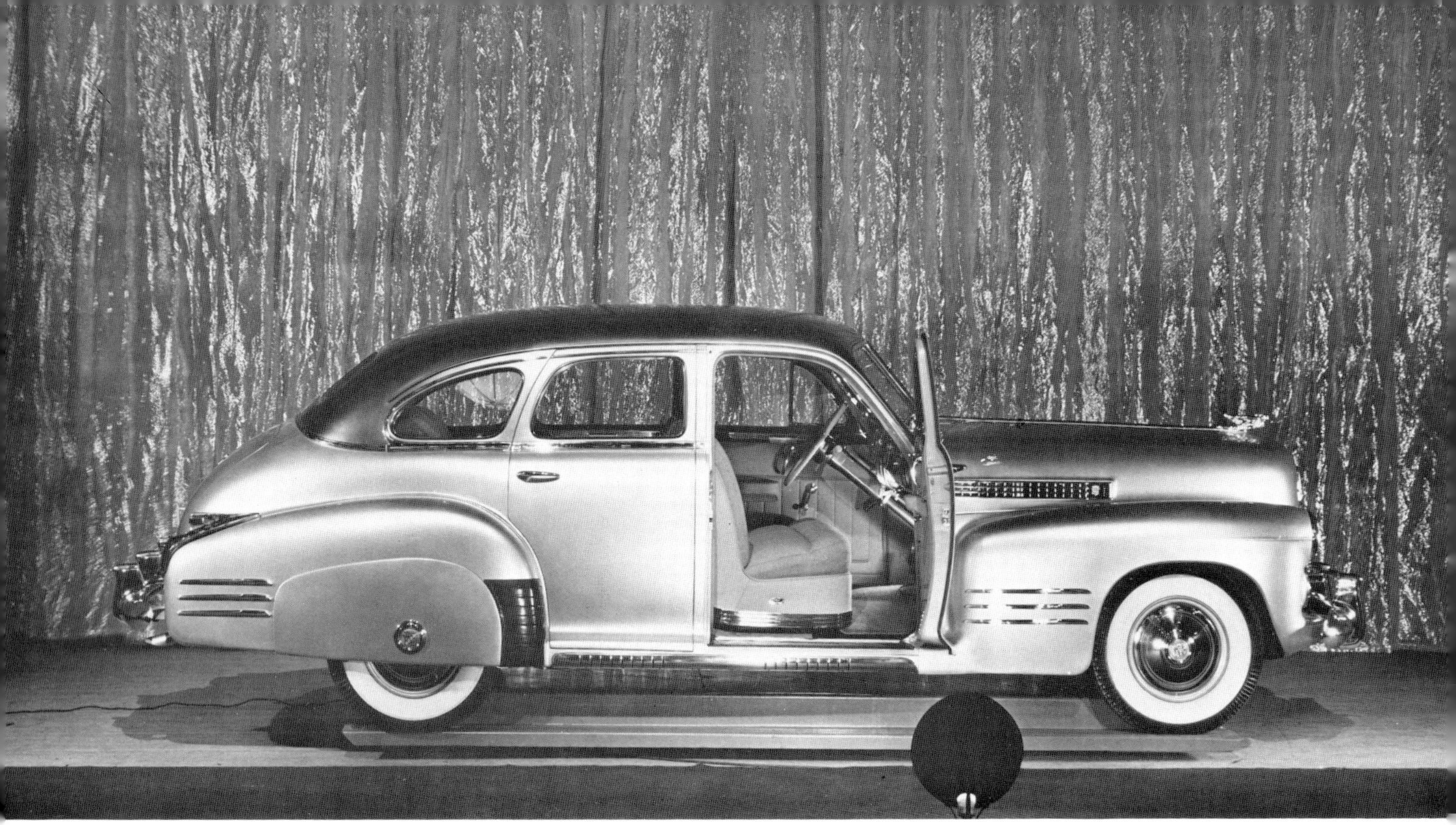

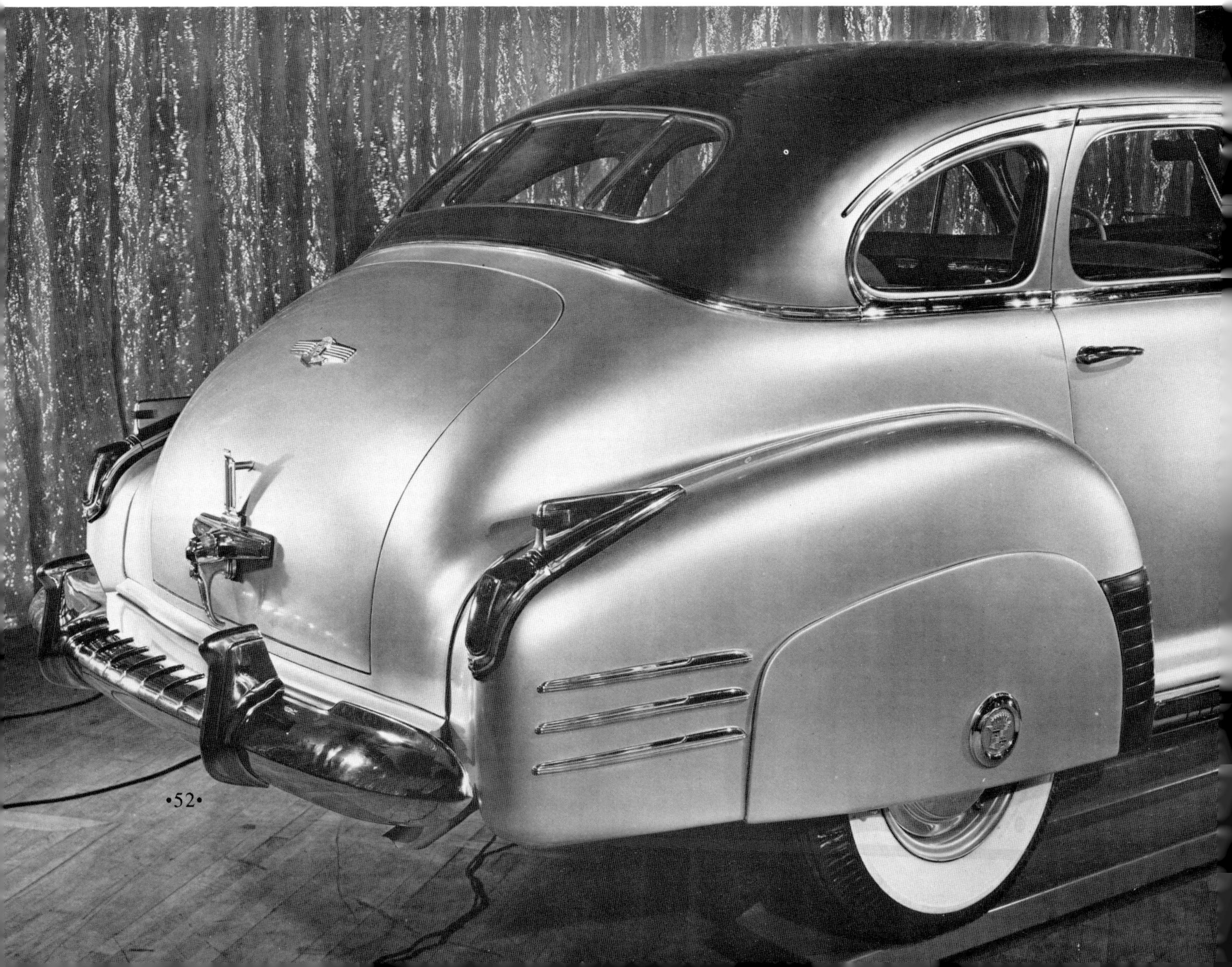

1941 SERIES SIXTY-THREE

Above, a proposal for the 1941 LaSalle employing the B-body that turned up on the 63-Series. Center and opposite, a 63-Series styling model. Mock-up building was such an advanced art at GM in the 1940s that it is sometimes difficult, when looking at original photographs, to tell a production car from a wood-metal mock-up. Advertising campaigns were normally planned well in advance of production and often retouched promotional photos, like the one below (Style 41-6319), used styling mock-ups instead of actual cars.

1941 FLEETWOOD SIXTY-SPECIAL

The 1941 Sixty-Special is a car that never has and never will go out of style. Its clean, beautifully proportioned design combined all the attributes of the evolutionary front end with the continental proportions of its predecessors. Low-slung lines, wide-vision windows and comfortable seating made the 60S the most imitated motorcar in America circa 1941. 13,800 had been produced through 1940, and the 1941 edition contributed an additional 4,100 units. Their survival rate was considerably better than average. Perhaps a score of original low-mileage 1941s are as pristine as the object of the factory photos at the center and bottom of this page; dozens more, like the example in the upper photo, have been meticulously restored.

Above, interior motifs exclusive to the Sixty-Special included three duo-tone fabric options using Bedford cord for the bolster roll on the seat backs and cushions and a harmonizing lighter fabric for inserts and door panels. Single-tone fabric interiors were, however, more common. Below, on models with formal divisions the rear seat cushion was 2¼ inches closer to the front seat back (in the rearward position) than in non-division styles.

THE DUCHESS

The Duke and Duchess of Windsor commissioned this magnificent Fleetwood soon after Rolls-Royce ceased passenger car production in World War II. Essentially the "Duchess," as the car is known, was a C-body sedan lengthened for the 136-inch wheelbase chassis through the use of wider doors and a 1942-type 60-S center body pillar. A special console incorporated into the division partition contained jewel case, vanity case, pipe rack, air cooling unit, heater and radio. Rear compartment foot rests could be adjusted manually from under the driver's seat. The car originally sold for $14,000 and was used by the Duke and Duchess until 1952. At that time the odometer had recorded 18,000 miles. Cadillac considered using this type of fender treatment for the 1942 model update but opted for the more compatible fender cap that terminated on the front door. At least one other custom C-body Cadillac sedan, with what became Buick-type fenders, was built in 1941; it was placed at the disposal of GM's Charles F. Kettering.

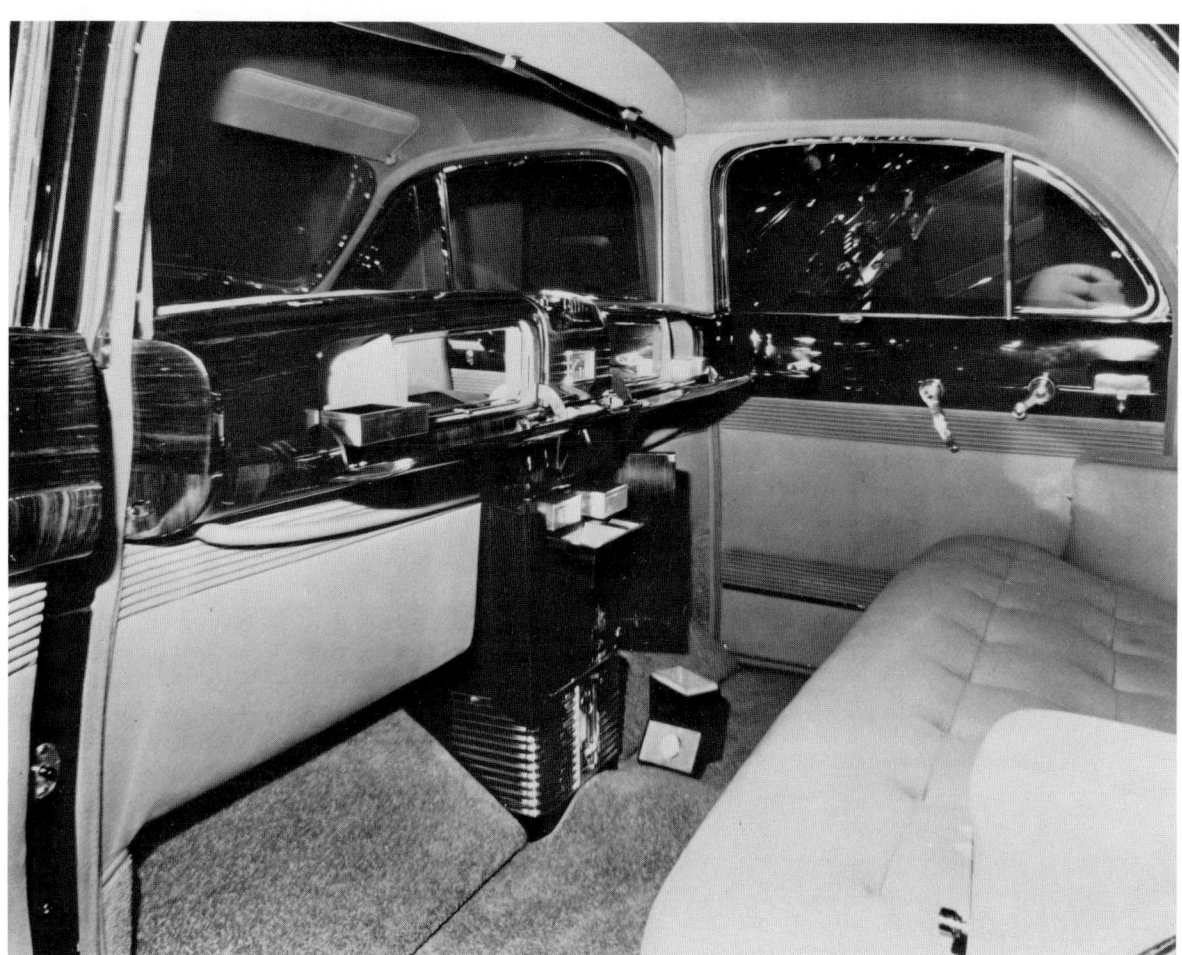

•57•

The pleasing visual aspects of the 1941 models were apparent from every perspective. Above and center, the 62-Series DeLuxe sedan (Style 41-6219D). Below, Style 41-6219. Although running boards were available on the 62s at no additional charge, they were rarely specified. To facilitate egress, wheel size was reduced one inch. The 15-inch wheels were standard on all series except the 67 and 75.

Opposite page above, the 41-6227D coupe had a bench seat in the rear providing seating for two. Opposite page below, the standard interior for the 62-Series sedan. Pleated door panels (DeLuxe models had a more intricately pleated pattern), pleated front seat back, imitation leather scuff pads and buttoned seat backs reflected Cadillac's contemporary tailored look.

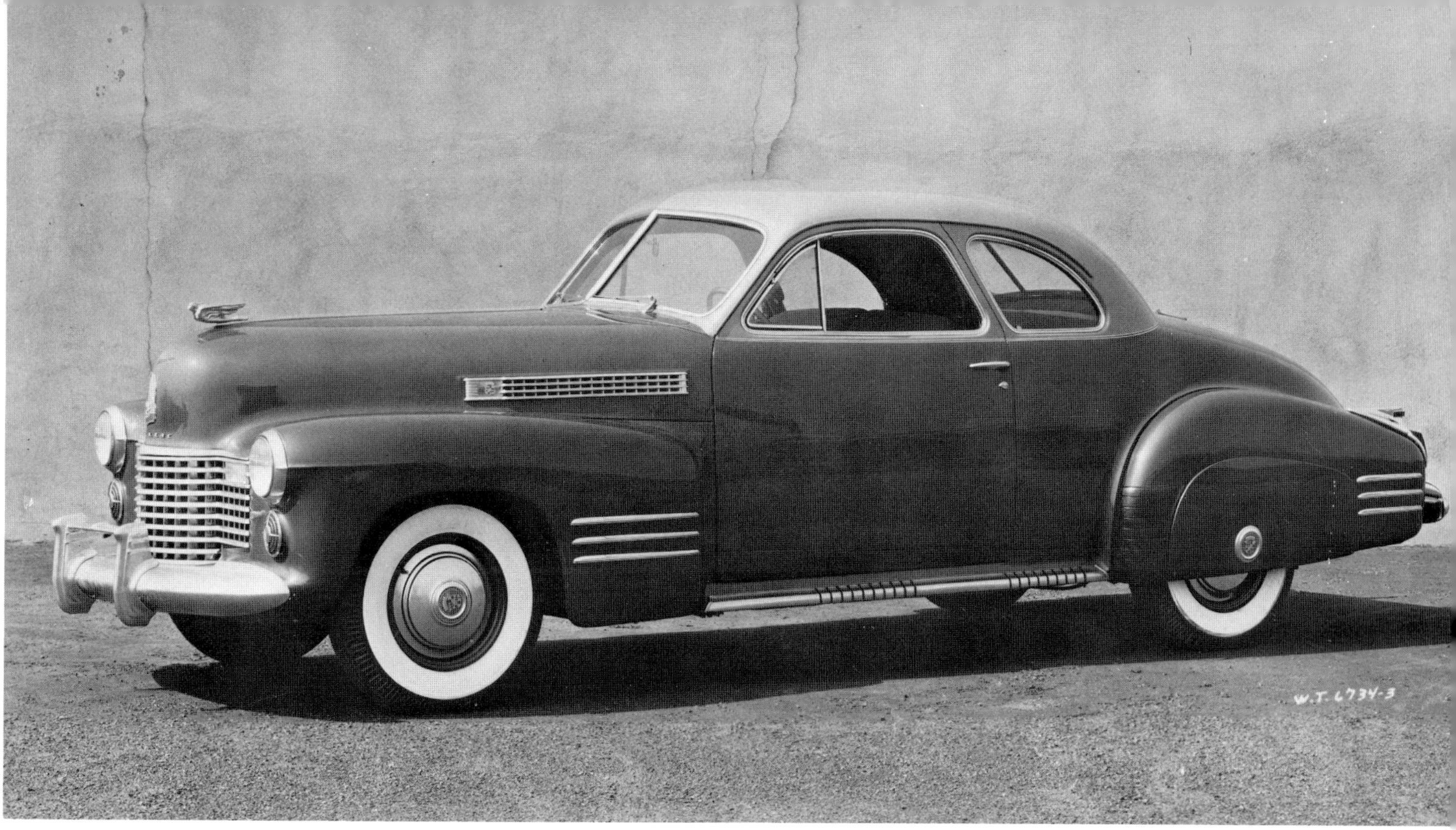
W.T. 6734-3

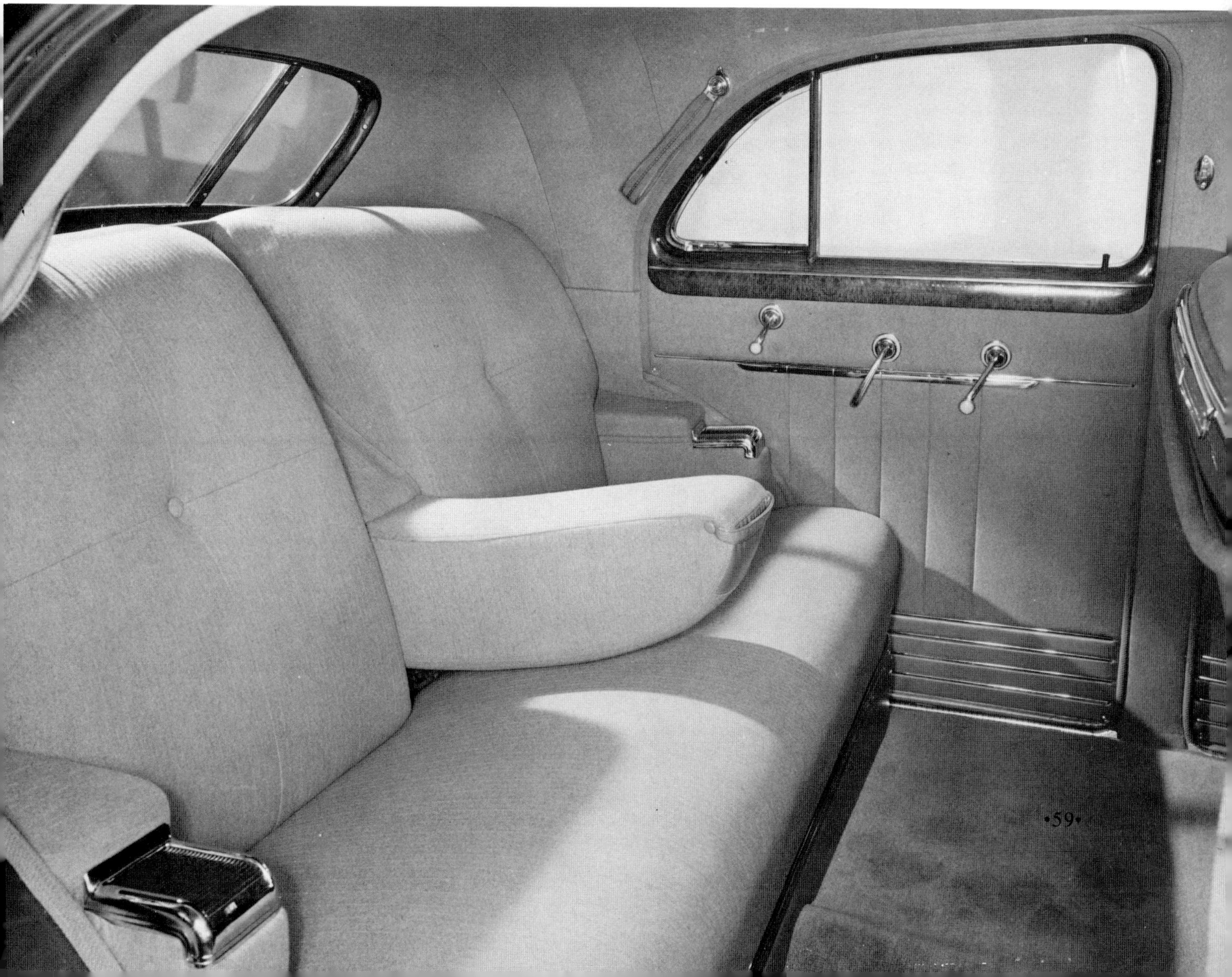

1941 SERIES SIXTY-TWO CONVERTIBLE

The 62-convertible continues to be heralded as a flawless work of automotive styling and a delight to behold from any angle. In the upper two photographs is a restored example while at the bottom is an original factory shot. 1941 was the last year in which Cadillac convertibles had solid rear quarters (no quarter windows).

THE CONVERTIBLE SEDAN

Cadillac's last production convertible sedan, Style 41-6229D. Its rakish lines are conspicuous in collectors' circles today even though a mere 400 were built. Standard convertible top fabric was tan, black or blue-grey; piping on the top and boot matched the leather upholstery.

Photographs at the top and bottom originated from the factory. The restored example in the center was an award winning entry in the West Coast's 1976 Ambassador Show.

With a base list price of $1,345 the 61-Series five-passenger coupe (Style 41-6127) was the lowest priced Cadillac since the one-cylinder models (1902-1908). Fastback styling proved so popular that this model became the overall sales leader for 1941. It was the first, and possibly the last, GM non-sedan in the post touring car era to earn this distinction. Two-tone paint plans, as shown, flattered this B-body.

A close runnerup in the production totals was the 41-6109 five-passenger sedan. Statistically the 61-Series accounted for 44 per cent of all 1941 production, yet surprisingly few have survived. Photos above and opposite are original; were it not for the disintegrating tail lamp jewels (now being reproduced), the attractive two-tone example below might, as the license plate suggests, have been taken in 1941.

CUSTOM *Fleetwoods*

Charles E. Wilson, who became President of General Motors in 1941, was chauffeured about in this custom lowered and lengthened Sixty-Special for several years. The apron in front of the grill was chromed, as were the wheels. The front compartment was trimmed in red leather and the rear was done in extremely pale beige. The California-based Liebendorfer Collection contains three custom 1941s including the Wilson car and the towncar on the opposite page. The Collection's third custom is a lengthened and lowered C-body sedan with 1941 Sixty-Special-type front fenders, a 1942 Sixty-Special-type center body pillar and windows of reduced height.

Below, a Sixty-Special with leather top (an option not cataloged in 1941, but offered at $650 on the 1939 Sixty-Special), 75-Series-type belt mouldings, unbarred rear window, and insignia abstinence. The total effect of these modifications, presumably by Fleetwood, is indeed handsome.

The last towncar built by Cadillac-Fleetwood was this one-off Sixty-Special, Style 41-6052LB. Shown above at its New York première and below as it appeared three decades later. (The much publicized El Dorado Brougham towncar built in the mid-1950s by GM Styling and exhibited at the Motorama shows was not motorized.)

Rerouted spark plug wiring and vertical ribbing on the cylinder heads were 1941 modifications that made the 150 HP engine perceptibly different from the previous L-head.

Commercial chassis developed into an important segment of Cadillac's business in the 1930s. Opposite page above, commercial chassis being loaded for shipment from the factory. A vast majority of the commercial chassis ordered in 1940 were based on the 159-inch wheelbase LaSalle 50-Series chassis, in 1941 the 163-inch wheelbase 62-Series chassis proved most popular and from then on the 75-Series and specially designated series prevailed. Opposite page below, a 1941 demonstration commercial chassis. Note the extra cross-member in the frame, heavy springs and jack shaft in the drive train.

·67·

Above, a convertible customized by Coachcraft, a Hollywood, California, coachbuilding firm. The attractive tapering fade-away front fender treatment was prophetic, the dechroming typical of the contemporary school of customizing. Below, a striking two-door station wagon based on the 61-Series chassis. Coachcraft was commissioned to build this *woodie* by cowboy actor Charles Starrett.

CUSTOM BODIES

A number of legendary custom body-building companies were still active in the eastern states in 1941. Above, a garish 61-Series coupe as modified by Brunn and Company of Buffalo, New York. In the center, two examples of Derham coachwork: The 75-Series towncar with fully collapsible rear quarter sold for a reported $10,000 in 1941, while the Sixty-Special towncar conversion was priced around $1,500 on customer-provided cars. Derham, located in Rosemont, Pennsylvania, a suburb of Philadelphia, is believed to have completed six 1941 Sixty-Special towncar conversions. Below, Rollson, successor to the Rollston Company of New York City, was active in modification work in the years immediately preceding the War. The most typical modification was to convert a three-window sedan into a formal sedan as seen here.

1942

CADILLAC V-8 ENGINE AND HYDRA-MATIC TRANSMISSION
POWER FOR CADILLAC MOTOR CARS AND IMPORTANT WAR VEHICLES

This elaborate cut-away engine and accompanying display made numerous appearances during the War years.

A PRELUDE TO WAR

The Cadillac Motor Car Company moved into the 1942 model year with new insights. In the wake of a depression that all but eradicated the ultra-luxury automobile business, low-end pricing parameters had been allowed to fall to new levels. But the captivating product line of the previous series had unleashed a burgeoning prosperity along Clark Avenue.

A combination of factors contributed to the bonanza: Lower prices on Cadillac prestige, the impending shortage of cars and the possible cessation of production because of the encroaching war, the floundering competition, and — last, but not least — the car itself. Cadillac had it all: Style, engineering, heritage, and perhaps the finest network of dealers in the industry.

Production of the 40th anniversary model began on October 1, 1941, precisely one month after the line closed down for the changeover. It took only one quick glance at the 1942 models for the public to realize that Cadillac was unveiling another masterpiece, another exciting new edition back-to-back with the runaway best-seller of 1941.

Earl's styling geniuses, under Bill Mitchell's direction, had changed the car's character, yet preserved an intrinsic traditional appeal. The horizontal grill was beautifully resculptured with fewer, more-dominant bars: Six horizontal and fourteen vertical. It was wider at the base, with integrated rectangular fog lamp provisions. Altogether the front ensemble was a dazzling combination of paint and plate complemented and embraced by the imposing contours of the hood and new flow-through fenders.

The car was a compendium of new styling details: Massive bumpers that swept around the fenders a little farther, bullet shaped bumper guards, updated tail light housings and more dominant body mouldings. Many observers agreed that here indeed was the ultimate in streamlined motorcars, the crescendo of modern design, a point beyond which there could be no advance.

Of course similar sentiments had been directed to GM's senior marque in other years. Some enthusiasts equate the differing appeals of the 1941 and 1942 models with those of the 1932 and 1933 cars. In both time frames successive Cadillacs were swathed in related, yet completely variant motifs, each endowed with a distinctive esthetic harmony. Mr. Earl's creative process remained the blackboard, model, mock-up route punctuated with endless days of trial-and-error and visual comparison. Consequently, each new model was the end result of an innovative and demanding process that synthesized imagination, perspective, shadow and line. In retrospect, there can be no denying that each Cadillac from 1928 on has been a perfected art form.

In short, attempts to grade one model year against another is utter folly, like attempting to evaluate the successive works of Rembrandt, Stradivari or Michaelangelo. The only truly valid index to such matters is personal preference, for each individual's assimilation of values, meanings, and style is dependent upon his own past experiences.

Cadillac's chief body engineer in 1942, William J. Tell, observed that the new fender lines historically represented a fifth stage in the evolution of fenders. Starting as accessory mudguards at the turn of the Century, they became flat metal shields through the mid-Twenties. Then came the stylish clamshells of the grand classic years, the aerodynamic pontoons of the Thirties and finally fenders that swept over the doors. The first Cadillac to use this form of design was the 1941 Sixty-Special, but its front fenders were unlike those gracing 1942 models since the cap on the door carried down to the sill rather than having a radius on the lower surface.

Operationally there were advantages in using the two-piece fender aside from appearance. The prevailing technology had made it necessary to stamp out earlier pontoon-type fenders in two sections and then weld them together. During the years when Cadillac-LaSalle used the pontoon with a crease along the upper surface, 30 percent of the stampings had to be scrapped because of severe splitting; others developed irreparable cracks when jigged up for the welding operation. The extra material in the 1942-type fender and the cost of attaching the cap to the door ostensibly represented a trade-off in costs with the earlier pontoon-types.

Cadillac utilized the three brand new Fisher C-bodies to full advantage. Newest in terms of configuration was the 62 fastback coupe known as the *sedanet,* the finest fastback design since the famed Aero-dynamic coupes of the mid-1930's. Like the other 62s, it was 220 inches in overall length and readily distinguishable from the five-inches-shorter 61-Series coupe. The vertical center body pillar and trailing belt moulding also gave it a character totally different from that of the 61 fastback.

The new convertible became recognized as the finest American-built open car of the mid-1940s. It had quarter windows and an enlarged rear compartment which incorporated a full width seat and added floor space. The convertible top was electrically powered.

A handsome two-window sedan completed the 62 line and it was the first Cadillac to have rear fenders that flowed onto the rear doors. The new 62s were larger cars with three inches of additional wheelbase (129 inches) and bodies three-and-a-quarter inches wider in the front and three-fourths of an inch wider at the rear. These new models again exemplified Cadillac's leadership in styling.

The new Sixty-Special was a distinct departure from the original design. Its body was seven inches longer and an inch lower, with generous increases in legroom and headroom. Fleetwood artisans performed more hand operations in the production of this body than perhaps any since. Starting with the basic main body stampings from the 62-Series sedan: The roof panel and floor pan were lengthened, special center body pillars installed, the lower portion of each door widened by two inches, the upper door frames modified, and the front seat frames fabricated. These were costly labor inputs

This mock-up illustrates the many avenues Styling explored in trying to establish a special identity for the successor to the original Sixty-Special. The late hour, evidenced by the clock and darkening skyline, actually meant business as usual in Harley Earl's departments where overtime was routine.

Here is the same mock-up pictured on the previous page one month later. The model was refinished after modifications to the deck and fenders. The trend toward integrating grills and front bumpers was especially influential at this time; it is reflected in the composition of this front ensemble. Fortunately, Cadillac opted for a more conventional approach for its front end, but many ideas incorporated in this mock-up were subsequently employed.

Again – A Great New CADILLAC ... AT A LOW PRICE!

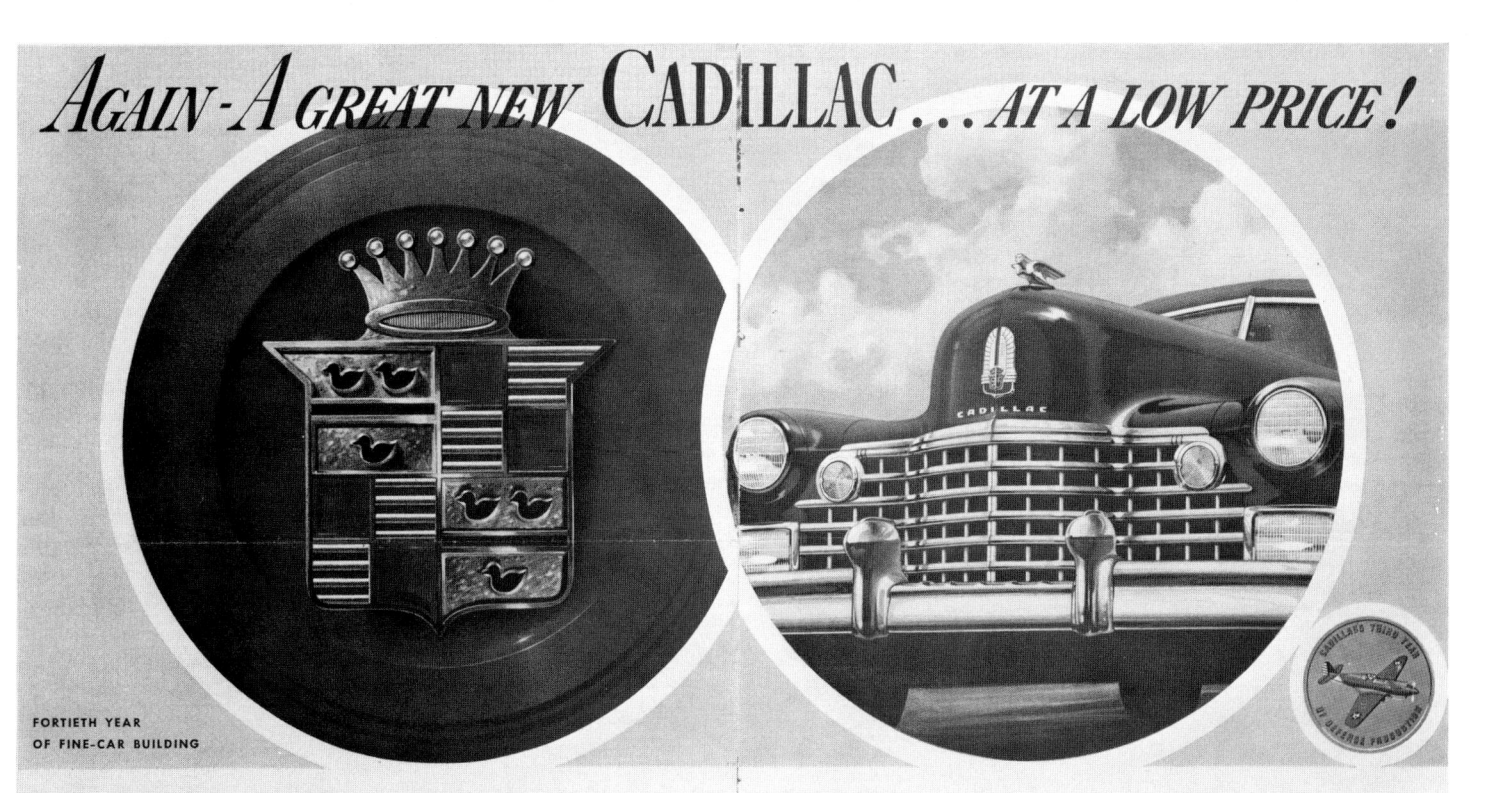

FORTIETH YEAR OF FINE-CAR BUILDING

SIX GREAT NEW SERIES
FOR 1942

The new Cadillac-Fleetwood Sixty Special—dynamically different in every way

CADILLAC HAS BUILT America's finest motor cars since 1902, *but never has a Cadillac announcement meant so much to so many people as it does today.* For Cadillac now presents exactly the kind of car everybody wants and *needs* for 1942—and it's priced within reach of every one who spends above a thousand dollars for a car.

This matchless value is a new and finer version of the most popular Cadillac ever built—the big, luxurious, thrifty Cadillac Sixty-One. Re-styled to give it the timeless beauty of perfect lines and proportions . . . years ahead in engineering . . . powered by Cadillac's mightiest V-8 engine . . . delivering 14 to 17 miles per gallon . . . and built to the highest quality standards in the industry, it stands ready to give you all that's best in motoring for years to come.

Moreover, like its companion cars—the ultra-smart Sixty-Two, the exclusive Sixty-Three, the spacious Sixty-Seven and the splendid Cadillac-Fleetwood Sixty Special and Seventy-Five—the new Cadillac Sixty-One is available, at extra cost, with Cadillac-engineered Hydra-Matic Drive—*and is the only car in its field providing this wonder-working advancement.*

Visit your Cadillac dealer today and confirm the welcome news that you can afford the finest—*just when you need it most!*

STYLED TO THE MINUTE
AND BUILT FOR THE YEARS

The new Cadillac Sixty-One—again available at a surprisingly low price

CONDENSED SPECIFICATIONS

ENGINE: Cadillac precision-built 90° Vee 8 design, L-head, bore 3½", stroke 4½", displacement 346 cu. in. Engine mounted in rubber at three points. Taxable horsepower 39.20—brake horsepower 150 at 3,400 r.p.m.

PISTONS: Lightweight, precision—manufactured to Cadillac quality standards. Surface treated to prevent scuffing. Pistons fitted with two compression rings and two oil rings which are surface treated with ferrous oxide for durability.

CARBURETION: Dual down-draft with equalized manifolding, mechanical fuel pump, oil bath type air cleaner, intake silencer, fully automatic choke.

GASOLINE TANK: Capacity 20 gallons; Series 75—24 gallons.

GENERATOR: Delco-Remy peak load current controlled generator maintains charging rate even when headlamps, radio, and heater are being used.

CLUTCH: 10½" semi-centrifugal single-plate torbend disc; Series 67 and 75: 11" diameter semi-centrifugal single dry plate torbend disc. Permanently lubricated ball throwout bearing reduces service expense.

TRANSMISSION: Cadillac pioneered and built Syncro-Mesh with pin type synchronizers, sliding low and reverse gears and constant-mesh second gear. Helical transmission gears fully carburized for hard use and long life.

LIGHTING: Sealed-Beam safety lighting system insures brilliant road illumination, accurate lamp adjustment and lasting reflector polish.

DIRECTIONAL SIGNALS: New, exclusive type which signal driver's intention to turn by flashing lights in parking and rear lamps. Operated by a lever located under left side of steering wheel which automatically returns to off position after turn is made.

FRONT SUSPENSION: Independent Knee-Action front wheels, simple and sturdy with large, helical coil springs for smoother riding comfort and effortless driving control. Thoroughly proven by nine years' use and millions of miles of testing.

SPRINGS: Independent helical type, front suspension, rear springs semi-elliptic type; spring leaves lubricated by wax-impregnated liners; 54½" long, 2" wide; Series 67 and 75: 56½" long, 2" wide.

BRAKES: New, Super-Safe hydraulic brakes operate in composite drums with 208 square inches braking area; Series 67 and 75: 233 square inches braking area.

DRIVE SHAFT: Two universal joints of the needle roller bearing type permanently packed with lubricant requiring no service attention.

REAR AXLE: Hypoid rear axle, Cadillac design and manufacture. Semi-floating type, insuring quiet, dependable performance. Gear ratio 3.77 to 1; Series 67 and 75: Gear ratio 4.27 to 1. Optional economy axle ratio, for Series 61, 62, 63, 60 Special, 3.36 to 1; for Series 67 and 75, 3.77 to 1.

STEERING GEAR: New ball bearing worm and nut gear—exceptionally smooth and practically frictionless. Design provides steering accuracy at all times.

FRAME: Tread—front 59"; rear, 63". Series 67 and 75: Tread—front 58½"; rear 62½". Rigid frame, X-type, with deep X-member junction and reinforced side members. Maximum depth 6⅝", flange width 2", thickness 9/64". Series 67 and 75: Maximum depth 7⅞", flange width Series 67, 2½"; Series 75, 2¼"; thickness, Series 60 Special, 67 and 75: 5/32".

RIDE STABILIZER: Double ride stabilizers—torsion bar-type front, cross link-type rear—hold car to level position and promote roadability and safety.

TIRES AND WHEELS: Slotted steel disc wheels with low pressure, 4-ply tires, 7.00x15. Series 67 and 75: Low pressure, 6-ply tires, 7.50x16.

FENDERS: Fenders and other sheet metal parts are bonderized to prevent rust.

WHEELBASE: Series 61 and 63, 126". Series 62, 129". Series 60 Special, 133". Series 75, 136". Series 67, 139".

BODY TYPES: Series 61—Two, Series 62—Five, Series 63—One, Series 60 Special—Two, Series 67—Four, Series 75—Six. No-draft ventilation and Turret-Top construction on closed models. Wide selection of color and upholstery options. Cadillac All-Weather Ventilation standard equipment on all models.

CADILLAC MOTOR CAR DIVISION OF GENERAL MOTORS SALES CORPORATION RESERVES THE RIGHT TO MAKE CHANGES AT ANY TIME, WITHOUT NOTICE, IN PRICES, COLORS, MATERIALS, EQUIPMENT, SPECIFICATIONS AND MODELS, AND ALSO TO DISCONTINUE MODELS.

The palpable Cadillac look that dominated the American scene through 1947, and beyond, developed in emulation of the considerable charm of the 1942 models.

even by pre-war standards. In 1940 the difference between the base list price of a 62-Series sedan and a Sixty-Special was $345. In 1941, with the greatly upgraded Sixty-Special, the difference jumped to $700; and then up to $781 in 1942, despite a $259 price hike on the 62 sedan.

Cadillac wanted to give the new version of the Sixty-Special an identity of its own. It had to have features that would make it readily distinguishable from the 62 sedan, features an already-established clientele could point to, and relate to, in terms of exclusivity. This philosophy dictated the use of character accents. The fender louvers, the rear quarter louvers, the longer body (four inches longer than the 62), the special center post treatment, the Fleetwood name script on the rear deck and the luxuriously appointed interior accomplished this objective in grand style.

The balance of the Cadillac line for 1942 followed closely the offerings of the previous year. Series 61, 63 and 67 cars employed refined 1942 front ensembles, fenders, trim and interiors using the same bodies that had proved so popular in 1941.

The 75-Series had several exclusive features not found on the other models: Fender spears, 1941-type fender skirts and tail lamps, and newly designed hood ports. Cadillac management embraced the concept that a car of this type required a restrained, less-progressive styling concept. Thus, this finest of Cadillacs perpetuated a strongly traditional dignity into the years of uncertainty that lay ahead.

New 1942 body features included an all-weather ventilating system consisting of two ventilating passages (left and right) which extended from the radiator grill to the front compartment. The flow of fresh air was controlled by valves operated by push-pull knobs on the instrument panel. The all-weather system obviated the cowl vent allowing the hood on all series except the 75 to extend back to the windshield. Air from the right duct could be directed to the heater-defroster when required.

Wheel shields (skirts) became standard equipment on all cars. With the exception of the 75s, removal and installation of the skirts was a quick and simple procedure requiring the rotation of a hex-head nut located on the lower edge of the shield.

Another new feature used on sedan bodies was a safety latch which allowed rear door locks to be set so that children couldn't operate the inner door handle until the lock button was raised. (This procedure is outlined in the appendix.)

Two types of dash panels were used on the 1942s. The 1941-type panel, with circular speedometer and clock and a rectangular instrument cluster, was continued on Series 61, 63, 67 and 75 cars. The 62-Series and the Sixty-Special had an all-new dash panel and radio grill with gauges located in two smaller round dials to the left of the speedometer. The clock was recessed into an enlarged glove compartment door.

Numerous other interior changes were incorporated. Redesigned gear shift and directional signal levers, a T-grip handle for the hand brake, a new DeLuxe steering wheel and fully adjustable sun visors were the most obvious.

Although the DeLuxe trim package was dropped on the 61-Series, many of the special interior upholstery and trim options available in 1941 were again offered at slightly increased prices. Special color on the garnish and finish mouldings, for example, was $15. Steering column assembly, brackets, instrument panel and front compartment painted parts were also $15 in a special color. A full listing of these special options is included in the appendix.

Cadillac discontinued thermostatically-operated radiator shutters in 1942. A single radiator thermostat was located in the top radiator tank. The use of one thermostat in a V-8 where the water pump was set in the right block could have created a problem in equal cooling for both blocks when the thermostat was closed, hence a by-pass pipe was run from the water outlet in the left block to the intake of the pump. This arrangement also reduced the time required to warm up the heater.

Another chassis improvement was thicker brake rims which absorbed and dissipated heat more readily in high speed stops. In addition, the open edge had a heavy new

Loading new cars into special boxcars for cross-country shipment was a tricky procedure — especially where the 75 was concerned.

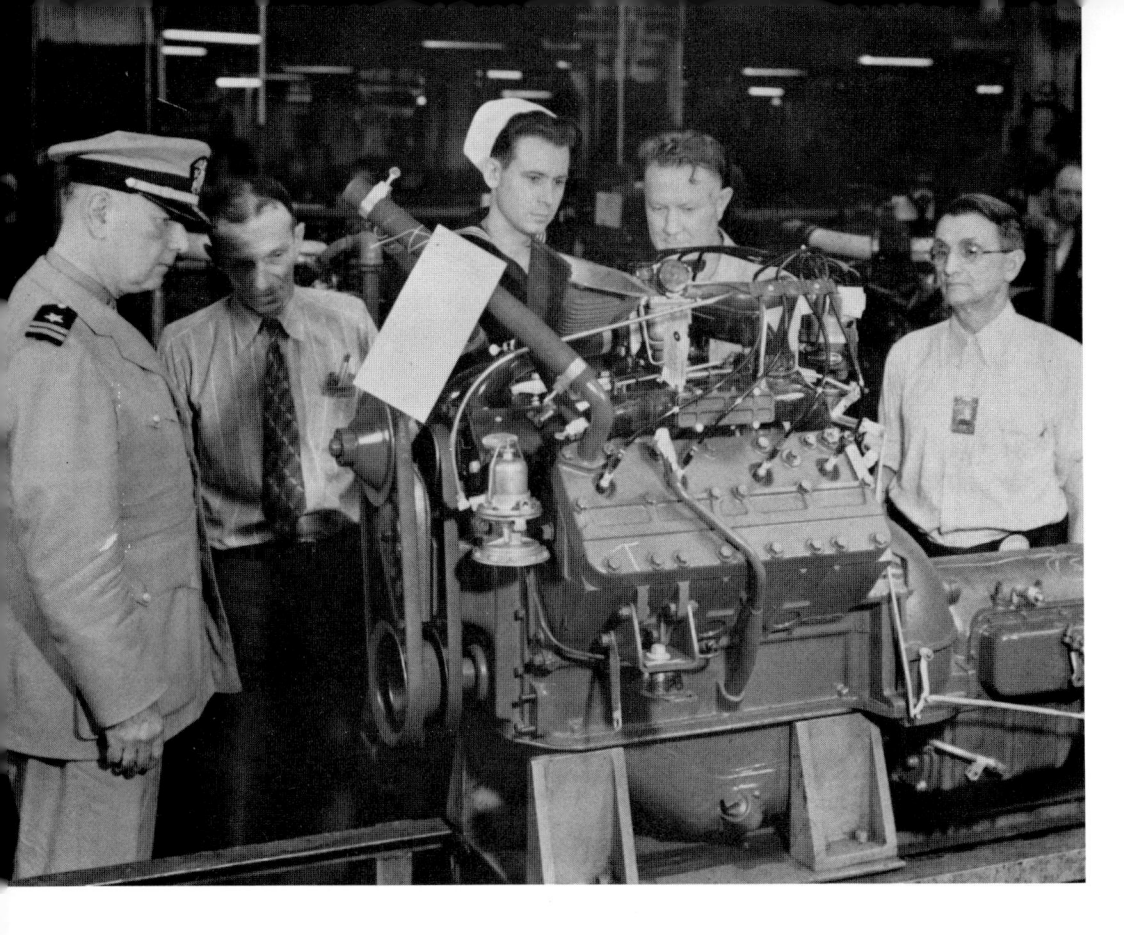

It has been estimated that as many as 200,000 various L-head V-8s were manufactured under government contracts during the war years. Many of these military engines were later successfully converted for passenger car installation, although the practice was frowned upon by the factory.

integral ring which helped radiate heat and also restricted the possibility that the drum might bell-mouth. The ring also acted to minimize the entrance of dirt and water.

Nineteen-forty-two might have eclipsed the triumph of 1941 had not car production stopped on February 4. Only 16,511 cars had rolled off the line in four months amid acute material shortages and restrictive Government allotments. Blackouts, those units produced between January 15 and February 4, which had painted rather than plated trim, constituted 2,150 of the total.

Actually, Cadillac was in its third year of war materiel production if the contract to provide components for the Allison aircraft engine is considered. Just two months after Pearl Harbor, Cadillac was assigned to constructing the M-5 light tank. It was superseded by the twin engined M-24 light tank which, like the M-5, was powered by Cadillac V-8s and Hydra-Matics — one engine and transmission for each track.

These Cadillac-built tanks were used extensively in both theaters of war. Other Cadillac L-head engines, thousands in number, powered military equipment of every description from anti-aircraft gun carriages (the M-19 built by Cadillac) to fleets of amphibious craft.

Coincidentally, the Allison aero-engine (for which Cadillac produced parts) had a significant bearing on the future design of automobiles. Bill Mitchell remembers the day Harley Earl dispatched a group of his top designers to a preview showing of the Allison-powered Lockheed P-38 fighter plane. *Earl knew the commandant out at Selfridge Field (Michigan), and he arranged for us to go out and see one of the first P-38s, actually the 13th P-38 made. Any designer seeing those booms coming back into the tails could visualize how you could take a fender and go right back into the tail. We went ahead and built some models then; called them the Interceptor.* Ultimately the events of that day would revolutionize the appearance of the postwar Cadillac.

There were no cars produced during the next several years along Clark Avenue although a few 75s were reportedly built by Fleetwood during the war as staff cars for military and political figures. Many 1941 and 1942 75s were seen around the world during the war years; they became internationally recognized symbols of American presence.

Town Brougham, was the Derham name for this Sixty-Special conversion. Modifications were carried out by the Pennsylvania coachworks during calendar 1942 on a 42-6069F with a special-order reinforced frame. The original owner was Mrs. William Deering Howe, but the stylish towncar gained more notice while in livery service on the streets of New York City in the 1950s.

Blackouts, those cars completed after January 4, 1942, in compliance with chrome, nickel and other conservation mandates, had little or no brightwork. As seen here, efforts to maintain some semblance of the original design concept were marginally successful. The only visible chrome on this 42-6109 is on the door lock cover and bumpers.

This unique convertible sedan was built expressly for Mrs. Harley Earl by GM Styling in 1942. In addition to the division glass, there was a removable secondary cowl and windscreen that could be installed in the rear compartment when the top was lowered. Note the blackout grill and extended fender line. There were low fins faired into the rear fenders.

·79·

·80·

4-21-41
DAWSON
SS493

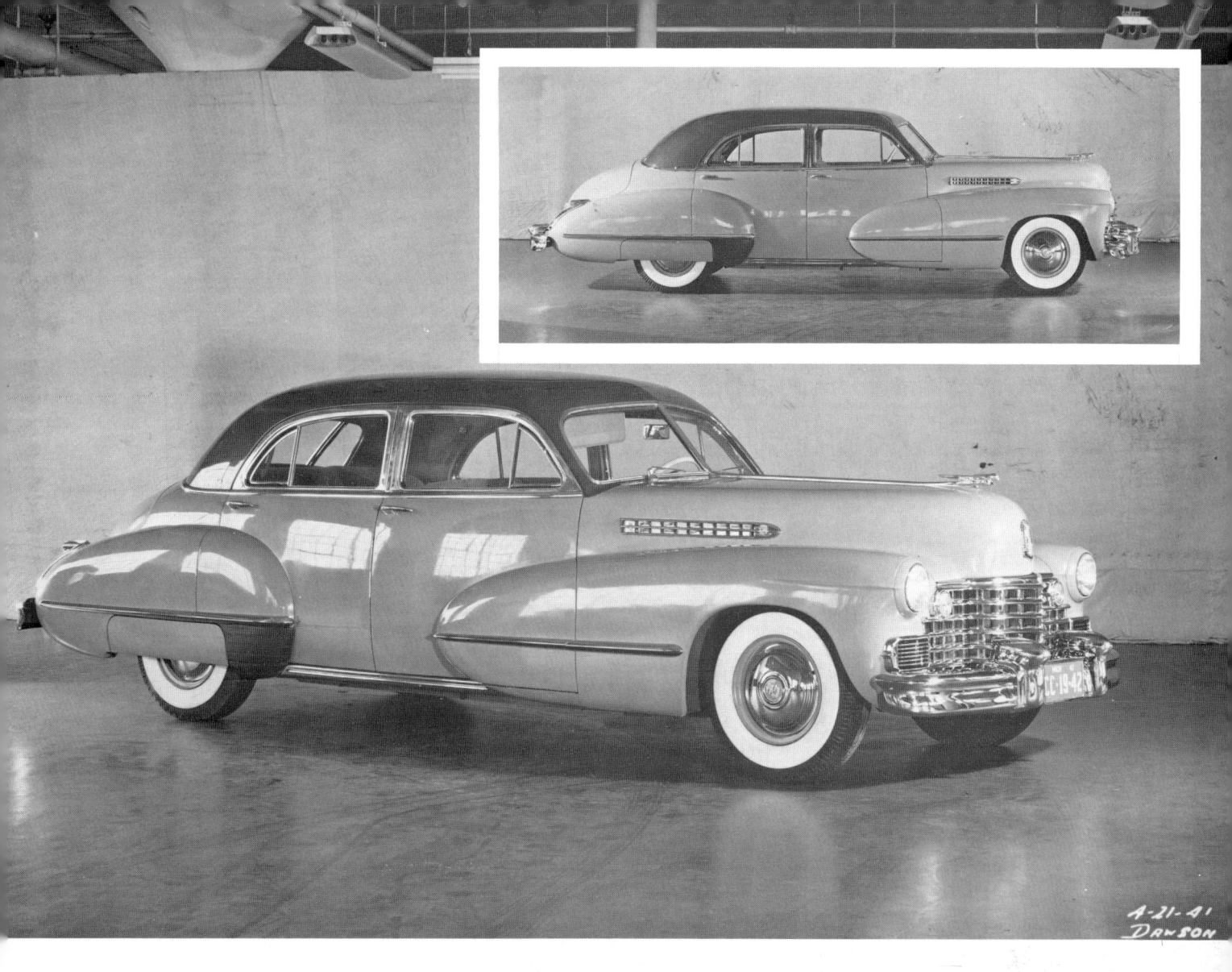

The photographs on this and the facing page represent a graphic demonstration of the precision and realism that Styling's modelers imparted to their creations. The proposed DeLuxe interior in this wood-based mock-up of the 62-Series sedan reflects the generous labor inputs affordable in 1942. Post-war wage-price spirals led to marked reductions in time-consuming trim operations like pleating. Hood ventilators, which proved such a handsome addition to the 1941 models, were unnecessary embellishments after the move to longer fender lines, but Cadillac wasn't convinced until this mock-up was completed.

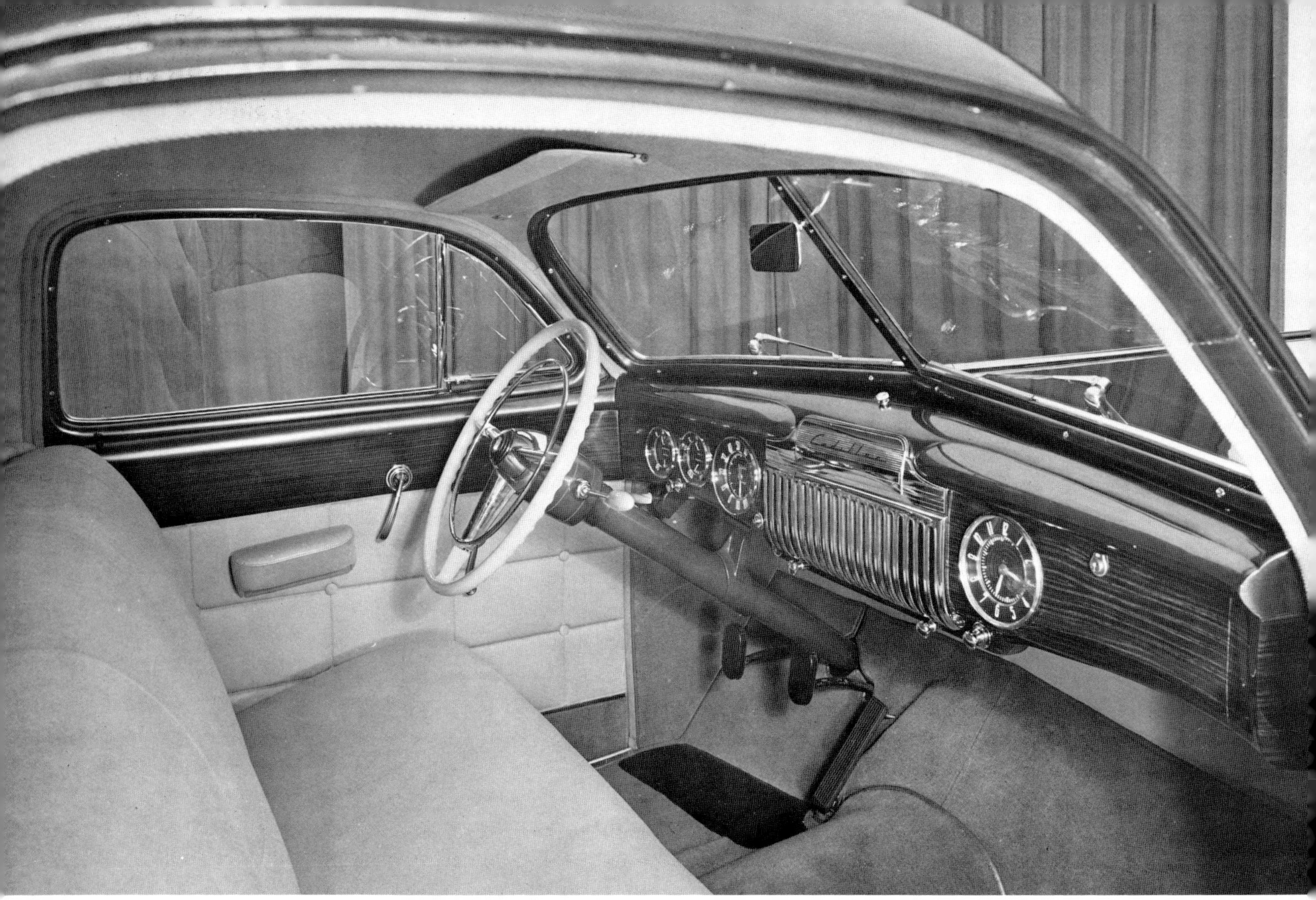

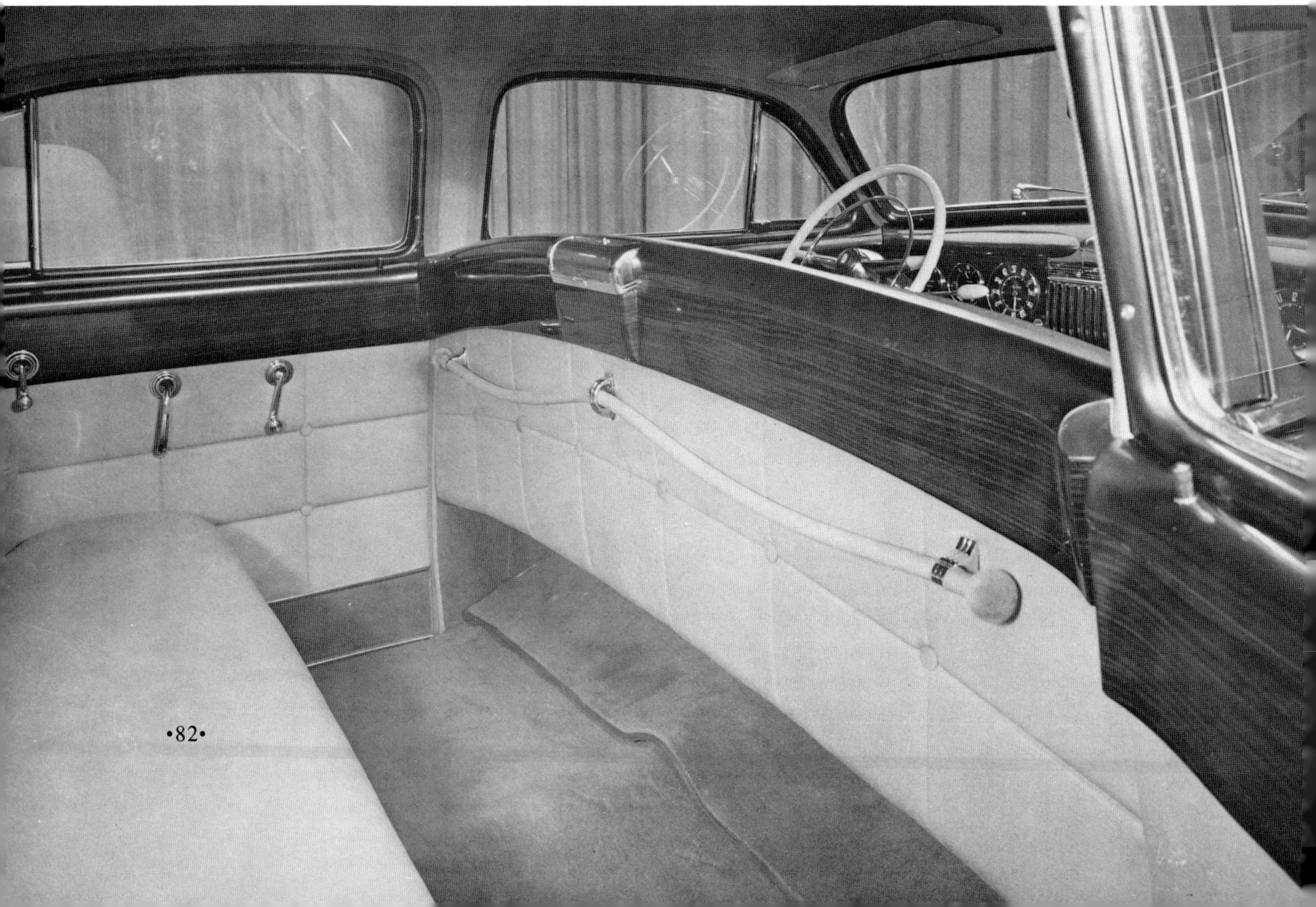

1942 FLEETWOOD SIXTY-SPECIAL

Sixty-Special production followed the format proposed in this styling model. Minor interior changes included the addition of adjustable foot rests in the foot recess under the front seat. The cowling-type instrument panel that curved onto the door finish panels, and the redesigned instrument faces, were exclusive features on the Sixty-Special and 62-Series. Inset, the prototype Sixty-Specials had chromed window reveals, but Cadillac rejected the idea and later adopted the louvers on the fenders which were designed to impart a lower look.

SERIES 62, OPTIONAL INTERIOR

Above, the 62-Series optional interior had bolstered and pleated seat backs and cushions (standard interiors were plain-paneled with a bolster on the seat back only). Optional interiors also had a pleated front seat back, carpeted — rather than leatherette — scuff pads, and duo-toned garnish mouldings (solid color on the upper areas with a wood grain below). Below, Style 42-6269 (with the optional interior it would have been a 42-6269D). Belt mouldings (stainless steel) appeared on all 62-Series models in 1942.

The 62-Series coupe had a magnificent sweeping roof line that was enhanced by the complementing curves of the belt mouldings, window reveals and rear fenders. The commanding grace of this rear treatment made it the epitome of motoring fashion for the balance of the decade. To many discerning collectors this styling represents the finest fastback design ever placed in production. Above, a 42-6207D factory study comparing it to the 61-Series at the top of the next page. Center and below, an attractively restored version that, with the exception of 1947-type stone guards, is stock. The raised-wing crest motif was carried through from 1941.

•85•

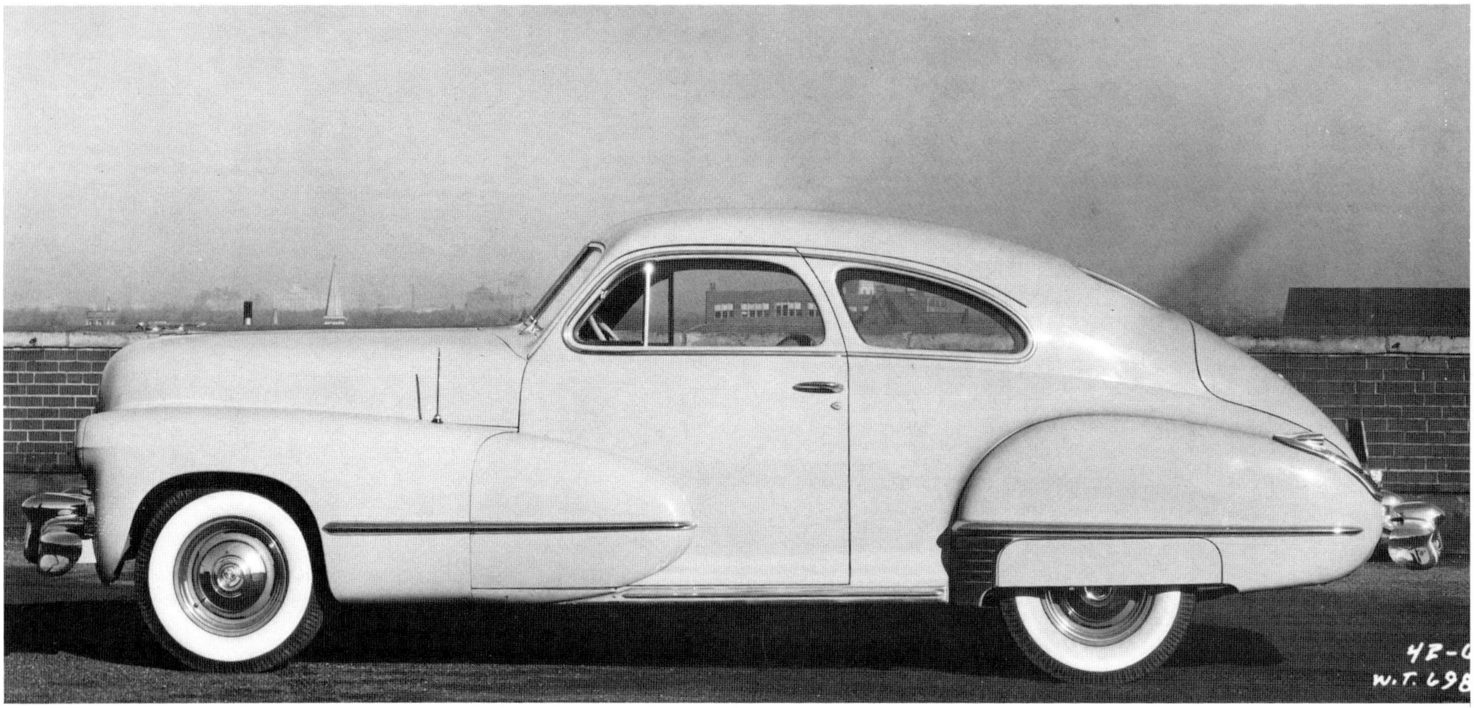

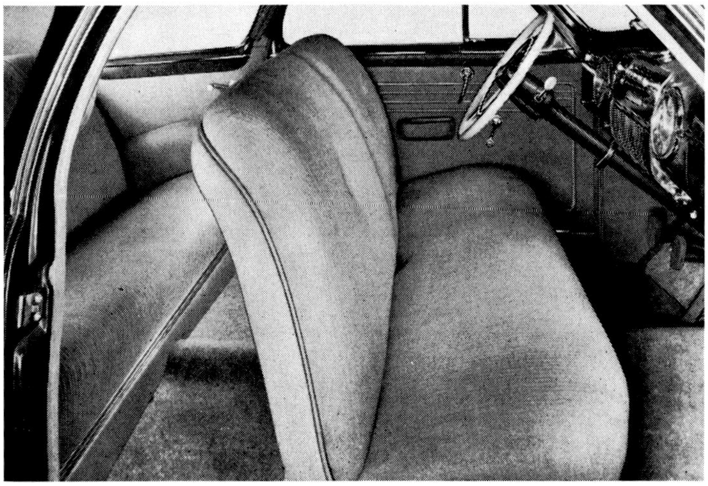

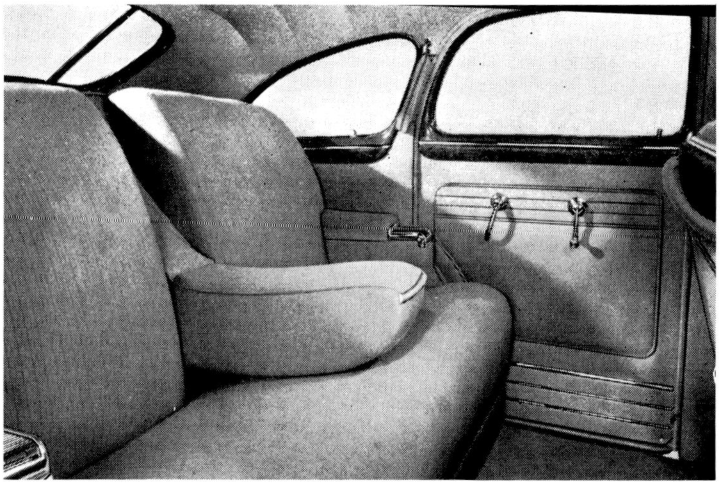

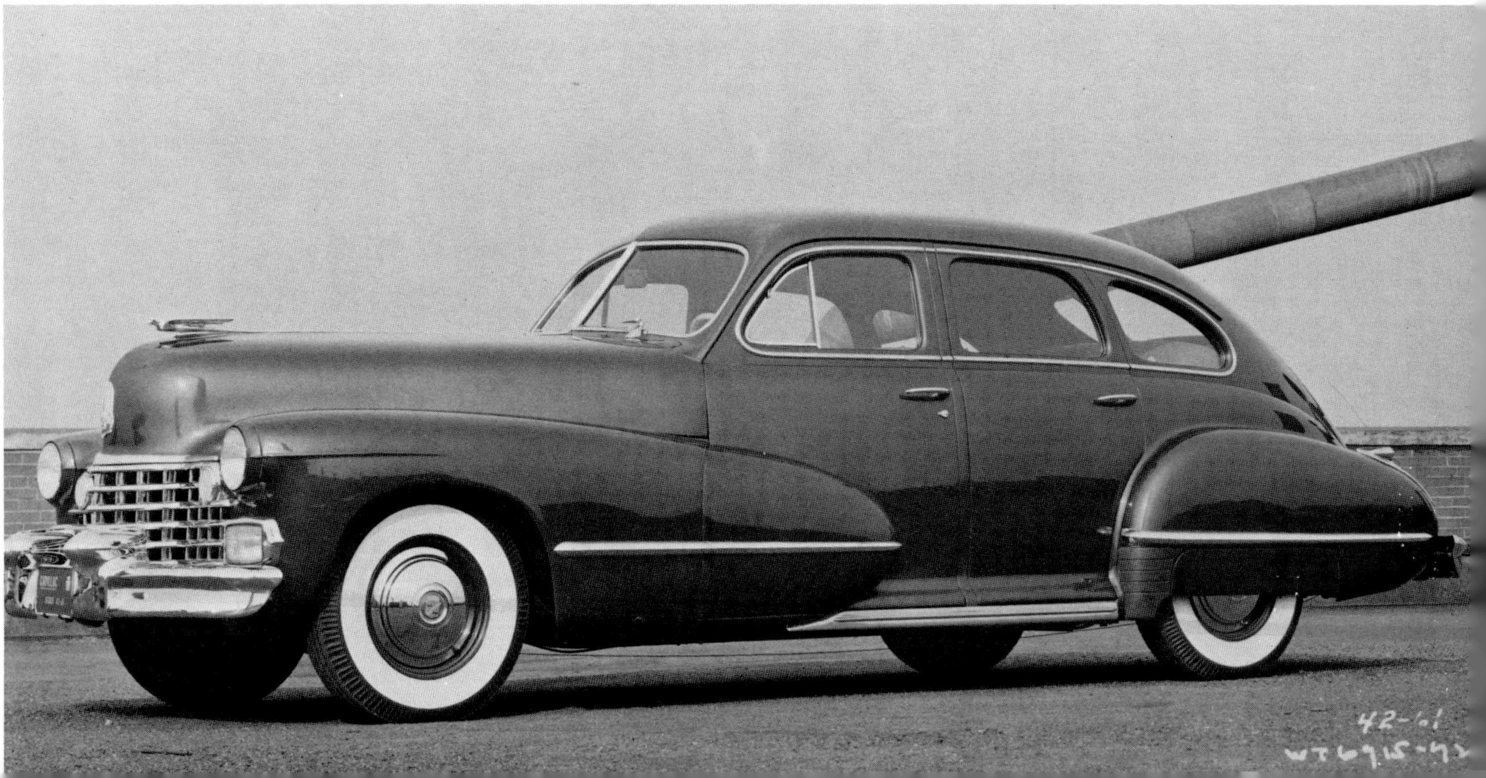
42-61

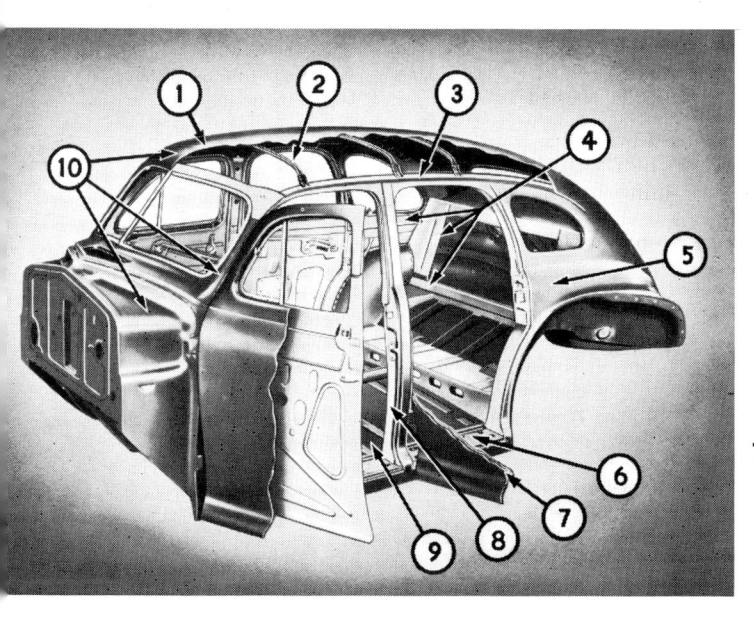

1. One-piece solid steel top.
2. Sturdy "U" shaped steel roof bows.
3. Steel roof rail welded to inner steel body framework.
4. Steel braces welded to sides of inner body structure joined by heavy steel cross member below rear window frame.
5. Steel body panels welded together.
6. Steel rocker panels welded to sides of underbody.
7. Steel door panels reinforced with steel.
8. Two "U" shaped steel bars welded together form each pillar post.
9. Steel floor welded integral with body.
10. Cowl structure one complete unit of reinforced dash, windshield posts and header panel welded to Turret Top. Also cowl structural support extends in straight line from front body bracket to windshield pillar for extreme strength and rigidity.

An interesting change in character was achieved when the 1942 front ensemble and fenders were married to the B-bodies. The revised 61-Series coupe, opposite page above, had especially well-balanced proportions. Opposite page center, Data Book illustrations of 61-Series interiors. Opposite page below, Style 42-6109. Below, not a leak test but a photographic session promoting All-Weather ventilation.

75-Series changes for 1942 were subtle. Grill, bumpers and hood louvers were apparent modifications to the classical 1941 edition. This exquisite 7519F Imperial five-passenger sedan was originally purchased by movie producer David O. Selznick, in December of 1941. Selznick and his actress wife, Jennifer Jones, accounted for most of the 44,000 miles put on the car by the mid-1960s. Right, the beautifully preserved original interior of the Selznick car. Cadillac made air conditioning available in 1941; the Selznick Imperial sedan had one of these rare trunk mounted units. (Only 300 air conditioning installations were made by the factory during the 1941 model run.)

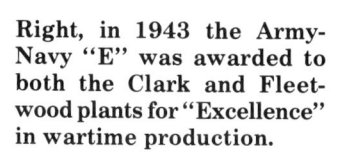

Right, in 1943 the Army-Navy "E" was awarded to both the Clark and Fleetwood plants for "Excellence" in wartime production.

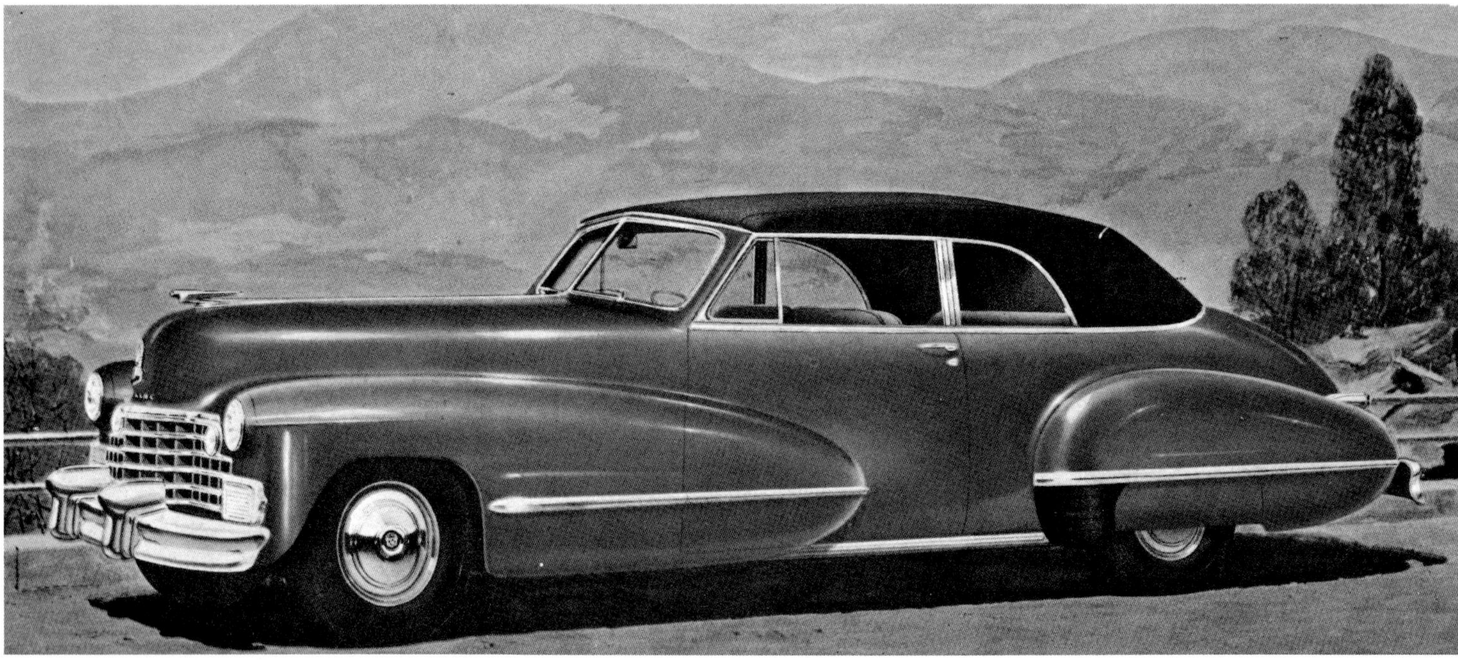

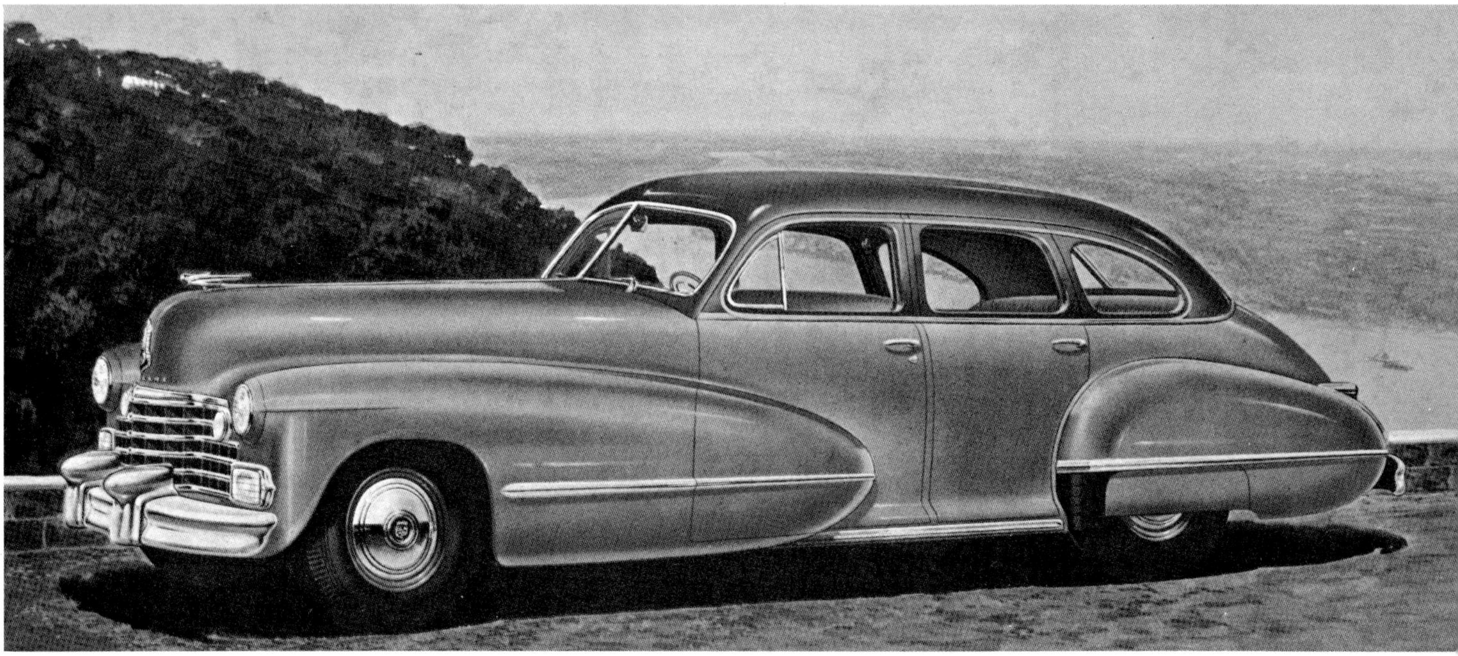

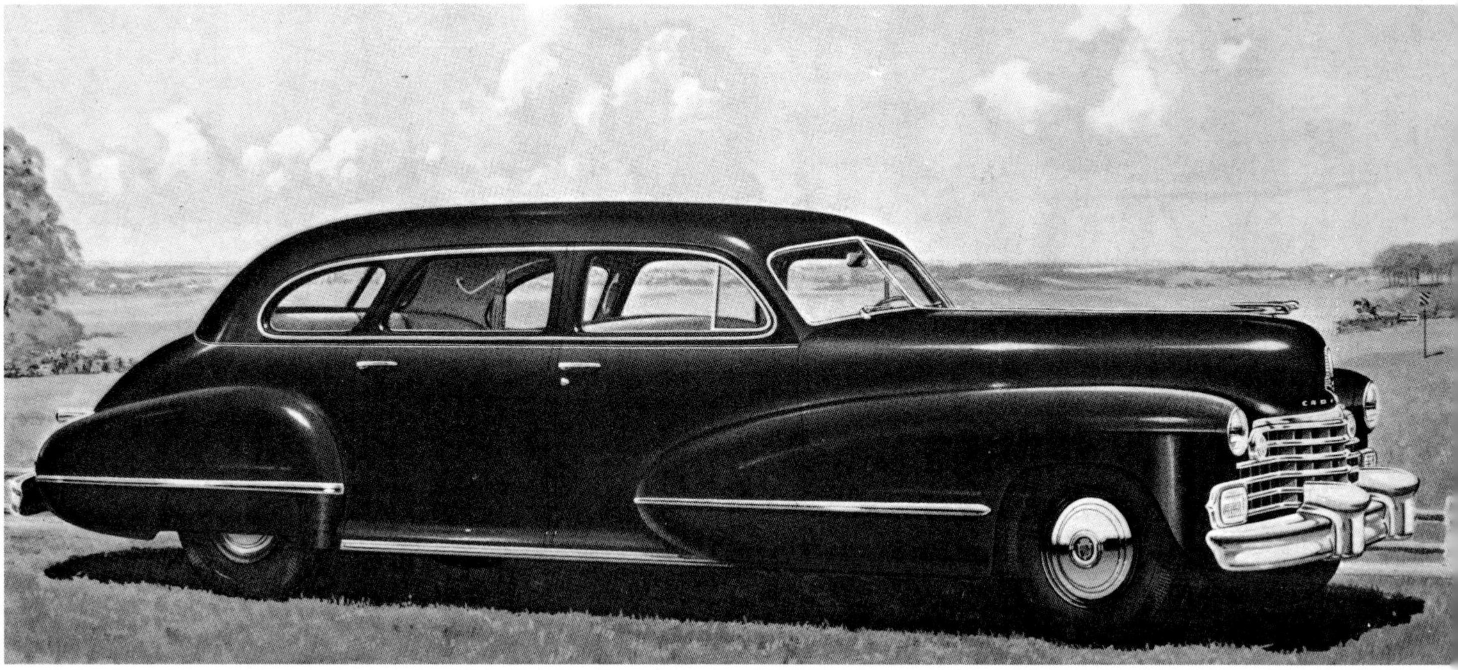

Opposite, three air brush renderings from the 1942 sales catalog: Top to bottom, the redesigned 62-Series convertible coupe, the the 63-Series five-passenger sedan and the 67-Series seven-passenger sedan. Right, the 67's lavishly appointed interior had a revised trim motif and special foot rests. Below, two L-head Cadillac V-8s in a military application.

1946-1947

Sights like this brought smiles to millions of Americans in the months following the War.

FROM RECONVERSION TO FULL PRODUCTION

    A profound peace settled over the United States following the upheaval of World War II. The feeling across the land was one of having completed a monumental job, of having enforced proper perspectives, of having righted the world order. It was a time of reunion, rehabilitation and, for the auto industry, reconversion to civilian production. Perhaps the ultimate realization that normalcy was returning came to Americans when they caught sight of those first postwar cars.

    The last Cadillac-built M-24 tank clanked down the line on August 24, 1945. Just 54 days later the first 1946 automobile moved out of the Division's final assembly area. There really wasn't any need to restyle the Cadillac in 1946. The extremely popular 1942 models had never been broadly merchandised and, besides, the dealers were already buried in orders that couldn't be met. But precedents don't fall easily along Clark Avenue, especially ingrained traditions like the annual model update. Cosmetic revisions included a restyled grill, three-piece bumpers that extended around the fenders, block lettering on the front fenders, a smoother hood ornament, and V-type hood and trunk emblems.

    Cadillac's tremendous role in the war effort had necessitated expansion of many manufacturing and engineering facilities. A huge new assembly building was constructed in 1943 and a large shipping and receiving court completed early in 1944. Two overhead conveyors had been installed in the plant, one to carry cylinder blocks and other major castings from the foundry to the machine shops, and the second to transport completed engines and axles from the machine shops to the final assembly building. The vastly modernized and supplemented engineering and research facilities included new engine test dynamometer rooms, and rooms for testing transmissions and axles.

Cadillac's service flag as it looked on April 3, 1946. The two-story overpass connects factory buildings on both sides of Detroit's Clark Avenue.

Body styles essentially paralleled the offerings of 1942. The first six months after Fisher Body reconverted to passenger car production were devoted to supplying Cadillac with C-body sedan stampings; C-bodied coupes and convertibles came later. As a result more than half of all the Cadillacs manufactured in 1945-1946 were 62-Series four-doors. A trickle of 61s began in May of 1946 and the first postwar 75s didn't appear until late August. Sixty-Specials began rolling through the Fleetwood plant in July of 1946.

Two 1942 models, the 63 and the 67, never did reach fruition after the War. The 67-Series, as well as the Buick Limited, was eliminated largely because of the diminished market for large sedan types. The 63 on the other hand was dropped because its DeLuxe trimmed B-body was overlapping other popular models in an otherwise complete product line.

The real story of Cadillac progress in 1946 was under the hood. The 346 cubic inch V-8 had literally never gone out of production during the war years. It had, in myriad military applications, survived three years under the severest of conditions in the same basic configuration, but improvements abounded: Redesigned 3-ring pistons with more durable rings, cylinder heads that provided better cooling, new bearings, redesigned valve guides, new tappet bodies of heavier construction, improved throttle controls, a modified thermo-plug for more accurate engine temperature readings, and refined carburetion that provided better acceleration under all conditions. Legions of Americans discovered in this Cadillac a minimum requirement for service work with maximum smoothness, power and dependability.

The battle-tested Hydra-Matic emerged from the War as the finest completely automatic system of drive theretofore placed in a motor vehicle. It had stronger and wider front and rear bands, a redesigned front pump, specially moulded clutch plates, new main shaft, new rear unit clutch hub, and it used vastly improved seals and hydraulic fluid. This transmission coupled to the L-head engine constituted a virtually indestructible combination that could master the most grueling driving conditions.

A fundamental change made in the 1946 cars, and carried thereafter, was

Cadillac's first negative battery ground. Reversing the ground of the electrical system did not affect the starter, solenoid, starter relay, or horn and lighting components. However, the voltage regulator, coil, ammeter, and temperature gauge were not interchangeable with previous models. Generators from earlier series cars could be interchanged providing the polarity of the units was reversed.

Beautiful new stainless steel running boards gave the 75-Series cars a distinction that set them apart from the prewar models. The running board motif continued on the rear fender with the use of a broad stainless steel moulding along the lower edge of the skirt. Excepting brightwork revisions, the 1946 Seventy-Fives closely paralleled the Fleetwood practices of 1942. The only major change incorporated in 1947, other than exterior plated parts, was the introduction of power windows.

The DeLuxe interior option was eliminated in 1946. Seats in the 61-Series continued the plain-paneled pattern of 1942, while the 62-Series closed cars had partially pleated seat backs and plain-paneled cushions. Trim options were blue-gray or tan dual-tone cord, or blue-gray or tan Heathertone broadcloth. Convertible interiors were black, tan, green, blue or red leather combined with Bedford cord. Door panels on all but the Fleetwoods were plain-paneled. Retaining the manufacturing set-ups of 1942, the 61 and 75-Series cars continued with a 1941-type dash through 1947.

The availability of special order finish options on interior fitments from 1946 on cannot be confirmed from existing sales and service documents in the factory archives. Cadillac apparently did not publish *Special Features* books after 1942 (these publications had detailed all special order options in the pre-war years). Although it is possible that deviations from the standard upholstery selections were made, it appears that the practice was strongly discouraged in the immediate post-war era due to the overwhelming demand for new cars. Another option not available after the war was the division glass in the Sixty-Special.

By the second postwar year, 1947, Cadillac dealers were holding 96,000 unfilled orders for new cars. Division Sales Manager, D. E. Ahrens, summed up the situation this way: *Cadillac will have but one merchandising goal in 1947 — to get a new Cadillac motorcar into the possession of every member of the greatest list of would-be purchasers in our history. Attainment of this objective may not be as difficult as it appears. Cadillac production, as 1946 ended, averaged 215 units a day. During 1941 — our largest*

The first cars down the line in 1945 had brackets to hold temporary wooden bumpers.

volume year — our daily production averaged 300 units. Thus it can be seen that we are narrowing the gap between waiting for a Cadillac and owning a Cadillac.

Shortages will continue to call the production tune during a good part of 1947. I do not know of any magical event which took place on New Year's Day which will make steel, and iron, and all the other vexing shortages vanish immediately. We are not at the top of the hill yet. But we may be closer to the top than we realize.

We have a peculiar problem at Cadillac. In the first place, our product — and I say this in all modesty — is one of the most sought-after, and most scarce items in the world today. The Cadillac car has become, in fact, a veritable success symbol. And, secondly, we are blessed with the greatest owner loyalty attached to any product — certainly the greatest commanded by an automobile. Our cancellations, despite long waits and price raises, have held at less than three percent.

The beauty of the 1946 front ensemble is strikingly portrayed in this view of the 62-Series. All the grills in GM's 1946 models, Chevrolet through Cadillac, were styled in the same studio in early 1945.

Officially the start of the 1947 models was January 2, 1947. There was no customary interval between annual models; workers along the assembly line simply came back from their New Year's holiday and began using components marked 1947 rather than 1946. The body styles that had become so familiar in 1946 were retained without change or exception. The only exterior modifications involved grill, emblems, stone guards, hubcaps and fender logo.

The appearance of the grill was perceivably altered by eliminating one of the horizontal members. The resulting increase of spacing between the bars gave the 1947 grill a huskier, wider look. All of the horizontal and vertical grill members, with the exception of the new concave top header bar attached to the hood, were stamped rather than cast in 1947.

Optional-equipment fog lamps similar to those used in 1946 combined parking and directional light functions through the utilization of an additional bulb in the same housing. When no fog lamps were present, cover plates designed to harmonize with the surrounding grill, and containing a round lens in the center, provided parking lights and directional signals.

A popular new wheel disc option was available in 1947. It was dubbed the *sombrero* because its shape suggested a wide brimmed hat. It was the most talked about hubcap of the Forties and variations were used on Cadillacs into the mid-Forties. The stainless steel *sombreros* seen on many 1947s today were produced by Cadillac in the Fifties as replacements.

The rubber stone guards which had been used on 1946 rear fenders were replaced with stainless steel guards which harmonized with the rest of the brightwork. Other stainless steel trim included the rocker sill extensions and belt mouldings on 61 and 62-Series cars.

The new V-type hood emblem placed the crest in a field of striped cloisonne, while on the deck lid was a winged crest — reminiscent of earlier Cadillac-LaSalle insignias. The winged crest was used on all series except the Sixty-Special; its trunk

Left, the 1946 75-Series with its full-length stainless steel running boards. Many early post-war limousines had cloth headliners and door panels in the front compartment rather than the full-leather treatment that was provided in 1947 models. Below, the 75-Series rear compartment radio. Including a separate vacuum-operated aereal, the installed price was $151.93.

carried the word Fleetwood in script continuing the tradition that began in 1942. The block style Cadillac name was replaced on the front fenders by the now-familiar script.

Chassis and drive train components were essentially identical in 1946 and 1947 although there was one major improvement in the '47 engine that actually went into production in late 1946. It was hydraulic valve lifters with hardened ball seats. The new lifters had the ability to crush or move aside anything that resisted proper ball seating. These units are more fully described in the appendix.

Few interior changes were noticeable in the 1947 cars. Most obvious perhaps was that the carpet in the front compartment was enhanced by a chrome moulding surrounding the steering column, brake, and, if there was one, clutch pedal. The accessory ivory plastic steering wheel had a semi-circular horn ring of slightly different construction from that supplied in 1946. Incidentally, most of the cracking problems experienced with these plastic steering wheels stems from the different expansion coefficients for the plastic and the inner steel core. Apparently all plastic of that era tended to deteriorate when left out in the weather, with sun being the worst enemy.

Hydro-Lectric window lifts became standard equipment on 1947 model 62 convertibles and 75-Series cars. A complex system by modern comparison, but nonetheless one that performed well especially in sedans where the glass guides were rigidly secured to the door pillars. The author's 1947 model 75 sedan has required the replacement of only two hydraulic window lift cylinders in 18 years, and presumably none before that.

A few facts should be remembered about the proper maintenance of these systems. First, all cylinders should be activated regularly. This will tend to keep the seals within the cylinders from drying up and generating leaks. Second, if a leak is detected, it is wise to repair it immediately. Cylinder and line replacement are relatively simple procedures and are outlined in detail in various Fisher Body Service and Construction manuals published during these years. (A few pertinent excerpts from the *1948 "C" Series Body manual* appear in the appendix.) Third, the fluid in the system should be changed every year. Dexron transmission fluid (type B) has been successfully used in place of the original brake fluid. Dexron won't damage paint and upholstery as severely as brake fluid. Other transmission fluids are not acceptable. Special flushing fluids are also available and should be used periodically to clean the system. Fourth, drainage slots on the bottoms of the doors must be kept clear so that, should a leak occur, the fluid can escape.

The advertised base price of a typical 61-Series Cadillac was up to $2,324 by 1947, a 38 percent increase over the price of the same car in 1941. Postwar inflation sent prices up an average of $567 on typical 61 and 62-Series cars in 1946 and another $156 in 1947. Similarly the 75-Series limousine carried a price tag in excess of $5,000 in 1947.

With the Office of Price Administration (OPA) still operational after the War, dealers realized extra revenues by merchandising every conceivable type of accessory. Sunvisors, locking gas caps, outside spare tire inflation valves, spotlights, fog lights, back-up lights, trunk lights, wipers on rear windows, seat covers, rear seat radio speakers, and even special chrome trim items — like the 1942-type Sixty-Special lower body louvers — radically increased the delivered prices on these first postwar cars. Dealer-installed specialties plus the broad range of factory-installed accessories brought considerable extra profits to dealers and salesmen in the midst of a booming, but product scarce, seller's market.

For the first time in as long as anyone could remember Cadillac kept right on building a previous model into a new calendar year. Actual production on 1947 cars didn't stop until January 13, 1948. By that date some 61,926 1947s had been assembled, more than double the 29,194 units produced during the 1946 model run. But still the unprecedented demand for both new and used Cadillacs kept growing.

The Cadillac Serviceman

JULY 1946

VOLUME XX   NUMBER 7

TOP CADILLAC EXECUTIVES PROMOTED
GENERAL MOTORS MANAGEMENT SHIFT AFFECTS CADILLAC

President C. E. Wilson of General Motors Corporation Names Nicholas Dreystadt as the General Manager of Chevrolet—Largest GM Division

CHIEF ENGINEER JOHN F. GORDON BECOMES THE NEW GENERAL MANAGER OF CADILLAC

On June 4, 1946, momentous things happened at the Cadillac Motor Car Division, for on that day Mr. C. E. Wilson, President of General Motors Corporation, announced that our beloved General Manager, Nicholas Dreystadt, had been transferred to another Division of the Corporation—Chevrolet. In his place, Cadillac has gained a most capable chief executive, John F. Gordon, the youngest General Manager in General Motors Divisions—a man who in twenty-three years has worked his way up from a 60-cent-an-hour laboratory assistant to Manager of his Division.

Mr. Dreystadt first became associated with Cadillac in 1916, when he began a decade of service with the Cadillac Branch in Chicago. In 1926, he was called to Detroit and, after a few months of traveling on sales and service, became the General Parts and Service Manager at the factory. In 1932, Mr. Dreystadt was appointed Works Manager, and in June, 1934, he became General Manager. Since that time he has done much to make Cadillac the most modern and efficient automobile manufacturing unit in the entire industry. In June, 1946, Mr. Dreystadt became General Manager of Chevrolet.

Born in Akron, Ohio, on May 15, 1900, John F. Gordon became interested in automobiles when his family moved to Colorado. There he joined a group of youngsters (including Floyd Clymer, famous as a motor car historian) who, not satisfied with what Detroit was doing, rebuilt cars for greater speed and better mountain climbing. In 1918, he entered Annapolis, having taken high honors in his entrance examinations. In 1922 when he graduated, the United States Navy was just scrapping its ships, but Detroit was continuing to build automobiles. So John F. Gordon headed for the University of Michigan, where in 1923 he obtained his Master's degree in Engineering.

After graduation, four companies made him offers, and he accepted the one with Cadillac. Here his career would truly have delighted the heart of Horatio Alger. Starting at the very bottom as a laboratory assistant or technician, Mr. Gordon worked his way progressively up to Foreman of the Experimental Laboratory in 1929; Motor Design Engineer in 1933; Assistant to the Chief Engineer in charge of

JOHN F. GORDON   NICHOLAS DREYSTADT

Allison engines at the Allison Division in 1940; and then back to Cadillac on June 1, 1943, as Chief Engineer. To his new assignment as General Manager, Mr. Gordon brings a wealth of practical experience in Cadillac interests, policies, and operations.

E. N. COLE APPOINTED CHIEF ENGINEER

One of General Manager Gordon's first official acts was the appointment of Edward N. Cole as Chief Engineer. Born in Marne, Michigan, September 17, 1909, Mr. Cole was educated in the public schools and at the Grand Rapids Junior College. On December 30, 1932, after completing his engineering course at the General Motors Institute, he became laboratory assistant at Cadillac. In 1938, he was appointed Research Engineer. In 1942, he was named to head up the tank development program. In 1943, he became Chief Design Engineer, and in 1944 was appointed Assistant Chief Engineer. Mr. Cole's appointment as Chief Engineer gives Cadillac one of the industry's youngest and ablest engineers as a top ranking executive.

EDWARD N. COLE

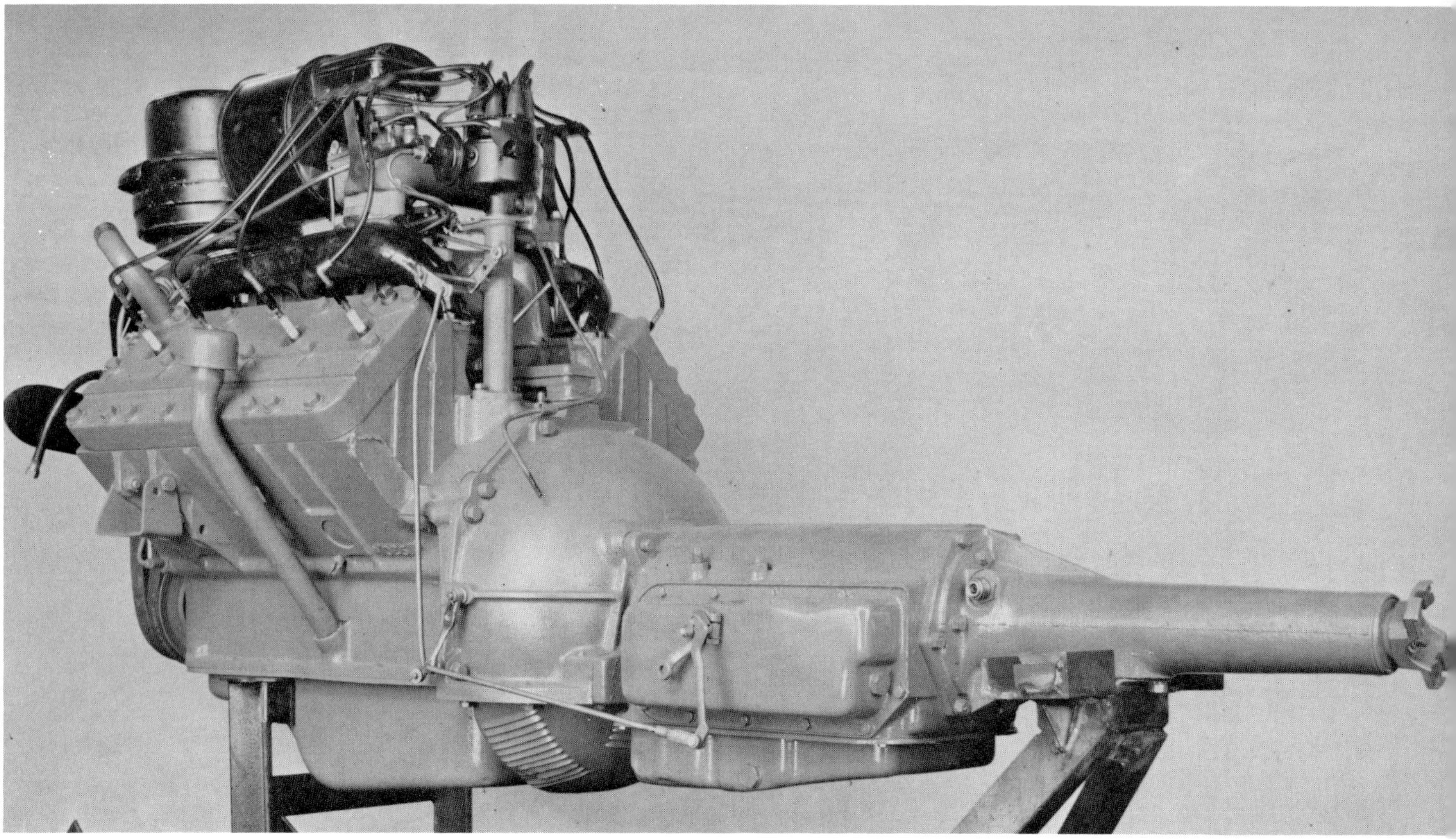

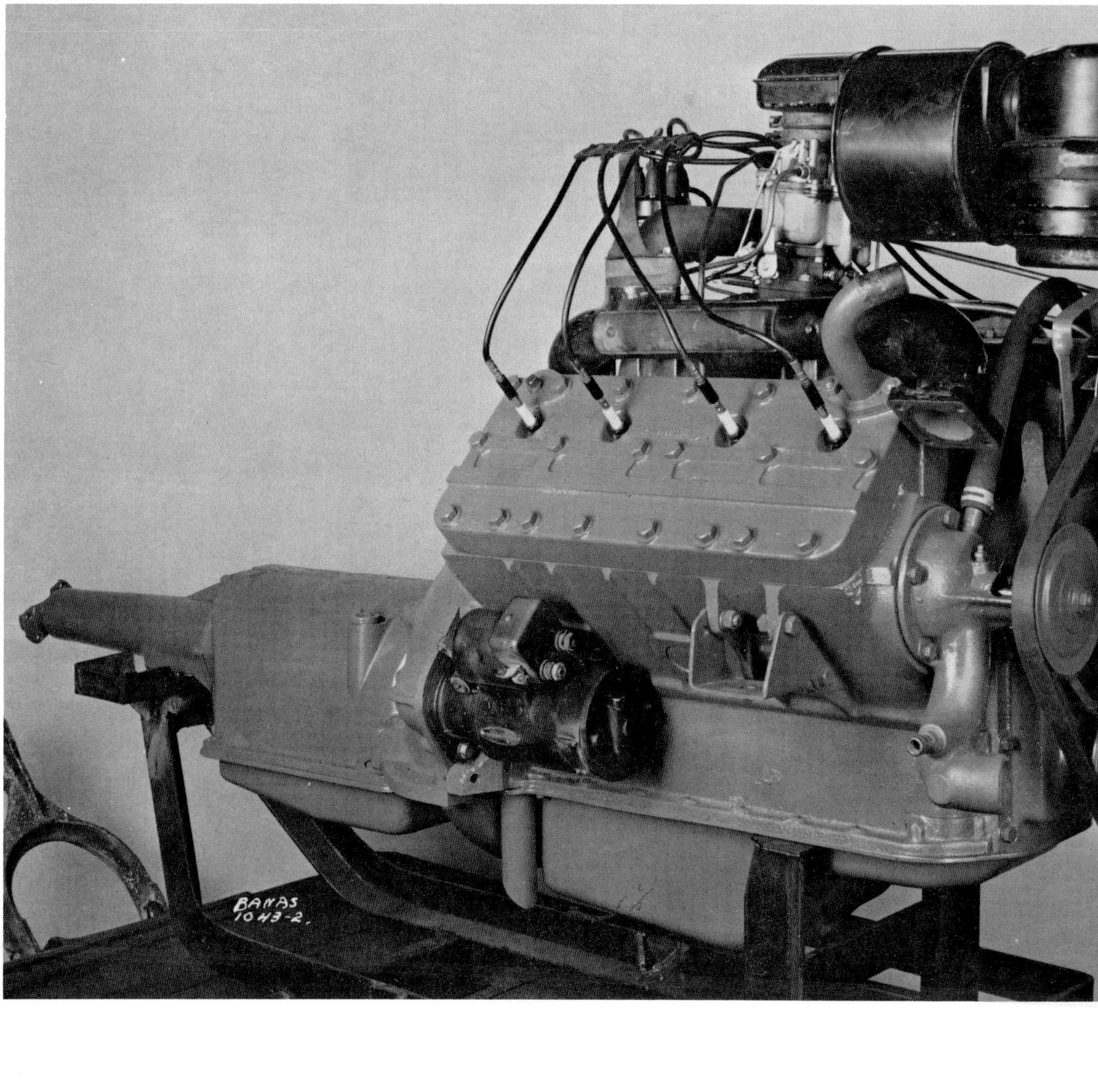
BANAS
1043-2.

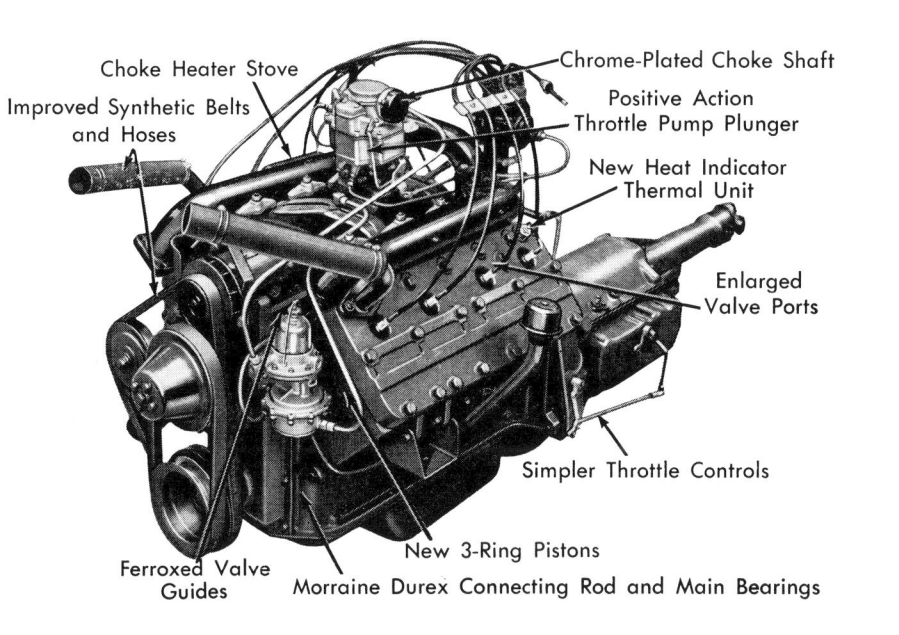

Engine diagram labels:
- Choke Heater Stove
- Improved Synthetic Belts and Hoses
- Chrome-Plated Choke Shaft
- Positive Action Throttle Pump Plunger
- New Heat Indicator Thermal Unit
- Enlarged Valve Ports
- Simpler Throttle Controls
- New 3-Ring Pistons
- Morraine Durex Connecting Rod and Main Bearings
- Ferroxed Valve Guides

Left, some of the changes made in the L-head engine for 1946. Opposite page, two views of the refined post-war powerplant. The distinctive bright green finish was used on flathead Cadillac V-8s through 1948. Below, an interesting view of a 1947 62-Series sedan on the production line.

·101·

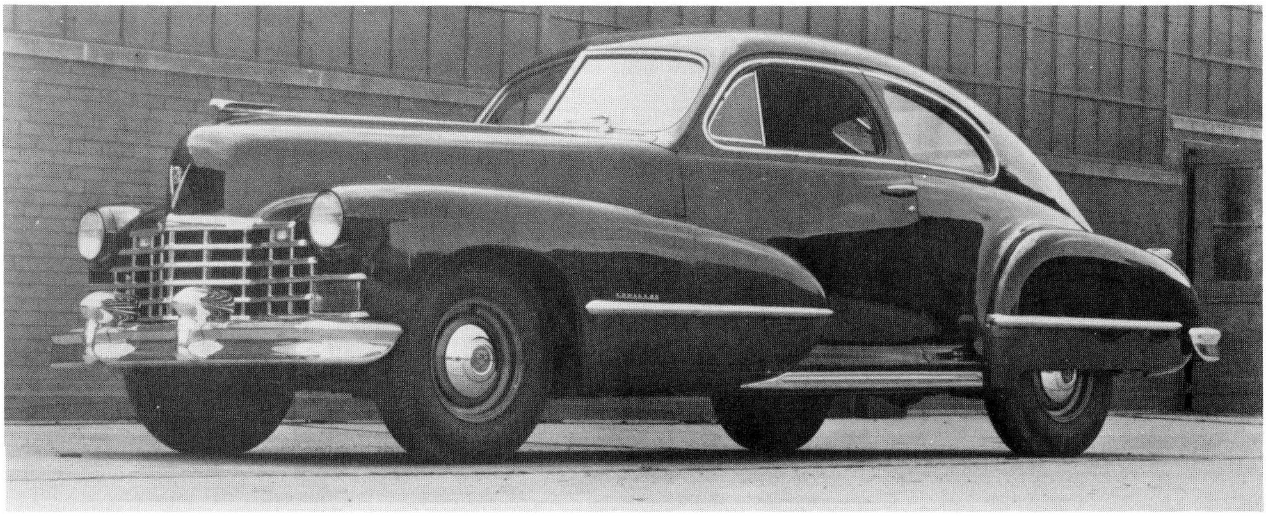

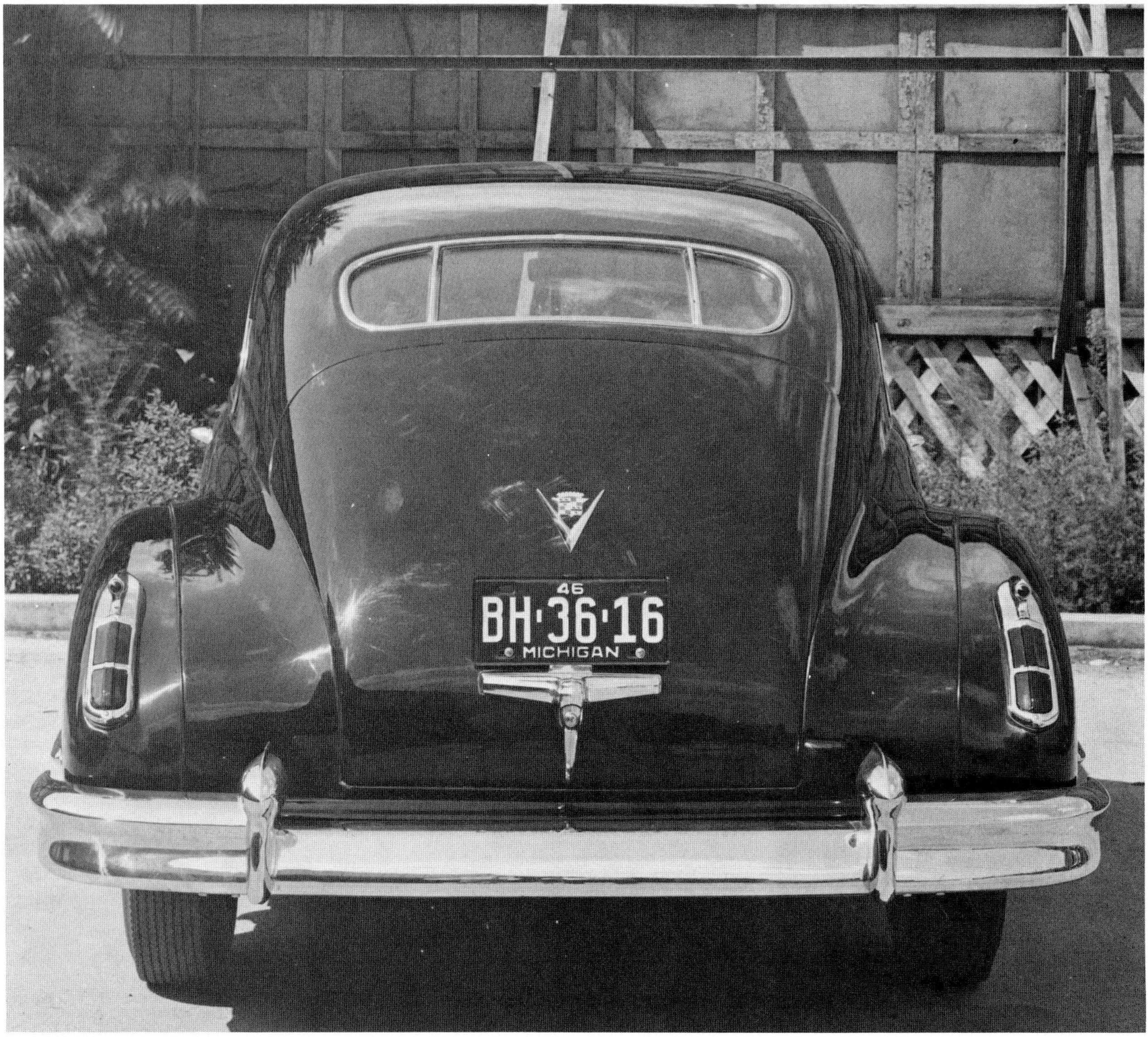
46
BH·36·16
MICHIGAN

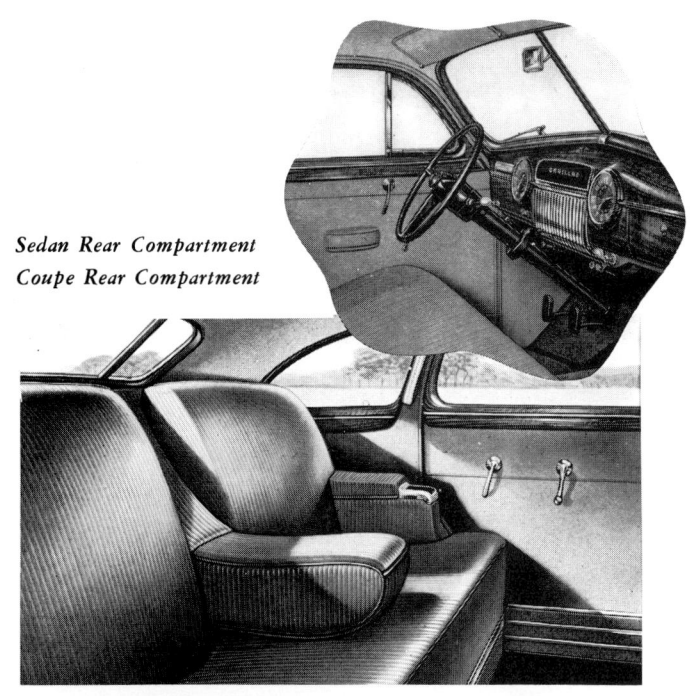

1946 SERIES SIXTY-ONE

Sedan Rear Compartment
Coupe Rear Compartment

The 61-Series continued with the two popular fastback models inaugurated in 1941. The 46-6107 coupe on the opposite page was relatively rare since only 800 units were manufactured during the 1946 model run. Although these bodies graced the Cadillac chassis during four model runs spread over seven years, each had distinctive variations on the basic theme that makes it possible to categorize proper vintage at a glance.

Above, the 1946 61-Series sedan Style 46-6109. Left, Data Book illustrations of 61 interiors. The lustrous finish on all Cadillacs of the Forties was the result of multiple coats of nitrocellulose lacquer and the required hand rubbing essential to a deep gloss. A rust-inhibiting undercoat also protected sheetmetal in event of scratches.

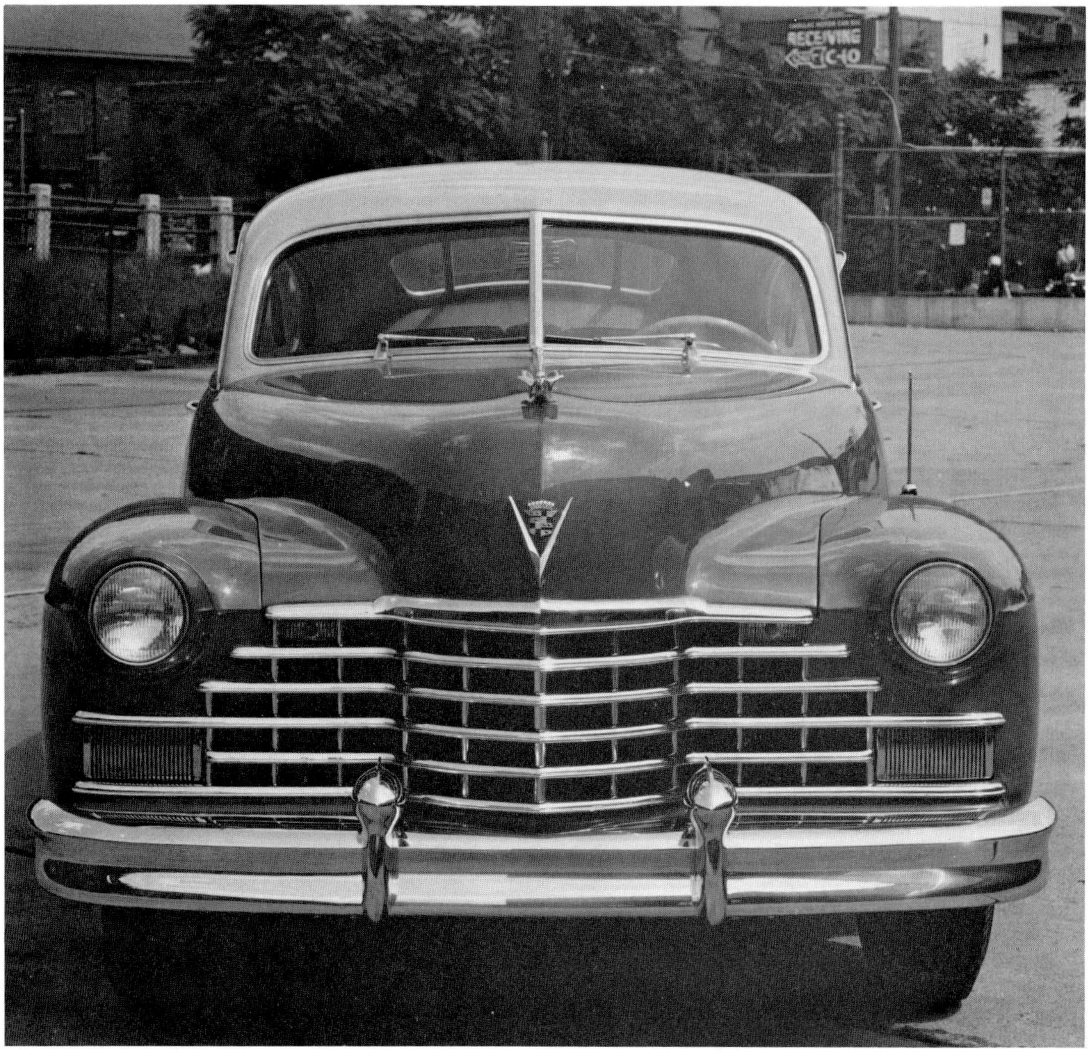
RECEIVING
C-10

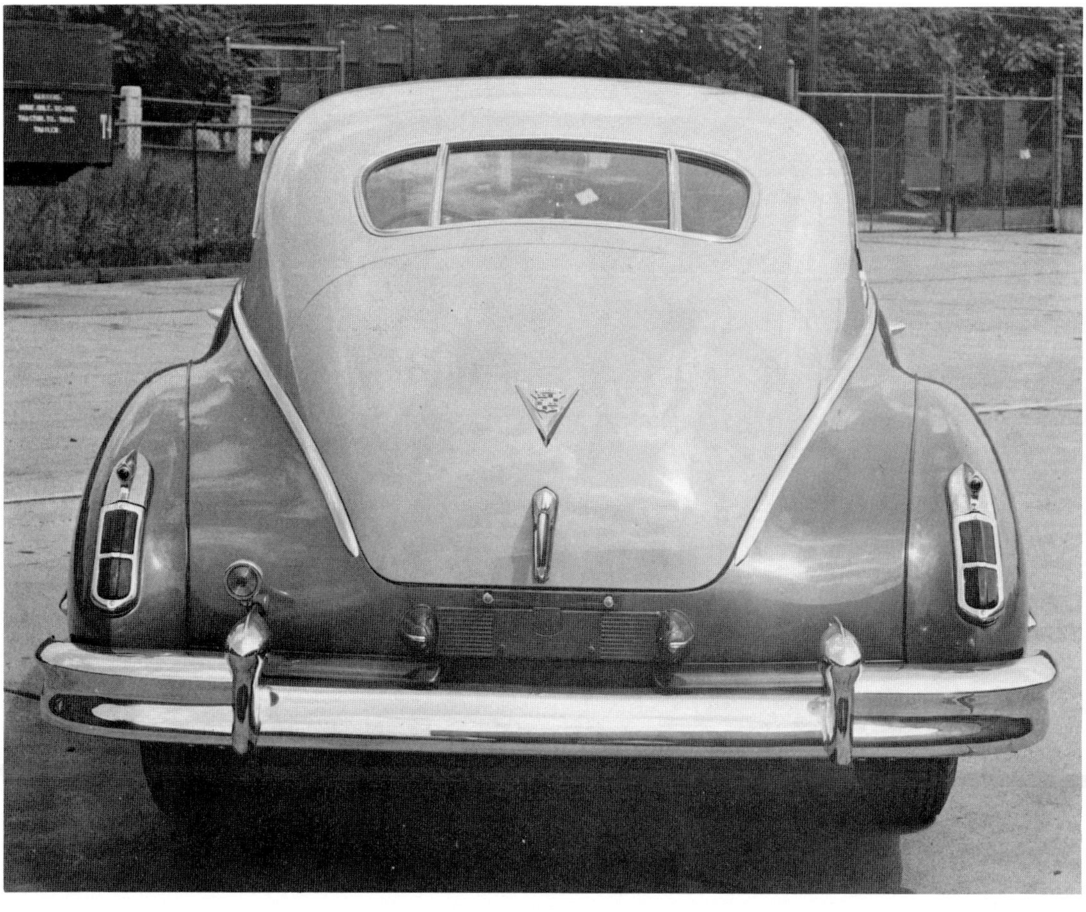

1946 FASTBACKS

The elegant lines of the C-body coupes were a welcome sight to war-weary Americans in 1946; Buick, Oldsmobile and Cadillac all fielded exciting versions. These original photographs illustrate the versatility in paint that was incident to the flowing lines of the 6207 coupe.

Left, block lettering on fenders and 1941-type wheel discs are quick references to 1946 models.

1946
SERIES
SIXTY-TWO

·106·

Opposite, the 1946 62 sedan, Style 46-6269. Above, the 62-convertible. Left, a catalog illustration of the convertible interior. The 62-Series models were all imbued with such carefully prescribed proportions that it is virtually impossible to fault their design: Hood length in relation to the deck is classically correct, fenders are precisely contoured to complement the body's architecture, glass areas are in balance with sheetmetal panels, brightwork is conservative, functional and esthetically positioned.

The convertible in the photograph above is the same car featured on the frontispiece of this volume. Its original color was gunmetal gray, but the reflected water and sky in the cover photograph, plus the age of the transparency (made in 1946), gave the car a bluish cast. The harbor view, however, was so typical of the period that the editors elected to use it in spite of the improbable combination of red leather and blue lacquer.

FLEETWOOD

1947 FLEETWOOD SEVENTY-FIVE

Fleetwood is a part of the Fisher Body Division of General Motors. It had its own management, engineering and manufacturing personnel, but its production during the 1940s, was directed exclusively by Cadillac. Most components for Fleetwood bodies were purchased from other specialized Fisher plants. Fleetwood never had a body drop operation in Detroit; throughout the 1940s it remained a traditional body building facility where body shells were assembled, trimmed and painted. Completed bodies were trucked to Cadillac's Clark Avenue plant for installation on chassis. Fenders and front end sheetmetal were painted and added at Cadillac. The 75s are superb road machines with the emphasis on comfort and luxury—capable of sustained cruising speeds above 70 mph. The author purchased the 47-7523, shown above and below, in 1958. With the exception of chrome headlight bezels, the car remains totally original; seemingly unassailed by the passage of time.

Above, postwar-type running boards and bumpers being evaluated on a 1942 model 75. The massive stainless steel running boards and harmonizing skirt mouldings (typical on 1946 through 1949 75s) unified the fenders and lower body with very attractive results. This expanse of brightwork at the base of the body (a Harley Earl benchmark) also tended to impart a lower appearance to large long wheelbase bodies. Below, President Harry S. Truman reviewing the Hydro-Lectrics on a newly delivered White House limousine.

The 1946 and 1947 Sixty-Special, sans louvers on the lower body, needed only the center body pillar motif, added length, and subtleties like the script on the deck and louvers on the quarters to express its individuality. Its Fleetwood interiors were more intricately trimmed and fitments more lavish than those of the 25 percent less costly 62 sedan. However, the major variance in interior physical dimensions between the two was limited to the leg room in the rear compartment. The Sixty-Special continued to be the ultimate expression of luxurious personal transportation in the 1940s, the last domestic beneficiary of the coachbuilder's craft in the traditional sense.

The upper photographs on this and the facing page are original factory shots of the 1946 and 1947 Sixty-Specials respectively. Other views on these pages are of a surviving 1947 in exceptionally fine original condition.

•110•

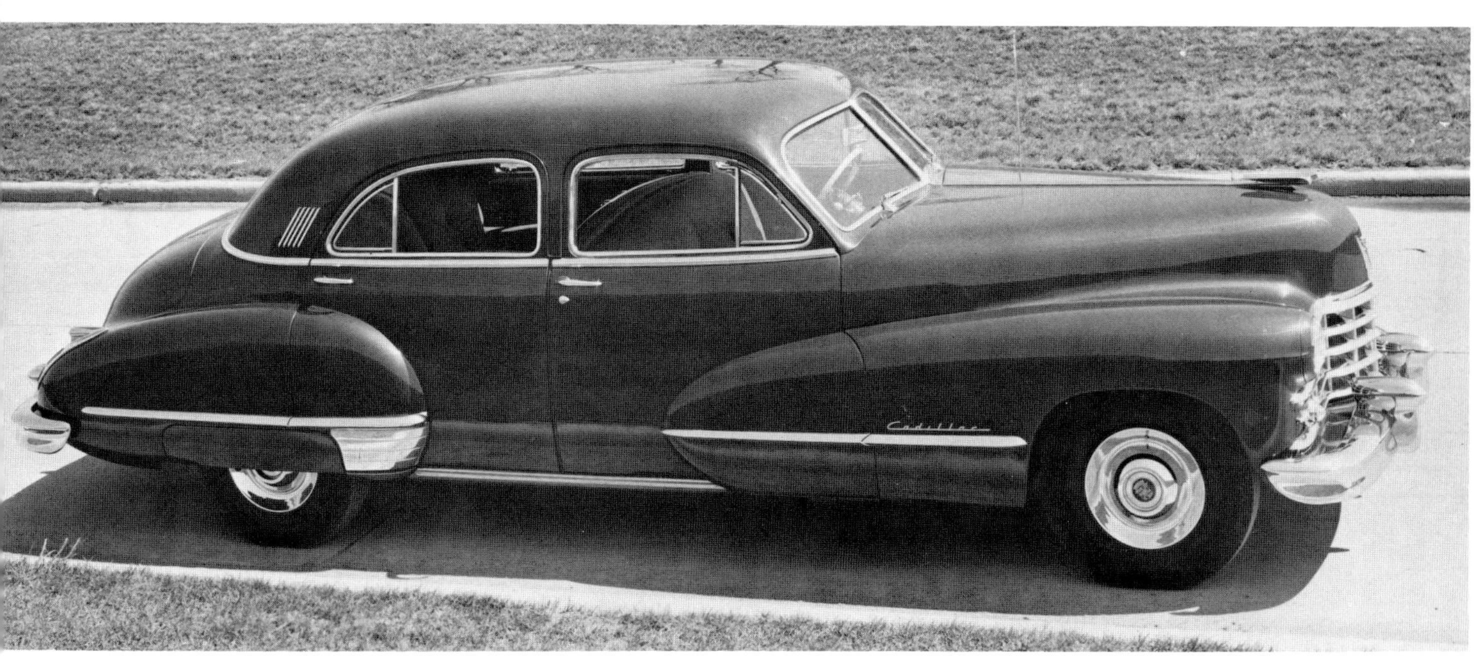

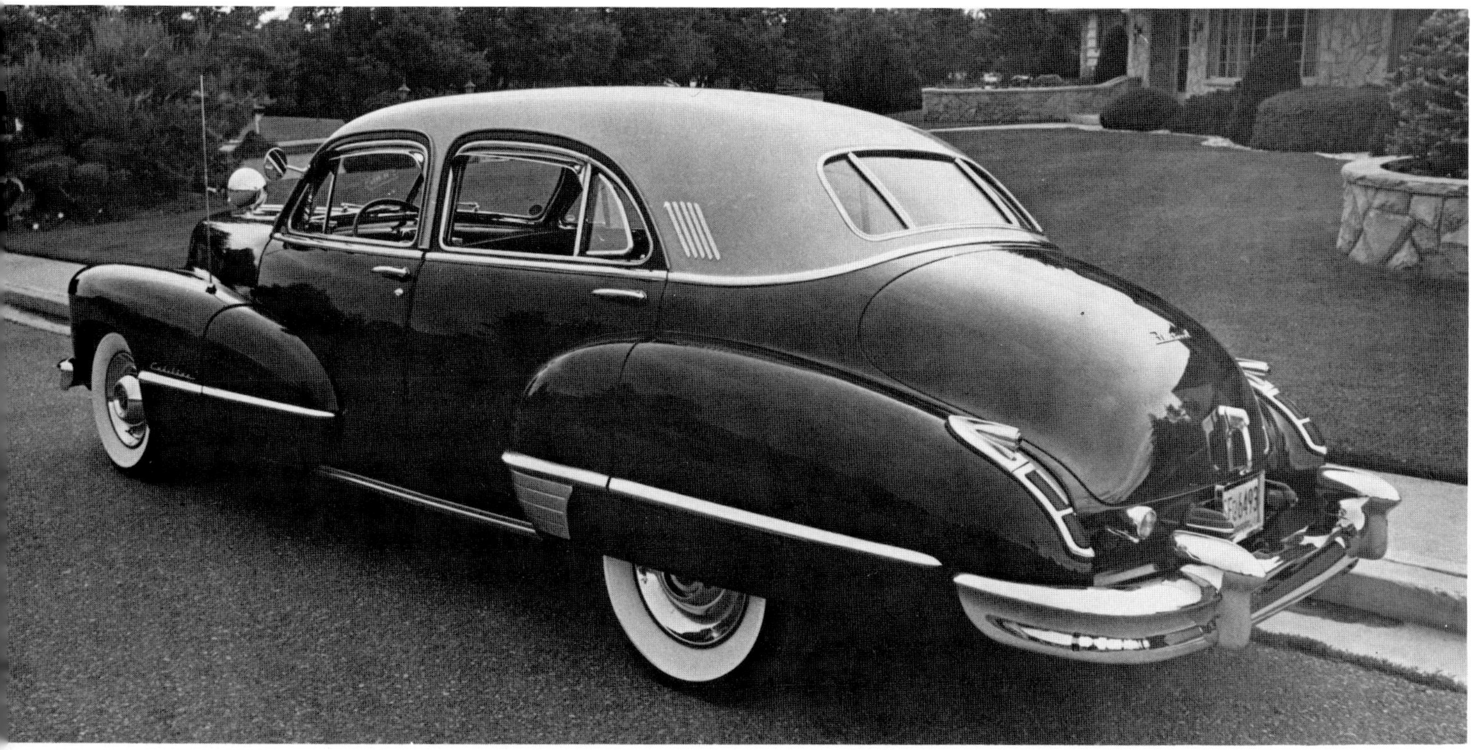

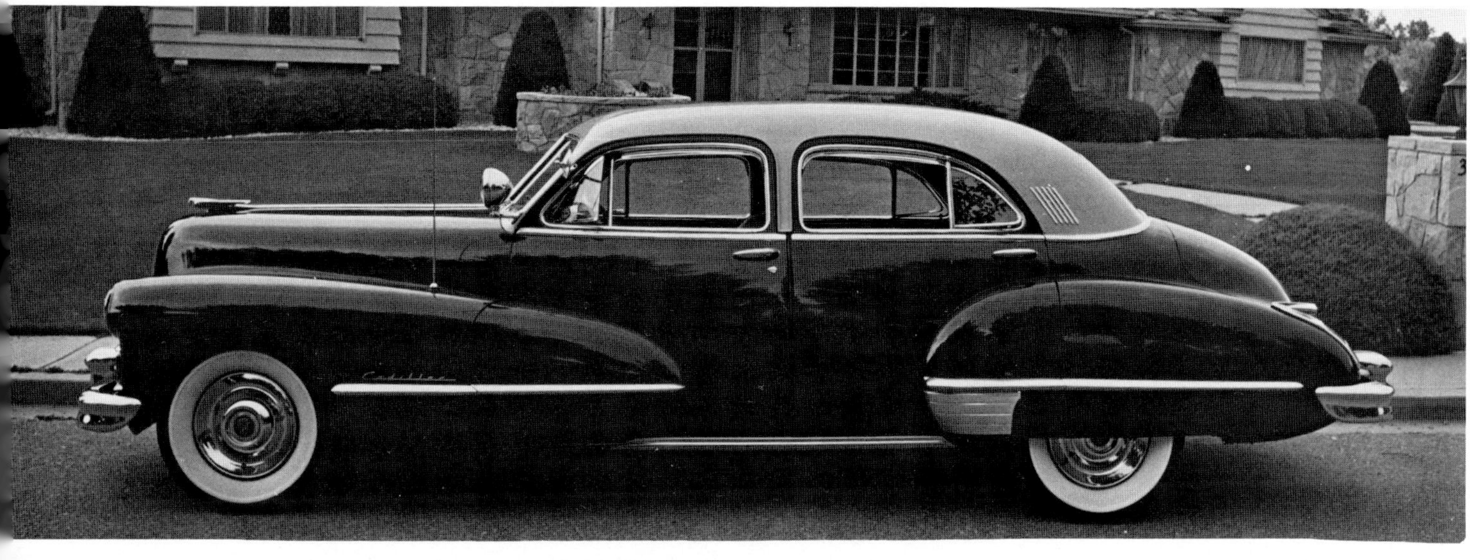

1947 FASTBACKS

Torpedo-bodied coupes were, in terms of performance, the standard bearers of the Cadillac line. Respectable power-to-weight ratios coupled with efficient aerodynamics gave these two-tone luxury machines the credentials they needed to effect some unexpected endings to street encounters with considerably lighter cars. For those with an aggressive attitude in such matters, there was an array of speed equipment on the market. Despite its weight, a Cadillac flathead V-8, fitted with an Edmunds dual-carburetor intake manifold, Cyclone aluminum heads, Mallory ignition and a Winfield cam, developed awesome power. In the period immediately following the war, hot rods with Cadillac fundamentals were regulars in the street racing scene. By 1947, when high-performance technology began expanding, a Cadillac-powered lakester could turn 130 mph at Bonnieville.

Opposite page, two 62-Series coupes (Style 47-6207). On this page, the 61-Series counterpart, an attractively restored 47-6107. At 4,145 pounds, the 61 coupe was only 70 pounds lighter than the 62 model. Because of low production and collector's preference of the 62, these stylish B-bodied coupes are rare.

•112•

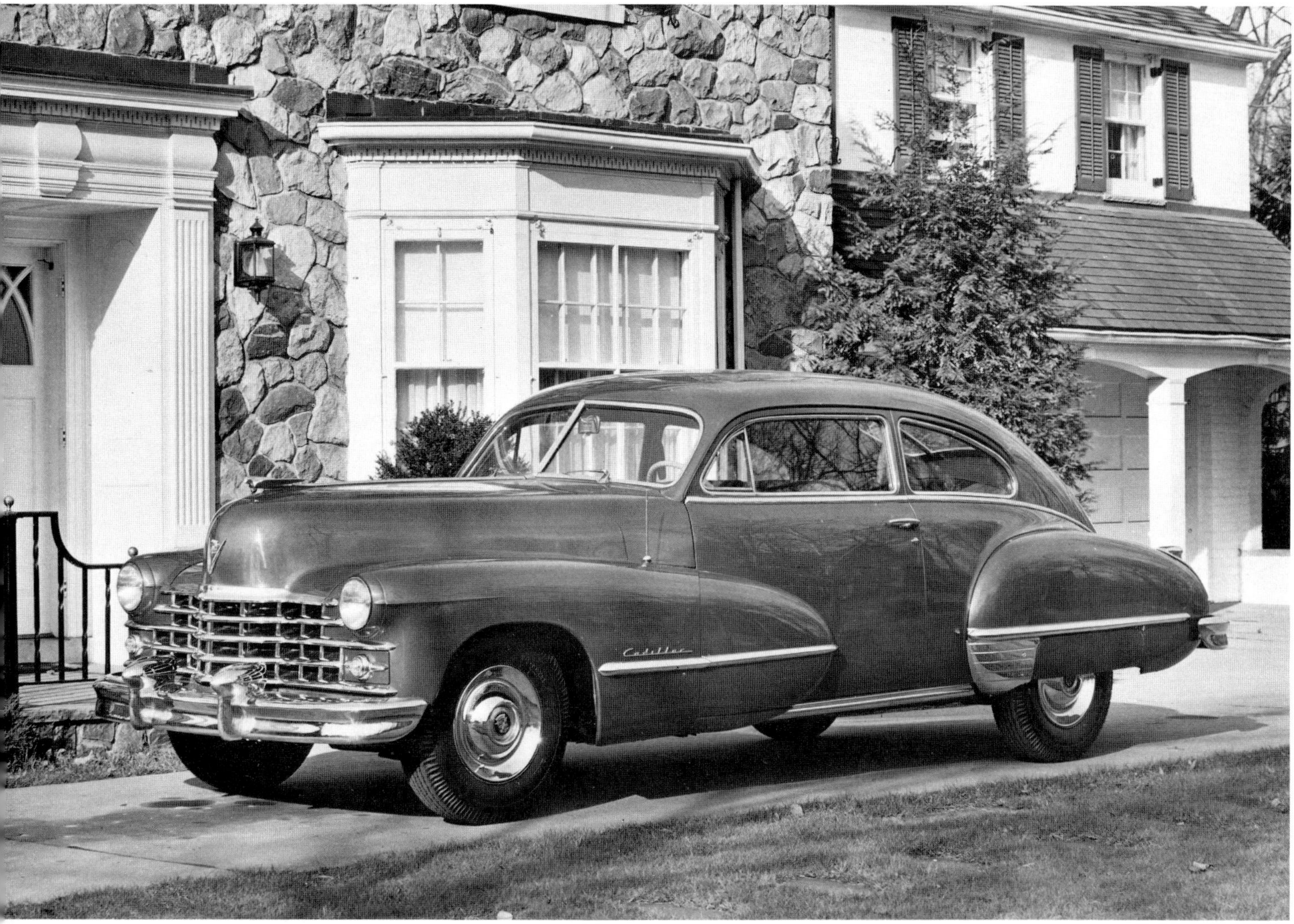

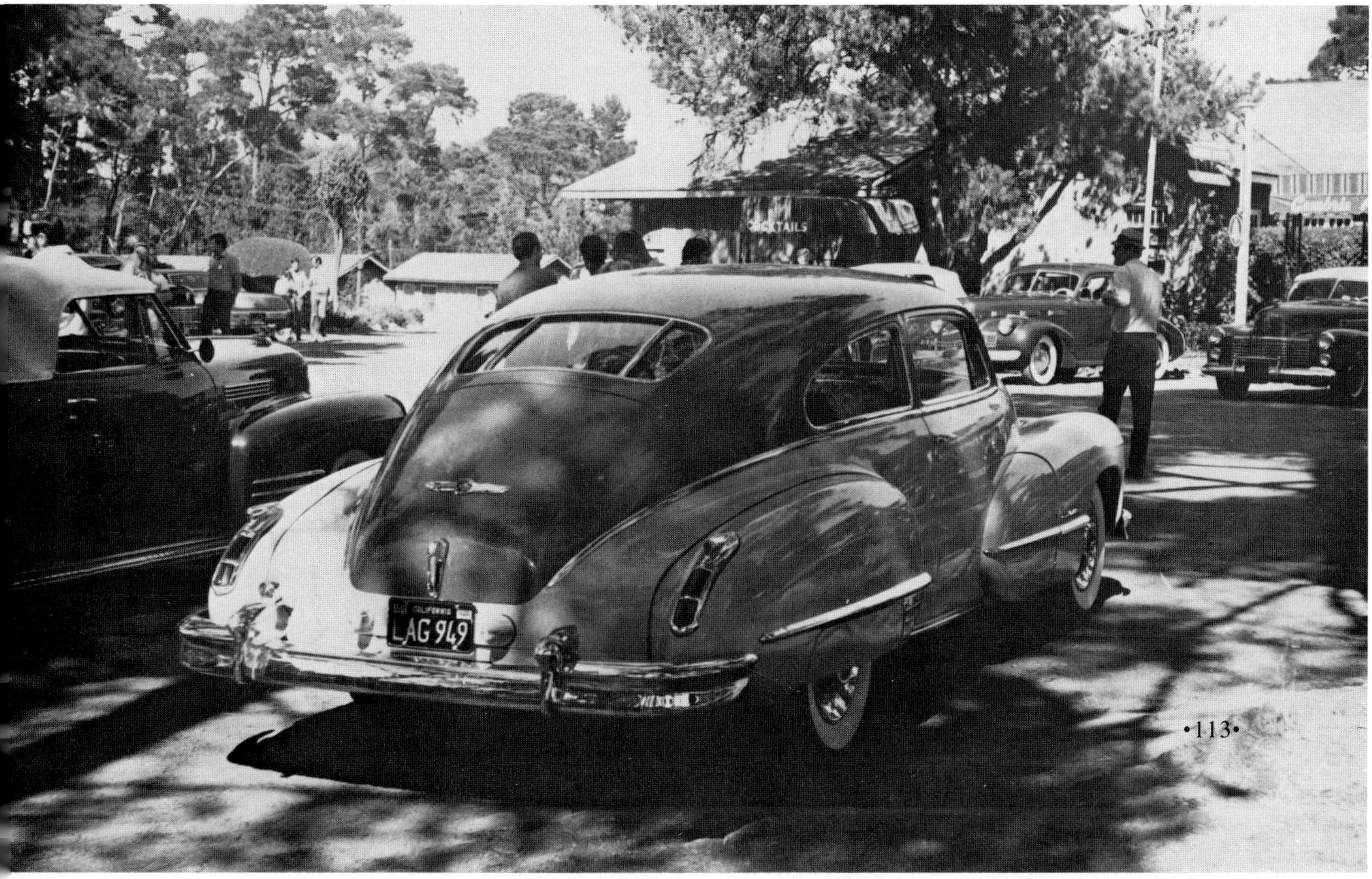
LAG 949

1947 SERIES SIXTY-TWO

On this page, three views of the 1947 6269 sedan. It was one of the most attractive mass-produced four-door sedans of the post-war era. Opposite, interior views of the 1947 62 sedan. The rear compartment, with its plain-paneled door panels and front seat back, had a decidedly Spartan look compared to pre-war models. The instrument panel, garnish mouldings and belt panels were finished with *Tick Grain Oriental Walnut Transfers* which was also typical of 1946 practice.

·114·

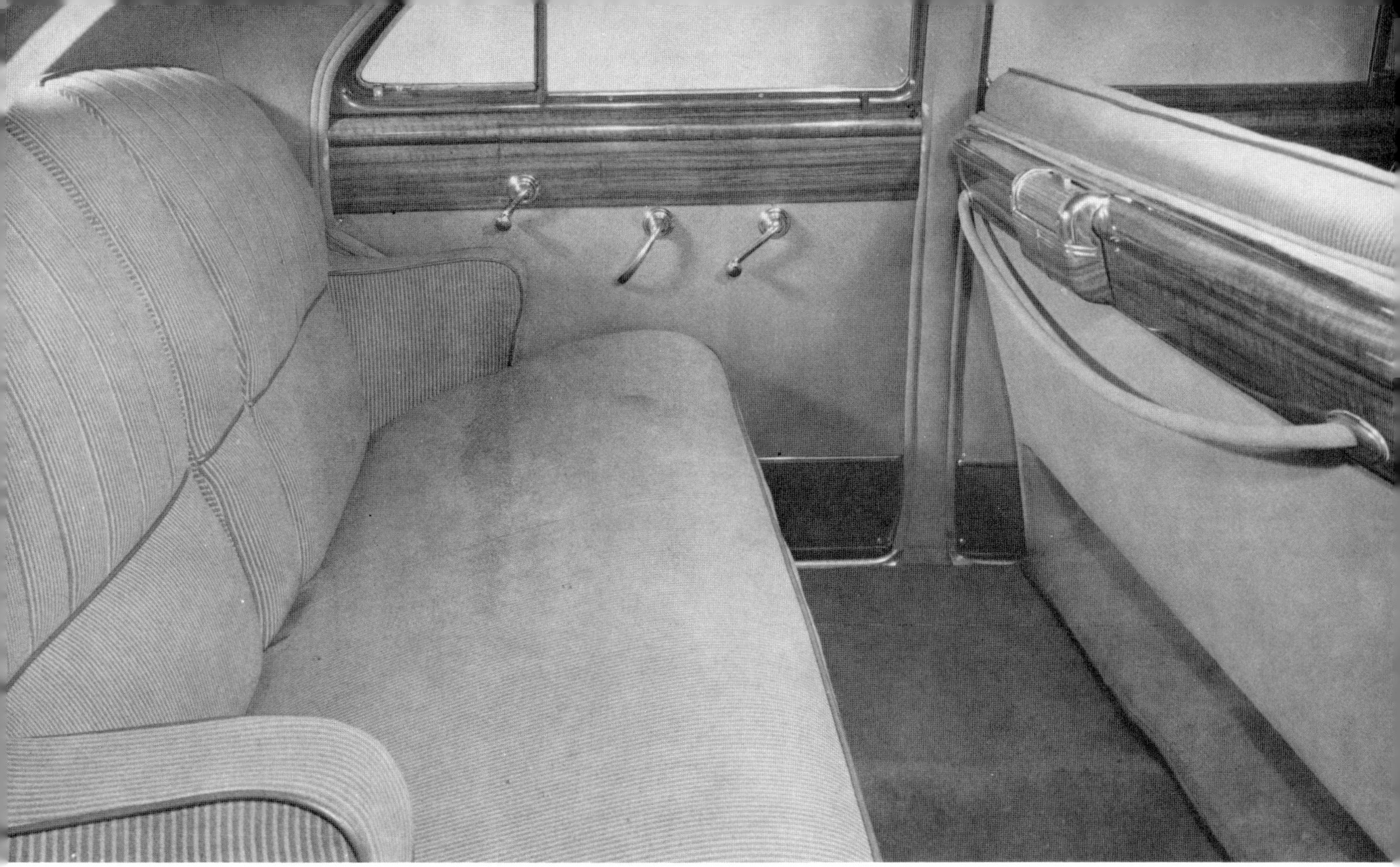

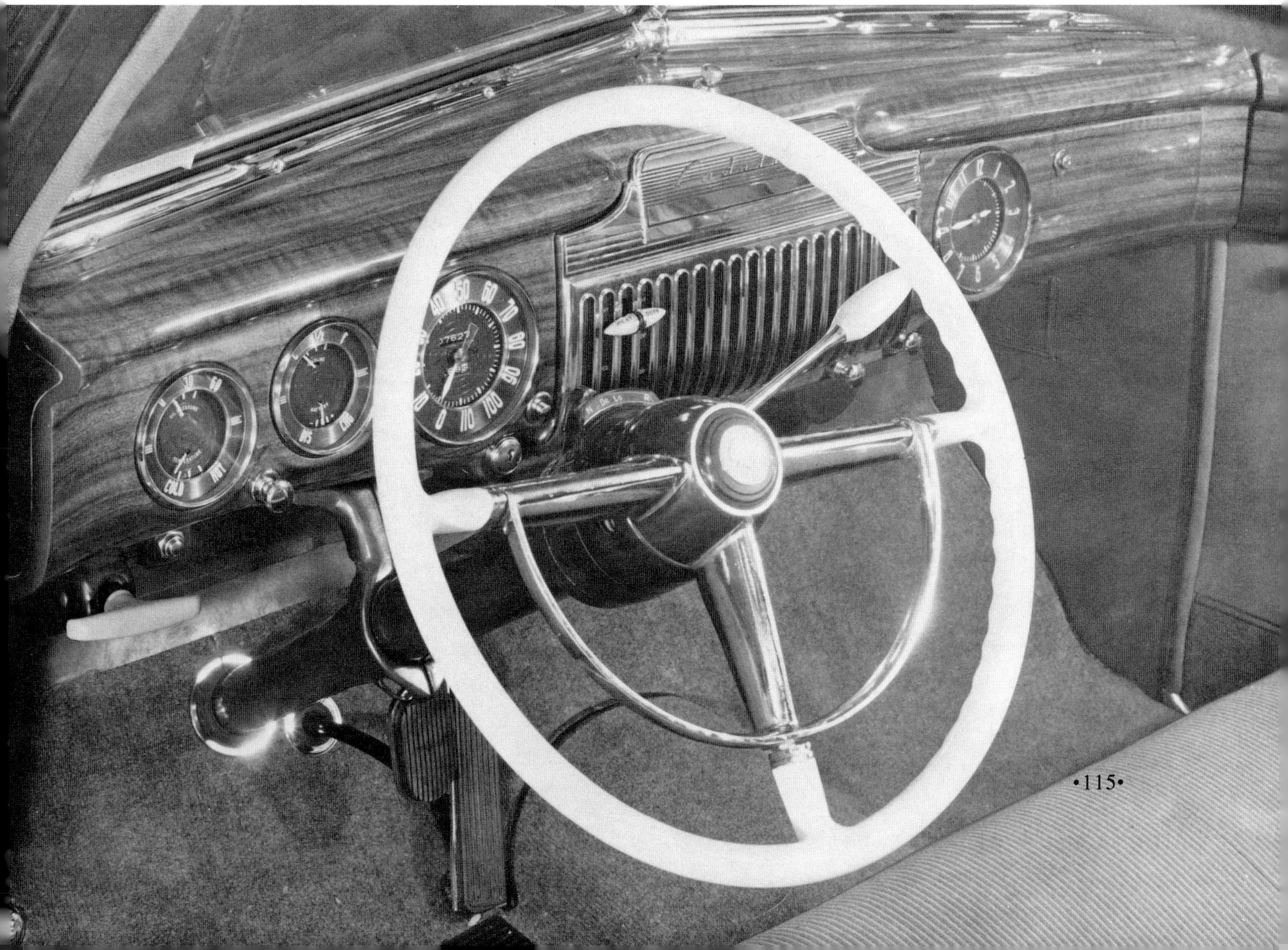

THE 1947 *Cadillac* CONVERTIBLE

A 1947 Cadillac convertible is probably one of the most nostalgia-invoking vehicles that ever rolled down American highways. Whether it was forging through a crowded business district or highballing along a country road, it took only a fleeting glimpse of GM's finest to know it was a sight to remember. With the possible exception of California, memories were all that did remain of most 1947 Cadillacs in the 1960s. Above, author's 47-6267 *circa* 1960. Below, two factory press release photographs.

Cadillac convertibles of this era are destined to become extremely valuable collectors' cars in the years ahead. A 1947 model, as shown on this page, or for that matter any Cadillac convertible manufactured during the Forties, presents an outstanding opportunity in terms of investment appreciation.

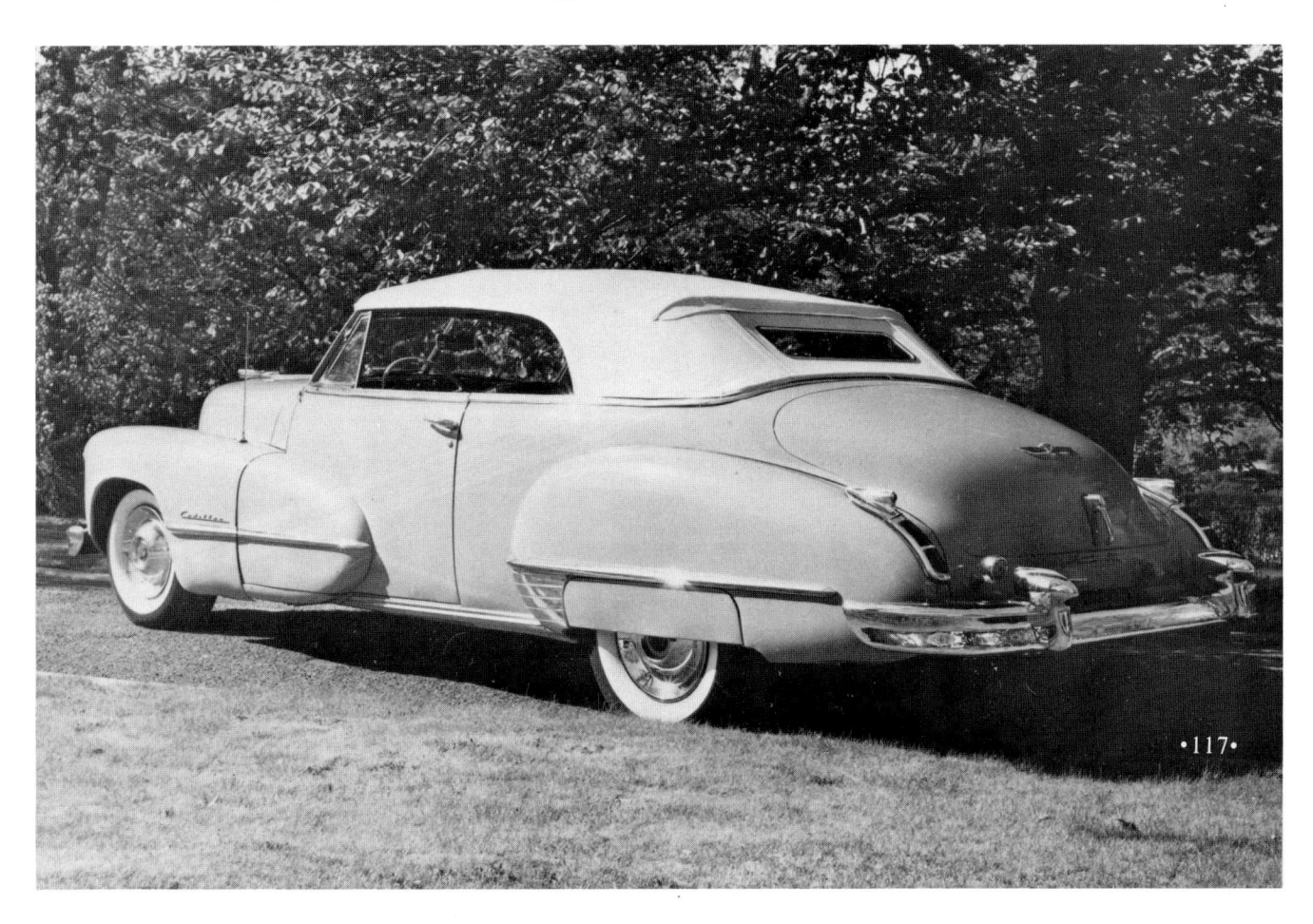

The Derham Body Co., through the medium of modification, continued to offer a wide range of traditional body types throughout the 1940s. Above, a convertible sedan beautifully evolved from a 1942 67-Series sedan. The script-type coachbuilders mark on the hood suggests this car was a post-war job. Derham used a three-sided shield in earlier years. Below, a 1947 75-Series convertible sedan. The convertible top, in the raised position, closely resembled the tops used on 1938 through 1940 75-Series convertible sedans.

COACHWORK BY DERHAM

Left, a 47-7533 converted to an attractive formal sedan by Derham. Below, a 75-Series limousine skillfully transformed into a Derham town-car. These photographs provide an interesting insight into what might have been if the full range of Fleetwood bodies had progressed beyond 1940.

·119·

COACHWORK BY MAURICE SCHWARTZ

When California coachbuilders Bohman and Schwartz parted in 1945, Maurice Schwartz stayed in Pasadena and continued the coachbuilding enterprise. Left, a six-door station wagon built for a major movie studio to transport acting personnel to and from shooting locations. Below, another six-door wagon custom built on a commercial chassis, this one for Gene Autry. Opposite above, a 1949 75-Series sedan transformed into a three-passenger coupe complete with golfbag door. Opposite below, a reconstructed 75-Series limousine as commissioned by Harry Karl as a gift for his wife Marie McDonald.

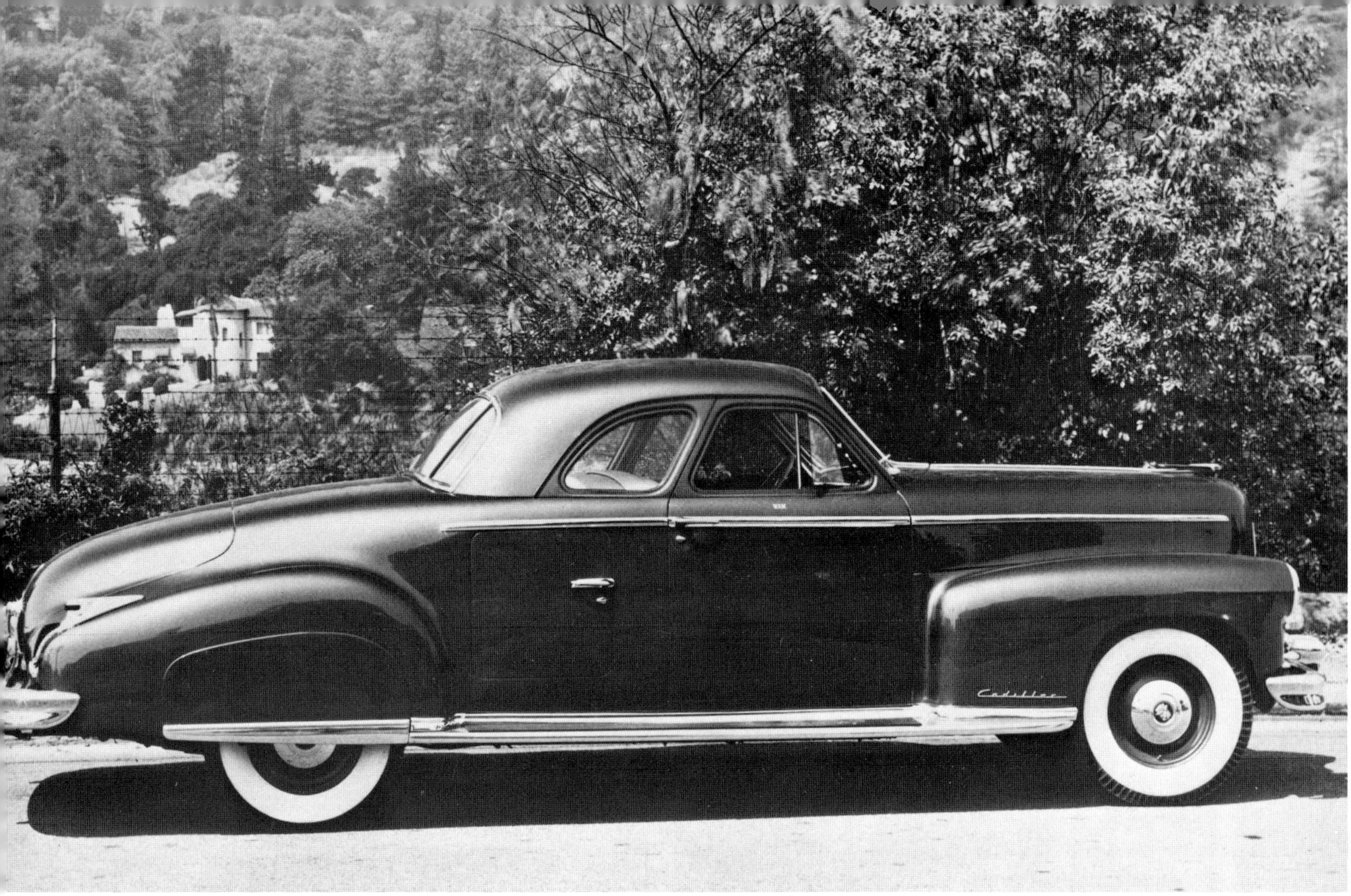

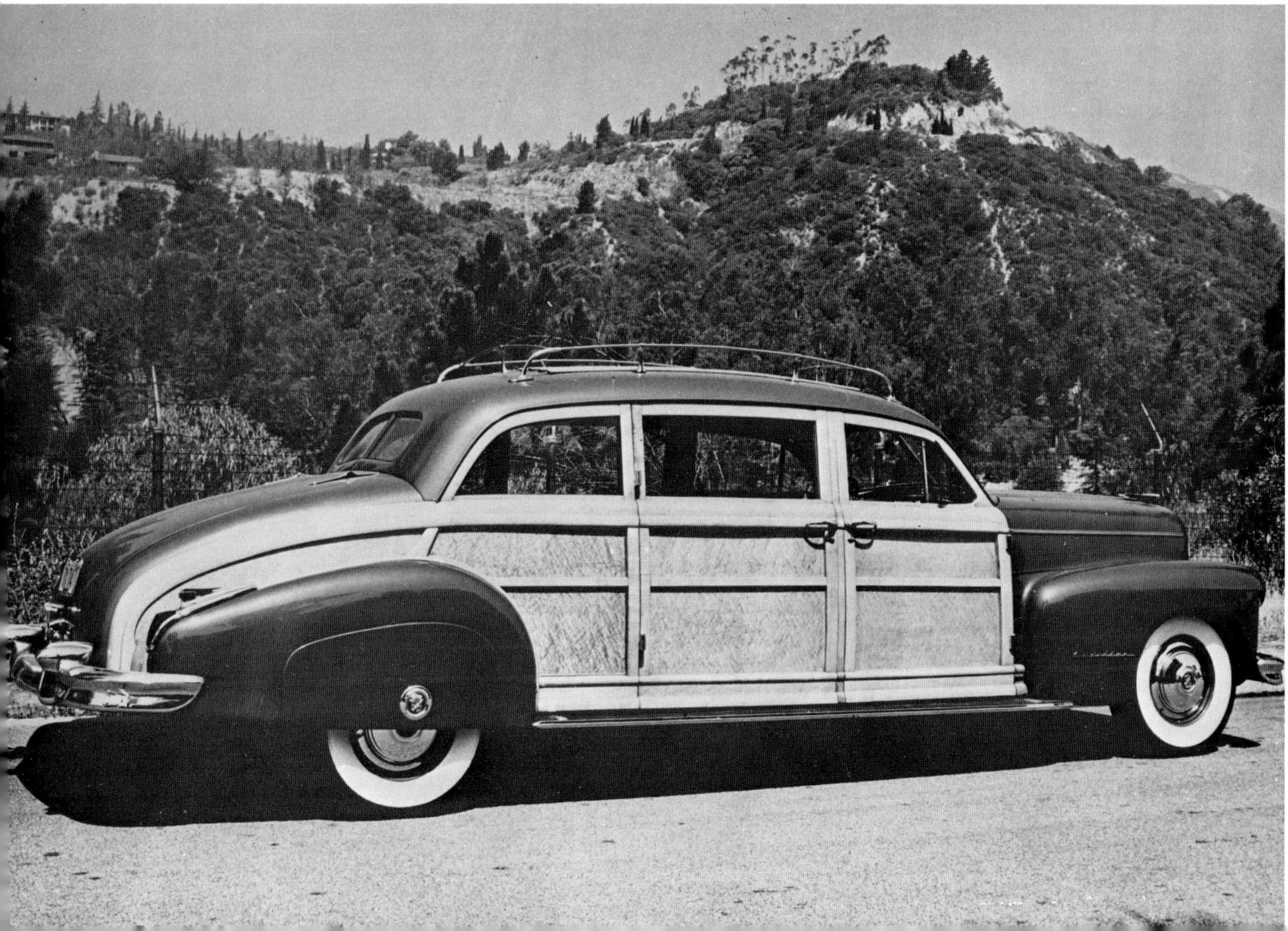

1948

Aeronautical settings were favored backgrounds for publicity photographs of the 1948 Cadillac — here a 62-Series coupe at the Detroit City Airport.

TAIL-FINS

The most fascinating, most influential and most popular automobile styling innovation of the 1940s was the tail-fin. Ironically the initial finned fender was never envisioned by its originators as a trend-setting breakthrough or the beginning of a major movement in postwar design. Cadillac had been affixing fins to tail lights since 1938. Bill Mitchell observes that, at least as far as Cadillac was concerned, the plastic jeweled tail lamp cover on the 1941 models signaled the onset of the fin era.

Inspiration for the 1948-type fin can be traced to the aeronautical developments that immediately preceded World War II. Harley Earl's people came away from their sojourn at Selfridge Field in 1939 duly impressed with the twin-tailed Lockheed P-38. But that was only the beginning. Within weeks GM stylists were sketching and evaluating a profusion of automotive designs that borrowed freely from contemporary aircraft. In 1940 Mr. Earl took the next step when he assigned the Advance Styling Studio, under Franklin Q. Hershey's direction, to preparing a series of 3/8 scale models; they were known as the Interceptor models and had dominant aerodynamic overtones.

The intervening war years dispersed the styling staff throughout the world and it was well after VJ Day before Bill Mitchell returned to Detroit. His immediate responsibility, upon reinvestiture as Cadillac Studio chief, became the review and dissemination of ideas advanced through the Interceptor investigations and the subsequent work by the Special Car Design Studio. Mr. Earl had set his sights on a revolutionary design for Cadillac and it was Mr. Mitchell's job to put it together and sell the concept to GM management and the Cadillac Division. To style a completely new automobile and to have it in the dealers' showrooms by the start of 1948 meant that Bill Mitchell and his staff would have to extend their creative powers as never before.

Cadillac's new General Manager, John F. "Jack" Gordon, who replaced Nicholas Dreystadt in 1946, was a conservative man with an engineering background. Convincing him that tail-fins on Cadillacs was a step in the right direction took consider-

In May of 1945 the Special Car Design Studio, under the direction of Franklin Q. Hershey, began sketching and modeling proposals for a new Cadillac. During the autoworkers' strike in 1946 the studio's personnel utilized the basement of the main house at Mr. Hershey's farm — 25 miles north of Detroit — to carry on with their work. This group made elemental contributions to the ultimate 1948 design concept. Frank Hershey is seated at the left and chief modeler Chris Kline is in the center (with fur coat and cigarette). Others are modelers and designers assigned to the Special Car Design Studio.

ably more than a Friday afternoon unveiling in the Styling Auditorium. There were countless meetings and conferences between Cadillac management and styling personnel before the aerodynamic, dorsal finned body was finally approved.

The production line closed out the 1947 models on January 13, 1948. Precisely three weeks later the first 1948 automobile made its ritualistic appearance in the final assembly area. It was the first week of February and Jack Gordon was still apprehensive as the first new cars were being loaded for transport to dealers. Indeed many dealers, prior to the public showings, expressed disbelief — even exasperation — when they caught sight of the new '48 models, but their misgivings were soon dispelled by the overwhelming clamor of public approval.

Tail-fins were, of course, only one element in the complete redesign of 1948. The principles of streamlining were manifest in each body component and from every perspective. From the rounded bumpers and curved windshield to the flowing body panels and faired-in tail lights the car was a compendium of new ideas.

There is evidence that the new wind tunnel testing installation at the GM Test Track in Milford, Michigan, played a role in the designing of these bodies. Wind drag was reduced to the point that a stock 346 L-head engine could pull the '48 models through Milford's high speed test track with better times than those of the several preceding years; and in spite of the 8.20" low-pressure tires introduced in 1948. In one test a stock Hydra-Matic-equipped 61-Series sedan with four passengers clocked a consistent 93.3 MPH. A fastback coupe with the 3.36 rear-end could exceed the century mark with ease.

The *rudder-type fenders,* as Cadillac referred to them in 1948 advertising, had solid styling logic behind them. Technically, raising the height or ends of the rear fenders had the visual effect of lowering the upper portion of the body. Another advantage incumbent to the finned fender was a car that looked longer in a front three-quarter view. This was true because the full rear fender stayed in sight from any viewing position. Cars with traditional rear fenders that curved inward toward the rear bumper appeared shorter than they actually were because the lines of the rear fenders tended to fade away when viewed from frontal angles.

During the 1940s, Cadillac used another ploy in combatting this fade-away phenomenon by consistently opting to invest in the extra metal it took to produce flat sided rear fenders rather than those with an inward curve. Thus plan views (straight down) tended to have overall flat sides. These were important techniques in advancing Harley Earl's avowed mission of giving the American automobile a longer and lower appearance.

The frontal approach to the new Cadillac emphasized the car's road-hugging lowness and massive width. The radiator grill was lower and wider, consisting of two horizontal chrome bars below the header, divided by seven vertical fins. Combination parking and directional lamps were recessed in the fender below the headlamps. If fog lamps were desired, an optional triple-function assembly replaced the standard unit. Front bumpers were heavier and designed to highlight the basic theme of the front ensemble. The broad hood sloped forward offering greater road visibility, while the curved windshield, narrowed front pillars and tri-sectioned rear window increased the arc of vision.

Fender lines were especially attractive. The trailing edge of the front fender faired into the doors and rear quarter panel without a perceptible termination point. Upper surfaces on both front and rear fenders were connected by a roll in the body panels creating an unbroken horizontal plane that carried the entire length of the body. Since this prominent body feature fell several inches below the actual belt line, it served as a focal highlight that effectively lowered the appearance of the car. The convex windsplit on the front fenders which had been relatively abbreviated up to 1947, now flowed to just short of the front door opening. The rear bumpers became an integral part of the overall design with outer ends that wrapped around and encased the lower rear trailing edge of the back fenders. Even the tail-fins were perhaps never again as restrained or complementary to the total design.

Yet this revolutionary new Cadillac retained a strong identity link with the previous series. The script on the fenders, the "V" and crest emblems, the double projectile bumper guards, the body mouldings, the flying goddess hood ornament, the hubcaps and the cross-hatched grill: All of these spelled Cadillac at a glance. In terms of recognition elements the tail-fins became, in a matter of weeks, among the most successful trademarks ever styled into an automobile body.

The consolidation of basic body stampings utilized by Cadillac continued into 1948. In 1941 there had been ten separate and distinctive body shells in use, then nine in 1942, seven in 1946 and 1947, and only five in 1948. Now both 61 and 62 Series sedans

Styling exercises like this incorporated ideas adapted from the Lockheed P-38 and foreshadowed the exciting contours of the 1948 Cadillacs.

and coupes used identical Fisher C-bodies. Exterior brightwork applied exclusively to the more expensive 62 ($163 separated the two sedans) were the three chrome stripes mounted just below each tail lamp, the front fender stone guard placed at the rear edge of the front wheel opening, and the rocker sill moulding extending between wheel openings. Interior refinements segregating the two series included the method of trimming door panels: The 62 had a horizontal pattern and ribbed kickpad as opposed to the plain paneled 61. Seat upholstery in the 62 utilized a two-tone motif versus the 61's conventional single fabric.

The esthetic appeal of the C-body coupe introduced in 1948 and manufactured through 1949 has become a major area of collector interest in recent years. This model articulated better than any other the theoretical shape and format expressed in GM's Interceptor investigations. Although its fastback styling retained a continuity with the earlier 1941 through 1947 models, the new interpretation lent itself best to being representative of the advancing state of the art *circa* 1948. The 61 and 62 coupes and sedans were built on a 126-inch wheelbase chassis that became standard for both series.

Convertibles enjoyed wide popularity during these years. The well-balanced proportions of the '48 version coupled with the delights of open car driving — in those pre-air conditioning days — made the Cadillac convertible a popular choice. In 1948, as in 1947, Division sales statistics show the 62 convertibles accounted for more than 10% of the production total. Deep leather-upholstered seats with cloth trimmed door panels and seat backs were available in many optional two-tone leather and cloth combinations including five colors of leather and two colors of cloth.

Perhaps the most memorable new Cadillac of 1948 was the Fleetwood-built Sixty-Special. Its manifest grace of line has resulted in its universal acceptance as a milestone in postwar automobile history. It was a large car by any standard with a bumper to bumper measurement of 226 inches — equal in length to the Seventy-Five. Exclusive trim features for the new edition included mouldings outlining all windows, five simulated louvers on the rear quarter panel, Fleetwood name script on the deck lid, a rocker sill moulding that extended back to the tip of the rear fender, and a rear fender stone guard that blended with the rocker sill moulding. Frank Hershey points out that the inspiration for the air-scoop motif used for this stone guard came directly from the early P-38.

The sharing of many basic body stampings among the Sixty-Special and the 61 and 62-Series sedans circumvented the costly modifications Fleetwood had performed in the production of the 1942 through 1947 Sixty-Specials. Interior dimensions for these three 1948 model sedans were the same except the Sixty-Special had a three-and-one-fourths-inch wider rear seat cushion. The eleven inches of additional length in the Sixty-Special was inserted between the rear quarter and the back bumper. In the rear half of the Sixty-Special there were non-interchangeable doors, fenders, trim, deck lid, and rear window. The Sixty-Special, as well as the 62 convertible and the 75s, was equipped with Hydro-Lectric windows and seat controls as standard equipment.

The instrument panel in the 1948 model car was as fresh as the exterior styling. A hooded rainbow-shaped instrument cluster projected from a massive dash panel that carried right down to the toe board. The lasting impression received when entering a 1948 Cadillac for the first time was the massive size and scope of the dash and instrumentation. These appointments were beautifully finished with leather-grained Di-Noc transfers in gray or brown tones depending on the series or the upholstery. A unique shrouded steering column and a centrally located package compartment were innovations not to be seen the following year.

That is not to say, however, that the 1948 dash proved unpopular. Its appearance aroused industry-wide acclaim, and in recent years enthusiasm for the 1948s has been heightened by its appealing front compartment. Even the 75 incorporated the new dash,

A full-size clay model of the Sixty-Special taking shape in the Cadillac Studio. The strong character lines incumbent to the 1948 Cadillac were generally retained in the redesigns of 1950 and 1954. Full-scale drawings on the boards in the background provided clay modelers with the precise contours of each component.

the first change in its instrumentation since 1941. Exterior styling on the 75 retained the previous configuration.

The special Tenite plastic steering wheels which were optionally available on the 61 and 62 sedans and coupes, but standard on the balance of the line, were available in ivory or black. The latter was less likely to develop cracks, a problem that had plagued all the plastic wheels that had gone before.

For most of 1948 it was business as usual in the Clark Avenue engine and transmission departments. Fully 97 percent of the 52,706 cars produced in an abbreviated nine-month model run were equipped with Hydra-Matic Drive. According to factory statistics the percentage of new Cadillacs with automatic transmissions was 30 percent in 1941, 60 percent in 1942, 87 percent in 1946, and 92 percent in 1947. It remained an extra-cost option throughout the decade: $110 in 1941, $176 in 1946, $186 in 1947 and 1948, and $200 in 1949.

The 1948 models again displayed Cadillac's ability to capture the spirit of American motoring and translate it into reality with uncanny consistency. Nineteen-forty-eight was a resounding success in the annals of Cadillac history that re-echoed the styling triumphs of 1927, 1932, 1934, 1938, 1941 and 1942.

This prototype was especially built to provide Cadillac's promotional departments and outside advertising agency with an advance look at what the 1948 sedan models would be like. Notice that one side of the car is 62-Series and the other simulates the Sixty-Special. These photographs are an interesting study in how variations in key bright metal details can modify the character of a body.

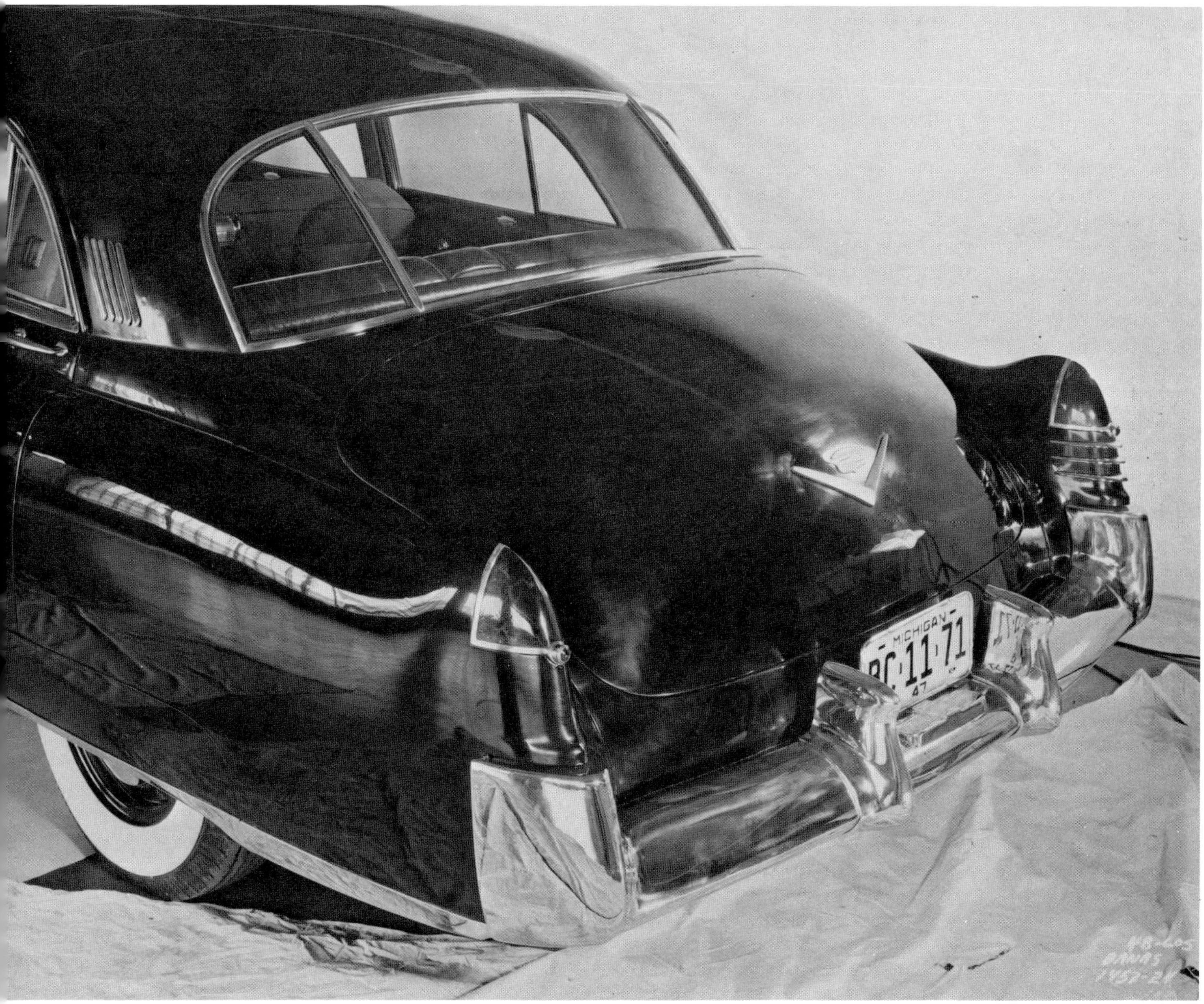
MICHIGAN

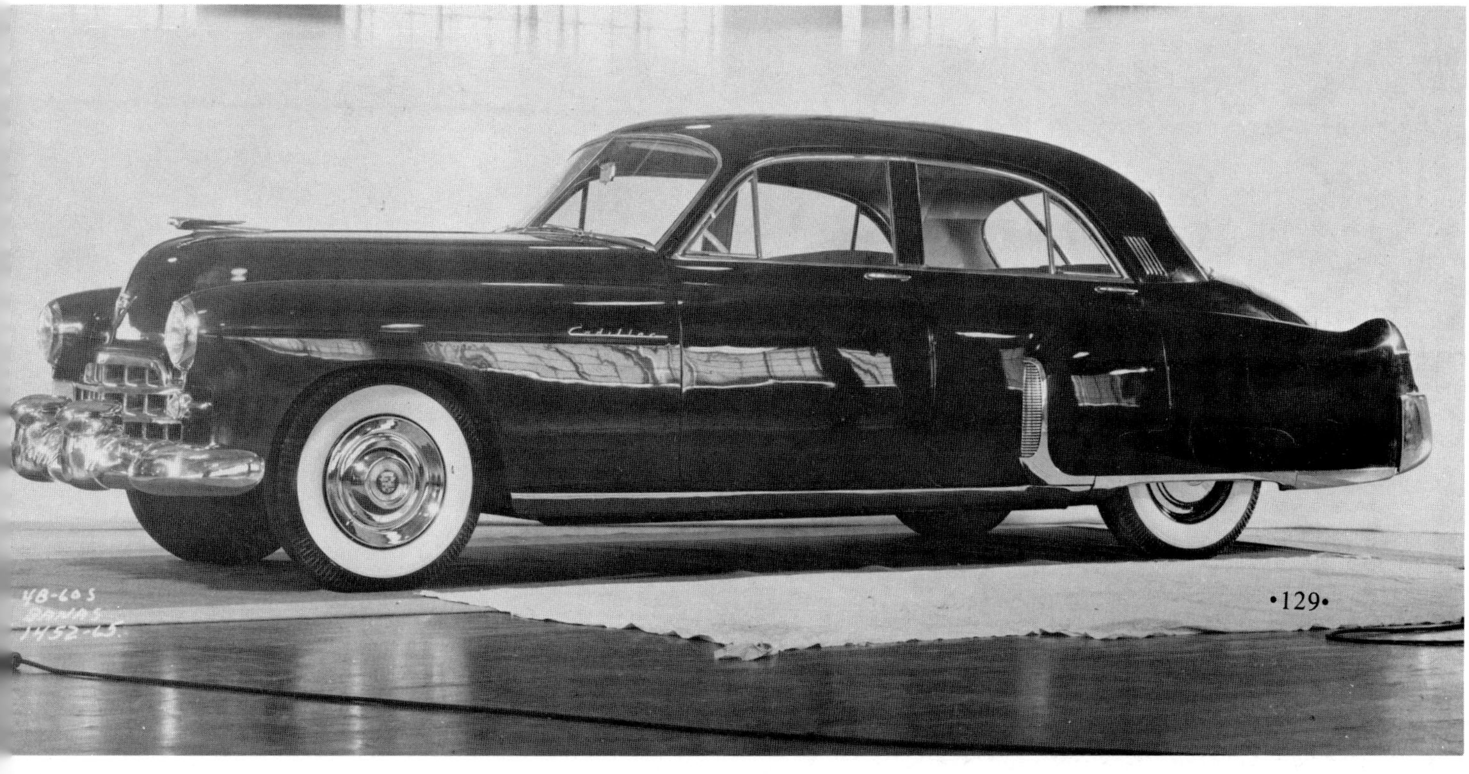

The revolution in automotive visual form that began with the 1948 Cadillac is underscored in a scene like this.

Above, the 62-Series sedan, Style 48-6269. Left, a Data Book illustration of the rear compartment in a 62 sedan with typical two-tone method of trim and horizontal pattern on door panels. 61-Series sedans employed single-fabric motifs set off by darker piping; door panels were plain and the seat backs had no bolsters. All 61 and 62-Series closed cars had instrument panels, door and quarter window mouldings, belt panels and back window mouldings finished with brown leather-grain transfers.

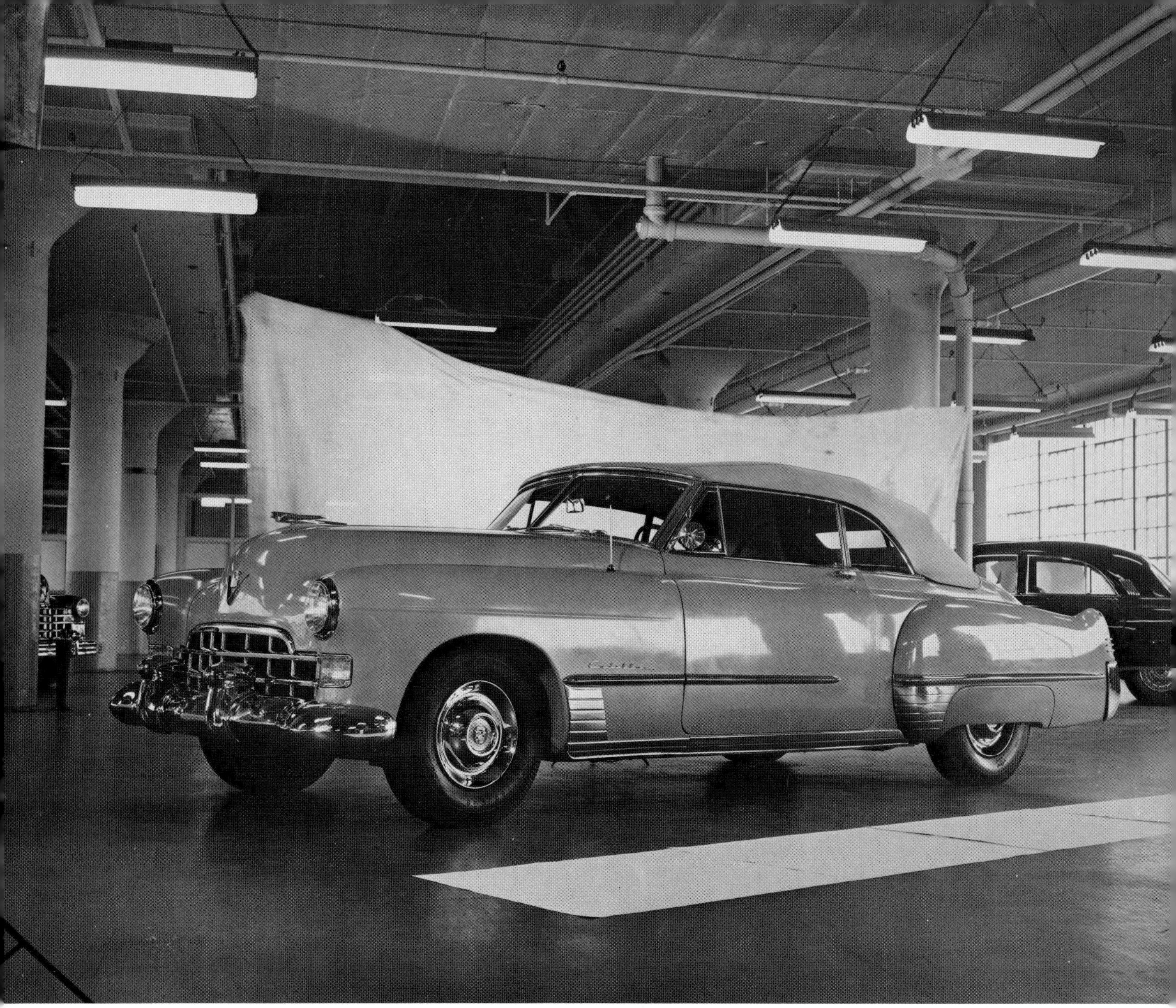

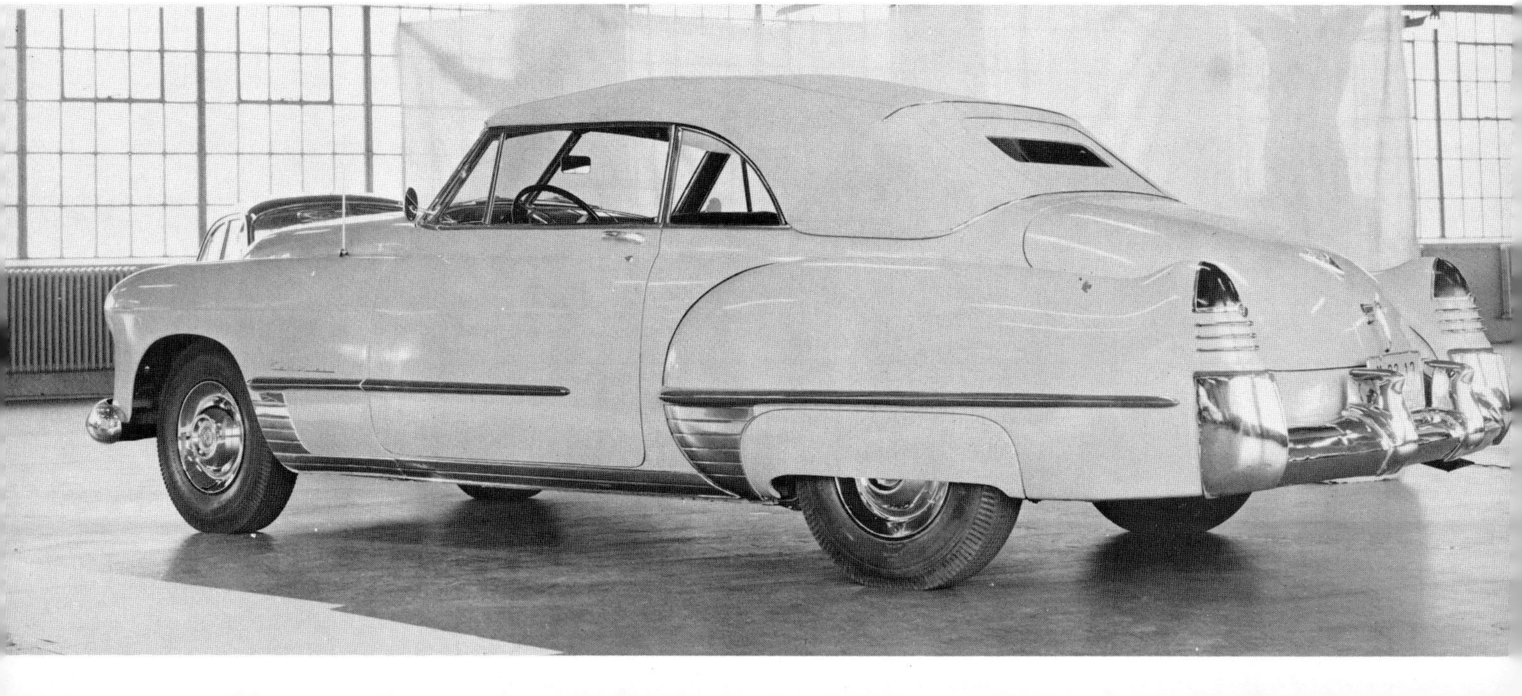

THE 1948 CONVERTIBLE

The svelte convertible body was a strikingly beautiful addition to the American motoring scene. The 1948 convertible was the first to have rear quarter windows, as well as door glass, front seat and top, activated by hydraulics. A conventional canvas top, with its diminutive rear glass, provided a traditional link with the past. The "X" in the style number indicated the presence of a Hydro-Lectric system on 1948 and 1949 Cadillacs. Opposite and above are factory photographs. Right, the author's 48-6267X circa 1962.

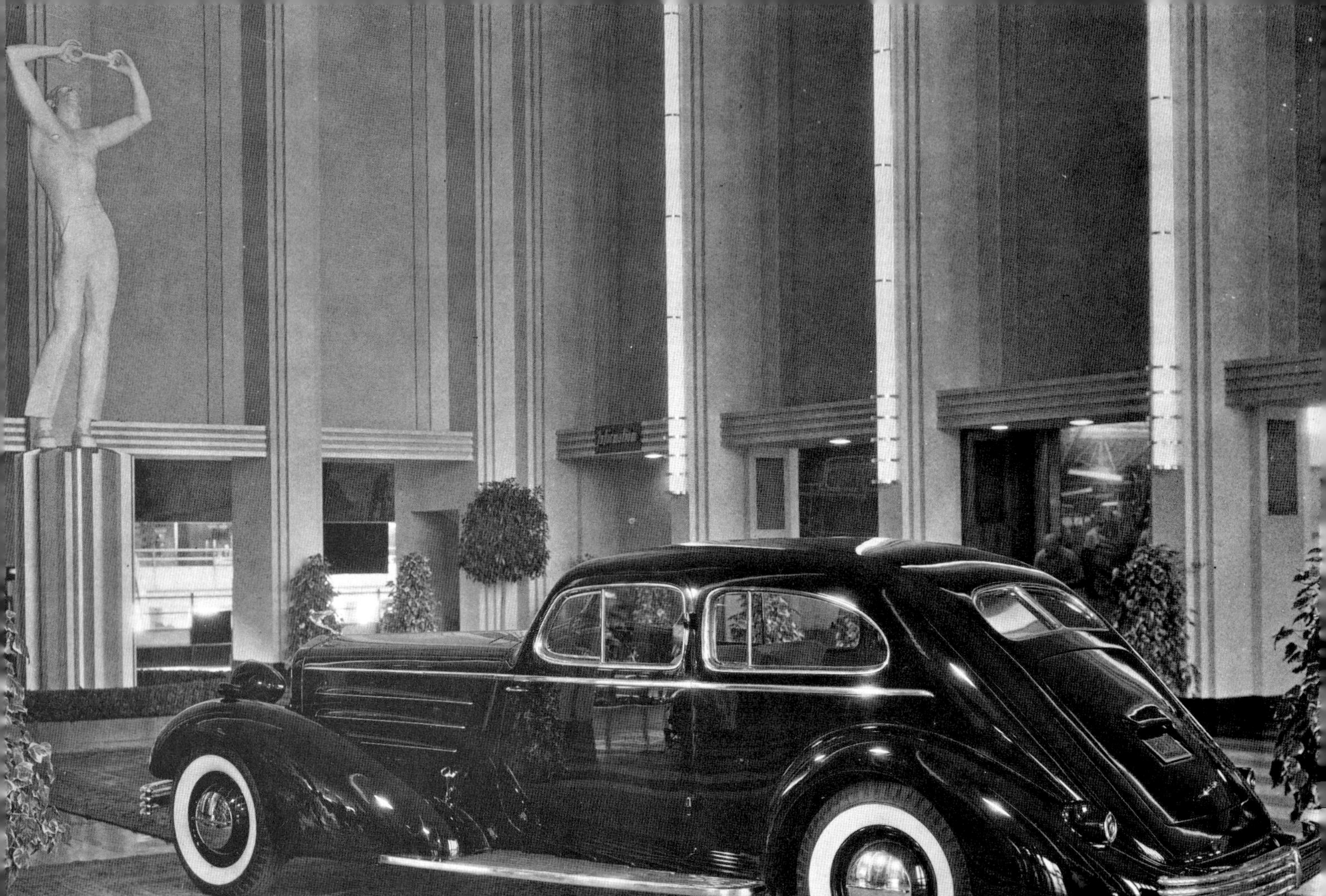

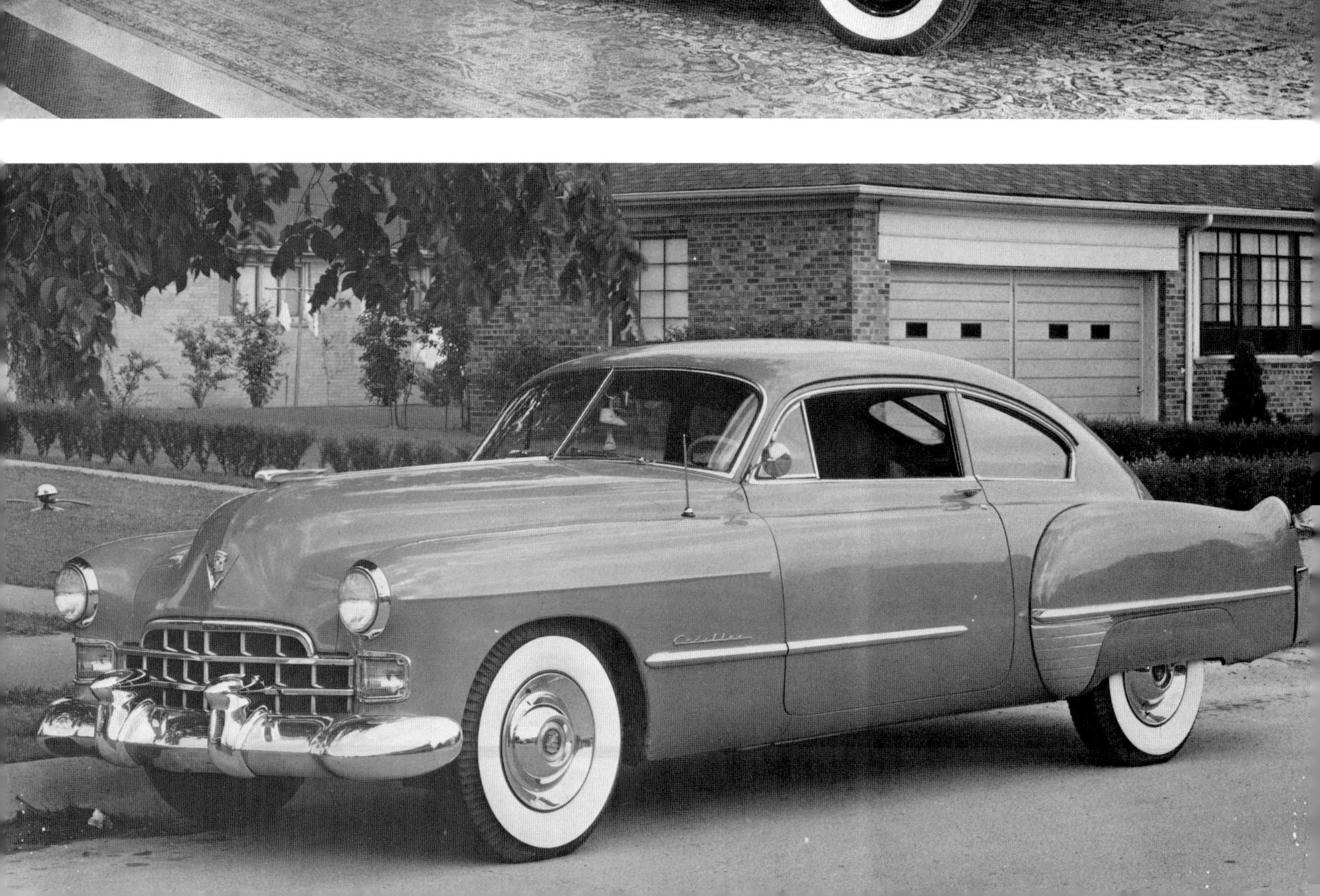

From 1934 through 1937 Cadillac had offered a fastback coupe for five passengers — the Aero-Dynamic Coupe which was based on the 1933 Chicago World's Fair exhibit (opposite page above). The expensive Fleetwood-bodied Aero-Dynamic Coupe accounted for 20 sales in four years. Then in 1941, the fastback was reintroduced at the opposite end of the price range and promptly became the hottest selling Cadillac in the line. A year later the highly acclaimed 62 sedanet appeared; it remained in production, along with the 61 coupe, through 1947. The 1948 and 1949 coupes continued the fastback revival for two more years. In 1950 Cadillac decided to put its money in hardtop styling, and thus closed the door on slantback exotica, making it strictly a phenomenon of the Forties. Opposite page below, Style 48-6107. Above, Style 48-6207.

The thrust of GM advance styling studies in the early 1940s was dominated by fastback themes. In the sketch at the right can be seen the emerging influences that were ultimately refined into the architecture of the 1948 Cadillac.

1948 FASTBACKS

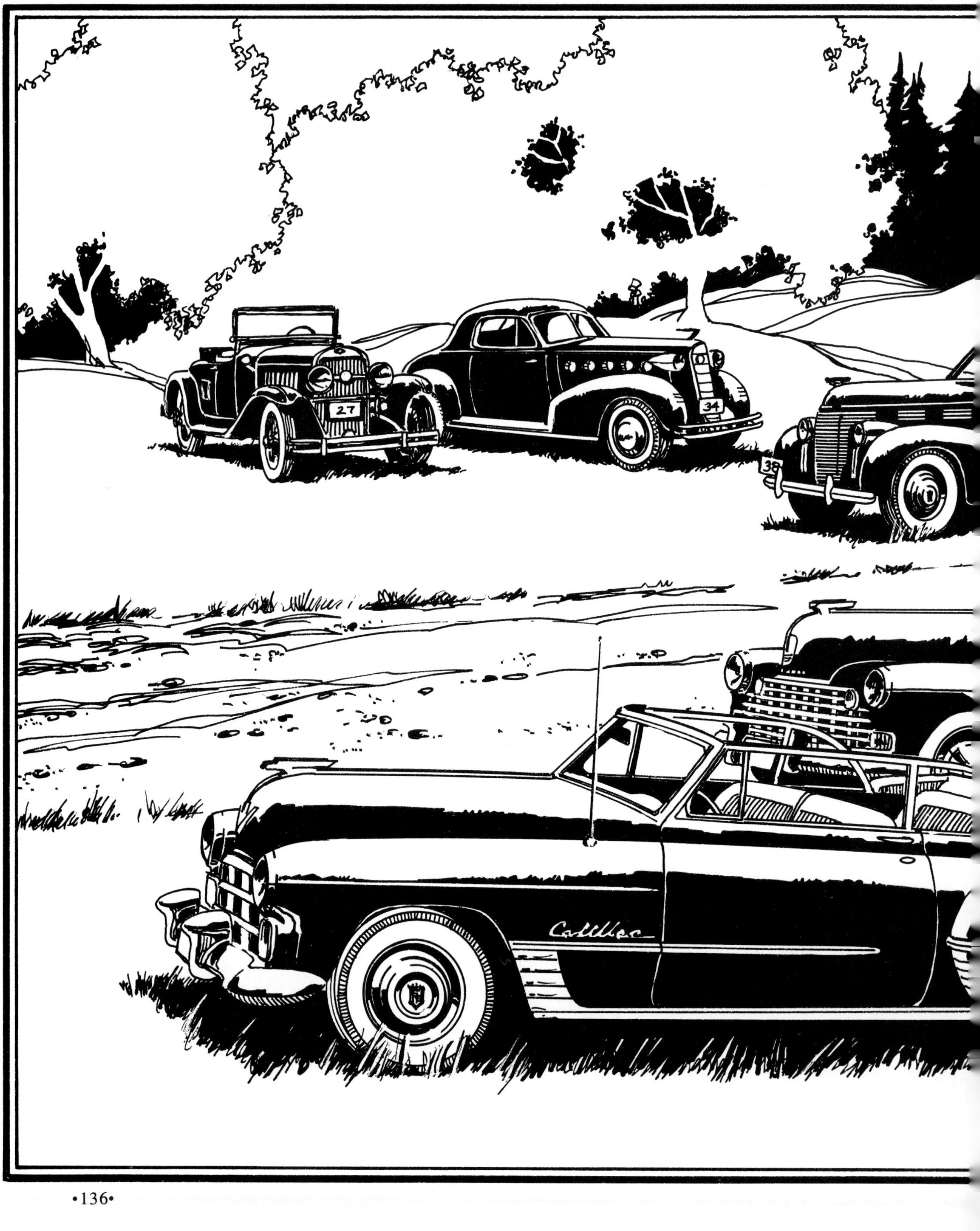
27
34
Cadillac

The lineage of the 1948 Cadillac can be traced through the succession of trend-setting vehicles in this drawing: 1927 LaSalle roadster, 1934 LaSalle coupe, 1938 Cadillac Sixty-Special, 1941 Cadillac 61-Series coupe, 1942 Cadillac Sixty-Special and 1948 62-Series convertible. This dramatic evolution in automotive form was accomplished under Harley Earl's direction in only 21 years.

The advertisements on this page typify Cadillac's magazine advertising campaign in the post-war years. Artists were inclined to take more liberties with realism than had been the case before the War. Backgrounds in most magazine advertisements were dominated by the V and crest superimposed on a field of color with the vehicular illustration and message confined to the lower third of the page.

Opposite page above, a pre-production Fleetwood Sixty-Special making its debut in the snow. Opposite below, a press kit photograph of the 48-6069X. Fabric and leather upholstery combinations were standard. Door trim panels and instrument panel were finished in black leather-grained transfers.

Cadillac

Today's Cadillac is the most beautiful ever built—and the new Cadillacs you see on the streets and highways are the most popular in Cadillac history. ☆ ☆ ☆ America's first look at these smart new cars was enough to win instant approval of their uncommon beauty—heralding, as it does, all that is best in modern motor car design. ☆ ☆ ☆ But beauty is only *half* the story of the great new Cadillacs—for the exterior smartness is matched completely by the new mechanical goodness. In all the things that make a motor car a joy to possess and a pleasure to drive—here, indeed, is the car of cars. ☆ ☆ ☆ Small wonder that thousands who have previously been content with lesser cars are turning to Cadillac —determined, once and for all, to be done with compromise. ☆ ☆ ☆ We feel sure you would enjoy a careful inspection of the car by which all others are measured and adjudged. You will be welcome at your Cadillac dealer's showrooms at any time.

★ CADILLAC MOTOR CAR DIVISION ★ GENERAL MOTORS CORPORATION ★

Cadillac PRESENTS THE *New* STANDARD OF THE WORLD!

Today, the world has a new standard by which to measure motor cars. For Cadillac has taken a great stride forward—one of the greatest, perhaps, in its entire history. As is always the case when a new Cadillac is introduced, the advancement embraces every phase of automotive goodness. The exterior appearance is *wholly* new, and represents the soundest principles developed in years of continuous research. Interior design and finish are a complete departure, and add immeasurably to comfort, beauty and convenience. Performance is finer in every way, for the great Cadillac chassis and engine have been thoroughly refined. And vital improvements in factory equipment have raised even Cadillac's high standards of manufacturing. In fact, *all* the attributes which have contributed to Cadillac's reputation as the world's premier motor car have been made more pronounced. Regardless of the price class from which you expect to select your next car, you are cordially invited to inspect the new Cadillacs—now on display. When the standard of the automotive world has been so decidedly raised, it should be of interest to everyone.

CADILLAC MOTOR CAR DIVISION ★ GENERAL MOTORS CORPORATION

·139·

CADILLAC MILESTONES—1902-1947

Year	Total Production	Type of Cars Produced	List Price (Typical Car)	Wheelbase	Milestones
1902	—	—	—	—	Detroit Automobile Co., established 1899, reorganized as "Cadillac Automobile Co."
1903	1,698	1 cyl. "A"	$ 850	76"	
1904	2,457	1 cyl. "B"	950	76"	Cadillac Automobile Co. and Leland & Faulconer consolidate as "Cadillac Motor Car Company" with Henry M. Leland, grand old man of the industry, as General Manager.
1905	3,942	1 cyl. "F"	950	76"	First Four Cylinder establishes Cadillac as the pioneer of multi-cylinder motor cars.
		4 cyl. "D"	2,800	100"	
1906	4,059	1 cyl. "M"	950	76"	
		4 cyl. "H"	2,500	102"	
1907	2,884	1 cyl. "M"	950	76"	Famous Johansson gauges, First imported into United States by Cadillac, enable Cadillac to become the following year the—
		4 cyl. "G"	2,000	100"	
		4 cyl. "H"	2,500	102"	
1908	2,377	1 cyl. "T"	1,000	82"	First American Car to be awarded the Dewar Trophy by Royal Automobile Club of London for being First to achieve interchangeability through standardization of parts.
		4 cyl. "H"	2,500	102"	
1909	7,868	4 cyl. "30"	1,400	106"	Cadillac purchased by General Motors Corporation. Four cylinder production increases six times over 1908 production.
1910	10,044	4 cyl. "30"	1,600	106"	First to offer Closed Bodies as standard equipment. Less than 10% of cars then produced had closed bodies
1911	10,166	4 cyl. "30"	1,800	116"	Custom Coachcraft by Fleetwood Body Company begins.
1912	12,547	4 cyl. "1912"	3,250	116"	First to equip cars with Electric Starting, Lighting, Ignition, for which Cadillac again was awarded the Dewar Trophy. First and only car in the world to win this award twice.
1913	17,290	4 cyl. "1913"	3,250	120"	
1914	7,823	4 cyl. "1914"	2,800	120"	First in this country to build a V-type, water-cooled eight cylinder engine. This engineeringly correct engine type is now used by every fine car manufacturer. First to use thermostatic control of cooling system.
		V-8 "51"	2,800	122"	
1915	13,000	V-8 "53"	2,950	122"	First to use Tilt-Beam Headlights for night driving safety.
1916	18,000	V-8 "53"	2,950	122"	Cadillac becomes "Division of General Motors."
1917	18,002	V-8 "55"	3,110	125"	Cadillac adopted as Standard Officers' car by U. S. Army after gruelling tests at Marfa, Texas.
1918	20,285	V-8 "57"	3,535	125"	Cadillac supplied 2,350 cars and 1,157 V-8 artillery tractor engines to U. S. Army.
1919	20,678	V-8 "57"	4,090	125"	
1920	19,628	V-8 "59"	4,750	125"	Cadillac completes new Clark Ave. plant, Detroit, most modern in the industry. Retail stores opened at Detroit and Chicago.
1921	5,250	V-8 "59"	4,950	132"	
1922	26,296	V-8 "61"	4,100	132"	First to use Thermostatic Carburetor Control.
1923	14,707	V-8 "61"	4,150	138"	First to build the inherently balanced 90° V-type eight cylinder engine. First to use the Compensated Crankshaft. Four wheel brakes featured.
1924	18,827	V-8 "V-63"	3,835	132"	First to provide wide choice of Duco Exterior Finishes as standard equipment.
1925	16,673	V-8 "V-63"	3,195	132"	First to use Crankcase Ventilation. $5,000,000 expansion program started. Cadillac contracts for entire output of Fleetwood Custom Body Co.
1926	20,732	V-8 "314"	3,250	132"	First to develop a comprehensive Service Policy and place it on a nationwide basis.
1927	30,641	V-8 "303"	2,685	125"	
		V-8 "341-A"	3,250	140"	
1928	36,037	V-8 "328"	2,495	125"	First to develop and use the Clashless Syncro-mesh Transmission. First to install Security Plate Glass as standard equipment.
		V-8 "341-B"	3,595	140"	
1929	40,965	V-8 "340"	2,595	134"	First to adopt Chrome Plating as standard.
		V-8 "353"	3,695	140"	
1930	25,991	V-8 "345-A"	2,595	134"	First to build a Sixteen Cylinder Automobile Engine. Later in the year the V-12 Cadillac was introduced. First to offer a complete line of multi-cylinder cars—all of V-type design. First to use Hydraulic Valve Silencers.
		V-8 "355-A"	3,695	134"	
		V-12 "370-A"	3,895	140"	
		V-16 "452-A"	5,950	148"	
1931	29,779	V-8 "345-A"	2,295	134"	
		V-8 "355-A"	2,795	134"	
		V-12 "370-A"	3,945	140"	
		V-16 "452-A"	5,950	148"	
1932	8,084	V-8 "345-B"	2,495	136"	First to introduce Super-Safe Headlights, Air-Cooled Generator, Completely Silent Transmission and Full Range Ride Regulator.
		V-8 "355-B"	2,895	140"	
		V-12 "370-B"	3,795	140"	
		V-16 "452-B"	5,095	149"	
1933	6,655	V-8 "345-C"	2,245	136"	First to provide fine cars with No-Draft Ventilation.
		V-8 "355-C"	2,895	140"	
		V-12 "370-C"	3,695	149"	
		V-16 "452-C"	6,250	149"	

•140•

Year	Total Production	Type of Cars Produced	List Price (Typical Car)	Wheelbase	Milestones
1934	13,021	Str. "8" "34-50"	$1,595	119"	**First** to introduce Today's Mode of Streamlining. **First** American Car with spare tire concealed within body. **First** to develop and use Knee-Action Wheels.
		V-8 "10"	2,695	128"	
		V-12 "40"	4,195	146"	
		V-16 "60"	6,750	154"	
1935	12,279	Str. "8" "35-50"	1,545	120"	**First** and **only** fine car equipped with one-piece solid steel Turret Top. For five years, more Cadillacs purchased than any other make of fine car.
		V-8 "10"	2,495	128"	
		V-12 "40"	3,995	146"	
		V-16 "60"	6,750	154"	
1936	25,905	Str. "8" "36-50"	1,225	121"	48.1% of all cars sold above $1,500 were Cadillacs.
		V-8 "60"	1,695	121"	
		V-8 "70"	2,445	131"	
		V-8 "75"	2,645	138"	
		V-12 "80"	3,145	131"	
		V-12 "85"	3,345	138"	
		V-16 "90"	7,750	154"	
1937	46,153	V-8 "37-50"	1,260*	124"	Cadillac-built V-8 proves stamina, dependability and speed of present day stock car by breaking all previous stock car records at Indianapolis Speedway. Deliveries at retail hit all-time peak in all Cadillac history.
		V-8 "37-60"	1,660*	124"	
		V-8 "37-65"	2,090*	131"	
		V-8 "37-70"	2,595*	131"	
		V-8 "37-75"	2,815*	138"	
		V-12 "37-85"	3,535*	138"	
		V-16 "37-90"	7,750*	154"	
1938	24,950	V-8 "38-50"	1,385*	124"	**First** to create and introduce a practical motor car of advanced styling. **First** to engineer and build the 135° V-type sixteen cylinder engine. A majority public recognition of **Cadillac Merit** and **Advanced Progress** is definitely established.
		V-8 "38-60"	1,775*	124"	
		V-8 "38-60S"	2,085*	127"	
		V-8 "38-65"	2,285*	132"	
		V-8 "38-75"	3,075*	141"	
		V-16 "38-90"	5,265*	141"	
1939	36,611	V-8 "39-50"	1,320*	120"	**First** to develop and introduce Controlled-Action, greatest advancement in riding comfort and safety since Knee-Action. More than half of all fine cars sold above $2,000 are Cadillacs.
		V-8 "39-61"	1,680*	126"	
		V-8 "39-60S"	2,090*	127"	
		V-8 "39-75"	2,995*	141"	
		V-16 "39-90"	5,140*	141"	
1940	37,162	V-8 "40-50"	1,320*	123"	**First** to offer custom car interiors at medium price. **First** to equip passenger cars with Ball Bearing Steering. **First** to introduce an *ultra-modern* large, luxurious motor car—The Cadillac Fleetwood 72. During first six months, 1939, Cadillac outsold all makes combined with series having 5 touring sedans priced at or above $1,300.
		V-8 "40-52"	1,440*	123"	
		V-8 "40-62"	1,745*	129"	
		V-8 "40-60S"	2,090*	127"	
		V-8 "40-72"	2,670*	138"	
		V-8 "40-75"	2,995*	141"	
		V-16 "40-90"	5,140*	141"	
1941	66,130	V-8 "41-61"	1,445*	126"	**First** to introduce to the medium price field a motor car of unquestioned prestige without a compromise in quality. **First** high price car to offer Hydra-Matic, the completely automatic transmission that eliminates the clutch pedal and all gear shifting. Cadillac outsold all makes of cars in both the Medium and High Price Groups.
		V-8 "41-62"	1,495*	126"	
		V-8 "41-63"	1,695*	126"	
		V-8 "41-60S"	2,195*	126"	
		V-8 "41-67"	2,595*	139"	
		V-8 "41-75"	2,995*	136"	
1942	16,511	V-8 "42-61"	1,647*	126"	**Presentation** of the Fortieth Anniversary Cadillacs. Introduction of sealed, ribbed Super-Safe Brakes and All-Weather Ventilation System.
(Production halted February, 1942)		V-8 "42-62"	1,754*	129"	
		V-8 "42-63"	1,882*	126"	
		V-8 "42-60S"	2,435*	133"	
		V-8 "42-67"	2,896*	139"	
		V-8 "42-75"	3,306*	136"	
1943		—	—	—	Cadillac-built light tanks and motor carriages contributed immeasurably to the struggle for victory and peace. Precision aircraft engine parts made by Cadillac helped power America's leading combat planes. Army-Navy "E" award to Cadillac for excellence in production of war equipment.
1944		—	—	—	Cadillac produced the M-24, one of the world's fastest and most maneuverable combat vehicles of its kind. This famous light tank, which served on all battle-fronts, was powered by Cadillac V-type engines and Cadillac Hydra-Matic Transmissions.
1945		—	—	—	Continued production of the world-famed M-24 light tank for distinguished use in both the European and Pacific theaters of war. Introduction of the M-19, a potent anti-aircraft gun motor carriage.
1946	29,194	V-8 "46-61"	$2,176*	126"	**Presentation** of the 1946 Cadillacs, using the battle-proved Cadillac V-type engine and Hydra-Matic transmission, the only automotive units of this kind to be produced and improved without interruption during the war.
		V-8 "46-62"	2,359*	129"	
		V-8 "46-60S"	3,099*	133"	
		V-8 "46-75"	4,298*	136"	
1947	61,926	V-8 "47-61"	2,324*	126"	**Postwar** production reaches over 90% of prewar peak. Cadillac increases fine car leadership with over 96,000 unfilled orders.
		V-8 "47-62"	2,523*	129"	
		V-8 "47-60S"	3,195*	133"	
		V-8 "47-75"	4,471*	136"	

(*Advertised Delivered Price at Detroit. State and local taxes extra.)

1949

THE OVERHEAD EIGHT

The 1949 Cadillac's position in postwar automotive history is without parallel. It combined the greatest engineering advance of the era with the ultimate in styling popularity. It was unquestionably the dominant American automobile of the late Forties. Its high compression overhead valve V-8 established industry standards that would prevail for decades.

The trend toward higher compression ratios had, since the days of the horseless carriage, prompted automakers to keep abreast of advances in fuel research. During the early 1930s Cadillac engineers determined that one of the best ways to prepare for the power demands and higher octane gasoline of the future was with continued exploration of the overhead valve engine configuration. Not that overhead valves were anything new at Cadillac; the classic V-12 and V-16 engines of the 1930 through 1937 era had all been valve-in-head designs. Active development of the overhead V-8 began shortly after the unit-cast L-head V-8 was introduced in 1936.

Compression ratios beyond the 7.25 to 1, which had remained standard from 1941 through 1948, were tested in the L-head configuration but, as E. N. Cole, Chief Engineer, reported: *We found that if we went above that (7.25 to 1) we restricted the volumetrics and started getting combustion roughness. We had experimental L-Heads on test using 8.0 to 8.6 to 1 compression ratios. The reason for going to overhead valves was to have higher compression, and you pick up rapidly on thermal efficiency when you go to higher compression . . . plus volumetric efficiency.*

By 1940 two important decisions on the design of the new Cadillac engine had been made. One was a commitment to use the slipper piston, a piston that was engineered to slip (nest) between crankshaft counterweights. The shorter stroke reduced piston

An early mock-up of the overhead valve engine executed primarily in wood. The actual engines shown on pages 142 and 146 are early 1949 versions with two bolts securing the valve covers. Head design was changed early in the 1949 production run to accommodate a revised four-fastener valve cover. The later design, typical on the majority of 49s, also necessitated revised plug wiring.

travel by approximately 20 percent; at 4,000 RPM the O.H.V. piston traveled only 2,400 feet per minute compared to 3,000 feet per minute for the piston in a 1948 L-head. Reduced piston travel also cut frictional power loss and made possible a reduction in reciprocating and rotating weight through the use of lighter, smaller engine components. Second, the crankshaft would be supported in five main bearings (rather than three) for more stability and minimization of the vibration characteristic of earlier overhead valve V-8 engines.

Early overhead valve experimental engines pursued the manifolding and accessory placement principles arrived at for the 1936-1937 L-head. Even up and over exhaust manifolding wasn't changed until after the War. Naturally, experimental work on the project had stopped at the onset of the War and it wasn't until after VJ Day that Mr. Cole and Harry Barr, Cadillac's engineer in charge of engines, got back to their research.

Official factory documents state that when design studies resumed two test engines were built, one an L-head, the other a valve-in-head. Experimental runs on these two proved conclusively that the valve-in-head engine was far superior for the higher compression ratios that Cadillac engineers were predicting for the future.

According to one factory press release, between 1946 and 1948 more than 25 prototype engines were built and subjected to the most demanding tests. In one laboratory endurance run a pre-production version of the 1949 engine was run for more than 100 hours at 4,250 RPM with wide-open throttle — the equivalent of over 108 miles per hour. At the conclusion of the test there was no appreciable wear on engine parts, there had been no mechanical failure, and the engine had run continuously except for stops to add fuel and oil.

With 12 years of research and more than a million test miles completed, the new overhead V-8 was ready. It was a bold step forward because it completely displaced the flathead at perhaps the height of its success. Factory literature went to great lengths to illustrate the differences between the old and the new engine. One booklet widely distributed to the general public, CADILLAC PRESENTS THE GREATEST AUTOMOBILE ENGINE EVER BUILT, made candid comparisons between the 1948 and 1949 powerplants. A number of comparative illustrations from the *1949 Data Book* are reproduced in this chapter as evidence of the reductions in size and weight. At 699 pounds the overhead edition was 188 pounds lighter than the flathead. Overall engine height was reduced four inches. The flathead's 346 inches of displacement and 3½" x 4½" bore and stroke overshadowed the overhead's 331 inches and 3³⁄₁₆" x 3⅝" dimensions, yet the latter had more horsepower; the 1948's 150 BHP at 3400 RPM compared to 160 BHP at 3600 RPM for the 1949. Even with two extra main bearings, the slipper technology and the use of thinner counterweights permitted a net decrease in engine length of five inches. Weight reductions realized with the lighter engine and lesser cooling requirements made the 1949 Cadillacs nearly 300 pounds lighter than counterparts in the previous series.

Below, pre-production testing in the low-temperature room at the GM Proving Grounds. All systems were tested and evaluated at temperatures down to 50 degrees below zero (Fahrenheit).

Above, the 1949 chassis employed a 1948-type frame. Modifications necessary for receiving the overhead powerplant were minimal.

Opposite page, 1949 Data Book illustrations showing the dramatic reductions in size between the L-head engine (old) and the valve-in-head powerplant of 1949 (new).

The end result was an engine capable of taking a 4,200 pound motorcar from 0 to 60 (MPH) in 12 seconds with a top speed of 100 MPH. Its outstanding accelerative ability impressed Cadillac's conservative clientele perhaps more than any other feature. The fact that it was possible to punch the throttle at a dead stop and be approaching 70 MPH before the Hydro shifted into fourth gear meant little to the average buyer. What did matter was that it took only four seconds to get from 45 to 75 MPH. That kind of performance gave the Cadillac driver the extra margin of safety that might be needed in traffic. Yet, despite this astonishing power, the new V-8 was exceptionally smooth and quiet. At cruising speeds, 60 to 75 MPH, there was little engine sound and wind noise was negligible.

There was an unexpected bonus in the overhead-valve V-8 which the public never anticipated, and that was remarkable fuel economy. A proving grounds report quoted a 12 to 17 percent increase in mileage over 1948, but that seems low in retrospect. Many 1949 owners reported yields as high as 22 and 24 miles per gallon (MPG) on the highway, and even the most conservative averagers granted 17 to 19 MPG. In one controlled English test a stock sedan was tested for 160 miles at speeds ranging from 80 to 90 miles per hour and received 15 to 17 MPG. Since the flathead's optimum mileage was close to 15 MPG at 50 MPH the net gain in fuel economy actually ran the spectrum from 12 to 60 percent!

An aerodynamically efficient body married to the singularly responsive new powerplant made the 1949 Cadillac a road-going machine. Driving was the kind of exhilarating experience not normally associated with large automobiles. Since the frame and suspension were essentially the same as that used in preceding years (Cadillac didn't re-engineer the chassis until 1950) handling characteristics were similar to those of 1948. Road adhesion was superb, as might be expected from a 4,000 pound vehicle and the ride

OLD

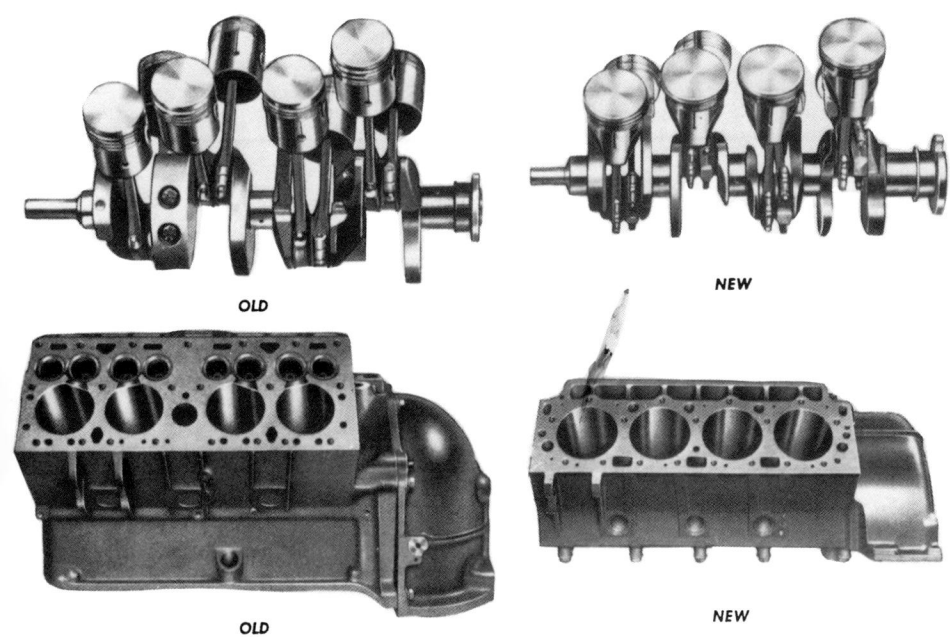

NEW

OLD

NEW

Above, this well detailed 1949 engine compartment illustrates the uncrowded and straight-forward arrangements found under the hood. Most routine service procedures were accomplished with relative ease. The OHV V-8 was designed with the future in mind. Provisions for displacement increases allowed the original 331-inch 1949 to be periodically expanded until it reached 429 CID in 1967.

measured up to the prevailing standards expected of luxury motorcars.

Industry and hobby journals have in recent years given rather complete coverage to the evolution and merits of Cadillac's valve-in-head V-8 engine. However, in the shower of praise and enthusiasm for the 1949 engine the important qualities of the 1937 through 1948 L-head are often forgotten or understated. It is well to remember that when a comparison of these two engines is being made the period which each served must be considered. Driving in the earlier period was not done on freeways, expressways or turnpikes with the same frequency that it is today. It was a slower traffic pattern that often required a greater dependence on low speed torque. This, plus the fact that the automatic transmission didn't proliferate until after the war, made the flathead well suited for the demands of Forties.

The major styling change in 1949 was a simplified grill which became another chapter in the reduction of horizontal bars that began in 1940. According to one report, Cadillac went from 38 horizontal members in 1939 to 20 in 1940, 10 in 1941, 6 in 1942, 5 in 1946, 4 in 1947, 3 in 1948 and 2 in 1949.

Harley Earl wanted something Tiffany for the 1948 grill, recalls stylist Frank Hershey. *Then after the car was out for six months they decided the grill had to have more punch. Everyone liked the general feeling in '48 so all that had to be done was heavy-up the bars and add some chrome.*

The added chrome swept over the parking-fog lamp provision and wrapped around the front bumper. Other frontal changes included a hood that extended farther forward and allowed the ornament to move ahead slightly. The raised bead in the sheetmetal of the hood, which had outlined the grill in 1948, was deleted in 1949.

At the opposite end of the car the three slashes below the tail lights were eliminated on the 62-Series cars. Below the tail light a band of chrome was added just below the red reflector. Another rear end change came mid-way during the model run in the form of a square deck lid. This modification was in response to requests for additional trunk space for luggage, but the new contours complemented the car's architecture perfectly. The new deck lid was designed to interchange with respective 1948 and early 1949 models. It was a feature that evolved from the squared trunk on the 1948 Sixty-Special.

Although it was almost unprecedented for Cadillac to discontinue a dash after only one year the 1949 instrument board was completely redesigned. The flatter upper surface of the new dash extended into the passenger compartment at hood level. In models with painted rather than grained dash panels (convertibles, limousines and Coupes de Ville) there was a pronounced illusion that the hood and cowl projected on past the windshield in roadster fashion. The hooded instrument cluster in front of the driver and the dash blending with door finish panels were reminiscent of previous years, but the total effect was both pleasing and fresh. The dominant finish used on the dash and finish panels in closed cars was *Cameo Grain* Di-Noc transfers with lighter harmonizing inserts. The duo-tone effect blended well with the two-tone upholstery options that prevailed in 1949.

The 62-Series interiors had seat and back inserts upholstered in pale tones of gray or brown broadcloth or Bedford cord. Seat back bolsters and arm rests were trimmed in darker harmonizing broadcloth. Sixty-one-Series interiors were upholstered in either tan or gray. Dual-tone cord was used on seat backs and cushions with door panels in plain fabric. In all models a broad heel pad extended up from the floor to create a finished appearance and protect the upholstery. All closed models (except the 75 with livery trim) had folding center arm rests.

Sixty-Special interiors were available in either cloth or leather- and cloth combinations. Black leather bolsters were used with either blue or green shadow-stripe broadcloth or Bedford cord. Tan leather was used with tan shadow-stripe cloth. As in all

Left, the re-styled Sixty-Special interior for 1949 was imbued with traditional Fleetwood workmanship and quality.

Cadillac models, floors were completely covered with wool pile carpeting to complement the interior trim. Door panels, seat backs, and the back of the front seat were tailored in block patterns, with buttons.

Convertible interiors were finished in all leather, with five color options, and either tan or black tops. Hydraulic power cylinders actuated the top, all windows and front seat in the convertible.

Hydraulic window lifts were also standard on the Fleetwood Sixty-Special and Seventy-Five. Automatic window regulators installed at the factory were $121.65 extra for 61 and 62-Series coupes and sedans. An interesting innovation in the accessory group was the heater-defroster unit that was designed to defrost the front door glass as well as the windshield.

All body offerings from the previous series were repeated in 1949: The 61 and 62-Series coupes and sedans, the 62 convertible and the ever-popular, still traditionally-attired 75. A pillarless coupe added to the line late in 1949 was perhaps the most significant body of the year. Copyrighters called Cadillac's first hardtop the Coupe de Ville, and both the name and the design expanded into the decades ahead. Only 2,150 Coupes de Ville were produced in this first year; the suggested list price was $3,497. Their construction was very similar to the 62 convertible and many body components such as deck lid and doors were interchangeable.

The perennial Cadillac of the 1940s was the Fleetwood Seventy-Five. Its timeless design was, and still is, the personification of luxurious transportation. Adding the 72-Series sedans of 1940 to the 75-Series cars produced between 1941 and 1949 finds a mere 10,000 of these classics were built. Because of their wide exposure in movies, television and magazines while in the service of heads of state, livery services, motion picture studios and so forth, they were the most visible luxury cars of the 1940s. In their final version — equipped with the overhead valve engine and '49-type dash and door finish mouldings — the 75s were as handsome and fleet as ever. But the pendulum of change was moving and the trend toward more current styling could not be ignored. Proposals incorporating the 1949 styling were explored; but, as traditionalists would have it, the old design survived the decade.

The rarest of the series were those cars with L-type interiors (known in the 1930s as *Livery Trim*) Styles 7533L and 7523L. These units had manually operated window regulators and division glass. Their interiors were much simpler with plain paneled door panels and seats. There were no finish panels on the doors (below the window garnish) and no center arm rests. Garnish mouldings in L-type cars were normally painted black.

The 1949 commercial cars, designated the 86-Series, did use passenger car styling. Independent ambulance and funeral coach builders purchased 1,861 163-inch wheelbase chassis in 1949, reflecting a somewhat lower volume than had been recorded in 1947 and 1948. The 1948 commercial chassis, also employing the 163-inch wheelbase, was known as the 76-Series and it was the last to use the 1941-type styling and L-head engine.

There was a fair amount of chromium plated die cast metal (pot metal) used on Cadillacs during the Forties. It is essential to the preservation of this material that it be kept sealed against moisture in the atmosphere. Special efforts taken to keep existing brightwork surfaces waxed with a non-abrasive product will tend to retard pitting and blistering. Pure carnauba paste wax is one of the best things to use on all plated areas. Waxes containing cleaners, rubbing compounds, and steel wool should be avoided since the chrome itself is extremely thin.

The original plating process of this era started with cleaning the virgin metal. Then layers of copper, nickel and chrome were successively applied. The final operation was merely a flash plating that deposited enough chrome on the surface to keep the nickel from tarnishing and provide a corrosion-resistant finish. If the thin coat of chromium does not cover completely or is subsequently polished away, a condition often referred to as *nickel shading* takes place — the visual color and luster variations between the remaining chrome deposit and the exposed nickel.

In choosing a shop to replate vintage auto parts, locate one that will take the time and care necessary to do the job correctly. The sequence that quality decorative chrome plating requires is: 1. Strip the part to bare metal and prepare it for plating by polishing. 2. Copper plating (sometimes it is necessary to build up the surface with multiple layers of copper). 3. Copper buffing (a thorough polishing that should remove all possible flaws). 4. Nickel plating (the lasting quality of the plating job is imparted with this operation). 5. Chrome plating (its primary function is to protect the porous deposit of nickel). There are many shortcuts a plater can employ; thus, each of the aforementioned steps should be specified.

It is also wise to talk to the plater prior to attempting to repair a pitted or broken die cast part because certain welding rod and solder will not accept plate in the tanks and baths used for plating die cast metal. Platers also normally advise stripping a die cast part before making welding repairs or filling pits with solder.

No more fitting comments could conclude this segment of Cadillac history than those of the Division's General Manager, John F. Gordon, on Friday, November 28, 1949. On this date the last 1949 model produced, a Coupe de Ville, became the one millionth Cadillac. Mr. Gordon said:

> *While Cadillac has continuously held to the principles of highest quality motorcar manufacturing, it has also been the constant aim in the Division to make more Cadillacs available at the lowest possible price. The over-all achievement of this aim is illustrated by a comparison of relative car prices. Fifteen years ago the average price of a Cadillac automobile was more than 4.5 times that of the average price of cars sold in the industry. At the present time, the average Cadillac price is only 1.6 times the average price of cars sold in the automotive field.*
>
> *This favorable price trend has been an important factor in Cadillac's steadily increasing sales volume which is currently emphasized by the 92,554 Cadillac automobiles built in the 1949 model year. This figure is 39 percent greater than the number of Cadillacs produced in any previous model. With this record volume in 1949 models, Cadillac's total production in the four years since the War has reached 236,380.*
>
> *Members of the organization, through long service and devotion to the Cadillac ideal "Craftsmanship a Creed – Accuracy a Law," have developed a fine car building know-how unequalled anywhere in the industry. More than 20 percent of Cadillac's employees have been with the Division for more than fifteen years. The high standard of workmanship to which the organization has been committed needs no further tribute than that established by a recent survey showing 453,000 of Cadillac's one million cars are still in service.*

Above, John F. Gordon, Cadillac's General Manager, standing next to the last Cadillac manufactured during the Forties. Next to him in the light suit is Donald E. Ahrens, the Division's General Sales Manager from 1935 through 1949.

THE 1949 AUTORAMA

In the heyday of the Classic Era, New York City — and to a slightly lesser degree the rest of Jazz-Age America — hosted spectacular automobile shows and lavish coachbuilders' salons. These crowded, almost ritualistic, extravaganzas established the luxury automobile as something more than personal transportation; indeed it was on these very occasions that many wealthy Americans paid enormous sums for what we now call classic cars, the ultimate status symbols of the Roaring Twenties. The sobering interlude of the depression didn't completely erase automobile shows but the prominence they once commanded was on the wane in the post-war years.

Harley Earl never forgot the excitement of the great salons that were so much a part of the industry when he first came to General Motors. After the war he continued to be a fervent patron of the European shows and a frequent visitor to New York. Thus it was only natural for him to gravitate toward a renewal of the promotional expositions of GM products in fashionable New York hotels.

The view on these pages is a portion of the Cadillac display at the January 1949 Autorama staged in the Waldorf-Astoria. There were seven Cadillacs in the show including four with special features that ranged from one-off coachwork to beautiful hand-tailored interiors. Each of the four customs is illustrated and described elsewhere in this chapter. The remaining models, including the 61-Series coupe and the 62-Series sedan in this photograph were standard in every respect with the exception of special exterior paint. None of the models on exhibit was available for purchase and orders were not taken for duplications in either trim or color.

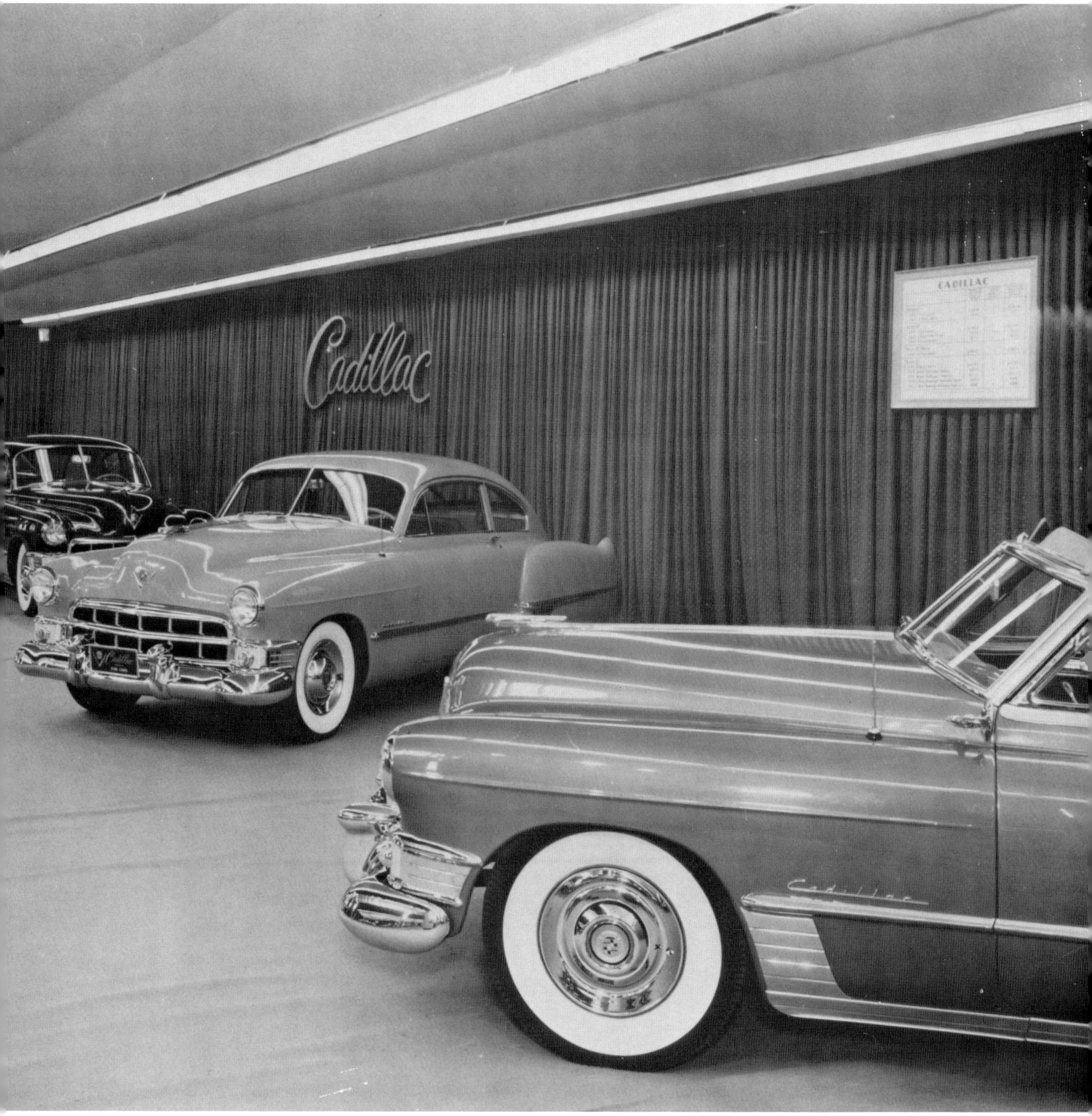
Cadillac
CADILLAC
Cadillac

1949 SERIES SIXTY-TWO CONVERTIBLE

The 1949 convertible, Style 49-6267X, is a highly-regarded collectors car. Above, a restored example and below, two views at the factory that were apparently made to evaluate the styling effect of the squared deck lid. The small hubcaps seen on the car at the bottom were standard equipment, trim rings optional.

Opposite page, three views of a restored convertible; dual exhaust and not-quite-authentic vinyl interior not withstanding, a real traffic stopper.

The first few hundred convertibles carried 1948-type torpedo-contoured deck lids. On these early units, the top well and its sub-structure were essentially the same as they had been in 1948, i.e., the top well and its supporting members were sheet-metal, whereas subsequent convertibles had fabric-type top wells. This change, coupled with the squared deck lid, allowed the spare tire to be mounted vertically in the trunk and increased luggage capacity.

Above, the 62-Series sedan Style 49-6269. The white paper on the ground was positioned to highlight the bright metal. Artists could then, through various techniques — airbrushing in particular — eliminate everything in the photo that was not desired. Below, the 61-Series sedan Style 49-6169.

In both 1948 and 1949 the 61-Series sedans were far outnumbered by their slightly - more - decorative 62-Series counterparts. This marked a major shift in consumer buying habits so far as Cadillac was concerned. In pre-war years the less costly models normally constituted the major sales volume. However, the trend in the later Forties ultimately led to Cadillac's discontinuance of the 61-Series after 1951. Even the Calais Series, which was begun in 1965, failed to recapture the market popularity enjoyed by the LaSalle and pre-war 61-Series.

Right, three views of an original 62 sedan interior; simple, dignified, but decidedly austere when compared to what went before and what was to follow. The interior of this car was photographed in 1976 and reflected the more than 27 years of dutiful care provided by the original owner; the second owner promptly installed tuck and roll naugahyde upholstery.

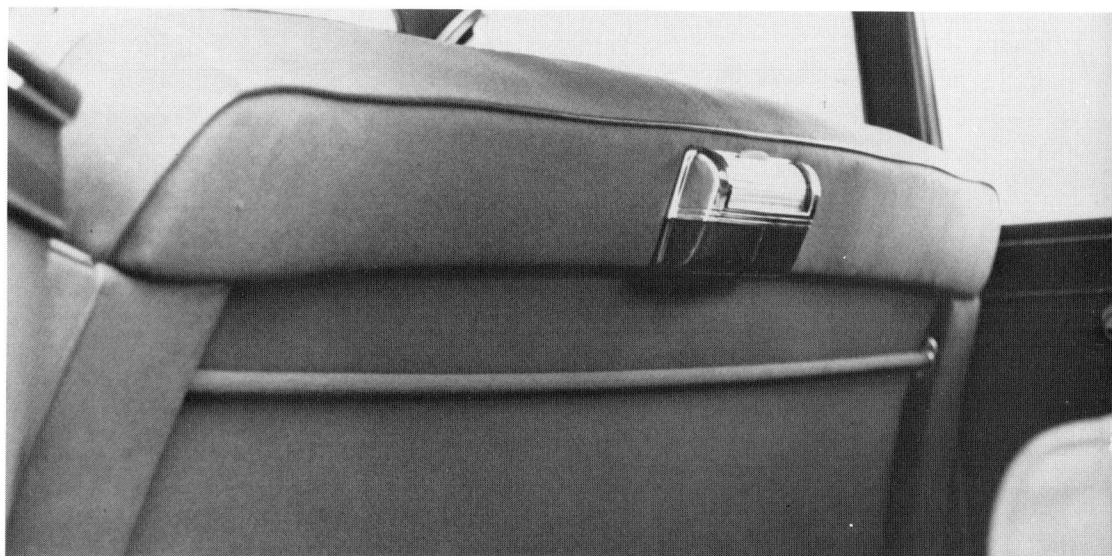

1949 FASTBACK

The 1949 coupes represented a perfect marriage of design and power. Aerodynamically, it's basic form was efficient; mechanically, it's OHV V-8 was invincible. Together they forged a new standard of personal transport. The glittering 49-6207, on this and the opposite page, is a veteran of the Pacific Northwest concours circuit; testament to the esthetic perfection inherent to this fastback design.

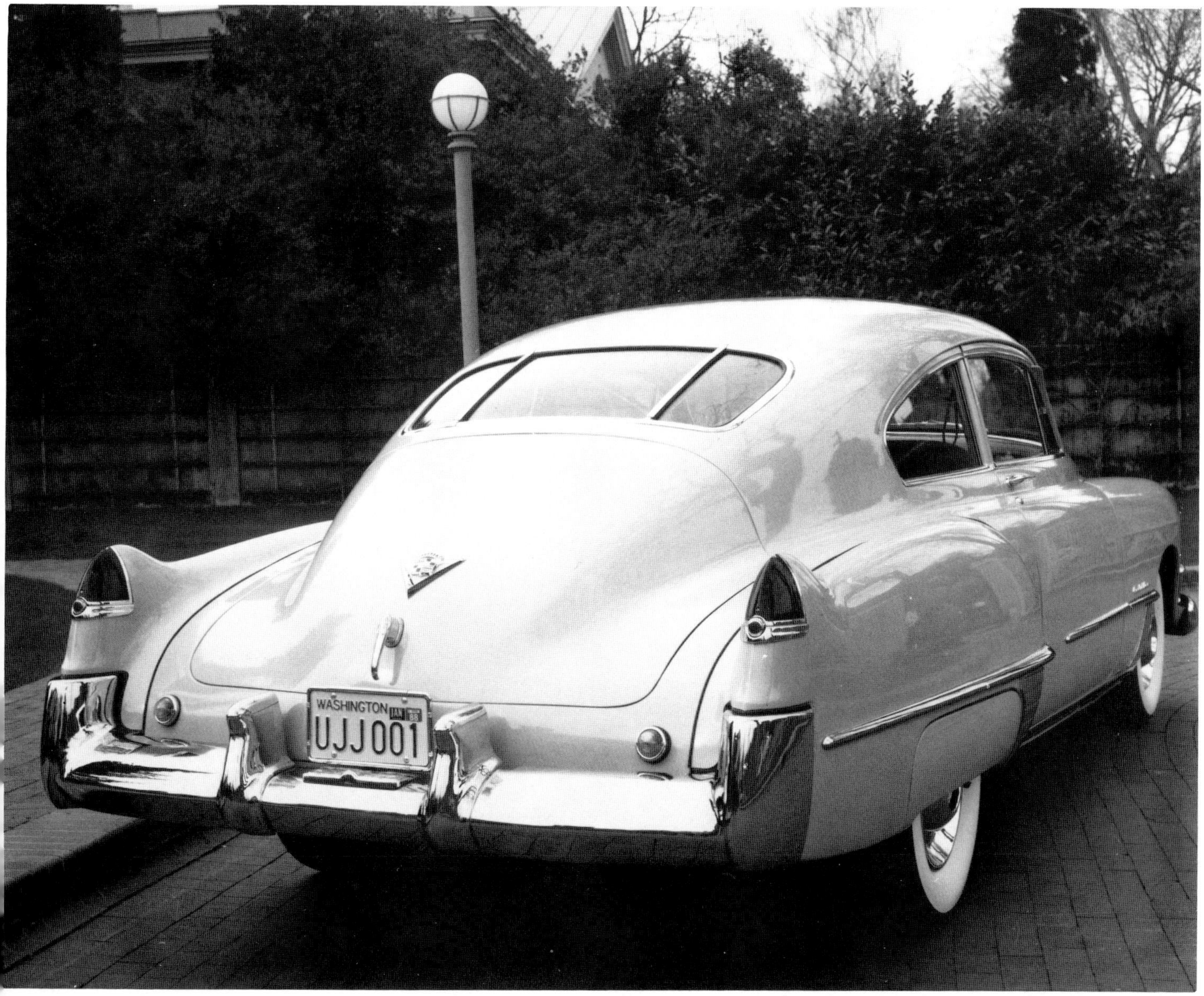
WASHINGTON
UJJ001

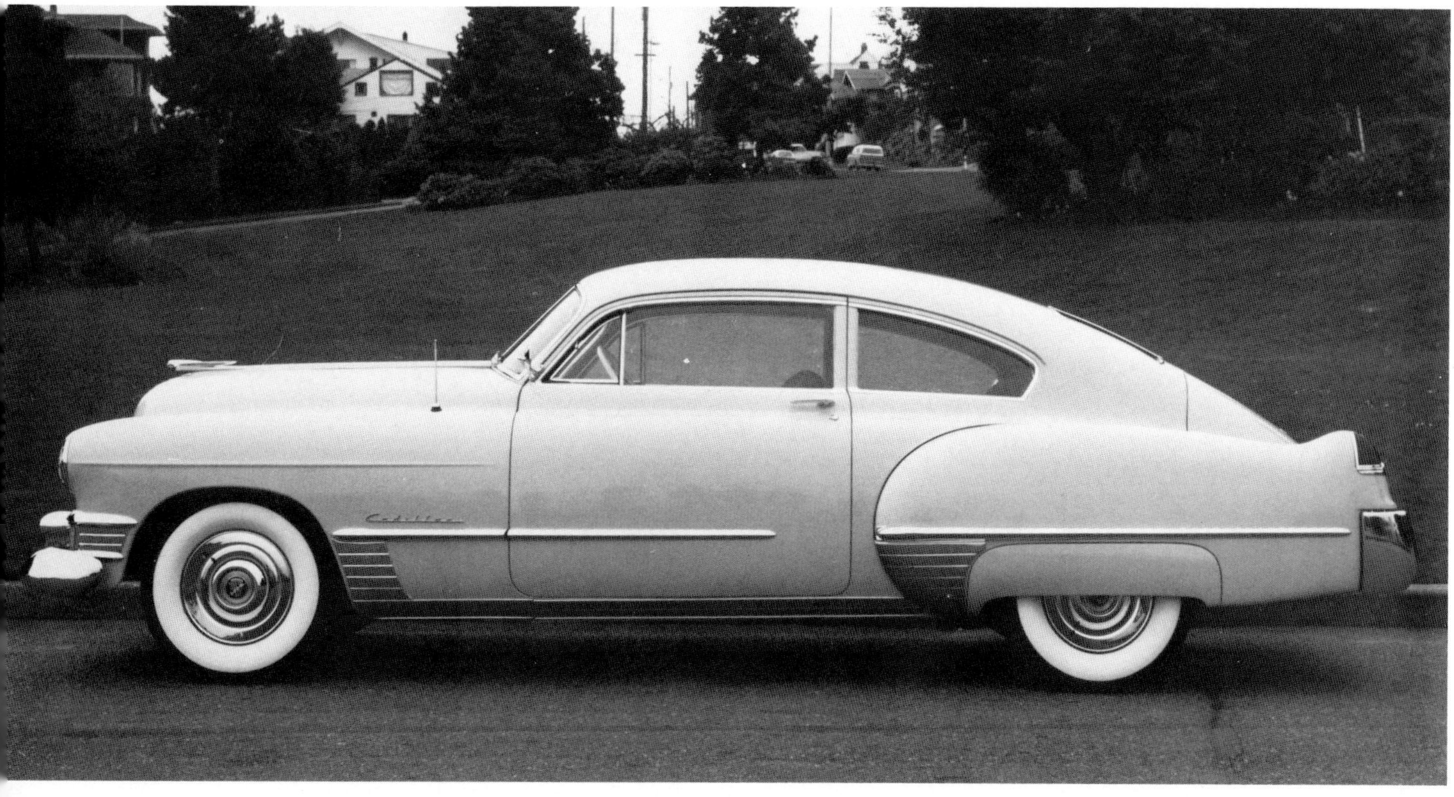

1949 FLEETWOOD SIXTY-SPECIAL

The length of the Sixty-Special (Style 49-6069X had a 133" wheelbase) was apparent from every perspective, yet it was exceptionally agile on the road; as pleasurable to drive as it was to look at. The restored example at the left shows the attractive possibilities in two-toned paint plans. Below, an equally appealing monotoned version.

Opposite below, the ever-popular 1949 instrument panel. The Sixty-Special, as illustrated here, had the deluxe steering wheel and automatic window lifts included as standard equipment.

Right, a Derham-modified Sixty-Special on New York's 54th Street. Zumbach's Motor Repair Service in the background, was a major gathering place for automobile enthusiasts during the 1930s and 1940s.

1949

COUPE

DE VILLE

·162·

The 1949 Coupe de Ville brought the sporty flair of convertible-type styling to the closed car. Although pillarless closed cars had been marketed by Cadillac as early as 1928, the concept didn't take off until 1949. Public acceptance was immediate and enthusiastic. The term *coupe' de ville* is rooted in 18th century coach building. The Cadillac Studio borrowed the name and bent the derivation into one of the most memorable of model designations. Opposite above, the interior of a styling model with its vinyl headliner highlighted with chromed strips simulating top bows; seats and door panels were trimmed in leather and cloth combinations. Opposite below, a favorite factory press photo. Above and center, an exquisite survivor illustrating the sweep of the wrap-around rear window. Below, a view of the historic millionth Cadillac that projects the size and roominess found in the luxury cars of this era.

1949 SERIES SEVENTY-FIVE

Left, a magnificently restored limousine Style 49-7533X. Center, a mocked-up rear compartment illustrating 1949-type finish panels at the waist, and the low-back jump seat, that became standard on 75s beginning in 1948. Below, the front compartment of a 1949 limousine — a symphony in black and chrome. Opposite page above, a handsome sketch of a proposal for the 1948 75-Series. Opposite page middle, a full size rendering of a proposed 1949 75-Series body. Opposite page below, a custom limousine built by GM Styling and Fleetwood: Here is the first use of the Florentine curve (as proposed in the upper sketch) on the quarter panels, a motif that proliferated on Cadillacs in the 1950s.

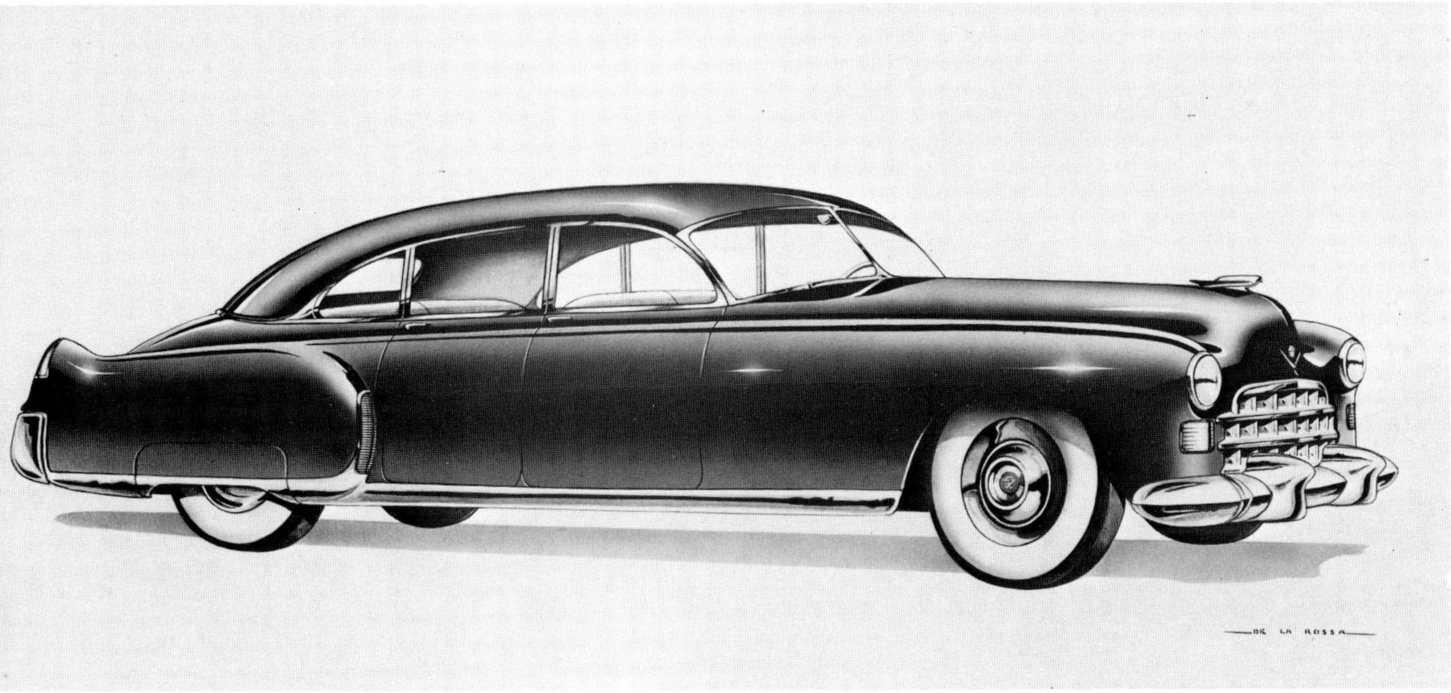
DE LA ROSSA

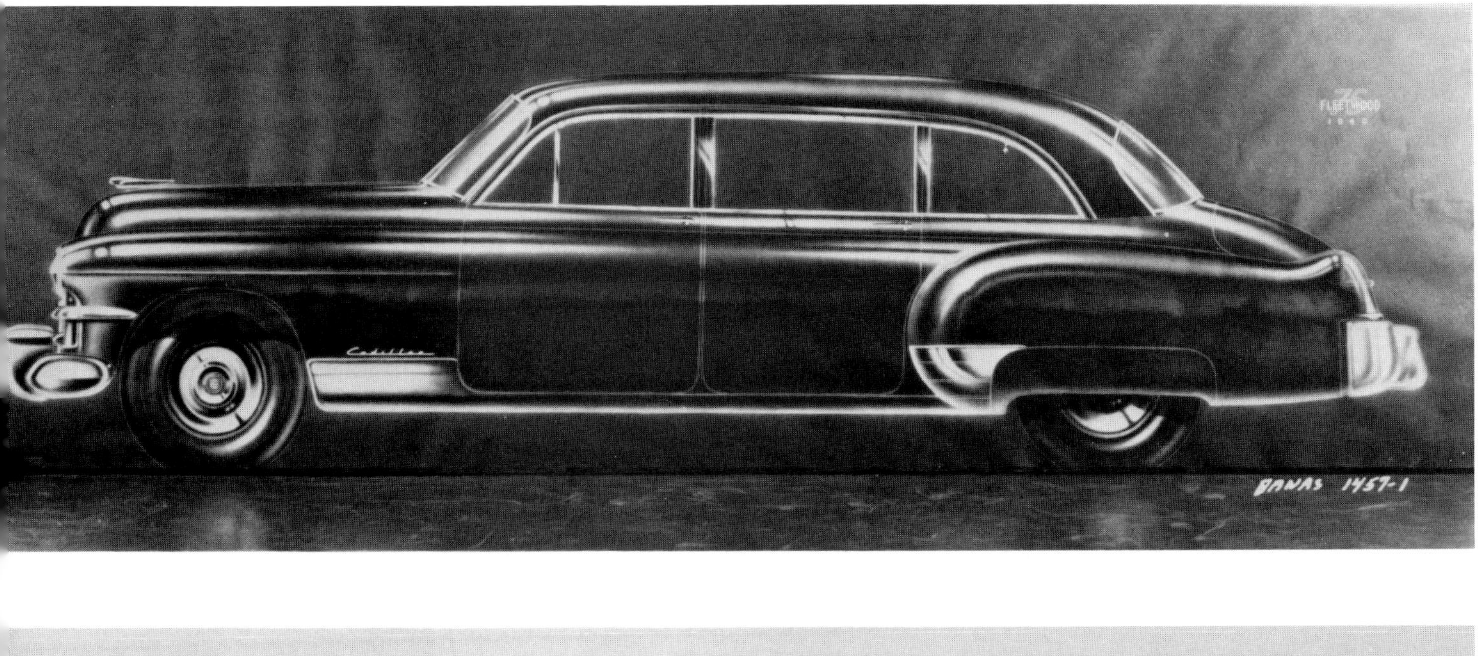
BANAS 1457-1

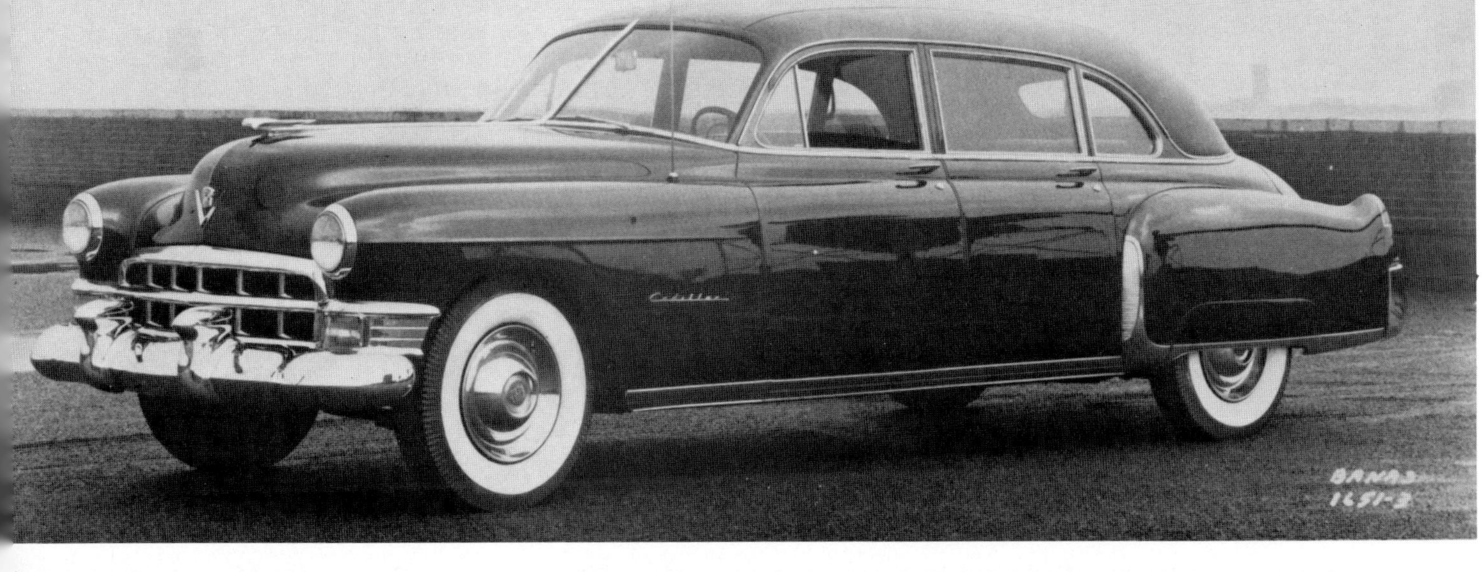
BANAS
1651-3

THE CARIBBEAN

On this and the facing page are two Sixty-Specials prepared for the 1949 Autorama. The model above was called the Caribbean. It featured a unique treatment at the body waist below the windows. In 1930 and 1931 this design detail was called a *door saddle* and was employed on many production Cadillacs. The Caribbean's interior was finished in French broadcloth piped and trimmed with iridescent green leather. The headliner was green broadcloth and the instrument panel was painted to match the exterior. The paint was a metallic-base lacquer called *Caribbean Daybreak*. Contrary to popular belief, GM show cars were not systematically destroyed after the show circuit was completed. Many were placed at the disposal of senior executives and a number of GM's most memorable dream machines are stored in a Michigan warehouse. They are not for sale and will probably remain in dead storage until suitable permanent exhibition can be studied and funded.

THE EMBASSY

This formalized Sixty-Special was called the Embassy. Its leather-covered top had a 75-type rear window. Rear fender stoneguards and mouldings were special and the front fender wheel openings were outlined with a chrome beading. The front compartment was trimmed completely in black leather. A recessed area in the right front door contained a tool kit fitted with chrome-plated tools. The left front door had a similar compartment for map storage. Under the front seat on the passenger side was a chrome plated umbrella receptacle complete with chauffeur's-type umbrella. A hydraulically operated division partition had a glass header inset with a clock. The back side of the clock and all rear compartment hardware were finished in brushed oxidized silver. A special case concealed in the left rear door contained a shortwave ship-to-shore telephone. A matching arrangement in the right rear door contained a special vanity case. Upholstery in the rear was custom-woven broadcloth with black leather door panels. The folding center arm rest in the rear was 11 inches wide.

COUPE DE VILLE
BY FLEETWOOD

This special hardtop coupe body mounted on a Sixt[y] Special chassis was the Autorama's Coupe de Vill[e.] Like the Embassy it had special air-scoop sty[le] stoneguards on the rear fenders and chrome trim ou[t]lining the front fender wheel-openings. Note t[he] 1950-type windshield and 1950 75-Series style rea[r] window. The interior, including the headliner, wa[s] immed in gunmetal leather which matched the exterior roof finish. In the glove box was a short-wave radio-telephone; related signal lights were in the instrument panel to the right of the radio. A vanity case and secretarial pad were built into the center arm rest of the rear compartment. All windows, including windwings, were operated by a hydraulic system. Interior hardware, as well as door mouldings, window mouldings and parts of the dash were finished in decorative chrome. The large photograph was taken at the Autorama while the three smaller views show what the car looked like in 1976. GM President Charles E. Wilson used this, the first Coupe de Ville, for several years before presenting it to his secretary in 1957.

The fourth specially outfitted Cadillac at the 1949 Autorama was this Westernized 62 convertible, the El Rancho. With the exception of paint the exterior was completely standard. However, the interior had a unique interpretation of western-style upholstering. Seats and backs were covered with select saddle leather, bolsters were dark brown sueded kip hides and all stitching was done with waxed white cord. Steering wheel and instrument panel were covered in natural leather. Door handles and other interior hardware were hand-engraved silver. Inside the pocket on each door was a pistol holster on which was branded the Cadillac crest. The rear quarter arm rests contained concealed provisions for liquid refreshment. The carpeting was selected Hereford hide tanned with the hair on and bound with russet leather.

COACHWORK BY SAOUTCHIK

This *coupe de ville* is evidence of the flamboyant trend in French coachbuilding that occurred in the years immediately following the War. Jacques Saoutchik had been during the Twenties and Thirties one of Europe's leading and most innovative coachbuilders. His exotic creations generally portrayed the advanced state of the art as practiced in France. This dramatic three-position drop head coupe on the 1948 Cadillac chassis is among the most imaginative, different and lavish of Saoutchik's later productions. The sheetmetal reflected outstanding craftsmanship, the body panels were beautifully blended and the brightwork was distinctive, yet, to the American taste, the styling was perhaps too theatrical. A very interesting feature on the car was the canework on the sides which was flawlessly applied by hand in a magnificent traditional pattern. The stock 1948 instrument panel was retained by Saoutchik and it serves as the only external clue to the origin and vintage of the chassis.

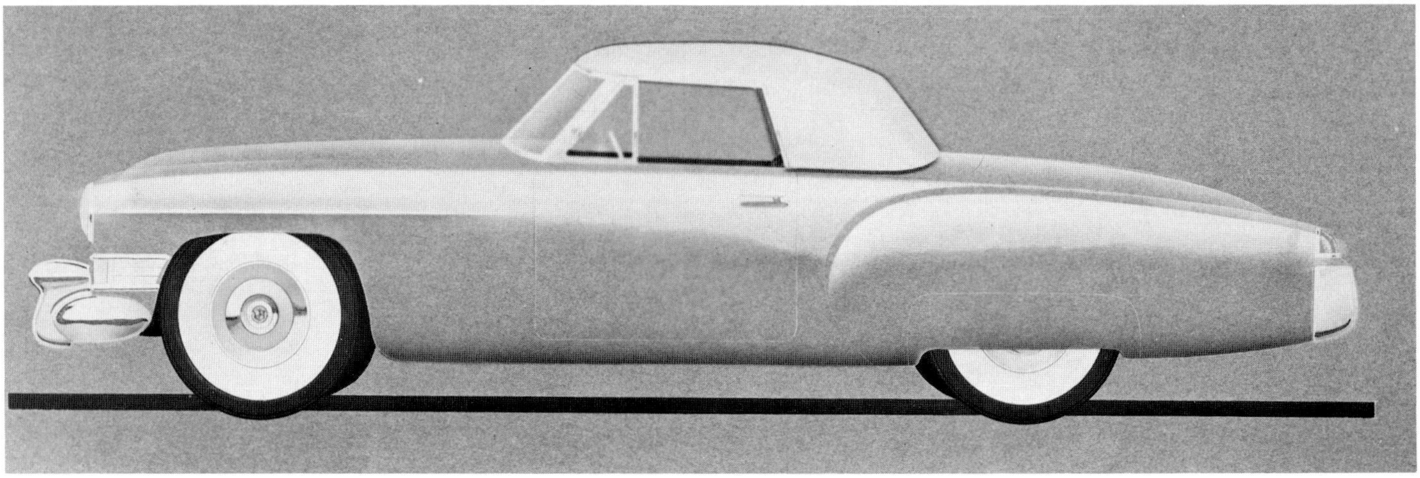

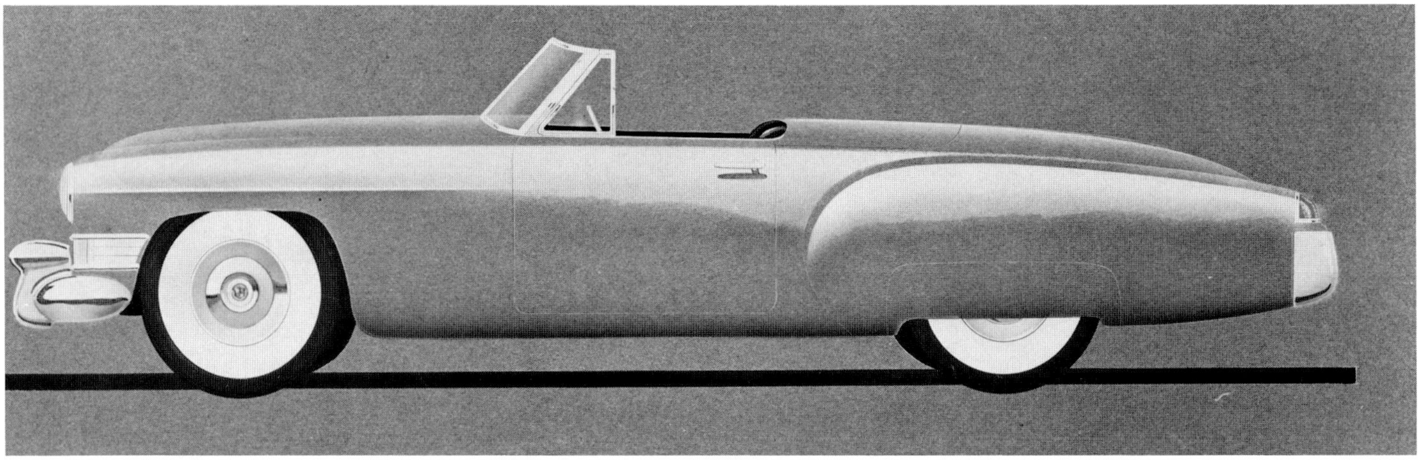

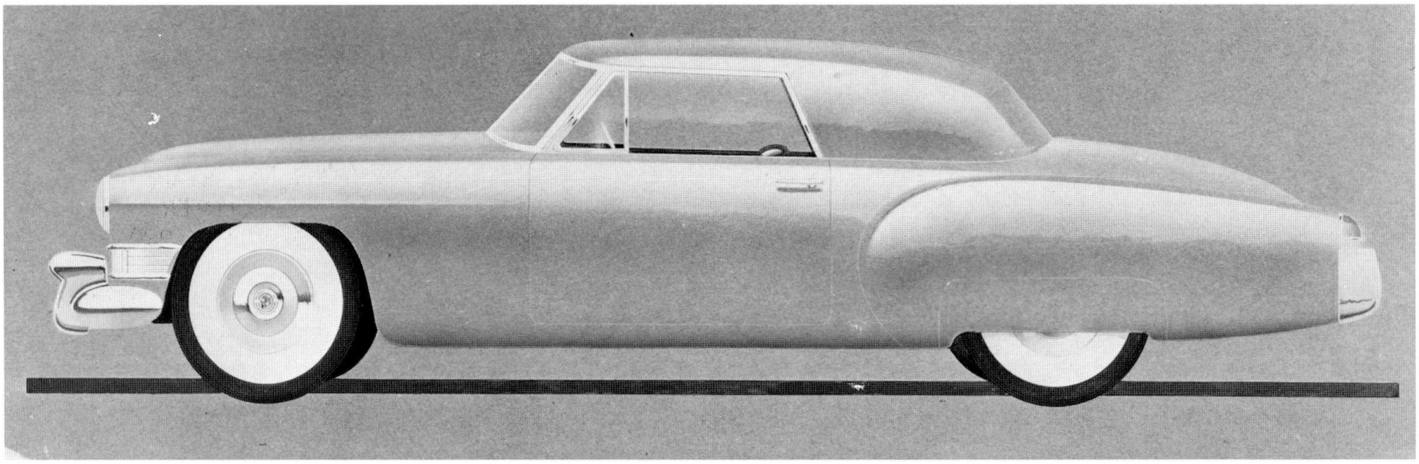

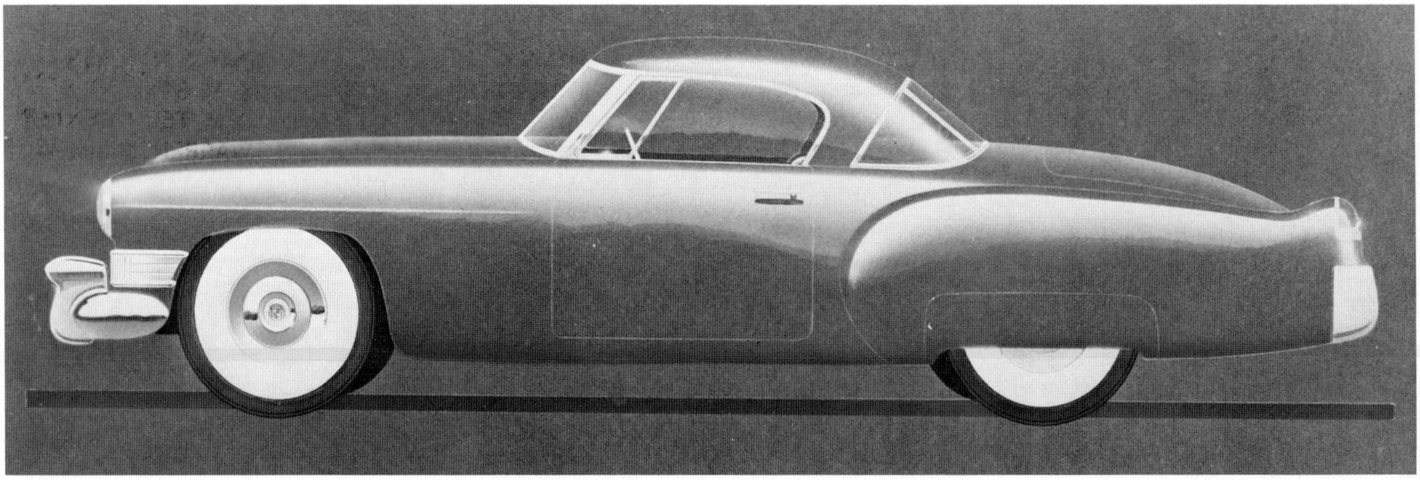

Opposite page, four design suggestions for 1949 Cadillac modifications from Coachcraft of Hollywood, California. On this page are two views of a shortened, de-chromed, highly customized coupe commissioned by Mrs. Morgan Adams. In its original form, as seen here, the Coachcraft coupe was quite handsome; later modifications to its appearance were less tasteful.

Two views of an extended wheelbase convertible sedan built by Derham for a Middle Eastern VIP. The car was equipped with oversized (wide) tires for increased traction on sandbound desert roads.

Above, Maurice Schwartz built this station wagon for Mexico's president Miguel Aleman on a stretched 62-Series chassis. Below, this exquisite towncar (on a commercial chassis) was the last formal body completed by Schwartz. Like the coupe on the preceding page, it was commissioned by Mrs. Morgan Adams. The rear compartment upholstery was a delicate powder blue. The car, with less than 30,000 miles since new, was sold on a Pasadena, California, used car lot in 1962 for $2,400.

APPENDIX I

1940 CADILLAC PRODUCTION DATA BY BODY TYPE

STYLE NUMBER	BODY STYLE	SHIPPING WEIGHT	PRICE FOB DETROIT	UNITS PRODUCED	SERIES TOTALS
	62-SERIES BODIES ON THE 129" WHEELBASE CHASSIS				5,900
6219	5P Sedan	4,030	$1,745	4,242	
6227	4P Coupe	3,940	1,685	1,322	
6229	5P Convertible Sedan	4,230	2,195	75	
6267	4P Convertible Coupe	4,045	1,795	200	
6219	5P Sedan CKD*			60	
62	Chassis only			1	
	SIXTY-SPECIAL BODIES ON THE 127" WHEELBASE CHASSIS				4,600
6019S	5P Sedan	4,070	$2,090	4,242	
6019SA	5P Sedan (with Sun-roof)	4,085	2,175	230	
6019F	5P Sedan (with division)	4,110	2,230	110	
6019AF	5P Sedan (with division & Sun-roof)	4,125	2,315	3	
6053LB	5P Towncar (with leather covered top)	4,365	3,820	6	
6053MB	5P Towncar (metal top)	4,355	3,465	9	
	72-SERIES BODIES ON THE 138" WHEELBASE CHASSIS				1,526
7219	5P Sedan	4,670	$2,670	455	
7219F	5P Imperial Sedan	4,710	2,790	100	
7223	7P Sedan	4,700	2,785	305	
7223L	9P Business Sedan	4,700	2,690	25	
7233L	9P Imperial Business Sedan	4,740	2,825	36	
7233	7P Imperial Sedan	4,740	2,915	292	
7233F	7P Formal Sedan (Imperial division)	4,780	3,695	20	
7259	5P Formal Sedan (X-type division)	4,670	3,695	18	
72	Commercial Chassis, 165" WB.			275	
	75-SERIES BODIES ON THE 141" WHEELBASE CHASSIS				959
7519	5P Sedan	4,900	$2,995	155	
7519F	5P Imperial Sedan	4,940	3,155	25	
7523	7P Sedan	4,930	3,210	166	
7529	5P Convertible Sedan	5,110	3,945	45	
7567	2P Convertible Coupe	4,915	3,380	30	
7557	2P Coupe	4,785	3,280	15	
7557B	5P Coupe (Bench seat in rear)	4,810	3,380	12	
7539	5P Town Sedan	4,935	3,635	14	
7533	7P Imperial Sedan	4,970	3,360	338	
7533F	7P Formal Sedan (Imperial division)	5,010	3,995	42	
7559	5P Formal Sedan (X-type division)	4,900	3,995	48	
7553	7P Towncar	5,195	5,115	14	
75	Chassis only, 141" WB.			3	
75	Commercial Chassis, 161" WB.			52	
	90-SERIES V-16 AND LA SALLE				
	50-Series LaSalle cars on the 123" Wheelbase Chassis			10,380	10,380
	52-Series LaSalle cars on the 123" Wheelbase Chassis			13,750	13,750
	90-Series Cadillac V-16 on the 141" Wheelbase Chassis			61	61
TOTAL PRODUCTION				37,176	37,176

NOTES: *"CKD" indicates COMPLETELY KNOCKED DOWN (export)

Shipping weights and pricing data based on information supplied to the National Automobile Dealers Association in 1940

Production figures determined from factory archives.

72-Series Business Sedans had livery trim and special jump seats which allowed three-across seating.

MOTOR NUMBERS: 62-Series 8320001 to 8325903, 60S-Series 6320001 to 6324600, 72-Series 7320001 to 7321525, 75-Series 3320001 to 3320956.

TIRES: 4-Ply 7.00-16 used on Series 50, 52, 62 and 60S.
6-Ply 7.50-16 used on Series 72, 75 and 90.

1940 ACCESSORIES*

Automatic Radio	$69.50
Defrosting Heater	26.50†
Ventilating Defrosting Heater	31.50†
Dual Ventilating Defrosting Heater:	
Series 40-50, 52, 62, 60	48.50
Series 40-72, 75, 90	52.50
†$5.00 Extra on V-16 Series 90	
Flexible Steering Wheel—LaSalle only	15.00
Automatic Cigarette Lighter—LaSalle only	2.25
Trim Rings—each	1.50
Wheel Discs—each	4.00
License Frames—pair	3.00
Grille Guard	10.00
NoRol—Series 40-50, 52, 62	11.00
Series 40-60	12.50
Series 40-72, 75, 90	13.50
Windshield Washer	6.50
Fog Lights—pair	14.50
Spotlight	18.50
Outside Rear Mirror	4.50
Automatic Battery Filler	7.50
Seat Covers—per seat	8.25
Robes—Fleetwood	50.00
Double Alpaca	30.00
Alpaca and Plush	30.00
Robe Monograms	5.50
Moto-Pack	6.85

Prices include cost of installation. State and Local taxes extra.

1940 ACCESSORY GROUPS*

"A"
Cadillac 5- or 6-Wheel

License Frames
Wheel Discs (4)
Grille Guard
GROUP PRICE, $29.00*

"B"
LaSalle 5-Wheel

Flexible Wheel
Automatic Lighter
License Frames
Trim Rings (5)
GROUP PRICE, $27.75*

"B6"
LaSalle 6-Wheel

Flexible Wheel
Automatic Lighter
License Frames
Trim Rings (6)
GROUP PRICE, $29.25*

"C"
LaSalle 5-Wheel

Flexible Wheel
Automatic Lighter
License Frames
Trim Rings (5)
Grille Guard
GROUP PRICE, $37.75*

"C6"
LaSalle 6-Wheel

Flexible Wheel
Automatic Lighter
License Frames
Trim Rings (6)
Grille Guard
GROUP PRICE, $39.25*

"D"
LaSalle 5- or 6-Wheel

Flexible Wheel
Automatic Lighter
License Frames
Wheel Discs (4)
GROUP PRICE, $36.25*

"E"
LaSalle 5- or 6-Wheel

Flexible Wheel
Automatic Lighter
License Frames
Wheel Discs (4)
Grille Guard
GROUP PRICE, $46.25*

Prices include cost of installation. State and Local taxes extra.

OPTIONAL EQUIPMENT AVAILABLE ON 1940 CADILLACS

Six Wheels, Fenderwells, and Tire Covers: (Series 62 and 60S)	$100.00
Six Wheels, Fenderwells, and Tire Covers: (Series 75)	120.00
Six Wheels, Fenderwells and Tire Covers: (Series 90)	130.00
Five Wheels and Right Hand Fenderwell: (Series 62 and 60S)	42.00
Five Wheels and Right Hand Fenderwell: (Series 75 and 90)	50.00
Six Wheels (two spares in trunk): (Series 72)	45.00
Sunshine Turret-Top Roof: (Available on 60S)	85.00
White Side Wall Tires: (4-ply tires each)	4.00
White Side Wall Tires: (6-ply tires each)	6.00

1941 CADILLAC PRODUCTION DATA BY BODY TYPE

STYLE NUMBER	BODY STYLE	SHIPPING WEIGHT	PRICE FOB DETROIT	UNITS PRODUCED	SERIES TOTALS
	61-SERIES BODIES ON THE 126" WHEELBASE CHASSIS				29,250
6109	5P Sedan	4,065	$1,445	10,925	
6109D	5P DeLuxe Sedan	4,085	1,535	3,495	
6127	5P Coupe	3,985	1,345	11,812	
6127D	5P DeLuxe Coupe	4,005	1,435	3,015	
61	Chassis only			3	
	62-SERIES BODIES ON THE 126" WHEELBASE CHASSIS				24,726
6219	5P Sedan	4,030	$1,495	8,012	
6219D	5P DeLuxe Sedan	4,050	1,585	7,754	
6219D	5P DeLuxe Sedan CKD*			96	
6227	4P Coupe	3,950	1,420	1,985	
6227D	4P DeLuxe Coupe	3,970	1,510	1,900	
6267D	4P DeLuxe Convertible Coupe	4,055	1,645	3,100	
6229D	4P DeLuxe Convertible Sedan	4,230	1,965	400	
62	Chassis only, 126" WB.			4	
62	Commercial Chassis, 163" WB.			1,475	
	63-SERIES BODIES ON THE 126" WHEELBASE CHASSIS				5,050
6319	5P Sedan	4,100	$1,695	5,050	
	SIXTY-SPECIAL BODIES ON THE 126" WHEELBASE CHASSIS				4,100
6019	5P Sedan	4,230	$2,195	3,693	
6019A	5P Sedan (with Sun-roof)	4,245	2,280	185	
6019F	5P Sedan (with division)	4,290	2,345	220	
6053LB	5P Towncar			1	
60	Chassis only, 126" WB.			1	
	67-SERIES BODIES ON THE 139" WHEELBASE CHASSIS				900
6719	5P Sedan	4,618	$2,595	315	
6719F	5P Imperial Sedan	4,755	2,745	95	
6723	7P Sedan	4,678	2,735	280	
6733	7P Imperial Sedan	4,810	2,890	210	
	75-SERIES BODIES ON THE 136" WHEELBASE CHASSIS				2,104
7519	5P Sedan	4,810	$2,995	422	
7519F	5P Imperial Sedan	4,860	3,150	132	
7523	7P Sedan	4,800	3,140	405	
7523L	9P Business Sedan	4,750	2,895	54	
7533L	9P Imperial Business Sedan	4,900	3,050	6	
7533	7P Imperial Sedan	4,935	3,295	757	
7533F	7P Formal Sedan (Imperial division)	9,915	4,045	98	
7559	5P Formal Sedan (X-type division)	4,905	3,920	75	
75	Chassis only, 136" WB.			5	
75	Commercial Chassis, 163" WB.			150	
TOTAL PRODUCTION				66,130	66,130

NOTES: *"CKD" indicates COMPLETELY KNOCKED DOWN (export)

Shipping weights and pricing data based on information supplied to the National Automobile Dealers Association in 1941.

Production figures determined from factory archives.

75-Series Business Sedans had livery trim and special jump seats which allowed three-across seating.

MOTOR NUMBERS: 61-Series 5340001 to 5369258, 62-Series 8340001 to 8364734. 63-Series 7340001 to 7345050, 60S-Series 6340001 to 6344101, 67-Series 9340001 to 9340922, 75-Series 3340001 to 3342104.

TIRES: 4-Ply 7.00-15 used on Series 61, 62, 63 and 60S.
6-Ply 7.50-16 used on Series 67 and 75.

OPTIONAL EQUIPMENT AND ACCESSORIES — SEE PAGE 192

1942 CADILLAC PRODUCTION DATA BY BODY TYPE

STYLE NUMBER	BODY STYLE	SHIPPING WEIGHT	PRICE FOB DETROIT	UNITS PRODUCED	SERIES TOTALS
	61-SERIES BODIES ON THE 126" WHEELBASE CHASSIS				5,700
6107	5P Coupe	4,055	$1,560	2,470	
6109	5P Sedan	4,115	1,647	3,194	
6107	5P Coupe CKD*			12	
6109	5P Sedan CKD*			24	
	62-SERIES BODIES ON THE 129" WHEELBASE CHASSIS				4,960
6207	5P Coupe	4,105	$1,667	515	
6207D	5P DeLuxe Coupe	4,125	1,754	530	
6269	5P Sedan	4,185	1,754	1,780	
6269D	5P DeLuxe Sedan	4,205	1,836	1,743	
6269D	5P DeLuxe Sedan CKD*			84	
6267D	5P DeLuxe Convertible Coupe	4,365	2,020	308	
	63-SERIES BODIES ON THE 126" WHEELBASE CHASSIS				1,750
6319	5P Sedan	4,115	$1,882	1,750	
	SIXTY-SPECIAL BODIES ON THE 133" WHEELBASE CHASSIS				1,875
6069	5P Sedan	4,310	$2,435	1,684	
6069F	5P Imperial Sedan	4,365	2,589	190	
60	Chassis only, 133" WB.			1	
	67-SERIES BODIES ON THE 139" WHEELBASE CHASSIS				700
6719	5P Sedan	4,605	$2,896	200	
6719F	5P Imperial Sedan	4,665	3,045	50	
6723	7P Sedan	4,680	3,045	260	
6733	7P Imperial Sedan	4,755	3,204	190	
	75-SERIES BODIES ON THE 136" WHEELBASE CHASSIS				1,526
7519	5P Sedan	4,750	$3,306	205	
7519F	5P Imperial Sedan	4,810	3,459	65	
7523	7P Sedan	4,800	3,459	225	
7523L	9P Business Sedan	4,750	3,152	29	
7533L	9P Imperial Business Sedan	4,810	3,306	6	
7533	7P Imperial Sedan	4,860	3,613	430	
7533F	7P Formal Sedan (Imperial division)	4,915	4,484	80	
7559	5P Formal Sedan (X-type division)	4,900	4,330	60	
75	Chassis only, 136" WB.			1	
75	Commercial Chassis, 163" WB.			425	
TOTAL PRODUCTION				16,511	16,511

NOTES: *"CKD" indicates COMPLETELY KNOCKED DOWN (export)

Shipping weights and pricing data based on information supplied to the National Automobile Dealers Association in 1942.

Production figures determined from factory archives.

75-Series Business Sedans had livery trim and special jump seats which allowed three-across seating.

MOTOR NUMBERS: (Second range of numbers for each series designates Blackouts) 61-Series 5380001 to 5385237 and 5386001 to 5386463, 62-Series 8380001 to 8384401 and 8386001 to 8386560, 63-Series 7380001 to 7381500 and 7386001 to 7386250, 60S-Series 6380001 to 6381500 and 6386001 to 6386375, 67-Series 9380001 to 9380520 and 9386001 to 9386180, 75-Series 3380001 to 3381200 and 3386001 to 3386327

TIRES: 4-Ply 7.00-15 used on Series 61, 62, 63 and 60S.
6-Ply 7.50-16 used on Series 67 and 75.

OPTIONAL EQUIPMENT AND ACCESSORIES — SEE PAGE 192

1946 CADILLAC PRODUCTION DATA BY BODY TYPE

STYLE NUMBER	BODY STYLE	SHIPPING WEIGHT	PRICE FOB DETROIT	UNITS PRODUCED	SERIES TOTALS
	61-SERIES BODIES ON THE 126" WHEELBASE CHASSIS				3,001
6107	5P Coupe	4,065	$2,022	800	
6109	5P Sedan	4,145	2,146	2,200	
61	Chassis only			1	
	62-SERIES BODIES ON THE 129" WHEELBASE CHASSIS				18,566
6207	5P Coupe	4,100	$2,249	2,323	
6267D	5P Convertible Coupe	4,462	2,521	1,342	
6269	5P Sedan	4,240	2,324	14,900	
62	Chassis only			1	
	SIXTY-SPECIAL BODIES ON THE 133" WHEELBASE CHASSIS				5,700
6069	5P Sedan	4,348	$3,054	5,700	
	75-SERIES BODIES ON THE 136" WHEELBASE CHASSIS				1,927
7519	5P Sedan	4,860	$4,238	150	
7523	7P Sedan	4,905	4,415	225	
7523L	9P Business Sedan	4,920	4,093	22	
7533	7P Imperial Sedan	4,925	4,609	221	
7533L	9P Imperial Business Sedan	4,925	4,286	17	
75	Commercial chassis, 163" WB.			1,292	
TOTAL PRODUCTION				29,194	29,194

NOTES: Shipping weights and pricing information based on information supplied to the National Automobile Dealers Association in 1946. Production figures determined from factory archives.
75-Series Business Sedans had livery trim and special jump seats which allowed three-across seating.
MOTOR NUMBERS: 61-Series 5400001 to 5403001, 62-Series 8400001 to 8418566 (for 1946 calendar year), 60-Series 6400001 to 6405700, 75-Series 3400001 to 3401927.
TIRES: 4-Ply 7.00-15 used on Series 61, 62 and 60S.
      6-Ply 7.50-16 used on Series 75.

OPTIONAL EQUIPMENT AND ACCESSORIES*

Hydra-Matic Drive	$176.49
Special Steering Wheel	17.74
License Frames (Pair)	3.39
Wheel Discs (4)	18.89
Glareproof Mirror	5.04
Windshield Washer	10.11
Back-up Light	13.03
Ventilating Defrosting Heater	39.32
Automatic Underseat Heater—Series 61, 62 & 60S.	70.07
Automatic Underseat Heater—Series 75	76.24
Trim Rings (5)	8.84
Fog Lights	29.14

*Suggested maximum installed prices as of May 22, 1946

1947 CADILLAC PRODUCTION DATA BY BODY TYPE

STYLE NUMBER	BODY STYLE	SHIPPING WEIGHT	PRICE FOB DETROIT	UNITS PRODUCED	SERIES TOTALS
	61-SERIES BODIES ON THE 126" WHEELBASE CHASSIS				8,555
6107	5P Coupe	4,145	$2,200	3,395	
6109	5P Sedan	4,225	2,324	5,160	
	62-SERIES BODIES ON THE 129" WHEELBASE CHASSIS				39,835
6207	5P Coupe	4,215	$2,446	7,245	
6267	5P Convertible Coupe	4,475	2,902	6,755	
6269	5P Sedan	4,295	2,523	25,834	
62	Chassis only			1	
	SIXTY-SPECIAL BODIES ON THE 133" WHEELBASE CHASSIS				8,500
6069	5P Sedan	4,420	$3,195	8,500	
	75-SERIES BODIES ON THE 136" WHEELBASE CHASSIS				5,036
7519	5P Sedan	4,860	$4,471	300	
7523	7P Sedan	4,905	4,686	890	
7523L	9P Business Sedan	4,920	4,368	135	
7533	7P Imperial Sedan	4,925	4,887	1,005	
7533L	9P Imperial Business Sedan	4,925	4,560	80	
75	Chassis only, 136" WB.			3	
75	Commercial Chassis, 163" WB.			2,423	
75	Business Chassis, 163" WB.			200	
TOTAL PRODUCTION				61,926	61,926

NOTES: Shipping weights and pricing data based on information supplied to the National Automobile Dealers Association in 1947. Production figures determined from factory archives.

75-Series Business Sedans had livery trim and special jump seats which allowed three-across seating.

MOTOR NUMBERS: 61-Series 5420001 to 5428555, 62-Series 8420001 to 8459835, 60S-Series 6420001 to 6428500, 75-Series 3420001 to 3425036.

TIRES: 4-Ply 7.00-15 used on Series 61, 62 and 60S
      6-Ply 7.50-16 used on Series 75.

OPTIONAL EQUIPMENT AND ACCESSORIES*

Hydra-Matic Drive	$186.34
Special Steering Wheel	19.54
License Frames (Pair)	3.63
Wheel Discs (4)	25.08
Glareproof Mirror	5.00
Windshield Washer	10.96
Back-up Light	11.50
Ventilating Defrosting Heater	43.28
Automatic Underseat Heater—Series 61, 62 & 60S.	76.15
Automatic Underseat Heater—Series 75	85.40
Trim Rings (5)	9.38
Fog Lights	30.12
Cadillac Radio	73.65
Vacuum Aerial (Front)	13.54

*Suggested maximum installed prices as of January 2, 1947

1948 CADILLAC PRODUCTION DATA BY BODY TYPE

STYLE NUMBER	BODY STYLE	SHIPPING WEIGHT	PRICE FOB DETROIT	UNITS PRODUCED	SERIES TOTALS
	61-SERIES BODIES ON THE 126" WHEELBASE CHASSIS				8,603
6107	6P Coupe	4,070	$2,728	3,521	
6169	6P Sedan	4,145	2,833	5,081	
61	Chassis only, 126" WB.			1	
	62-SERIES BODIES ON THE 126" WHEELBASE CHASSIS				34,213
6207	6P Coupe	4,125	$2,912	4,764	
6269	6P Sedan	4,180	2,996	23,997	
6267X	6P Convertible Coupe	4,450	3,442	5,450	
62	Chassis only, 126" WB.			2	
	60-SPECIAL BODIES ON THE 133" WHEELBASE CHASSIS				6,561
6069X	5P Sedan	4,370	$3,820	6,561	
	75-SERIES BODIES ON THE 136" WHEELBASE CHASSIS				3,329
7519X	5P Sedan	4,865	$4,779	225	
7523L	9P Business Sedan	4,925	4,679	90	
7533L	9P Imperial Business Sedan	4,930	4,868	64	
7523X	7P Sedan	4,910	4,999	499	
7533X	7P Imperial Sedan	4,930	5,199	382	
75	Chassis only, 136" WB.			2	
76	Commercial Chassis, 163" WB.			2,067	
TOTAL PRODUCTION				52,706	52,706

NOTES: Style numbers with an "X" suffix have hydraulic systems to operate windows and seats as standard.

Shipping weights and pricing data based on information supplied to the National Automobile Dealers Association in 1948.

Production figures determined from factory archives.

MOTOR NUMBERS: 61-Series 486100001 to 486148663, 62-Series 486200001 to 486252704, 60S-Series 486000001 to 486052706, 75-Series 487500001 to 487546088.

TIRES: 4-Ply 8.20-15 used on Series 61, 62 and 60S.
6-Ply 7.50-16 used on Series 75.

OPTIONAL EQUIPMENT AND ACCESSORIES*

Hydra-Matic Drive	$200.00
Automatic Window Regulators (6107, 6169, 6207, 6269)	121.65
Special Steering Wheel	19.50
License Frames (Pair)	3.80
Wheel Discs (4)	25.00
Glareproof Mirror	5.00
Windshield Washer	11.00
Back-up Light	11.00
Ventilating, Defrosting Heater	60.00
Automatic Heating System, Series 61, 62 & 60S	90.00
Automatic Heating System, Series 75	123.50
Trim Rings (5)	9.50
Fog Lights	38.00
Cadillac Radio (Front)	85.50
Cadillac Radio (Rear-Series 75 only)	147.00
Vacuum Aerial (Front)	13.60
Vacuum Aerial (Rear-Series 75 only)	15.00

*Suggested maximum installed prices as of July 26, 1948

1949 CADILLAC PRODUCTION DATA BY BODY TYPE

STYLE NUMBER	BODY STYLE	SHIPPING WEIGHT	PRICE FOB DETROIT	UNITS PRODUCED	SERIES TOTALS
	61-SERIES BODIES ON THE 126" WHEELBASE CHASSIS				22,148
6107	6P Coupe	4,070	$2,814	6,409	
6169	6P Sedan	4,145	2,919	15,738	
61	Chassis only			1	
	62-SERIES BODIES ON THE 126" WHEELBASE CHASSIS				55,643
6207	6P Coupe	4,125	$2,992	7,515	
6267X	6P Convertible Coupe	4,450	3,523	8,000	
6269	6P Sedan	4,180	3,076	37,617	
6237X	6P Coupe de Ville	3,857	3,497	2,150	
6269	6P Sedan CKD*			360	
62	Chassis only, 126" WB.			1	
	60-SPECIAL BODIES ON THE 133" WHEELBASE CHASSIS				11,400
6037X	6P Coupe de Ville			1	
6069X	6P Sedan	4,370	$3,859	11,399	
	75-SERIES BODIES ON THE 136" WHEELBASE CHASSIS				3,363
7519X	5P Sedan	4,865	$4,865	220	
7523L	9P Business Sedan	4,925	4,691	35	
7533L	9P Imperial Business Sedan	4,930	4,890	25	
7523X	7P Sedan	4,910	5,011	595	
7533X	7P Imperial Sedan	4,930	5,211	626	
75	Chassis only, 136" WB.			1	
86	Commercial Chassis, 163" WB.			1,861	
TOTAL PRODUCTION				92,554	92,554

NOTES: Style numbers with an "X" suffix have hydraulic systems to operate windows and seats as standard.

Shipping weights and pricing data based on information supplied to the National Automobile Dealers Association in 1949.

Production figures determined from factory archives.

MOTOR NUMBERS: 61-Series 496100001 to 496192554, 62-Series 496200001 to 496292554, 60S-Series 496000001 to 496092554, 75-Series 497500001 to 497592554.

TIRES: 4-Ply 8.20-15 used on Series 61, 62 and 60S.
6-Ply 7.50-16 used on Series 75.

OPTIONAL EQUIPMENT AND ACCESSORIES*

Hydra-Matic Drive	$200.00
Automatic Window Regulators (6107, 6169, 6207, 6269)	121.65
Special Steering Wheel	19.50
License Frames (Pair)	3.80
Wheel Discs (4)	25.00
Glareproof Mirror	5.50
Windshield Washer	11.00
Back-up Light (Dual)	17.50
Back-up Light (Single)	11.50
Automatic Heating System, Series 61, 62 & 60S.	107.00
Automatic Heating System, Series 75.	140.50
Trim Rings (5)	9.50
Fog Lights	37.00
Cadillac Radio (Front)	85.50
Cadillac Radio (Rear-Series 75 only)	147.00
Vacuum Aerial (Front)	13.60
Vacuum Aerial (Rear-Series 75 only)	17.00

*Suggested maximum installed prices as of May 23, 1949

APPENDIX II
SPECIAL FEATURES

During the mid-Thirties Cadillac formalized its special features program by publication of booklets prescribing extra charges for variations from standard paint, upholstery and trim practice. These special features could be incorporated into a car only when specified on the production order. Hence special features were production line modifications and had no connection with the miscellaneous equipment offered by the factory Parts Department or accessories sold by dealerships. The vast majority of Cadillacs produced while the special features program was in effect during the 1940s were standard in terms of color, upholstery and body. However, the present-day restorer can benefit from a knowledge of what special features were available at the time his car was manufactured. For example, pre-war Cadillacs were literally available in any color of the rainbow. The factory's color policy as stated in the 1941 Special Features book was: *Any discontinued standard color previously offered by the factory is subject to the same extra charge as quoted for special color. The use of white or colors of delicate shade, which are difficult to apply, should be discouraged. Although some such colors are included in the durable line of lacquers, the use of these colors involves additional labor to apply and are necessarily furnished on individual quotations.* Hence the restorer can employ the color of his choice assured that even the most stringent judging regulations, such as those used by the Classic Car Club of America, will not penalize him on authenticity. Similarly, interior special features options provide the restorer with a wide range of choices. But some discretion is essential; even though most 1941 and 1942 instrument panels can be painted or grained, it would, for instance, be unwise to arbitrarily remove a salvageable grained transfer and apply paint.

An examination of materials published after the war relative to 1946 through 1949 models has not verified the availability of special features, thus the restorer must necessarily be guided by contemporary standard practice relative to paint, upholstery, interior finish and method of trim. The apparent absence of a published program does not mean that every car manufactured during this period was strictly standard. On the other hand there is no compelling evidence among surviving cars that suggests an unpublished *de-facto* program existed.

SPECIAL FEATURES AVAILABLE ON 1940 CADILLACS

SPECIAL FEATURE NUMBER	*EXTRA CHARGES FOR SPECIAL COLOR FEATURES*	SERIES 62 & 60S	SERIES 72, 75 & 90
40-1	ENTIRE CAR ONE COLOR (any non-standard durable color)	$25.00	N/C
40-2	TWO-TONE COMBINATIONS — Body below beltline, including hood and fenders painted one color, body above beltline in contrasting color.		
	A. Combination of any two standard colors	12.50	
	B. Combinations of non-standard colors	25.00	
40-3	WHEELS IN SPECIAL COLOR		
	A. When body is standard color. Per wheel	1.00	N/C
	B. When body is special color. Per wheel	N/C	N/C
40-4	FENDERS FINISHED IN COLOR OTHER THAN BODY COLOR	$10.00	$10.00
40-5	MOULDINGS - EXTERIOR, FINISHED IN COLOR Body and hood mouldings not including door handles		10.00
40-6	STRIPING - Stripe above and below body and hood mouldings or on mouldings when painted — Except gold or silver leaf.		10.00
40-7	MOULDINGS - INTERIOR, FINISHED IN COLOR Garnish mouldings, windshield and ventilator division strips, and back of rear view mirror painted in a special color	15.00	
	Chrome door belt garnish mouldings painted in color on 60S.	7.50	
40-8	FRONT COMPARTMENT - Instrument panel, steering column, steering wheel hub, horn button, and hand brake lever painted in one special color.	15.00	
40-9	PLASTIC PARTS - INTERIOR, FINISHED IN COLOR Flexible steering wheel rim, shift lever knob, cowl ventilator knob, all instrument panel knobs, and all body hardward plastic parts painted in special color.	10.00	
40-10	MONOGRAMS (Three ⅜" Block Letters) Painted on doors — special designs on request. Per Pair	15.00	15.00

SPECIAL FEATURES AVAILABLE ON 1940 CADILLACS (Continued)

EXTRA CHARGES FOR SPECIAL FABRICS AND TRIM STYLES

SPECIAL FEATURE NUMBER		SERIES 62	SERIES 60-S	SERIES 72	SERIES 75 & 90
40-13	SIXTY-SPECIAL TRIM STYLE (62 Fabrics)	$125.00			
40-14	72 & 75-SERIES TRIM STYLE (62 Fabrics)	80.00			
40-15	90-SERIES TRIM STYLE (Standard Materials)		$90.00		
40-17	72-SERIES FABRICS SUBSTITUTED FOR LEATHER (Style 7233 front compartment only)			N/C	
40-18	75 & 90-SERIES FABRICS SUBSTITUTED FOR STANDARD FABRICS.	75.00	100.00	$80.00	
40-19	SPECIAL QUALITY FABRICS (Including some leather parts)	200.00	250.00	240.00	$225.00
40-20	SPECIAL TOP FABRICS - CONVERTIBLE MODELS (Black or Blue Gray in standard quality)				10.00
40-21	LEATHER PIPING (with standard cloth trim)		25.00		
40-21A	LEATHER PIPING (top and boot of convertible models piped in special quality leather)				20.00

EXTRA CHARGES FOR LEATHER UPHOLSTERY

COMBINATION "A" -   Genuine leather throughout.
COMBINATION "B" -   Leather below beltline with standard cloth above.
COMBINATION "C" -   Seat cushions and backs in leather; balance in standard cloth.

		SERIES 62	SERIES 60-S	SERIES 72	SERIES 75 & 90
40-25	50-SERIES LEATHERS (Priced for sedan models*)				
	COMBINATION "A"	175.00	175.00	200.00	**
	COMBINATION "B"	125.00	110.00	**	**
	COMBINATION "C"	60.00	60.00	**	**
40-26	75 & 90-SERIES LEATHERS (Priced for sedan models*				
	COMBINATION "A"	225.00	225.00	300.00	225.00
	COMBINATION "B"	150.00	150.00	**	**
	COMBINATION "C"	100.00	100.00	**	**
40-27	SPECIAL QUALITY LEATHERS (Priced for sedan models*)				
	COMBINATION "A"	300.00	300.00	350.00	275.00
	COMBINATION "B"	200.00	200.00	**	**
	COMBINATION "C"	100.00	100.00	**	**
40-28	LEATHER PIPING WITH LEATHER TRIM		25.00		
40-29	LEATHER IN FRONT COMPARTMENT USING SPECIAL QUALITY LEATHER SUBSTITUTED FOR FABRIC (Styles 6019F, 7219F, 7259, 7519F, 7559, 9019F, 9059)***		120.00	125.00	100.00

NOTES: *Prices on coupe models approximately 20% less
 **Quotations on request.
 ***Lesser quality leathers were available at lower prices.

SPECIAL FEATURES AVAILABLE ON 1940 CADILLACS (Continued)

EXTRA CHARGES FOR SPECIAL BODY FEATURES

SPECIAL FEATURE NUMBER		SERIES 62	SERIES 60-S	SERIES 72	SERIES 75 & 90
40-30	MARSHALL SPRINGS installed in seat cushion or back in place of standard All-body type. (Standard on 72, 75, 90 and 60-S cushions) Price per seat or back	$10.00	$10.00		
40-32	ROLLER CURTAINS (Exposed type shades)				
	A. Back window all body styles	2.50	2.50	STD.	STD.
	B. Rear quarter windows	N/A	N/A	20.00	$20.00
	C. Rear door windows	N/A	N/A	15.00	20.00
	D. Division glass (Styles ending in 33 or 33F)	N/A	N/A	25.00	25.00
40-33	FOOT HASSOCKS (replaces foot rail in 72, 75 & 90)	15.00	15.00	10.00	10.00
40-34	FOOT RAIL IN PLACE OF STANDARD HASSOCKS				10.00
40-35	ROBE RAIL IN PLACE OF ROBE CORD			30.00	30.00
40-36	GRIP HANDLES IN PLACE OF ASSIST STRAPS			10.00	7.50
40-37	LULL STRAPS AND RODS AND GRIP HANDLES (in place of standard assist straps)			20.00	20.00
40-39	ASSIST STRAPS IN PLACE OF GRIP HANDLES (7557 & 7557B)				N/C
40-40	POCKETS ON DOORS (Shirred Type) (14½" x 9" deep)				
	A. With cloth trim PER PAIR	20.00	20.00	25.00	25.00
	B. With leather trim PER PAIR	25.00	25.00	30.00	30.00
40-41	SHEEPSKIN MAT (Closed body types)			45.00	45.00
40-42	FOLDING CENTER ARM REST IN FRONT SEAT	75.00	75.00	75.00	75.00
40-43	SLASH POCKET AND MIRROR IN REAR QUARTER			10.00	10.00
40-44	VANITY MIRROR AND NOTEBOOK (In place of ash tray and lighter in rear arm rest)			25.00	25.00
40-45	CIGAR LIGHTER (In back of front seat)	15.00	15.00		
40-46	ELECTRIC CLOCK (Installed in back of front seat) (Styles 7519, 7519F and 7523*)				30.00
40-47	MOTOR PHONE FOR STYLE 7519F, 7219F*				50.00
40-48	AUTOMATIC DOME LIGHT SWITCH (For left rear door)	7.50	7.50		
40-49	REAR QUARTER LAMPS (Styles 6219, 6019, 7557*)	30.00	30.00		12.50
40-53	EXTRA RADIO SPEAKER (In package tray)			35.00	35.00
40-54	AUXILIARY SEATS OMITTED (Floor blocked in, carpets uncut)			25.00	25.00
40-55	OPERA SEATS ON DIVISION WALL (Styles 7529, 9029)				100.00
40-56	DIVISIONS				
	A. Imperial type with package compartments — 7519 & 7539*				300.00
	B. X-type, less opera seats with compartments—7519 & 7539*				400.00
	C. X-type with opera seats—7519*				350.00
40-57	VENTI-PANES OMITTED ON FORMAL SEDANS & TOWNCAR				150.00
40-58	ROOF & REAR QUARTERS IN SPECIAL TOP FABRIC —7533F & 7559*				N/C

*Indicates inclusion of same body on 90-Series chassis

SPECIAL FEATURES AVAILABLE ON 1941 CADILLACS

EXTRA CHARGES FOR SPECIAL COLOR FEATURES

SPECIAL FEATURE NUMBER		SERIES 61 & 62 STD.	SERIES 61, 62 & 63 DeLuxe	SIXTY SPECIAL	SERIES 67	SERIES 75
41-1	ENTIRE CAR (ONE COLOR)					
	A. Std. optional paint combination	N/C	N/C	N/C	N/C	N/C
	B. Lower color of std. two-tone combination	N/C	N/C	N/C	N/C	N/C
	C. Upper color of std. two-tone combination	$12.50	$12.50	$12.50	N/C	N/C
	D. Any other accepted durable color	25.00	25.00	25.00	N/C	N/C
41-2	TWO-TONE COMBINATIONS					
	A. Std. optional two-tone combinations	N/C	N/C	N/C	N/C	N/C
	B. Reverse std. two-tone combination	12.50	12.50	12.50	N/C	N/C
	C. Combination of any two std. colors	12.50	12.50	12.50	N/C	N/C
	D. Any other combination of accepted colors	25.00	25.00	25.00	N/C	N/C
41-3	WHEELS PAINTED A SPECIAL COLOR					
	A. When body is std. color (PER WHEEL)	1.00	1.00	1.00	N/C	N/C
	B. When body is special color (PER WHEEL)	N/C	N/C	N/C	N/C	N/C
41-4	FENDERS PAINTED A SPECIAL COLOR	N/A	N/A	S/O	N/A	N/A
41-5	MOULDINGS — INTERIOR					
	A. Garnish & finishing panels in one special color (excluding windshield).	N/A	10.00			
	B. Garnish & finishing panels in two colors (excluding windshield moulding).	N/A	12.50			
	C. Chrome windshield garnish moulding painted a special color.	N/A	4.00	4.50	$4.00	
	D. Chrome windshield garnish moulding grained to match door mouldings.	STD	N/C	10.00	10.00	
41-7	FRONT COMPARTMENT SPECIAL FINISH Instrument panel, steering column, and hand brake lever painted a special color.	N/A	12.50	S/O	12.50	
41-8	MOULDINGS — EXTERIOR (HOOD & BODY) Finished in color rather than chrome					$8.00
41-9	PLASTIC PARTS — INTERIOR — IN A SPECIAL COLOR Steering wheel rim, horn button, shift lever knob, cowl ventilator knob.	N/A	12.50	11.00	11.00	
41-10	STRIPING BODY IN STD. LOCATION IN SPECIAL COLOR Only exception gold & silver leaf	N/A	4.00	4.50	4.00	14.00
41-11	MONOGRAMS (THREE ⅜" BLOCK LETTERS) Painted on doors (PER PAIR)	12.50	12.50	12.00	12.00	12.00

SPECIAL FEATURES AVAILABLE ON 1941 CADILLACS (Continued)

EXTRA CHARGES FOR SPECIAL FABRICS AND TRIM STYLES

SPECIAL FEATURE NUMBER		SERIES 61 & 62 STD.	SERIES 61, 62 & 63 DeLuxe	SIXTY SPECIAL	SERIES 67	SERIES 75
41-16	SIXTY-SPECIAL TRIM STYLE (STD FABRICS)*	N/A	$115.00			
41-17	75-SERIES TRIM STYLE (STD. 67 FABRICS)	N/A			$150.00	
41-18	61-62-SERIES DELUXE FABRICS	N/A			N/C	
41-19	67-SERIES FABRIC IN 6733 FRONT COMPARTMENT				N/C	
41-20	SIXTY-SPECIAL FABRICS	N/A	7.50			
41-21	75-SERIES FABRICS*	N/A	105.00	$100.00	110.00	
41-23	SPECIAL QUALITY FABRICS WITH SPECIAL CARPETS*	N/A	245.00	240.00	275.00	$230.00
	EXTRA CHARGES FOR LEATHER UPHOLSTERY					
	COMBINATION "A" - Genuine leather below beltline with imitation leather above including headlining.					
	COMBINATION "B" - Genuine leather below beltline with standard cloth above, including headlining.					
	COMBINATION "C" - Seat cushions and back rests only in genuine leather with balance in standard cloth.					
	COMBINATION "D" - Genuine leather throughout including headlining.					
41-30	62-SERIES LEATHERS AS USED IN DELUXE CONVERTIBLES					
	COMBINATION "A"*	120.00	110.00	105.00	110.00	
	COMBINATION "B"*	105.00	95.00	92.50	100.00	50.00
	COMBINATION "C"*	60.00	55.00	52.50	60.00	45.00
	COMBINATION "D"*					100.00
41-31	SPECIAL QUALITY LEATHERS (FINEST AVAILABLE)					
	COMBINATION "B"*	200.00	200.00	185.00	215.00	170.00
	COMBINATION "C"*	130.00	125.00	120.00	140.00	115.00
	COMBINATION "D"*	275.00	265.00	250.00	350.00	270.00
41-32	SPECIAL QUALITY CARPETS TO MATCH S.F. 41-31	50.00	50.00	40.00	N/C	N/C
41-33	LEATHER IN FRONT COMPARTMENT (STYLES 6019SF, 6719F, 7519F & 7559)					
	A. 62-Series DeLuxe leather			52.00	55.00	27.00
	B. 75-Series black leather				75.00	50.00
	C. Special quality leather			120.00	120.00	84.00
41-35	MODIFY HEIGHT & CONTOUR OF SEAT CUSHIONS & BACKS (S.F. Numbers 35 through 41 are related)	18.00	17.50	20.00	16.00	17.50
41-42	MARSHALL SPRINGS IN SEAT CUSHION OR BACK (in place of standard All-body type) (PER SEAT OR BACK)	9.00	9.00	10.00	10.00	STD.

SPECIAL FEATURES AVAILABLE ON 1941 CADILLACS (Continued)

EXTRA CHARGES FOR SPECIAL BODY FEATURES

SPECIAL FEATURE NUMBER		SERIES 61 & 62 STD.	SERIES 61, 62 & 63 DeLuxe	SIXTY SPECIAL	SERIES 67	SERIES 75
41-45	ROLLER CURTAIN (Exposed type shade) (on back window only—closed body types)	N/A	$6.00	$5.00	$4.50	N/C
41-46	ROLLER CURTAINS IN SILK OR COATED MATERIAL**					
	1. Installed on quarter windows	N/A	N/A		N/A	14.00
	2. Installed on rear door windows	N/A	N/A	N/A	N/A	22.50
	3. Installed on division					22.50
41-47	FOOT HASSOCKS (In place of foot rail)				20.00	14.00
41-48	ROBE RAIL (In place of robe cord)				30.00	30.00
41-49	GRIP HANDLES (In place of assist straps)				4.00	2.00
41-50	LULL STRAPS & RODS (In place of assist straps)				20.00	17.00
41-51	LULL STRAPS & RODS & GRIP HANDLES				22.50	20.00
41-54	SHEEPSKIN MAT (For all body styles)				45.00	45.00
41-55	FOLDING CENTER ARM REST IN FRONT SEAT BACK	N/A	75.00	75.00	95.00	95.00
41-56	MOTOR PHONE (Installed in Style 6019SF)			50.00		
41-57	REAR QUARTER LAMPS	N/A	30.00	25.00	STD	STD
41-58	EXTRA RADIO SPEAKER (in package tray)				22.50	20.00
41-59	AUXILIARY SEATS OMITTED (Floor blocked in, uncut carpet & std. division wall)				N/C	N/C
41-60	75-SERIES FOOT RAIL (In place of 67 rail)				12.00	
41-63	UMBRELLA COMPARTMENT INSTALLED IN FRONT SEAT (Styles 7533, 7533F & 7559)					
	A. With umbrella					50.00
	B. Less umbrella					40.00

*Prices quoted are for sedan models— small variance for other body types.

**Prices quoted are for silk shades. When S.F. 41-46.3 is installed the division was not entirely covered due to the shape of the division header (available on Styles 7533 & 7533F only).

NOTES: N/A — NOT AVAILABLE, N/C — NO CHARGE, S/O — SPECIAL ORDER
If no price or code is designated the SPECIAL FEATURES BOOK had no entry.

SPECIAL FEATURES AVAILABLE ON 1942 CADILLACS

EXTRA CHARGES FOR SPECIAL COLOR FEATURES

SPECIAL FEATURE NUMBER		SERIES 61 & 62 STANDARD	SERIES 62 & 63 DELUXE	SIXTY-SPECIAL	SERIES 67	SERIES 75
42-1	ENTIRE CAR (ONE COLOR)					
	A. Std. optional paint combination	N/C	N/C	N/C	N/C	N/C
	B. Lower color of std. two-tone combination	N/C	N/C	N/C	N/C	N/C
	C. Upper color of std. two-tone combination	$12.50	$12.50	$12.50	N/C	N/C
	D. Any other accepted durable color	25.00	25.00	25.00	N/C	N/C
42-2	TWO-TONE COMBINATIONS					
	A. Std. optional two-tone combinations	N/C	N/C	N/C	N/C	N/C
	B. Reverse std. two-tone combinations	12.50	12.50	12.50	N/C	N/C
	C. Combination of any two std. colors	12.50	12.50	12.50	N/C	N/C
	D. Any other combination of accepted colors	25.00	25.00	25.00	N/C	N/C
42-3	WHEELS PAINTED A SPECIAL COLOR					
	A. When body is std. color (PER WHEEL)	1.00	1.00	1.00	N/C	N/C
	B. When body is special color (PER WHEEL)	N/C	N/C	N/C	N/C	N/C
42-4	FENDERS PAINTED A SPECIAL COLOR—NOT RECOMMENDED					
42-5	MOULDINGS-INTERIOR					
	Garnish mouldings and finishing panels painted in a special color.	15.00	15.00	15.00	15.00	15.00
42-6	FRONT COMPARTMENT IN SPECIAL FINISH					
	Steering column assembly, brackets, instrument panel and painted parts in special color.	15.00	15.00	15.00	15.00	15.00
42-7	MONOGRAMS - PAINTED ON DOORS					
	Three 3/8" block letters- (PER PAIR)	12.50	12.50	12.50	12.50	12.50
42-8	CONVERTIBLE TOP FABRICS INCLUDING BOOT - 6267D					
	A. Optional black or blue gray top fabrics		N/C			
	B. Jonarts Cleaneasy top fabrics		85.00			
	C. Jonarts Harmony Line top fabrics		55.00			
42-9	SPECIAL PIPING ON CONVERTIBLE TOP					
	In contrasting color to trim		15.00			

SPECIAL FEATURES AVAILABLE ON 1942 CADILLACS (Continued)

EXTRA CHARGES FOR LEATHER UPHOLSTERY

	COMBINATION "B" -	Genuine leather below beltline and imitation leather above including headlining.					
	COMBINATION "C" -	Genuine leather below beltline with Standard cloth above including headlining.					
	COMBINATION "D" -	Genuine leather on seat cushions and back rests only with balance in Standard cloth.					
	COMBINATION "E" -	Genuine leather entirely.					
42-11	62-SERIES LEATHERS AS USED IN DELUXE CONVERTIBLE						
	COMBINATION "B"*		$125.00	$115.00	$150.00	$150.00	$75.00
	COMBINATION "C"*		115.00	105.00	140.00	140.00	65.00
	COMBINATION "D"*		70.00	65.00	75.00	75.00	60.00
42-12	SPECIAL QUALITY LEATHERS (FINEST AVAILABLE)						
	COMBINATION "C"*		175.00	175.00	200.00	200.00	150.00
	COMBINATION "D"*		100.00	100.00	115.00	115.00	90.00
	COMBINATION "E"*		250.00	250.00	315.00	315.00	250.00
42-13	SPECIAL QUALITY CARPETS						
	To match special quality leathers on SF 42-12		50.00	50.00	N/C	N/C	N/C
42-14	LEATHER IN FRONT COMPARTMENT						
	(Styles 6069F, 6719F, 7519F, 7559)						
	A. 62-Series DeLuxe leather				60.00	35.00	35.00
	B. 75-Series leather				90.00	60.00	60.00
	C. Special quality leather				100.00	80.00	80.00
42-21	SUBSTITUTE 62 DELUXE FABRICS FOR STANDARD FABRICS		25.00	STD.	N/C	N/C	N/C
42-22	SUBSTITUTE 60-S FABRICS FOR STANDARD FABRICS		50.00	25.00	STD.	N/C	N/C
42-23	SUBSTITUTE 67 FABRICS FOR STANDARD FABRICS		50.00	25.00	N/C	STD.	N/C
42-24	SUBSTITUTE 75 FABRICS FOR STANDARD FABRICS		115.00	90.00	65.00	65.00	STD.
42-25	SUBSTITUTE LAIDLAW VICTORIAN FOR STANDARD		200.00	175.00	150.00	150.00	85.00
42-26	SUBSTITUTE LAIDLAW DELUXE FOR STANDARD FABRICS		315.00	290.00	265.00	265.00	200.00
42-27	SUBSTITUTE CLOTH FOR LEATHER IN FRONT COMPARTMENT (Styles 6733, 7533 and 7533F)				N/C	27.50	27.50
42-31	MODIFY HEIGHT & CONTOUR OF SEAT CUSHIONS & BACKS (S.F. Numbers 31 through 36 are related)		20.00	20.00	20.00	20.00	20.00
42-37	MARSHALL SPRINGS IN SEAT CUSHION OR BACK (In place of Standard) (PER SEAT OR BACK) (Standard on 60-S cushions)		10.00	10.00	10.00	STD.	STD.

EXTRA CHARGES FOR SPECIAL BODY FEATURES

42-40	ROLLER CURTAIN ON REAR WINDOW (EXPOSED TYPE)**		N/A	N/A	N/A	5.00	STD.
42-41	ROLLER CURTAINS IN SILK OR COATED MATERIAL**						
	X. Installed on quarter windows					N/A	7.50
	Y. Installed on rear door windows					N/A	7.50
	Z. Installed on division					N/A	15.00
42-42	FOOT HASSOCKS (In place of foot rail)				25.00	25.00	20.00
42-43	ROBE RAIL (In place of robe cord)					35.00	35.00
42-44	GRIP HANDLES (In place of assist straps)					3.50	3.50
42-45	LULL STRAPS AND RODS (In place of assist straps)					20.00	20.00
42-46	LULL STRAPS, RODS AND GRIP HANDLES (In place of assist straps)					22.50	22.50
42-47	SHEEPSKIN MAT				45.00	45.00	45.00
42-48	RADIO SPEAKER IN REAR COMPARTMENT				50.00	15.00	15.00

NOTES: *Prices quoted are for 4-door sedan models, cost variable on other body types approximately 20 percent.
**Prices quoted are for coated material. Silk shades ran an average of $5.00 more per window.
N/A - NOT AVAILABLE, N/C - NO CHARGE, STD. - STANDARD
If no price or code is designated the SPECIAL FEATURES BOOK had no entry.

1941

OPTIONAL EQUIPMENT AND ACCESSORIES

	INSTALLED PRICE
Group A—Special Steering Wheel, License Frames, Trim Rings (5); Style No. 6127, 6109, 6227, 6219	$25.50
Group B—Special Steering Wheel, License Frames, Wheel Discs (4); Style No. 6127, 6109, 6227, 6219	34.00
Group C—Wheel Discs, License Frames, Windshield Washer All Series except Style No. 6127, 6109, 6227, 6219	26.50
Group D—Wheel Discs, License Frames, Windshield Washer, NoRol; All Series except Style No. 6127, 6109, 6227, 6219	38.00
Sixth Wheel Tire and Tube Mounted in Trunk—Series 61, 62, 63, 60S (All Styles except Coupes)	$32.50
Sixth Wheel Tire and Tube Mounted in Trunk—Series 67, 75	45.00
White-Black Reversible Sidewall Tires per Tire—Series 61, 62, 63, 60S	3.50
White-Black Reversible Sidewall Tires per Tire—Series 67, 75	5.00
Sunshine Turret Top—Style No. 6019 only	85.00
Radio and Vacuum Aerial	69.50
Rear Compartment Radio and Vacuum Aerial	125.00
Automatic Heating System—Series 61, 62, 63 Sedans and Style No. 6019	59.50
Automatic Heating System—Series 61 and 62 Coupes	62.00
Automatic Heating System—Series 67, 75 and Style No. 6019-F	65.00
Ventilating Defrosting Heater	33.00
Defrosting Heater	26.50
Special Steering Wheel	15.00
Trim Rings—Each	1.50
Wheel Discs—Each	4.00
Wheel Shields—Pair, Style No. 6127, 6109, 6227, 6219	17.50
License Frames—Pair	3.00
NoRol, all Series	11.50
Windshield Washer	7.50
Fog Lights—Pair	14.50
Spotlight Left or Right	18.50
Back-Up Light	7.50
Day-Nite Rear View Mirror	4.50
Outside Rear View Mirror Left or Right	4.50
Seat Covers—Per Seat	8.75
Fleetwood Robes	50.00
Fleetwood Robe Monograms	5.50

**ABOVE PRICES SUBJECT TO CHANGE WITHOUT NOTICE
ANY STATE OR LOCAL TAXES SHOULD BE ADDED TO ABOVE PRICES**

PRINTED IN U.S.A. 12-40.

1942

OPTIONAL EQUIPMENT AND ACCESSORIES

	INSTALLED PRICE
Group A—Special Steering Wheel, License Frames, Trim Rings (5), Gas Cap Lock; Style Nos. 6107, 6109, 6207, 6269	$28.00
Group B—Special Steering Wheel, License Frames, Wheel Discs (4), Gas Cap Lock, Windshield Washer; Style Nos. 6107, 6109, 6207, 6269	45.00
Group C—License Frames, Wheel Discs (4), Gas Cap Lock, Windshield Washer, Back-Up Light—All Series except Style Nos. 6107, 6109, 6207, 6269	42.50
Hydra-Matic Drive	$
Sixth Wheel Tire and Tube Mounted in Trunk—Series 61, 62, 63, 60 Spec. (All Styles except 6107, 6207, 6207-D, 6267-D)	$35.00
Sixth Wheel Tire and Tube Mounted in Trunk—Series 67, 75	50.00
Radio, Complete with Aerial	75.00
Rear Compartment Radio, Complete with Aerial—Series 67, 75	125.00
Automatic Heating System—Style Nos. 6109, 6269, 6269-D, 6319, 6069	59.50
Automatic Heating System—Style Nos. 6107, 6207, 6207-D, 6267-D	62.00
Automatic Heating System—Series 67, 75 and Style No. 6069-F	65.00
Ventilating Defrosting Heater	29.50
Rear Window Wiper	14.50
Rear Window Defrosting Fan	8.25
Special Steering Wheel	15.00
Trim Rings—Each	1.50
Wheel Discs—Each	4.00
Gas Cap Lock	2.75
License Frames—Pair	3.00
NoRol, All Series (Not available with Hydra-Matic Drive)	12.50
Windshield Washer	8.25
Fog Lights—Pair	24.50
Spotlight, Left or Right	19.50
Back-Up Light	12.50
Day-Nite Rear View Mirror	4.50
Outside Rear View Mirror, Left or Right	4.50
Seat Covers—Per Seat	9.75
Fleetwood Robes	50.00
Fleetwood Robe Monograms	5.50

**ANY STATE OR LOCAL TAXES SHOULD BE ADDED TO ABOVE PRICES
THE RIGHT IS RESERVED TO MAKE CHANGES AT ANY TIME WITHOUT NOTICE, IN PRICES, COLORS, MATERIALS, EQUIPMENT, SPECIFICATIONS AND MODELS, AND ALSO TO DISCONTINUE MODELS.**

PRINTED IN U.S.A. 9-41

Home of Cadillac and LaSalle

The CADILLAC LA SALLE SERVICE·MAN

APPENDIX III

Volume XIII, Number 9   October, 1939

New Features of 40-Series Cadillacs and La Salles

THE NEW CADILLAC-LA SALLE cars for 1940, which are now ready for public announcement, cover the entire range of the fine car field. Seven new series with 46 different body styles comprise the 40-Series line. These seven series are indicated in the chart below.

In spite of the extensiveness of the new line, the changes in the mechanical features and in service procedures are not too numerous. Servicemen can master them easily by careful study of the service literature which is now available.

Service Literature

Servicemen will be glad to know that the complete Shop Manual for 1940 is now ready, and that copies have already been sent to all Cadillac-La Salle distributors and dealers. These copies have been sent to the Service Manager in each organization, and he will distribute them to the other men.

In style and layout, the new Shop Manual follows closely the 39-Series and previous manuals. The familiar group index is used and within the groups information is given in the form of service notes, illustrations and specifications.

The Shop Manual does not emphasize which mechanical features are new in the 40-Series cars. Description of new features has heretofore been a function of the Preliminary Service Information Booklet. No booklet of this type is being prepared this year. In its place, the following description of new features has been compiled.

Body and Sheet Metal

Outstanding changes in appearance and numerous improvements in construction characterize the bodies of 40-Series Cadillac and La Salle cars. The basic construc-

Chassis Model Designation

Series	W.B.	Displacement
La Salle 40-50	123"	322 cu. in.
La Salle 40-52	123"	322 cu. in.
Cadillac 40-62	129"	346 cu. in.
Cadillac 40-72	138"	346 cu. in.
Cadillac 40-60S	127"	346 cu. in.
Cadillac 40-75	141"	346 cu. in.
Cadillac 40-90	141"	431 cu. in.

tion of the bodies is, however, much the same as the corresponding 39-Series, all bodies being of the familiar all-steel turret top design.

The most striking innovation is the "projectile" body design used on the 40-52, 62 and 72 series cars. This body style has low, sleek lines, chrome window reveals, an increased slant in the windshield and a curved rear window, all of which add to the modern streamlining and to the impression of speed.

Construction features of the "projectile" body design include concealed door hinges, a one-piece cowl construction that provides increased rigidity, and a safety lock on the rear doors. This safety lock operates on both the inner and outer door locks to prevent accidental opening. This type of lock is also used on the 40-50 La Salle.

The changes made in the sheet metal are of special interest to Servicemen, because they simplify considerably, work on the engine or the front end. All of the front end sheet metal has been rearranged, starting with a new radiator cradle and frame, to which virtually all front end sheet metal parts are attached.

(over)

193

October, 1939 — The Cadillac-La Salle Service Man

New Mechanical Features of the 40-Series Cars

With this new design, the radiator grille can be removed without disturbing other parts; the radiator can be removed without taking off any sheet metal; and the hood and sheet metal parts can be realigned more easily than on previous series cars. All of these operations are covered in detail in the Shop Manual.

Front Suspension

The front suspension system used on 40-50, 52, 62, 72 and 60S cars is new, although it is based upon the design used for 39-50 and 61, strengthened by a number of detail changes.

The lower suspension arms are of pressed steel, mounted at the inner ends on threaded bushings instead of the rubber bushings previously used. These bushings are protected from dirt and water by seals made of "Neoprene," a synthetic rubber not affected by oil or grease. The bushings require lubrication with chassis lubricant every 1,000 miles.

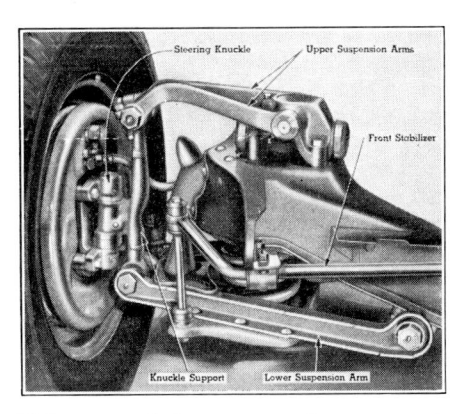

This type of front suspension system is typical of 40-50, 52, 62, 72 and 60S series cars.

The front suspension system used on 40-75 and on 40-90 cars is exactly the same as that used on 39-75 and 90.

The recommendations for caster and camber are new on 40-Series cars, but the methods of checking and correction are the same as before. The new specifications are given in the Shop Manual.

Rear Suspension

The rear suspension system used on 40-50, 52, 62, and 72 differs from that used on 39-50 and 61 in that inverted shackles are not used and the springs themselves are several inches longer. Rubber mountings are used both for the spring bolts and the spring shackles.

A cross-link rear stabilizer is also used on these series. It is the same in principle as the stabilizers used on the larger cars, although somewhat different in construction.

The complete Shop Manual on the 40-Series cars has been sent to all Distributors and Dealers.

The assembly and adjustment of the stabilizer is explained in the new Shop Manual.

The rear spring suspension systems used on the 40-60S and on the 40-75 and 90 cars are unchanged from those used on the corresponding 39-Series.

The rear axle and differential remain substantially unchanged from '39 construction. The axle ratios correspond with the '39 ratios, and all service procedures are unchanged. One precaution, however, is worth repeating: Always use the proper tools when installing rear axle and pinion shaft oil seals. These tools, announced in the September SERVICE MAN, should be available for use in every service station.

Brakes

The brakes on the 40-Series cars are unchanged from those used on 39-Series, except for a few minor changes. The chief of these is the use of dust seals around the brake drums and dust shields on all 40-Series cars. Several changes have been made in the brake master cylinder on 40-50, 52 and 62 cars to accommodate the new mounting location in the frame.

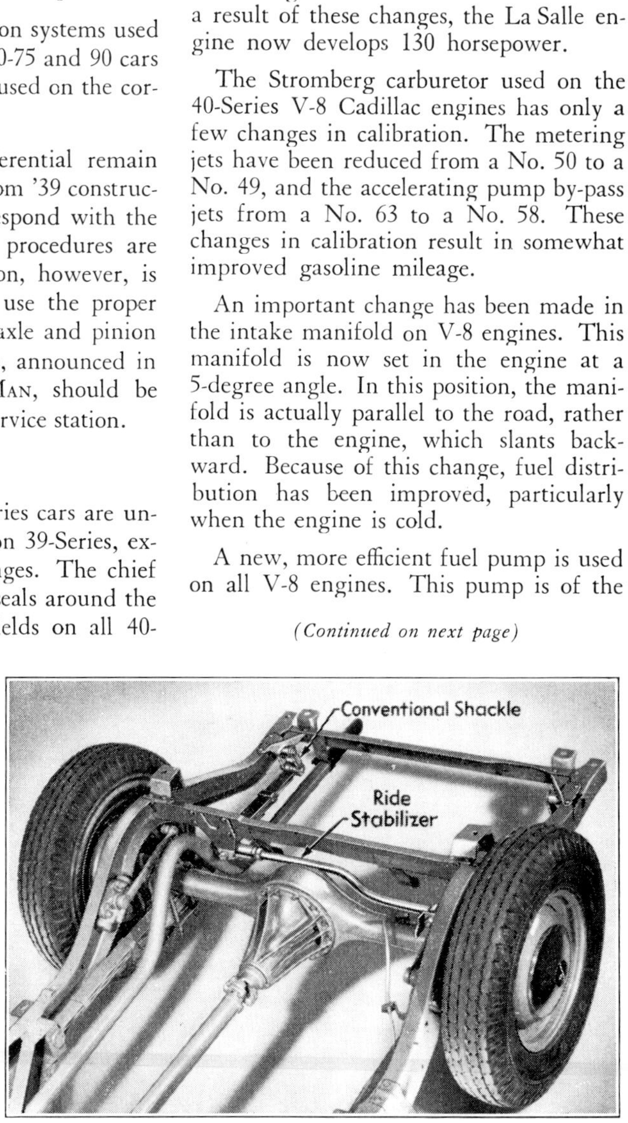

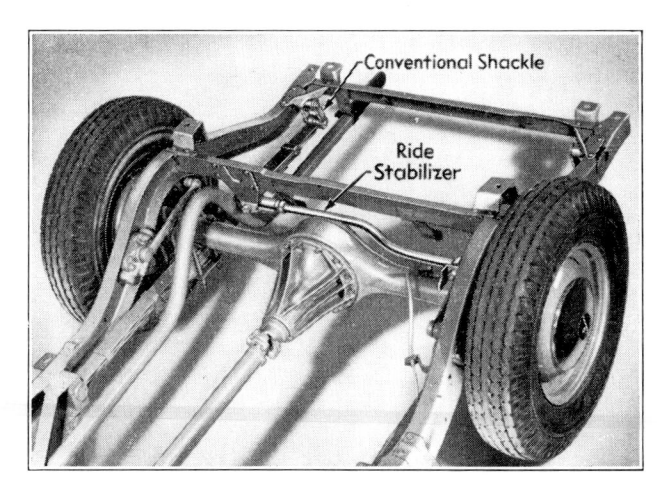

Longer rear springs with conventional type shackles are used in the 40-50, 52 and 62 rear suspension systems.

There is no change in the brake adjustment procedures and none in the disassembly operations, except that the dust seals must first be removed before the wheels are removed.

Engine

The 322 cu. in. V-8 engine is continued in the 40-50 and 40-52 La Salle cars and the 346 cu. in. V-8 engine is continued in the 40-62, 72, 60S and 75 engines. There are, however, several minor changes in the engines, mostly in the fuel and ignition systems, and designed primarily to provide added economy and performance.

Several changes have been made in the Carter carburetor which is used on the 40-50, 52 and 90 series. The carburetor throat size has been increased from 1⅛" to 1¼". A new vacuum controlled metering system is used. The accelerating pump has been improved by means of a new operating rod and more direct jets, and a float bowl vent similar to that used on the Stromberg carburetor has been added. As a result of these changes, the La Salle engine now develops 130 horsepower.

The Stromberg carburetor used on the 40-Series V-8 Cadillac engines has only a few changes in calibration. The metering jets have been reduced from a No. 50 to a No. 49, and the accelerating pump by-pass jets from a No. 63 to a No. 58. These changes in calibration result in somewhat improved gasoline mileage.

An important change has been made in the intake manifold on V-8 engines. This manifold is now set in the engine at a 5-degree angle. In this position, the manifold is actually parallel to the road, rather than to the engine, which slants backward. Because of this change, fuel distribution has been improved, particularly when the engine is cold.

A new, more efficient fuel pump is used on all V-8 engines. This pump is of the

(Continued on next page)

New Mechanical Features of the 40-Series Cars

"beehive" design similar to the pumps used on the V-16 engine. This construction provides better pump cooling. In addition, the new pump has greatly increased fuel and vapor handling capacity due to a compression ratio of 3 to 1, which is greater than on pumps previously used.

The timer distributor used on all 40-Series V-8 engines has a vacuum advance mechanism which can advance the spark a maximum of 18°, in addition to the 22° advance provided by the mechanical spark advance mechanism. The addition of the vacuum advance will provide better performance and increased economy as well.

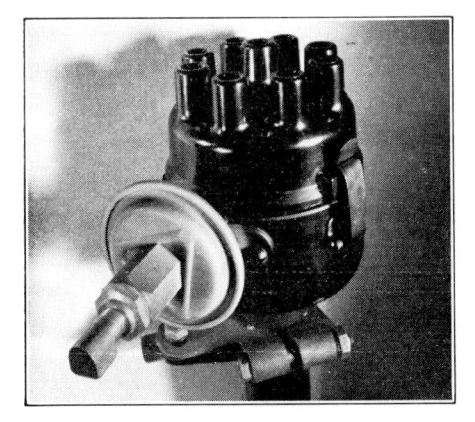

The vacuum advance timer-distributor is used in all 40-Series V-8 engines.

The vacuum advance mechanism does not change ignition service except in checking the ignition timing. The vacuum advance should always be disconnected when the timing is being adjusted.

Clutch

A new "Torbend" clutch driven disc is used on all 1940 Series Cadillac and La Salle cars. This disc differs from the disc previously used in that it has no separate cushioning spring between the facing and the disc. It has instead a spring-type construction in the disc itself. Because of this feature, the new driven disc is nearly 30% lighter than the conventional disc, a feature which materially reduces clutch spinning. The clutch facings are of a new material that is especially wear resistant and permits smooth engagement. Clutch servicing operations are unchanged.

Transmission

The transmissions used on 40-Series cars are unchanged from the previous transmission, except in minor details. The transmission shifting mechanism, however, has been changed in several ways to provide easier shifting and to simplify adjustment.

The Torbend clutch driven disc has no separate cushion springs as the disc itself provides this action.

Easier shifting is accomplished largely by increasing leverage through an increase in the length of the shifter levers at the transmission case.

The second change is in the construction of the shifting shaft and shifting tube at the lower bracket on the steering column. The adjustment between the inner shaft and the outer tube is maintained definitely by a collar on the lower end of the inner shaft. With this construction the low and reverse shifter lever does not require any adjustment, although the high and second speed lever is still adjusted with Tool No. J-1204.

Detailed information on adjustments and on assembly and disassembly are given in the Shop Manual.

Steering

The steering gears for all 40-Series, except the 40-72, are the same as for the corresponding previous, and require the same adjustments. The steering gear used on 40-72 Series cars is of an entirely new type, called the "Recirculating Ball Steering Gear."

This type of steering gear, illustrated on this page, has a nut which contains a large number of steel balls that run on the circular worm teeth. As the worm turns, the nut rises and falls with the balls circulating around inside the nut, thus moving the sector. Instead of having a sliding contact between the worm and nut, the balls provide an almost frictionless rolling contact.

Only two adjustments are required by the Recirculating Ball Steering Gear. The

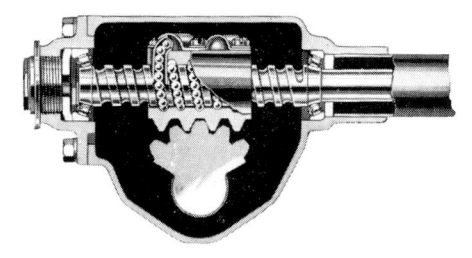

The re-circulating ball type of steering gear is used on 40-72 series cars only.

end-play of the worm should be adjusted until there is between ¾ to 1-pound tension, as measured at the rim of the steering wheel with the pitman arm disconnected.

The end-play of the sector shaft should be adjusted until a tension of 1½ to 2 pounds, as measured at the rim of the steering wheel, is required to pull the steering gear through the high spot range.

Complete information on this new type of steering gear is given in the Shop Manual. This includes not only the adjustment procedure, but also the disassembly and reassembly procedure. For the present,

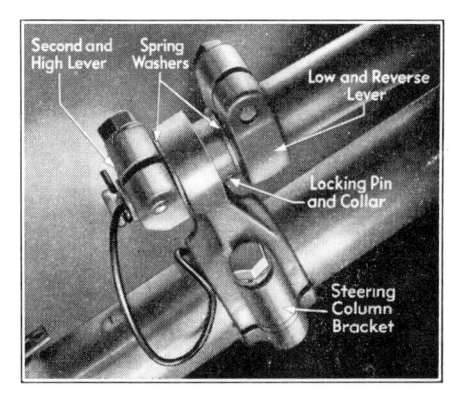

The new lower shifting column construction, used on all 40-Series, requires new adjustment and disassembly procedures.

however, we are asking that none of these steering gears be disassembled and serviced except here at the factory. If any attention is required other than adjustment, the steering gear should be replaced and returned to the factory for this attention.

Electrical

The most outstanding change in the electrical system is, of course, the "Sealed Beam" headlamps. Complete information on these lamps has already been provided in the September issue of the SERVICE MAN and in the Shop Manual as well.

A new generator is used on all 40-Series cars. This generator has a maximum charging rate of 34 amperes and is both current and voltage controlled to provide the correct output under all driving conditions.

Minor changes have been made in other parts of the electrical system which are described in detail in the Shop Manual, but service operations are in the main the same as previously.

Radiator

Although the radiators used on the 40-Series Cadillac and La Salle cars are of the familiar tube and fin construction, they are mounted in a different manner and re-

(over)

New Mechanical Features

(Continued from page 195)

quire a different procedure for removal and installation. The service adjustments on the radiator itself, however, remain unchanged.

The radiator may now be removed without removing the radiator grilles after first removing the fan, air cleaner, hoses, thermostat connections, etc. The radiator is mounted on a cradle assembly from which it must be disconnected. The radiator grilles and fenders are also supported by this cradle assembly.

Lubrication

Four new lubrication points—each end of the lower suspension arm mounting shafts—have been added to the lubrication instructions of the Series 40-50, 52, 62, 72 and 60S cars. The lubrication of the front wheel bearings has been simplified as they are now to be repacked only every 12,000 miles.

Although the periodic lubrication of the generator rear bearing with engine oil every 1,000 miles is unchanged, it must now be repacked with wheel bearing grease if it is disassembled for any reason. Other lubrication points on all 40-Series cars and the lubrication schedule are the same as for the previous corresponding series.

« »

Air Leakage at Tail Lamps Prevented by Rubber Tape

IN THE EVENT that any dust or exhaust fumes are found to be leaking into the bodies of 40-Series cars through small openings around the rubber grommet between the tail lamp and the body, they may be stopped by sealing the grommet with soft rubber tape. Ordinary gum rubber tape, such as used by electricians, is particularly effective in making an air-tight seal and may be easily obtained at any electrical supply house.

Servicemen should not try to seal openings around this grommet with two gaskets cemented back to back, as this practice may cause a clicking or creaking in the tail lamp housing.

« »

NOTICE

BECAUSE INQUIRIES are still coming in, we repeat the following information—"Sealed Beam" headlamp units cannot be installed on previous model cars.

New Cylinder Block Cleaning Procedure

CARS THAT HAVE SEEN considerable service over a period of a year or more may accumulate a considerable amount of sludge, rust and scale in the water passages of the cylinder blocks. This is particularly true of cars which have not had the benefits of regular cooling system cleaning.

This accumulation of scale and sludge cannot always be cleaned out by ordinary reverse flushing of the cylinder blocks with water and compressed air as prescribed in the cooling system cleaner instructions. It is very important, however, that this sludge be removed because if it is left in the cylinder blocks, there is the possibility that it will be recirculated and will plug the radiator core a short time after the system has been cleaned.

After cleaning the cooling system on cars with over a year's use, the cylinder blocks should always be inspected for deposits of sludge, rust or scale. The inspection, and the correction of this condition, can best be made in the following manner:

1. Remove water pump.
2. Plug right cylinder head outlet and connect water supply to left cylinder head outlet.
3. Remove cylinder head cap screw in lower rear corner of left cylinder head.
4. Insert a length of $\frac{5}{16}$" copper tubing connected to an air supply, through bolt hole to bottom of water jacket.
5. While water is reverse flowing through cylinder blocks, give several strong blasts of air through tubing.

The air should be forced into the water passages through the cylinder head bolt holes indicated on both cylinder heads.

6. If considerable sediment is dislodged and flows out of water pump opening, repeat above instructions on first and second bolt holes of lower row of bolts at each end of cylinder heads and end bolt holes on center row of bolts.
7. If little or no sediment is dislodged by Operation No. 5, it may be assumed that there is no loose sediment and the operation need not be continued.

Valve Lifters Must Be Oiled To Prevent Rust and Wear

WHEN THE HYDRAULIC VALVE lifters used on all recent series Cadillac and LaSalle cars are disassembled for cleaning they should be well oiled with engine oil before they are reassembled. The gasoline with which the parts are washed leaves them dry and if they are reinstalled in this condition the parts may wear considerably before engine lubricant reaches them.

Servicemen should bear this fact in mind, and make certain to oil all valve lifter parts when they are assembled.

Valve Lifters Oiled to Prevent Rust

Several reports also have been received at the factory that new hydraulic valve lifters were found to be badly rusted in distributors' and dealers' Parts Departments. These valve lifters are machined to a very high polish and, if they are not protected from dust and moisture, they will rust in a very short time.

When valve lifters are sent out from the factory they are very carefully oiled and wrapped in wax or oiled paper. If they are removed from these wrappings they should be carefully reoiled and tightly wrapped in oiled paper before they are put back in the parts bin.

Incorrect Wheel Balance Affects Steering & Handling

THE IMPORTANCE OF proper wheel balance, particularly front wheel balance, in securing easy handling and shock-free steering, has been emphasized in automotive service ever since the introduction of the low pressure tire nearly 20 years ago.

It should, therefore, be second nature for every Serviceman to check wheel and tire balance right away in any complaints of steering or handling conditions. It should also be second nature to remember to check and correct wheel balance whenever the original tires are removed and reinstalled, or whenever new tires are installed on any of the wheels.

This is particularly important when the new tires are of some of the special types that are being distributed by several manufacturers. The weight and weight distribution of these heavy tires and tubes often causes serious wheel unbalance.

Before a car is put into service with these types of tires, it is important that the wheel and tire assembly be carefully balanced, both statically and dynamically. If the service station does not have equipment for accurate wheel balancing, the wheels must be sent out for balancing.

The Cadillac-La Salle Service Man

Fuel and Vacuum Pump Tests on the Car Permit Accurate Diagnosis of Conditions

THE FUEL AND VACUUM PUMPS used on Cadillac and LaSalle cars have a large and important job to do and are consequently precision instruments that operate at peak efficiency. Complete service on fuel and vacuum pumps requires special tools, replacement parts and a considerable degree of skill.

Although any service station can secure the parts and tools required and train Servicemen for major fuel pump service, an exchange program has been established by the factory Parts Division where fuel and vacuum pumps needing overhauling are sent to the factory for repair and rebuilding and returned to the distributor. This exchange program, which is fully outlined in General Service Letter No. GS-316, dated November 3, 1939, is much more convenient for distriubtors and dealers and is also advantageous to the customer.

There are many inspections and minor service operations, however, which may be performed on the fuel and vacuum pumps by Cadillac-LaSalle Servicemen without any special tools. These inspections and adjustments, which are outlined below, should always be performed before the pump is removed, either to fix the pump or determine accurately any need for removal.

Fuel Pump Pressure

The first thing to check when a fuel pump is not operating properly is the pressure. This may be done by attaching a pressure gauge to the carburetor inlet end of the gas pipe and running the engine. The pressure should be from 3½ to 5 pounds for 40-Series and 3 to 4½ pounds for all past model cars, with the engine at idling speed. This pressure should be maintained by the fuel pump for a few minutes after the engine is stopped.

If the pressure is low, it is probably due to leakage through the diaphragm or valves. If the pressure drops immediately after the engine is stopped after two or three tests, it is an indication that the discharge valves are leaking.

The diaphragm may be inspected in a few minutes' time without removing the pump from the car. If the fuel pump diaphragm is broken, the fuel and vacuum pumps should be removed for repair.

Leaky fuel pump valves may be caused either as a result of normal wear or by foreign material preventing the valves from operating properly. Foreign material can be cleaned out, of course, but if the valves are worn the pump should be removed for repair.

Fuel Pump Capacity

The fuel pump capacity may be checked easily on the car without disassembling the pump. To make this check, disconnect the gas line from the pump to the carburetor at the carburetor, loosen it slightly at the pump and swing it out toward the side of the car as illustrated.

Hold a one-quart can under the open end of the pipe and turn the engine over several revolutions with the starter. When gasoline is coming from the end of the pipe in regular spurts, put another empty

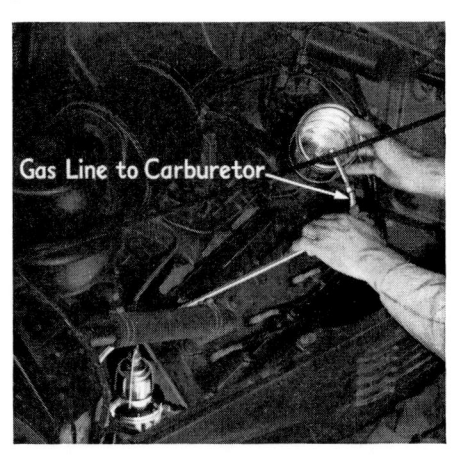

Measure ten spurts of gasoline into a can to check the capacity of the fuel pump.

can under the pipe and measure out exactly ten spurts, or ten strokes of the pump. The fuel pump should deliver at least five ounces of gasoline in ten strokes *with the engine and fuel lines cold.*

If the capacity of the fuel pump is low, it may be due to air leaking into the system. Check the glass sediment bowl for looseness and also the gasoline line from the tank and the inlet fitting on the pump for air leaks. Most air leaks may be detected by bubbles in the glass sediment bowl when the engine is cold.

If tightening the gasoline fittings and sediment bowl does not eliminate the air leaks, the pump should be removed.

Vacuum Pump Tests

The principal test that can be made on the vacuum pump is a check of its output. First, make sure the windshield wipers operate satisfactorily with all lines connected. Then disconnect the vacuum line from the manifold to the pump and check the operation of the windshield wipers again. If they slow down a trifle, the pump is satisfactory but the wipers should not stop.

When the vacuum is not sufficient to operate the wipers, it is an indication that the valves are worn or not clean, or that the diaphragms are leaking. Foreign material in the valves should be cleaned out, but if the valves are worn or if the diaphragms are leaking, the pump should be removed for repair.

———*———

Do not replace the complete pump assemblies without first making these inspections and adjustments to actually determine the need for replacement.

Important Note

Fuel and vacuum pumps have no relation to oil consumption on all cars with V-8 cast-en-bloc engines; that is, since the Series 355-D. *Do not replace* diaphragms or entire pump assemblies on late series Cadillac and LaSalle cars to correct oil consumption.

« »

Hold the Radiator Ornament Up When Closing the Hood

WHEN CLOSING the hoods on 40-Series cars, Servicemen should either hold the radiator ornament up or let it stay loosely in its normal position. The ornament should *never* be held down when closing the hood.

If the ornament is forcibly held down while the hood is being closed, the latch on the ornament will strike the stationary catch and tend to bend it backward. If this

Holding the radiator ornament up when closing the hood will prevent the latch from damaging the stationary catch.

practice is continued, it may do considerable damage to the catch with the possible result of releasing the hood accidentally.

« »

197

The CADILLAC LA SALLE SERVICE·MAN

Volume XIV Number 9

September-October, 1940

Service Notes for the 41-Series Cadillacs

THE CADILLAC PROGRAM for 1941 comprises six new 41-series Cadillac cars blanketing the former Cadillac-LaSalle price class range. The new series are listed in the box below.

Servicemen know that the first requisite of a successful service business is to *know the product*. That means that you must familiarize yourselves with the features and servicing of the 41-series cars at once.

Service Literature

In this respect Servicemen will be glad to know that copies of the 1941 Shop Manual have been mailed to your Service Manager. Get your copy right away, if you do not already have it, and study it over from cover to cover as soon as you can.

The 41-series Shop Manual follows closely the familiar style of the 40-series and previous manuals. Many new detailed service write-ups and a greater number of illustrations, however, combine to make this manual more valuable and easier to use than ever before.

The new Shop Manual does not list or emphasize the mechanical features which are new on the 41-series cars. This information is given instead in the following discussion.

The 41-Series Cadillacs

Series	Wheelbase	Starting Engine No.
41-61	126″	5,340,001
41-62	126″	8,340,001
41-63	126″	7,340,001
41-60S	126″	6,340,001
41-67	139″	9,340,001
41-75	136″	3,340,001

Body and Sheet Metal

The bodies of the 1941 cars have a striking new appearance with many different features, but in structure they resemble closely the 40-series bodies with the turret top and uni-steel construction.

Among the body features of interest to Servicemen are concealed running boards on Series 61, 63 and 67 and concealed door hinges at all points on most series. The spare tires on all series closed sedans are now mounted vertically on one side of the luggage compartment, permitting easy removal and installation, yet providing more accessible trunk space.

A new feature of the Fleetwood bodies is the glass division between front and rear compartments, which is now operated electrically and controlled by small switches in the rear compartment. Special service procedures which this electrical division may require are discussed in a separate article in this issue.

The hood on the 41 Series Cadillac cars is the same alligator type, opening at the front. The hood side panels have been eliminated and the hood top panel now contacts the edge of the front fenders. This type of hood greatly increases the accessibility of most parts of the engine.

(Continued)

September-October, 1940 — *The Cadillac-La Salle Service Man*

Mechanical Features of the 41-Series Cars

The gasoline tank filler cap is located underneath the top section of the left tail lamp body.

New hood hinges, counterbalancing springs and brackets are used with this type hood and require a special service procedure for alignment. This procedure is covered in the new Shop Manual.

The radiator cradle assembly, fenders and radiator grilles have a simplified mounting that makes for easier removal.

Frame

The frames used on the 41 series cars are all similar in design to the 40 series frames but have several improvements. Construction features include deeper reinforced channels and increased width at the rear, which provide considerable increase in rigidity.

Front Suspension

The front suspension system used on the new Cadillac cars is essentially the same as the 40-62 system but with several new features.

The eccentric pin for caster and camber adjustment is increased in eccentricity to permit almost twice as great a camber adjustment range as was obtained previously. In addition, threaded bushings at the inner ends of the lower control arms permit an increased caster adjustment. The caster adjustment may also be made within much narrower limits than was previously possible.

The recommendations for caster and camber on 41 series cars are new, but the methods of checking and corrections are practically the same as before.

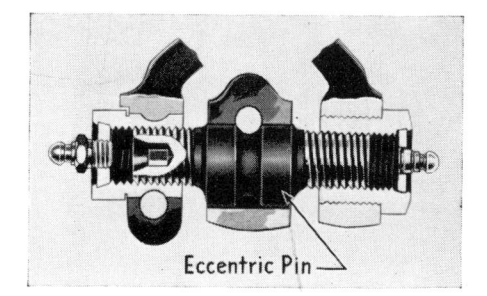

The new specifications and procedures are, of course, given in the new Shop Manual.

Rear Suspension

The most interesting change in the rear suspension system is the adoption of an optional or "Economy" rear axle ratio for series 41-61, 62, 63 and 60S cars. The Economy gear ratio is 3.36 to 1, whereas the standard ratio is 3.77 to 1. Economy ratio axles can be identified by a figure "6" stamped on the bottom of the differential case beneath the center of the pinion shaft. The standard ratio axles have no marking at this point.

The 41-67 and 75 series cars have an axle ratio of 4.27 to 1. These axles can be identified by a figure "4" stamped in the location just mentioned. In addition, a 3.77 to 1 ratio is also available for these cars.

Rubber bushings are now used in the rear spring bolts and shackles on all 41 series cars. This means that no lubrication is required either by the rear springs or

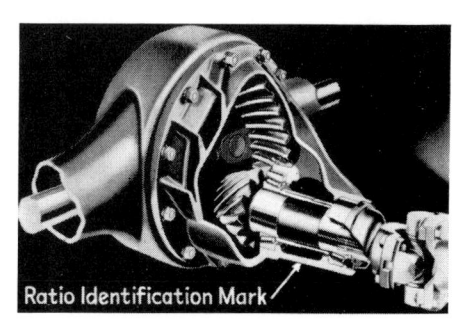

The gear ratio identification mark is located underneath the center of the pinion shaft.

spring bolts and shackles on any 41 series cars. Disassembly of the spring bolts and shackles is the same as for 40-62 series.

Improved riding qualities are obtained through the use of resilient rear springs and the addition of auxiliary rubber bumpers on the frame to lessen the likelihood of rear springs bottoming.

Brakes

The hydraulic braking systems used on the 41-series cars are very similar to those used on the 40-series Cadillac cars. All series use the 12-inch diameter brake drums, but differences in lining widths provide 208 square inches of lining area on 41-61, 62, 63 and 60S, and 233 square inches on 41-67 and 75 and commercial cars.

The slotted brake shoes used on cars on late 1940 production are continued on all 41-series cars. New dust seals are used around the front brake drums on all series as a protection against dirt and splash.

The hand brake linkage is new. The cable from the brake lever extends to a sheave just behind the center of the frame X-member. A cable runs through this sheave to both the rear brake shoes. Adjustment is made by means of a nut at the sheave.

Engine

The large 346 cubic inch engine is used in all 41-series Cadillac cars but several changes have been made to provide greatly increased performance and economy.

The compression ratio has been increased to 7.25 to 1 on all series with a corresponding increase in horsepower up to 150. This high compression ratio requires the use of premium fuel to obtain the best performance.

Connecting rod bearing life has been doubled through the use of new type, thin babbitt-lined, steel-backed bearings.

Quiet engine operation is assured even under difficult conditions by redesigned valve silencers. The compression ratio of the silencers has been increased and the oil bleeder hole has been raised to prevent oil from draining out of the silencer while the engine is not being used.

The exhaust valves are constructed of a new alloy steel which reduces valve stem wear.

A new cast iron camshaft is used on all 41 series engines. This camshaft reduces

(Continued on page 200)

The eccentric pin now provides an increased camber adjustment and a finer caster adjustment.

Features of the rear suspension system include rubber spring bumpers and a new type stabilizer.

The new clutch release linkage provides easier clutch pedal operation.

New 41-Series Mechanical Features

(Continued from page 199)

any tendency toward scoring on the cam lobes. With this new camshaft, it is important not to overtighten the nut on the front end of the shaft. Correct torque tightness is from 90 to 95 foot pounds.

The timing chain and sprockets also are new and of a design that will minimize wear on the timing sprockets.

Only two adjustments are required by the recirculating ball steering gear used on all series.

Another improvement is new ignition wire spacers, providing wider spacing between ignition wires, which in turn lessens the effect of induction between the wires.

The successful "Syncro-Flex" flexible flywheel is used on all 41-series engines.

Both Carter and Stromberg carburetors are used on 41-series cars, with minor changes to provide increased performance and economy.

Clutch

The clutch pressure plate assembly and clutch disc used on 41 series cars are the same as for 40 series except for the addition of anti-squeak washers on the clutch release lever pivot shafts.

A new clutch pedal adjustment procedure is required by the use of a different clutch linkage, as illustrated on page 34. This linkage gives easier clutch pedal operation.

Transmission

A redesigned shifting linkage is used on new cars, providing easier, more positive shifting, and requiring some changes in adjustment procedure as outlined in the Shop Manual. The transmission extension shaft is splined for the slip joint, which is now contained within the extension housing and no longer in the propeller shaft.

The extension shaft rear bearing consists of two diamond bored babbit bushings for increased performance through the life of the car. As these bushings cannot be installed and bored in service stations, replacement can be made only by exchange of the extension housing.

Steering

The re-circulating ball type steering gear, which proved so successful on the series 40-72 cars, is used on all 41 series cars. This steering gear should now be

(Continued on page 201)

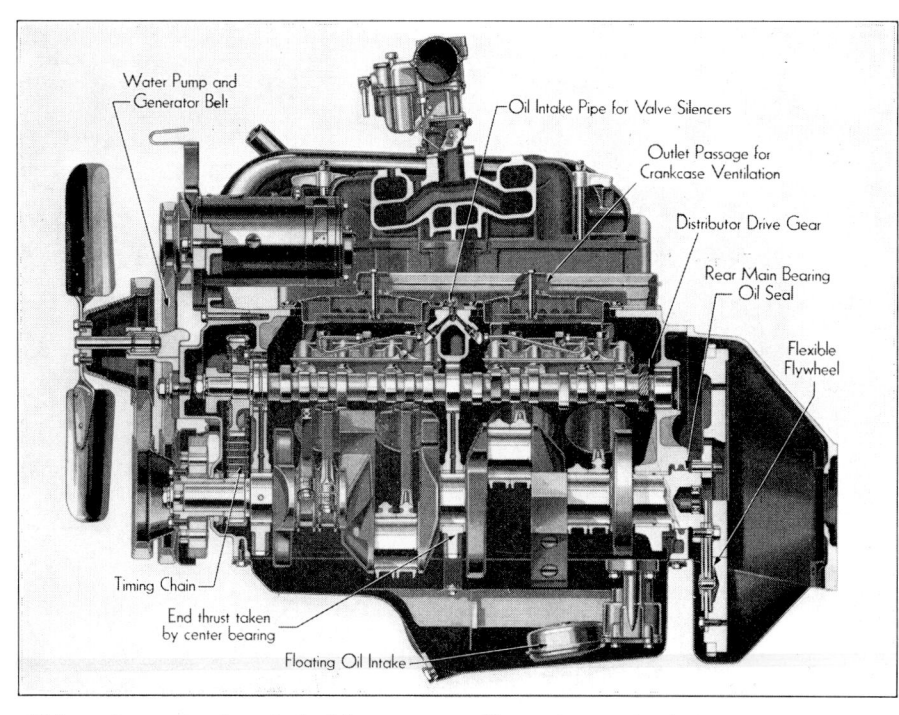

This engine section is typical of the many new illustrations in the 41-Series Shop Manual.

Fleetwood Center Division Now Operated Electrically

THE GLASS DIVISION on 41 Series Fleetwood cars equipped with this feature is now operated electrically. A neat "up and down" switch on each rear seat arm rest actuates a small motor through relays in the division just back of the front seat.

This motor is connected by a worm drive to a grooved drum which winds up and unwinds two cables. One end of each cable is attached to the bottom channel of the glass division so that one cable pulls the glass down as it winds around the drum and the other lets the glass be pushed up by pivoting arms and springs, as it unwinds from the drum.

The glass may be raised or lowered any desired amount depending on how long the "up or down" switch is depressed. Its limit of travel up and down, however, is controlled by an automatically operated cut-off switch in the mechanism so that the motor is stopped when the glass is all the way up or down, even though the switch on the arm rest is held depressed.

The only adjustment which the mechanism ordinarily may require is the limit of travel of the glass up or down. The unit is easily reached for service by opening a small door at the bottom of the division. The control rod and cut-off switch are shown in the accompanying illustration.

To adjust the lower limit of travel of the glass, loosen the top lock nut "A" on the control rod and turn down the threaded bushing "B" the required amount, retighten the lock nut.

To adjust the upper limit of travel of the glass, turn the lower adjusting and lock nuts "C" and "D" up or down as required. Be sure to retighten the nuts after adjustment is completed.

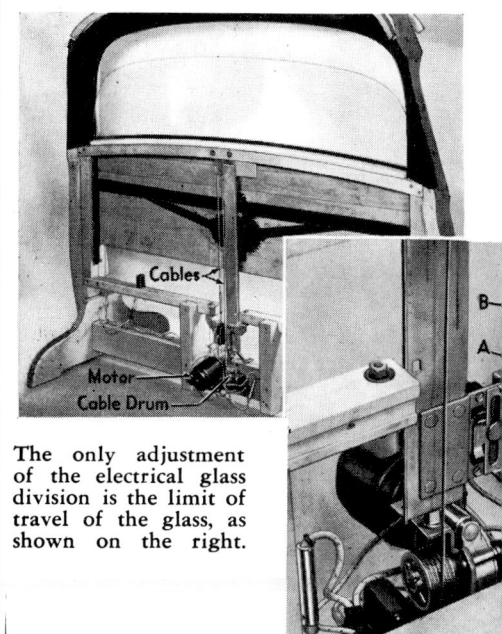

The only adjustment of the electrical glass division is the limit of travel of the glass, as shown on the right.

Two Types of Stromberg Carburetors Used on 41 Cars

TWO DIFFERENT TYPES of Stromberg carburetors have been used on 1941 Series cars. The first type carries Strom-

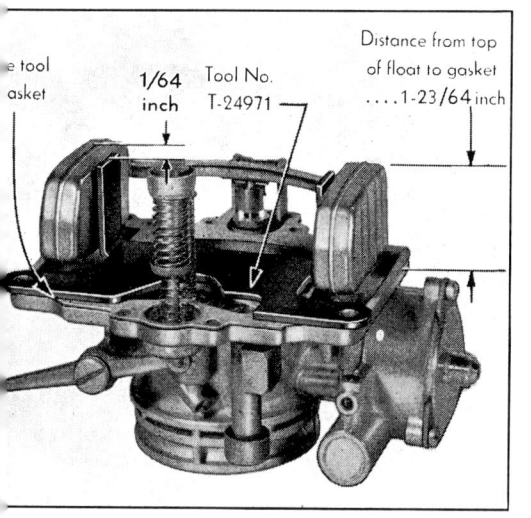

Revised float level specifications, as shown, apply to second type Stromberg carburetors

berg No. 380015 and Part No. 1441513, while the second type carburetor has Stromberg No. 380048, and Part No. 1442538. Only the second type is supplied for complete replacement by the factory Parts Department.

The service adjustments on both type carburetors are precisely the same except that the second type carburetor has different fuel level adjustment specifications, due to a difference in floats.

The fuel level should be set so that the top of the float is 1/64" above the tops of the vertical guides on Tool No. T-24971, or 1-23/64" from the gasket on the carburetor upper body.

When checking the float level on 41-Series cars, Servicemen must determine from the number stamped on the body which type carburetor is used. All Hydra-Matic cars are equipped with the second type carburetor and require the revised float level adjustment.

Float Level Correction

The Stromberg carburetor float gauge setting listed on pages 40 and 43 of the 1941 Shop Manual and on pages 35 and 37 of the 1940 Shop Manual is incorrect. The distance from the top of the float to the gasket should be 1-11/32" instead of 1-13/32" as listed. (1-23/64" on second type 41-Series carburetors.)

Servicemen should note this change in their copies of the 1940 and 1941 Shop Manuals.

41-Series Features
(Continued from page 200)

serviced in the field. Complete sets of replacement parts are available at the factory Parts Department.

Minor changes in the steering gear have simplified the adjustments and the disassembly procedure as well. These operations are clearly explained in the Shop Manual.

Wheels and Tires

Fifteen-inch wheels are used on 41-61, 62, 63 and 60S series cars, to provide lower body height and a better overall appearance.

Rear wheel shields are standard equipment on most 41 series cars. This new

The long lever simplifies removing and installing wheel shields.

wheel shield, illustrated on this page, is removed by reaching up under the bend at the rear, clasping the handle of the tightening lever and pulling the lever inward and then down and forward. The shield will then drop outward at the top and can be lifted clear of the fender brackets at each end.

A new type wheel jack is used on all cars. This jack has a separate stand which supports the car after the wheel has been raised with the jack. The use of the jack is pictured in the Owner's Manual and Shop Manual.

Electrical

The electrical system units which proved so efficient in 1940 are being continued in 1941. These include the generator, starter and "sealed beam" headlights. The major improvement in the electrical system is the new style battery filler plug which prevents overfilling.

Retouching Is Practical on Grained Instrument Panels

A SMALL BLEMISH or scratch on an instrument panel with a grained finish may be satisfactorily touched with a pencil hair brush if the proper procedure is observed.

Before finishing over the scratch or blemish, thoroughly clean the surface of all polish or dirt. Next, mark in the darker lines of the grain in the damaged spot, so that the grain matches up with the surrounding portions of the instrument panel.

Begin touching over the spot with a slightly colored clear lacquer and gradually darken it until it matches with the rest of the panel, allowing ample time for drying between touches. After the lacquer is matched, cover the refinished spot with a mist coat of clear lacquer and let it dry.

Sand and compound the spot lightly after it is thoroughly dry. Finally, the entire panel should be polished.

« »

Tire Valve Literature

A COPY OF a Schrader Tire Valve Company's bulletin and booklet to service station operators is included with the Service Managers' issue of this SERVICEMAN. This literature not only contains interesting information on balanced tire pressures; it uses comparisons with balancing tricks to clarify its tire balancing information. It can well be passed around the shop or posted on the shop bulletin board.

This filler plug, known as the "Electro-Level," uses a movable lead valve which traps air in the battery when the cap is removed and prevents the addition of excessive battery water.

When the battery filler plug is reinstalled, this lead valve automatically vents the battery chambers.

Lubrication

Lubrication has been simplified on 41 series cars by the elimination of lubrication points at the rear springs and at the propeller shaft splines. Other lubrication points on all 41 series cars are the same as for the previous corresponding series. The lubrication schedule and chart appear in the Shop Manual.

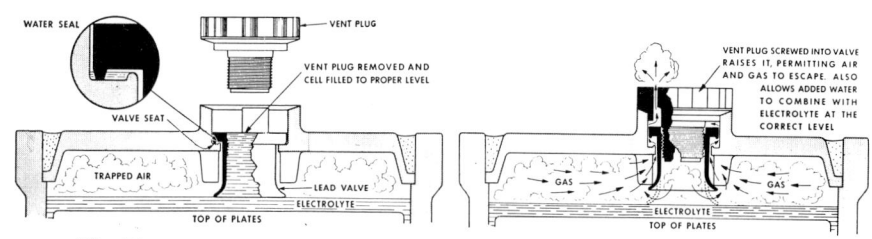

The Electro-Level is open for filling, at left, and closed and vented, at right.

Installation and Adjustment of 41-Series Wheel Shields Is Discussed In Detail

THERE HAS BEEN some confusion regarding the proper method of removing and installing the wheel shields used on most 41-Series cars. In order that everyone will be thoroughly familiar with this removal and installation, the following detailed discussion is provided.

There are two types of wheel shields used on 41-Series cars. Those used on 41-61 and 62 De Luxe models and the 63, 67 and 75 models are all the same. A larger wheel shield is used on the 41-60S Series cars because of the different style of the fender. The removal and installation of the two types of wheel shields used on 41-Series cars are quite similar, although small differences occur in the adjustment of the wheel shields to the fenders.

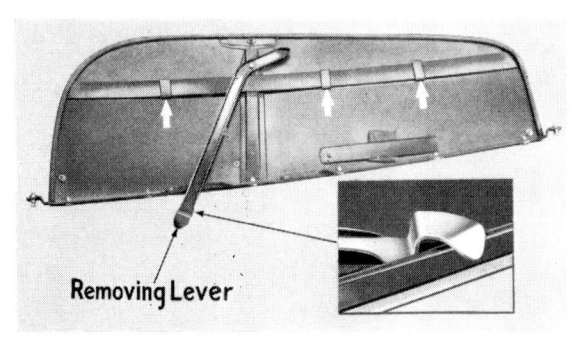

The three rubber anti-rattle rings on the 41-60S shield are indicated by arrows. The inset shows the removing lever locked in place over the shield flange.

To remove wheel shields, first reach in under the bottom of the wheel shields toward the rear, and grasp the removing lever at the bottom. Then push inward to unlock the lever and move it forward until the wheel shield comes loose at the top.

Holding the top of the shield out at about a 60° angle, slide the shield backward until the mounting brackets on the bottom of the shield at the front and rear slide off the fender flange. The shield may then be removed.

To install a wheel shield, slip the rear mounting bracket over the fender flange just in back of the fender baffle (except on 41-60S cars) and slip the front mounting bracket in place over the flange. Slide the shield forward until it contacts the rubber gravel guard at the front, push the top of the shield in place and move the removing lever backward until it locks in position over the edge of the shield flange as shown.

The hook on the rear mounting bracket of the 41-61 and 62 De Luxe cars and the 41-63, 67 and 75 cars is adjustable in order that the wheel shield may be moved inward or outward at the rear to secure the best fit. To adjust this hook, loosen the attaching bolt and move the hook inward or outward as required.

The mounting brackets used on 41-60S shields have an adjusting bolt and lock nuts on both the front and rear brackets so that the wheel shield may be raised or lowered to make it fit properly on the fender. The bolts should be tightened to raise the wheel shield and loosened to lower it.

41-60S Rubber Anti-Rattle Rings

In the event that a rattle occurs in the wheel shields of early 41-60S Series cars, three rubber anti-rattle rings, Part No. 1442398, should be installed on the tension bar. One of these rings should be installed in front of the center lock support and two about equally spaced in back of the support.

To install the rings, remove the locking wire and loosen the rubber anti-squeak down to a point just above the tension bar. Spring the tension bar out of the flange and install three rubber rings on the bar.

If the wheel shield rattles against the gravel shield behind the rear wheel, roll the edge of the gravel shield back ½" to provide adequate clearance, using a dolly block and hammer. As an extra precaution, place one of the rubber rings mentioned above, on the tension bar in position opposite the gravel shield.

Correct Window Regulator Handle Position Explained

WHEN A CASE occurs of a window working itself open the first thing to do is to make sure the window regulator handle is installed in the proper position.

The handle must be installed on the shaft so that when the window is fully raised, the handle is in a horizontal position and in a direction such that its weight will tend to keep the window up.

Tightening Battery Clamps

SERVICEMEN ARE CAUTIONED not to overtighten the clamps when reinstalling batteries in cars. The battery clamps need only be turned up snug enough to avoid their working loose. They are not under any strain which would require a severe tightening.

This precaution is important as overtightening these clamps will crack the seals on top of the battery cells.

Gasoline Tank Cap Vent Must Always Be Kept Open

IT IS EXTREMELY IMPORTANT to keep the vent in gasoline tank caps clean and open at all times. If this vent is obstructed, there is danger of the suction of the fuel pump drawing gasoline from the tank causing the tank to collapse.

Occasionally, a car may be found where gasoline spilled on the gas tank filler neck rubber grommet has caused the grommet to swell and close off the vent. In this event, the filler neck should be raised to give $\frac{1}{8}$-inch to $\frac{3}{16}$-inch clearance.

On 60S Series cars where no adjustment is possible, a small hole drilled through the knurled flange of the cap makes a satisfactory vent without detracting from the appearance.

« »

Spring Clip Must Seat Down Against Hood Emblem Letter

WHENEVER IT IS NECESSARY to refinish the hood top panel of a 41-Series car, which has been in an accident for example, particular care should be exercised while reinstalling the small "Cadillac" letters on the sides of the hood. If these letters and their spring clips are not installed properly, the letters may become loose and even drop out.

The metal letters are held in place with small spring clips which fit over the stem of the letter and down into a recess in the back of the letter itself. Before installing the letters on the hood, be sure the spring clips are *all the way* on the stem of the letters. The small flange on the end of the spring

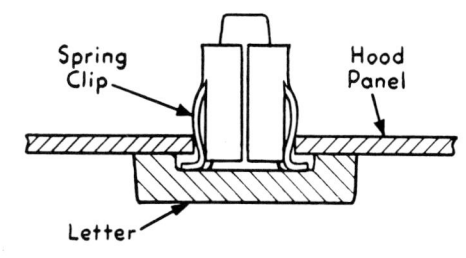

Both the spring clip and the letter must be installed properly to keep the letter tightly in place on the hood.

clip should seat firmly and lie flat in the bottom of the recess in the back of the letter as shown.

Push the stem of the letter with the spring clip, through the rectangular hole on the hood panel. Be sure that the back of the letter seats firmly against the hood panel.

If any spring clips, Part No. 1314433, are discovered which are cracked or broken, they should be replaced.

Additional Specifications for Distributor Testing

DISTRIBUTOR IGNITION TESTERS are widely used by distributors and dealers alike for precision testing distributors. The use of these testers require a considerable number of detailed distributor specifications.

These specifications are usually furnished by the manufacturers of the equipment. At the beginning of a new model season, however, it is difficult for the manufacturer to distribute specifications on all of the new model cars until three or four months after the cars reach the field.

A request has been received for the required additional 41-Series specifications for use in distributor testing that are not included in the 41-Series Shop Manual or heretofore in the SERVICE MAN. We are pleased to furnish this information for the benefit of all distributors and dealers who use distributor ignition testers. In addition, the information will be incorporated in future series Shop Manuals.

The additional specifications required for distributor testing include the centrifugal spark advance at various engine speeds, cam or dwell angle of the distributor, and vacuum advance specifications.

The degrees advance of the centrifugal spark advance for various ignition speeds for all 37, 38, 39, 40 and 41-Series cars is listed below:

Engine Speed R.P.M.	Centrifugal Spark Advance *Distributor Degrees
1000	0 to 1°
1200	0 to 2.5°
1400	1 to 4°
1600	2.5 to 5.5°
2000	5.5 to 8.5°
2400	9 to 12°
2800	12 to 15°
3200	15 to 18°
3600	18 to 21°
4000	21 to 24°

*Distributor degrees equal 1/2 flywheel degrees.

The vacuum required to start plunger movement of the vacuum advance mechanism on all 40 and 41-Series cars equals 5.5 to 7.5" of mercury. The vacuum required for full travel of the plunger equals 15 to 18" of mercury. The total plunger travel is .190" to .212". The range of travel of the vacuum advance expressed in cam degrees equals 9 degrees, plus or minus one degree.

The cam or dwell angle of the distributor is 31 degrees plus or minus 2 degrees for all V-8 Series cars.

Tightness and Lubrication of Hood Hinge Screws Listed

THE SCREWS that hold the hood hinge links to the hood hinge brackets on the cowl of 41-Series cars are designed with shoulders which bear against the brackets when the screws are properly tightened. It is very important that these screws be turned all the way in until the shoulder seats firmly against the bracket as shown below.

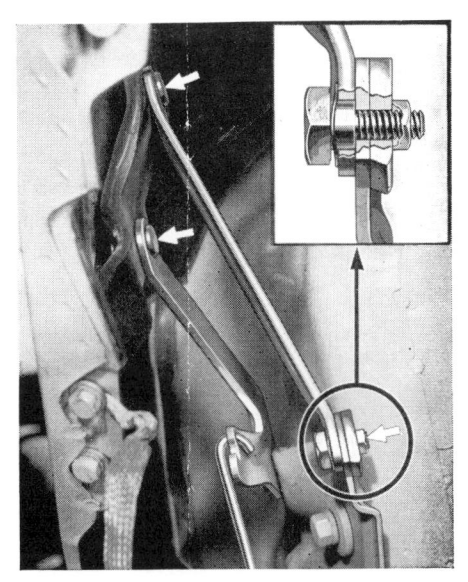

The three arrows indicate parts requiring lubrication. Inset shows construction of hinge screw.

On the first 41-Series cars, these screws were locked in place by staking the threads. On later 41-Series cars, a lock nut is employed at this point.

Should any of the first type, staked screws be discovered which are not tight against the bracket, they should be retightened and locked in place with the lock nut used on the second type. The lock nut is available from the Parts Department under Part Number 124824.

When tightening hood hinge screws equipped with a lock nut, the proper method should be employed to make certain that the shoulder of the screw bears tightly against the bracket. First, tighten the screw to about 15 ft. lb. torque. This is sufficient to seat the shoulder, and excessive torque may break the screw or strip the threads.

Second, hold the head of the screw with a wrench while the lock nut is tightened. Otherwise, the screw may turn with the lock nut enough to back the shoulder away from the bracket.

Hood Hinge Screw Lubrication

The hood hinge screws holding the hood hinge links to the hood hinge brackets on

New Cylinder Block Test For Sludge Deposits Given

IT IS VERY IMPORTANT to inspect the cylinder blocks for the presence of any rust, sludge or scale at the time of cleaning the radiator, particularly on cars which have seen a great deal of service. If the cylinder blocks do contain a certain amount of sludge or rust, these deposits must be removed to prevent any possibility of their being recirculated through the cooling system and plugging the radiator again in a very short time.

A simple test may be performed to determine whether or not any sludge is lodged in the cylinder blocks. To make this test proceed as follows:

1. Drain water.
2. Remove two or three lower rear cylinder head cap screws on both of the cylinder blocks.
3. Insert a long rod or tube through the bolt holes to the bottom of the water jacket.
4. Remove the rod or tube and note the presence of any sludge clinging to it.

If any sludge, rust or scale are found in the cylinder blocks, the blocks themselves

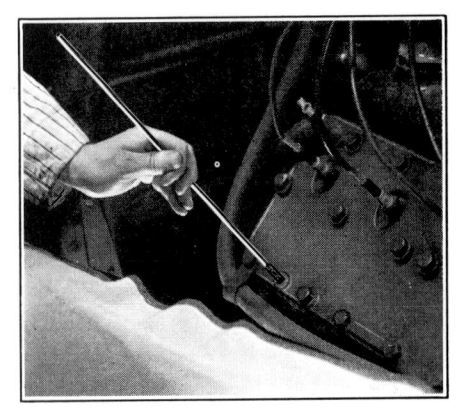

The amount of sludge on the tube or rod indicates the amount of sludge in the water jacket.

must be given a thorough cleaning. The best cleaning procedure for clogged cylinder blocks is that given in the August, 1939 "Service Man," on page 27.

cars. The function of the Automatic Battery Filler is only to regulate the solution level and does not affect the specific gravity of the solution. Making the test involves no more labor on these cars, except that this opportunity should be taken to add more water to the filler bottles.

The fluid in these bottles does not freeze because of the presence of sulphuric acid from the battery. To preserve this antifreeze quality, it is important to add small quantities of water frequently rather than to let the bottles get low and then add a large amount.

The CADILLAC SERVICEMAN

Volume XV, Number 9   October, 1941

SERVICE Information on the 42 Series Cadillacs

THE NEW 1942 SERIES Cadillac cars, which were just announced to the public, include six different series with 22 different body styles. These six series, which are listed below, are similar to the six series which proved so popular last year.

Although the 42-Series cars have a brand new and extremely modern appearance, and a number of new mechanical features, there are not many changes in service procedure. Servicemen can easily master these changes if they study the 1942 service literature which will soon be in the mail. Knowledge of the product is essential to good service and must not be neglected because of the evident similarities to the previous series.

1942 Service Literature

The 1942 Shop Manuals will be mailed to all Service Managers within the next week, so be on the watch and get one as soon as they arrive.

The new 42-Series Shop Manual is bigger and better than ever before, containing a total of 160 pages. A large "General Description" section is included in each division of the manual for the benefit of new and old Servicemen alike.

In addition, many new service operations are covered and other familiar ones have been discussed in greater detail. More illustrations have also been incorporated in the manual.

Cadillacs for 1942		
Series	Wheelbase	Starting Engine Number
42-61	126"	5,380,001
42-62	129"	8,380,001
42-63	126"	7,380,001
42-60S	133"	6,380,001
42-67	139"	9,380,001
42-75	136"	3,380,001

All Servicemen will be pleased to know that a complete cross reference index is included in the 1942 Shop Manual. This index, which is similar to the popular "SERVICEMAN" index, makes the Shop Manual handier to use than was previously possible.

The new Shop Manual does not list or emphasize the mechanical features which are new on the 42-Series cars. This information is provided instead in the following discussion.

Body and Sheet Metal

Although the 1942 bodies have a striking new appearance incorporating graceful sweeping lines and extra long, sleek fenders, the fundamental design has not been changed. The familiar all-steel turret top Fisher and Fleetwood bodies are used in all models.

(Continued on page 205)

Service Information on the 42-Series Cadillacs

An interesting feature on sedan bodies is the system of locking rear doors. The rear doors are fitted with the familiar lock buttons in the garnish mouldings. These buttons differ from the front doors, however, in that they can be set to operate in one of two ways.

The buttons are normally set so that the inside door handles will operate regardless of whether the outside door handles are locked or not. They can also be set so that the *inside* as well as the outside door handles are locked or inoperative. This feature is of special benefit when small children ride alone in the rear seat. It will eliminate any possibility of their opening the doors accidentally.

In order to open a door which has been locked in this manner, it is first necessary to raise the lock button before operating the door handle.

In order to set the locks so that the lock button makes the inside door inoperative, it is merely necessary to insert a rounded, slightly bent rod through the clearance hole in the lock plate, as shown in the illustration, and trip the remote control link upward to engage the intermittent lever. To reset the locks to positive action, simply insert the rod and trip the remote control link downward to engage the lock bolt.

All body styles are equipped with the Cadillac all-weather ventilating system. This feature consists of two (right and left) ventilating passages which extend from the radiator grille back to the driver's compartment. The flow of fresh air is controlled by shut-off valves operated by push-pull knobs on the instrument panel. Hinged deflectors permit guiding the air stream.

The Cadillac Automatic Heating System and the Ventilating Defrosting Heater, supplied as accessories, have a takeoff from the right fresh air passage in providing home-like warmth in the interior of the car.

The glass divisions in Fleetwood bodies so equipped are operated automatically. Small control buttons on both rear seat side arm rests raise or lower the glass division. This device is powered by a small electric motor in the back of the front seat.

The front fenders on all 42-Series, except the 42-75, have extensions on the front doors and the rear fenders have extensions on the rear doors on 42-62 and 60S sedans, providing an extremely modern touch to the appearance of the car. Because of these extensions, fenders must be aligned to the body as well as to the hood.

While the alignment operations of the front end sheet metal are different, they are not difficult. The procedures given in the Shop Manual must be followed exactly, however, to assure accuracy in alignment.

An exploded view of the various front end sheet metal units is shown in the accompanying illustration.

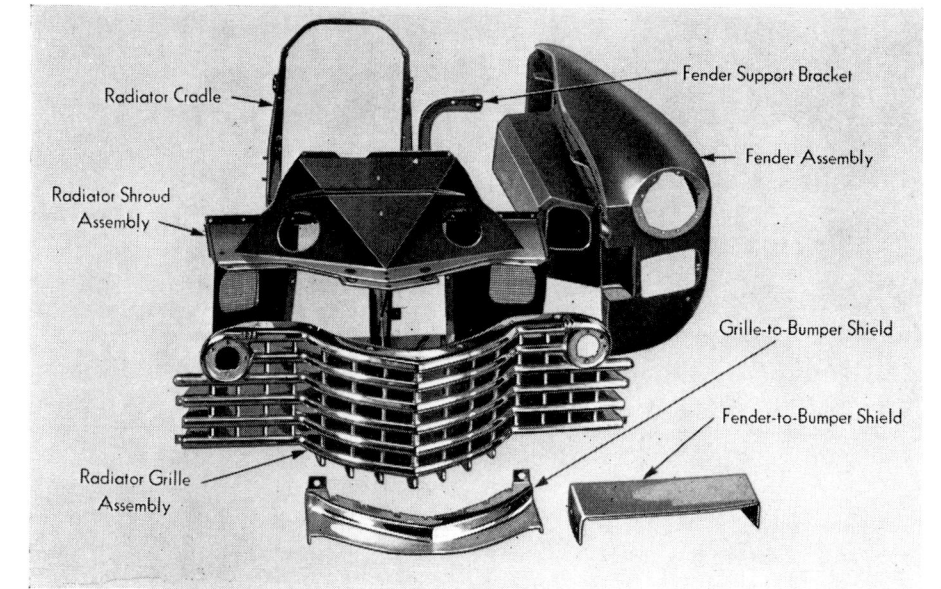

Frame

The frames used on all 42-Series cars have the rugged X-type construction, with

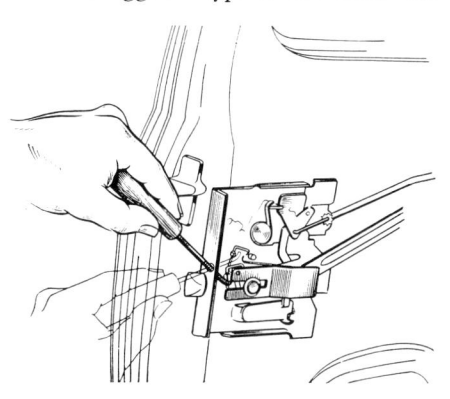

A short rod inserted through the lock plate releases and engages the double door locking mechanism.

deep, wide, reinforced channels. Six different frames are used on the six different models, thus providing the best and strongest type frame for each series. In addition, the frames used on convertible coupes are equipped with special reinforcements to provide extra strength.

(Continued on page 206)

Service Precaution

Trunk Lid Support

For any service work where the trunk lid has to be left open, the lid support should be locked in position. If the trunk lid were accidentally bumped upward, the support catch would release and the lid would bang shut with the grave danger of personal injury to anyone in the way.

The lid support may be locked securely in the open position, merely by inserting any suitable sized bolt or hook through the hole in the support as pictured in the illustration.

This exploded view of the front end assembly shows the various units and their relation to each other. It is also typical of the many new Shop Manual illustrations.

The trunk lid support must be locked in the open position with a bolt or rod to prevent it from closing accidentally during service.

1942-Series Service Notes

(Continued from page 205)

Front and Rear Suspension

The individual front suspension system used on 42-Series cars is essentially the same as that used on 41-Series cars. There are no changes in service procedures. The limits for adjusting the various factors of front wheel suspension such as caster, camber and toe-in remain the same.

The Hotchkiss drive with a hypoid rear axle is continued on 42-Series cars. All features of this type construction are the same. The rear stabilizer has been changed in its geometry to provide finer riding qualities.

The same rear axle ratios used on the 41-Series cars are continued on the 42-Series. These are listed as follows: A 3.77 to 1 ratio is used as standard equipment on a 42-61, 62, 63 and 60S series cars; a different axle with this same ratio is used on 42-67 and 75 series cars equipped with Hydra-Matic Drive; a 3.36 to 1 "Economy" ratio is optional equipment on 42-61, 62, 63 and 60S series cars, and standard equipment on cars of these series equipped with Hydra-Matic Drive; and a 4.27 to 1 ratio is standard equipment on 42-67 and 75 cars.

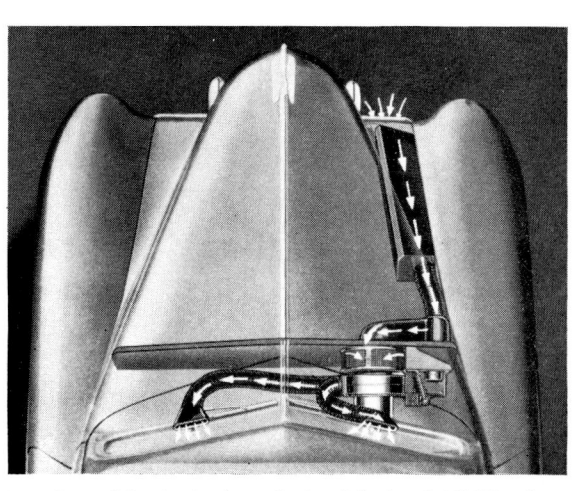

The flow of fresh air through the right hand All Weather Ventilator and the Automatic Heating System Defroster is shown by the white arrows.

The rebound valves on all 42-Series shock absorbers are fitted with special collars which centralize the shock absorber valve springs. By centralizing the valve springs, any tendency toward squeaks is eliminated. Valves containing this collar can be identified by a vee groove in the valve cap (illustration above right).

Brakes

Although the hydraulic braking system

(Continued on third column)

Proper Methods of Checking Spring Heights Discussed

WHEN CHECKING SPRING HEIGHTS on 41-Series cars, Servicemen should check the car against the specifications given in the 41-Series Shop Manual. Spring heights for both front and rear springs on all 41-Series cars are given in the manual and a ¾" variance between left and right front springs, and a ½" variance between left and right rear springs is permissible.

When complaints of low spring heights are received, and before any replacement is attempted, Servicemen should check to see that shock absorbers are filled with oil and that the sheet metal parts or bumpers are not aligned too low on one side simulating the appearance of weak springs.

Metal shims, Part No. 1433474, are available to raise front springs within the proper limits on all 41-Series cars. The installation of these shims will bring the springs back to a level position between the left and right sides. However, no more than 3 shims per spring should be used.

A slight difference in height between right and left side, front or rear can sometimes be corrected by reversing the springs from right to left, etc.

If a 41-Series car is low at the rear, and the condition is found to be due to habitual overloading, the only correction would be the installation of heavier springs which is the owner's responsibility and not covered by the Warranty.

Rear spring sag on 41-67 and 75 Series cars may be corrected by the removal of the ¾" shims with which the cars are originally equipped as explained in the December, 1940, issue of the SERVICEMAN.

Heavier front or rear springs are available at the factory Parts Department upon special request. When ordering heavy-duty springs Partsmen should be sure to specify the actual weight on each wheel, left and right, front and rear, of the car when it is carrying the load usually carried, engine number and body style.

1942-Series Service Notes

(Continued from first column)

used on 42-Series Cadillac cars is similar to that used on the 41-Series, a number of changes have been made. Among the more important of these are a new hand brake control and adjustment and new dust seals at the brake drums.

The new seal, called the "labyrinth"

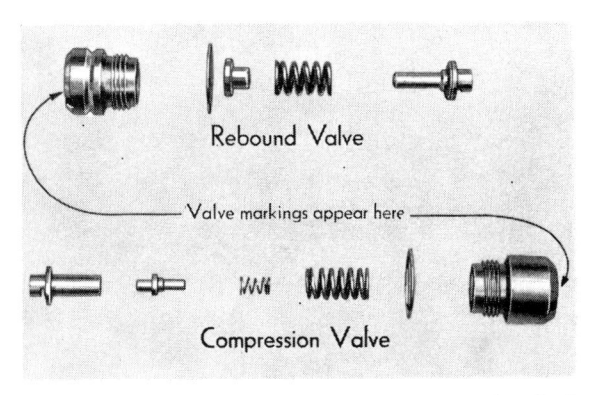

The small collar (upper center) centralizes the shock absorber rebound valve spring and prevents valve squeaks.

seal because of the intricate path which keeps water from getting into the brakes, is cast into the brake drum. Besides effectively sealing the brakes against water, the "labyrinth" seal increases the exposed area of the brake drum, thus increasing heat dissipation and reducing "fading" at high speeds.

Rubber plugs are now used over the brake adjusting holes to provide a better seal against water leaks.

The new hand brake lever has a tee handle mounted on the instrument panel at the extreme left that is much more accessible than the previous lever handle. The tee handle is pulled straight out to apply the brakes, and a ratchet arrangement automatically holds it. To release the brake, the lever is twisted counter-clockwise, which releases the ratchet and allows the lever to return to the released position.

Engine

The powerful 346-inch V-8 engine is used on all 42-Series cars with several improvements to provide increased performance and economy.

The pistons in 42-Series engines are the same as those used on the last 41-Series engines. Although the use of these pistons does not require any changes in service operations, they are fitted to different limits as specified in the new Shop Manual. Two piston compression rings and two oil control rings are used as heretofore.

(Continued on page 207)

Mechanical Features of the 42 Cadillacs
(Continued from page 206)

The crankshaft and connecting rods used on 42-Series cars are heavier and more rugged than ever before. For this reason the 42-Series rods and crankshafts are not interchangeable with past models.

An important change is found in the long connecting rod bolt. This bolt now has a $^{15}/_{32}$—24 thread, instead of the $^{7}/_{16}$—24 thread, which is still used on the short bolt. It is extremely necessary that no past model long bolt be interchanged with the new 42-Series long bolt. Although a $^{7}/_{16}$—24 bolt could be installed, the fit is very poor.

The most outstanding single change in the engine is in the cooling system, where a new blocking-type radiator thermostat

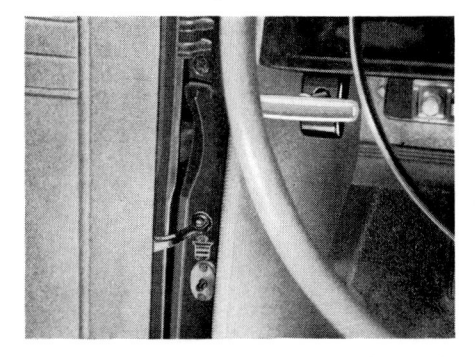

The new "Labyrinth" brake seal not only provides a positive seal against water but aids heat dissipation as well.

The handy emergency brake handle locks automatically in position when pulled out to engage the brakes.

is incorporated in a new hot water return elbow. The hot water return hoses from each cylinder to the radiator inlet are joined together and enter the radiator in the center of the upper tank.

When the engine is cold, the blocking type thermostat prevents the solution from flowing through the radiator. Instead, the liquid is bypassed from the left cylinder block back to the water pump and is recirculated through the cylinder blocks. As the engine warms up the thermostat allows more and more liquid to circulate through the radiator and maintains the engine temperature in the most desirable range.

A detail change in the water pump is the use of only three chevron packings. Recent investigations have shown that the spring loading on the packings is more effective when only three are used. *In addition, only three packings will be supplied in the service parts kit, as they are satisfactory for all past models.*

The exhaust manifolds used on 42-Series engines are ribbed to restrict the flow and so increase the heat of the exhaust gases. This provides better heat-ing to the heated section of the intake manifold and better choke thermostat performance.

Stromberg carburetors are used on the 42-Series cars. A Carter carburetor of new

(Continued on page 208)

Sticking Carburetor Float Causes Engine to Stall

THERE HAVE BEEN a few instances in which the solder covering the vent hole in the Stromberg carburetor float has contacted the side of the float bowl, causing the float to stick. This solder is added to plug the vent hole after the float is assembled.

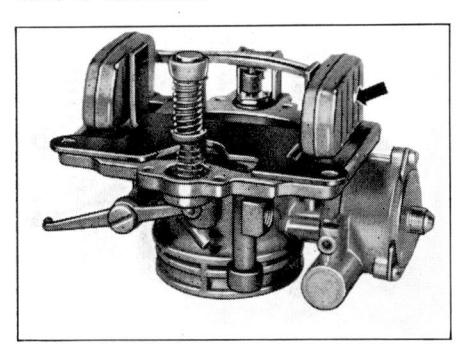

Arrow points to soldered vent hole on carburetor float

Some complaints regarding flooding and stalling have been traced to this cause. The clearance between the carburetor float and the float bowl should be checked whenever flooding and stalling is encountered and no other cause is apparent.

In some cases it may be possible to correct this condition by filing away some of the solder at the vent hole so as to prevent its contacting the wall of the float bowl. It may be, however, that the floats are adjusted too close to the bowl, in which case the arm connecting the float should be bent slightly to provide sufficient clearance.

SLOW IDLE ADJUSTMENT IS MADE WITH SELECTOR LEVER IN DRIVE

WHEN SETTING THE SLOW IDLE speed on either Stromberg or Carter carburetors on all Hydra-Matic equipped 1941, 42, 46, and 47 Series Cadillac cars, the adjustment should be made with the selector lever in DRIVE and the r.p.m. set at 375 with the engine at operating temperature and on slow idle.

Although our shop annuals do not state whether the selector lever should be either in NEUTRAL or DRIVE, it has been found that the idle speed drops about 30-50 r.p.m. from NETURAL to DRIVE, so that if the r.p.m. was set at 375 in NEUTRAL, the drop in r.p.m. to DRIVE would increase the tendency to stall the engine. Servicemen should note this change in their copies of the Shop Manual.

42 Engine Oil Level Gauge Has Been Recalibrated

THE ENGINE OIL LEVEL gauge plunger on 42-Series Cadillac engines is calibrated to show "Full" when seven quarts of oil have been added after the engine crankcase has been drained. This is, in other words, a "re-fill" calibration.

On 41 and previous series V-8 engines, however, the plunger was calibrated to show "Full" when seven quarts are added to a "dry" engine—that is, right after an engine has been assembled.

In consequence, the addition of seven quarts of oil to a 41 or previous engine after draining will bring the oil level slightly above the "Full" mark. This extra oil is not sufficient to cause aeration

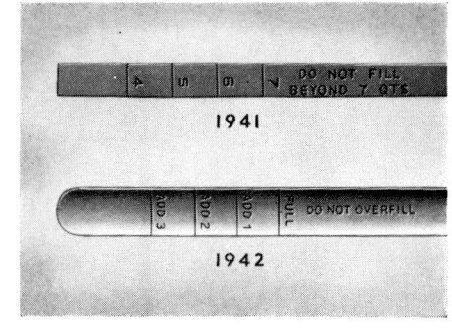

The 1942 engine oil level gauge reads full when exactly seven quarts have been added after draining the oil.

of the oil supply or other harmful effects.

When adding oil between changes on 41 and earlier series cars, however, Servicemen should be sure to fill the crankcase only up to the "Full" mark. This will minimize the possibility of the crankcase being overfilled.

The Cadillac Serviceman — *October, 1941, Page 41*

Service Information on the 42-Series Cadillacs

design will also be used optionally. Service information on the Stromberg carburetor is in the 1942 Shop Manual, but information on Carter will be released at a later date.

Transmission

The inertia type syncro-mesh transmission used on 42-Series cars is exactly the same as that used on the 41-Series. The shifting mechanism is entirely new, however, and requires new service procedures.

The shifter lever on the steering column is shifted into low, second, etc., in the usual manner, but the shifting mechanism is concentric with the steering column, thus giving a much neater, more compact appearance.

The shifter lever is pivoted on a carrier which is mounted below the steering wheel hub, so that the carrier revolves with the shift lever as the crossover from low and reverse to second and high is made, but does not move up and down with the lever.

The various parts of the new thermostat and radiator inlet elbow are shown in this exploded view.

The inner end of the shifter lever is connected to a yoke, which in turn is connected to the shifting tube. Thus, the shifting tube moves up and down and rotates as the position of the shifter lever is changed.

Slots cut into the shifting tube close to its lower end engage one of the two keys in the shifting levers mounted loosely in the steering jacket as the shifting tube is moved up or down. Rotation of the shifting tube then causes the shifting levers to rotate.

The two shifting levers are connected to the transmission by control rods so that when the shifting levers rotate the transmission shifts from one speed to another.

Several improvements in the Hydra-Matic Drive have been made for 1942. The selector lever shifting mechanism, which operates the manual control valve and reverse linkage, is entirely new, being similar to the shifting mechanism on the standard transmission.

A new front oil seal housing and oil seals are used in the 1942 Hydra-Matic Drive, which minimize oil leakage.

The flywheel cover is now doweled to the flywheel in addition to the cap screw mounting, to provide a definite location between the flywheel and cover.

Another improvement is the riveted joint between the torus members and torus hubs. By riveting the hubs to the torus members a much more rigid joint is obtained.

A new type intermediate shaft and new output shaft thrust washers are other changes that have been made in the Hydra-Matic.

The Hydra-Matic service information is now included in the regular Shop Manual.

Fuel and Exhaust

The fuel and exhaust system has remained unchanged with a few exceptions. The exhaust manifolds are ribbed to provide better heat to the carburetor stoves, as explained in the Engine Section.

The gasoline tank filler neck is inside the left rear fender and is reached by lifting the top section of the tail lamp body. A new feature is the Cadillac Gas Cap Lock, an accessory which is concealed underneath the tail lamp body and uses the same key as the trunk and glove compartment locks.

Steering

The efficient recirculating ball type steering gear, which proved so successful in the 1940 and 1941 cars, is used again in all 42-Series cars. A new worm adjusting nut is incorporated, which makes for an easier adjustment. Another improvement in the steering gear is the use of larger balls than last year.

Wheels and Tires

Wheel shields are now standard equipment on all 1942 Series cars. The mounting attachment of the shields has been improved and the removal and installation procedure simplified accordingly.

To remove all wheel shields, except the

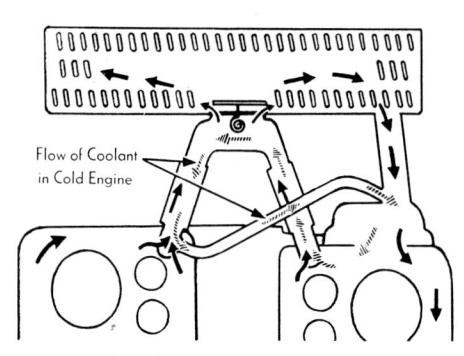

In a cold engine the water is blocked from the radiator by the thermostat and is by-passed back to the water pump.

42-75, it is merely necessary to turn the hex head nut (same size as wheel stud nuts) clockwise and lift the lower edge of the shield outward and upward. Installation is the reverse of the removal. The 42-75 wheel shields are removed and installed in the same manner as the 41-Series shields.

(Continued on page 209)

« » »

Fill All Shock Absorbers When Removed for Service

INFORMATION IS GIVEN in the Shop Manuals and in the July, 1941, issue of THE SERVICEMAN as to the correct procedure for adding fluid to shock absorbers while they are mounted on the car. Whenever shock absorbers are removed from the car for service, they should be completely refilled on the bench before reinstalling them in the car.

The way to bleed shock absorbers out of the car is, first, to fill the shock absorber with as much fluid as possible while holding it in the horizontal position. Then reinstall the filler cap and check the movement of the arm.

If there is any free movement in the arm between compression and rebound strokes in the *center* of the arm travel, this indicates air in the shock absorber. In such cases, place the shock absorber on end and pump several times; then remove the upper end cap and add fluid until the shock absorber is completely filled. Recheck the arm for free movement after the end cap has been replaced, and repeat the operation if necessary.

This method of bleeding shock absorbers should also be employed when difficulty has been experienced in bleeding shock absorbers on the car.

Service Information on the 42-Series Cadillacs

A sturdy heavy duty, bumper-type jack is used on all 42-Series cars. This jack has an exceptionally wide base for greater stability. The jack handle also serves as a wheel wrench and wheel shield remover.

Electrical

The electrical system of the 42-Series cars remains much the same as the highly efficient 41-Series system. Smaller generator pulleys are used, however, to provide an increased charging rate for extreme conditions.

A new type 3-position illuminated ignition switch is featured on the new cars. When the key is turned to the left, accessories such as the heater, radio and instruments are on but the ignition is off. When the key is in the center, accessories, instruments and ignition are all off. When the key is turned to the right, everything is turned on. Owners should be carefully instructed on this feature.

This 3-way system has the advantage of being able to play the radio and run the heater while the car is stopped and ignition turned off and yet the accessories cannot be accidentally left on when the ignition key is removed.

Sealed Beam headlamps are used on the 1942 Series Cadillacs to provide the maximum in lighting efficiency. The combination headlight light and instrument light switch is continued on the 42-Series. Pulling the control knob out turns on the headlights and revolving the knob turns on, brightens, and dims the instrument lamps.

The various auxiliary lights supplied as accessories, combined with the standard Sealed Beam headlamps, make probably the most complete set of lighting equipment ever offered to the public. These lights include the Fog Lights, the automatic Back-up Light, and the Cadillac Spotlight.

The tail lamp arrangement on 42-Series cars is new in that the tail and stop lights are in a separate compartment than the signal lamp and have separate lenses. Another new feature is the condensing lens with which the lights are fitted.

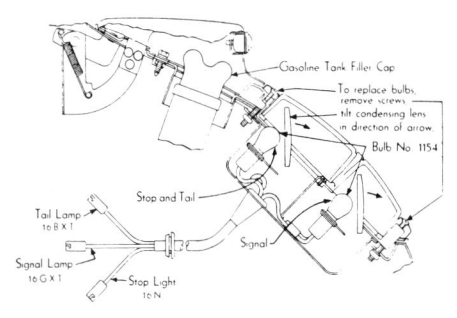

The directional signal assembly (bottom) is now entirely separate from the tail and stop light assembly (top).

These condensing lenses direct the light in a horizontal direction and compensate for the slanting outer lens. Assembly and disassembly of the rear lamps are new, and are completely described in the Shop Manual.

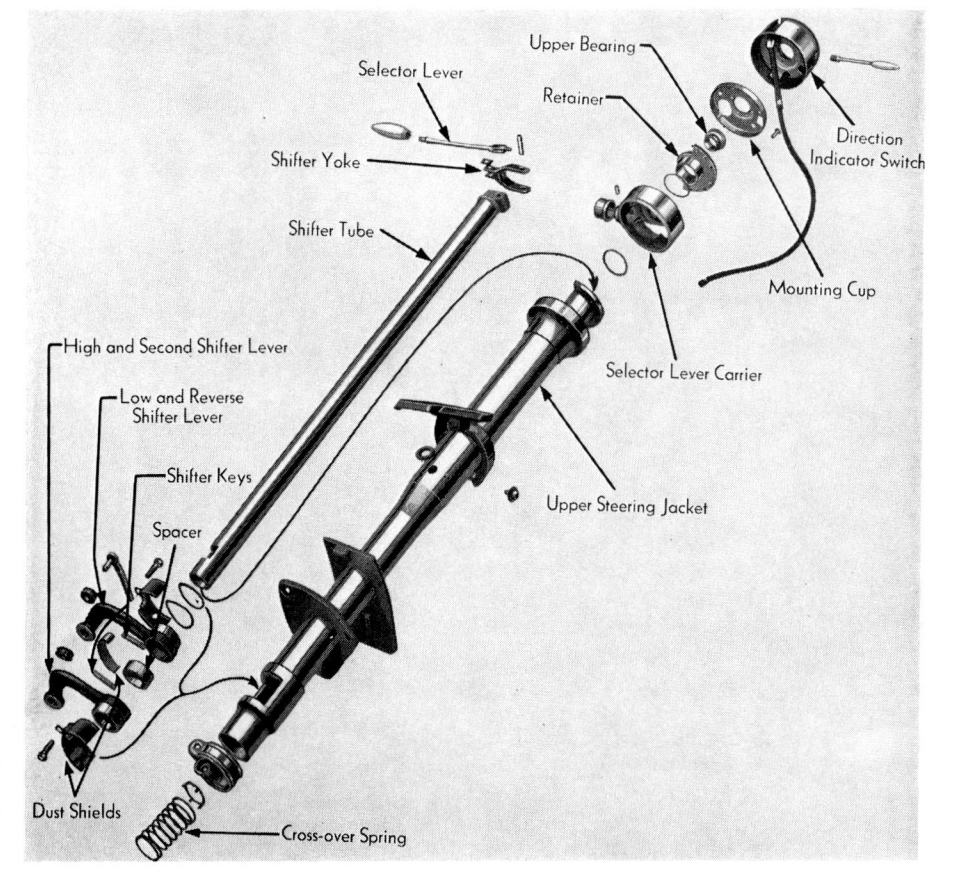

Cadillac Inhibitor Prevents Formation Of Rust & Scale

ALL SERVICEMEN are familiar with the fact that much of the rust and scale which can accumulate in the cooling system occurs during the summer season. This is due largely to hard and fast driving during hot weather, which causes the cooling system to operate at higher temperatures with increased aeration or bubbling. This bubbling is the strongest contributing factor to scale and rust formation.

In addition, when owners are touring, during the vacation season, they may have to add water which contains numerous minerals that cause formation of scale in the cooling system.

A cooling system which has been treated with Cadillac Cooling System Inhibitor will never be troubled with rust or scale formation as long as the inhibitor is left in the system. Servicemen should stress to each of their new and old car owners alike, the advantage of using Cadillac Cooling System Inhibitor. Cadillac Cooling System Inhibitor is installed in all new cars at the factory and should be made a regular part of the conditioning procedure in the spring and fall tune-up campaigns.

In addition, Servicemen should be on the lookout for owners who are going touring during the summer. The subject of Cooling System Inhibitor should be mentioned again to each one of these owners to make sure that their car's cooling system is protected against rust and scale.

The shifting mechanism for both the standard transmission (shown) and the Hydra-Matic Drive is concentric with the steering column, providing a neat, compact installation readily accessible for service.

Carter Carburetor of New Design Used In Some '42 Engines
Complete Service Information Is Given In This Article

THE FIRST 42-Series Cadillac cars shipped from the factory were equipped with Stromberg carburetors, and the 1942 Shop Manual contains service information only on the Stromberg carburetor.

Since that time, however, an entirely new Carter carburetor has been developed, and is now used on some of the cars being shipped. This new carburetor, Carter Type WCD, is illustrated below.

The WCD carburetor is similar in principle to the Carter carburetor used in 1941, but with several important changes. The first of these is the use of double floats which provide better control of the fuel level. Another is the addition of a sight plug for checking the float level. Still another is a change in the anti-percolating feature which eliminates the need for a separate adjustment.

Engine Starting

When starting a cold engine on cars with Carter carburetors, the accelerator should be pressed slowly to the floor boards and released *before* cranking engine. This will set automatic choke correctly. This procedure is the same as for Stromberg carburetors and previous model Carter carburetors.

Idling Adjustment

1. Run engine until it is thoroughly warm so that choke valve is wide open and throttle stop screw on slow idle.
2. Set throttle stop screw so that engine speed approximates 7 to 8 m.p.h. in high gear on level road.
3. Adjust two idling adjustment screws so that engine runs smoothly without loping or stalling at this speed. Turn screws clockwise to lean mixture and counter-clockwise to enrich mixture.

Float Level Adjustment

A sight plug is provided for checking the float level without disassembling the carburetor. This plug is so located, however, that the correct level is up to the centerline of the hole. This means that a small quantity of gasoline will spill out when the plug is removed. **Because of this, the level should *not* be checked while the engine is running.** If level is incorrect:

1. Remove upper body assembly and float bowl cover and disengage metering rods by removing metering rod arm pins.
2. Invert float bowl cover, holding needle seat away and float in horizontal position.
3. Measure distance between metal rim for cover gasket and nearest point of float. Be sure gasket is removed.
4. Bend lip on float lever if measurement shows improper setting. The correct float level setting is $9/64$". A new tool, No. J-1884, Carter No. T 109-160, is available from Hinkley-Myers for measuring this distance.

Automatic Choke Adjustment

If initial and part throttle running mixture is too lean or too rich, revolve thermostat housing as indicated on housing face. Ordinarily, choke setting mark in housing should be set exactly opposite large mark on carburetor flange.

Metering Rod Adjustment

The metering rod adjustment is slightly different than that on the 41-Series Carter carburetor in that it requires the use of new gauges. The procedure is as follows:

1. Remove metering rods and washers at top of metering rod chambers.
2. Insert the two metering rod gauges, tool No. J-1883, Carter No. T 109-163, length identification 2.940, in place of the metering rods. Be sure gauges seat in metering jets.
3. Press metering rod pin carrier down until pins rest on shoulders of notches in both gauges.
4. Back off throttle stop screw until throttles are completely closed.
5. The center bracket on the metering rod pin carrier should now touch metering rod arm. If necessary, bend arm until it just makes contact.
6. Remove gauges and reinstall washers, metering rods and springs.
7. Before reinstalling cover, put a drop or two of a light oil and graphite mixture into the two screw holes.
8. Readjust throttle stop screw.

Slow and Fast Idle Adjustment

1. Make sure that correct slow idle adjustment (7 to 8 m.p.h.) has been made.
2. With fast idle screw resting against high lobe of fast idle cam, check clearance between throttle lever adjusting screw and carburetor casting stop.
3. Adjust clearance to final setting of .015" for correct operation.

Dechoking Adjustment

1. Check distance between upper edge of choke valve and wall of carburetor upper body when throttle is fully open.
2. Measure opening, which should be approximately $3/16$" and bend lip on fast idle connector rod that contacts choke trip lever, if it is necessary to change position of valve.

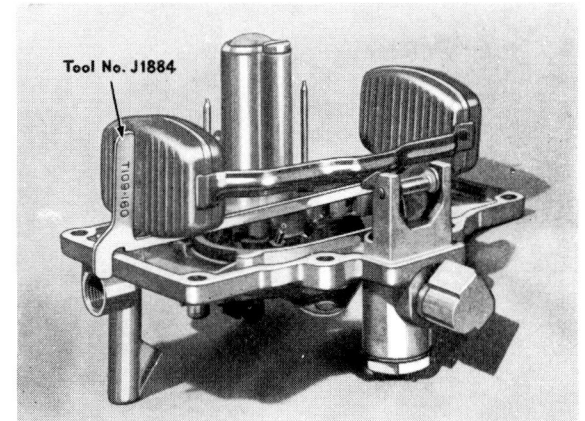

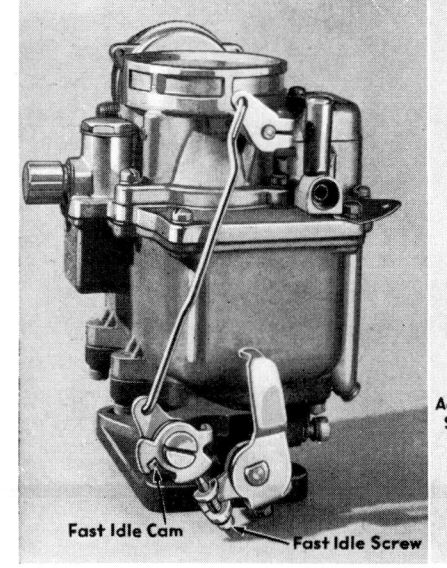

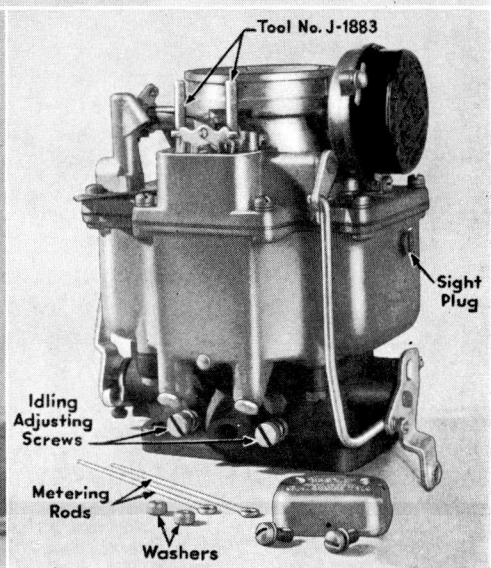

These views of the new Carter Carburetor show (lower left) the fast idle connections, (lower right) the metering rod adjustment, and also the float level sight plug and the idling adjustment; and (upper right) the float level setting, using the gauge.

Proper Procedure for Storage of New Cars Is Required to Provide Maximum Protection

WITH THE LARGE NUMBER of new cars now being put in longtime storage, it is important that servicemen understand thoroughly the procedures to be followed in properly preparing cars for storage and the necessity for each of the steps recommended.

Servicemen are well aware of the fact that the deteriorating effects of idleness are much more harmful to a car than the wear brought about by normal usage. It is well, therefore, that they acquaint themselves with all the things that should be done to help prevent or minimize the ill-effects of longtime storage. Too much emphasis cannot be placed on the thoroughness of the storage preparation procedure because one overlooked operation may result in many dollars of damage.

Preliminary Preparation

The first step in properly preparing the car for storage is to clean the car thoroughly inside and out, as well as underneath. This is necessary to remove grease, grime, mud, tar, salt and any other foreign substance that may be present and which could cause harm if not removed.

A thorough chassis lubrication is then advised, although it is not always necessary. If the car has been standing idle for some time before storage or, more particularly, if it has been subjected to the weather, the lubrication should be performed.

Tires

After the car has been cleaned and lubricated as necessary, it should be driven to the spot where it will be stored. If this is a dark, cool place, it will not be necessary to remove the wheels and tires. All that will be required for adequate protection is to raise the car on jack stands (horses) so as to release the weight from the tires.

In the event the storage place is not dark and cool, the tires and wheels should be removed, wrapped and stored in the basement or some other suitable location. Whether left on the car or stored in the basement, it will not be necessary to deflate the tires before storage.

In order that the car jack stands normally used in the shop will not be tied up with car storage, it is advisable that temporary stands be procured. An inexpensive stand is illustrated below. Detailed instructions for making these stands locally were given in General Service Letter No. G. S. 423.

Fuel System

In preparing the fuel system for storage, the gasoline tank should be completely drained and the filler cap should be reinstalled to prevent the entry of dust.

All the gas should be removed from the carburetor by the following procedure: Disconnect the gasoline line at the fuel pump, start the engine and allow it to run at a speed slightly above idle until all the gasoline has been pumped out of the fuel pump (approximately two minutes). Just before the engine runs completely out of fuel, pour one-half pint of 20-W engine oil into the carburetor air intake rapidly enough to stall the engine.

On cars equipped with Stromberg carburetors, both of the carburetor main discharge jet plugs should be removed and all the gasoline allowed to drain out of the carburetor. The throttle valve should also be opened rapidly two or three times right after draining the carburetor to make sure the accelerator pump is properly drained. The plugs should then be reinstalled.

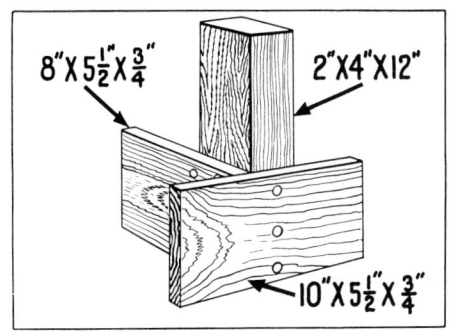

This type of car jack stand has been found very satisfactory for storing cars.

On cars equipped with Carter carburetors, the entire carburetor must be removed, turned upside down to drain it completely and reinstalled.

Clutch

To prevent the clutch-driven disc from rusting or sticking to the flywheel or the pressure plate, the clutch pedal should be held in a released position by blocking it down between the pedal and the underside of the toe-board, using a small piece of wood.

Cooling System

The cooling system should be completely drained by opening the drain cock at the bottom of the radiator as well as the drain cocks on both cylinder blocks. All drains should be left open to permit the circulation of air.

All hose connections, including the heater hose and also the windshield wiper blades, should be removed, wrapped in heavy paper and stored in a dark, cool place.

Battery

The battery should be removed from the car and stored separately, preferably in a battery room where it can be given regular attention and occasional recharging. Batteries in storage should be checked at six-week intervals and recharged at any time the specific gravity falls below 1.220. If the battery is not properly cared for, the plates will become sulphated and the battery will be useless.

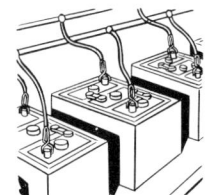

Brakes

In order to prevent the brake lining from adhering to the brake drums, it is necessary that the hand brake control be left in the fully released position.

Chrome-plated Parts

All chrome-plated parts should be thoroughly cleaned and covered with a light coating of vaseline, light chassis lubricant or wax in order to prevent rusting and pitting.

Body

The preparation of the body is vitally important because improper preparation may result in faded or moth-eaten upholstery, faded finish, deteriorated rubber weatherstrips, etc.

After thoroughly cleaning the upholstery, a moth-proofing treatment should be applied. This may be of the liquid type or crystal type, but in either case a well-known brand of moth preventive should be used for maximum protection.

If the cars are in storage for a prolonged period of time, a second moth-proofing treatment may be required, depending on the type of chemical applied and the recommendations of the supplier.

If the car is not to be completely covered with a special car cover, all the windows should be covered with heavy wrapping paper fastened in place with masking tape to prevent the sunlight from fading the upholstery.

(Continued on page 212)

Car Storage Procedure
(Continued from page 211)

All rubber weatherstrips around doors, ventilators and trunk openings should be coated with DuPont Orel to counteract their tendency to dry out when not in use.

Doors and ventilators should not be closed tightly but should be left resting lightly on their openings or, in the case of body doors, they should be left on the safety catches in order that the rubber will not be kept under compression.

Floor mats should be thoroughly cleaned and left in their normal position on the floor.

Wherever possible, it is suggested that a car cover be applied in order to protect the complete car from dust and light.

The tops of convertible cars should be left in the raised position and should be completely covered with the shipping covers or with heavy paper taped securely in place.

The list of precautions which must be taken in properly preparing a car for storage is rather long but each of the steps recommended must be performed if the cars are to be fully protected while stored.

Servicemen should remember that these cars will eventually go into the hands of Cadillac owners and proper preparation *now* will mean better satisfied owners *later*.

Shop Manual Corrections

SINCE the distribution of the 1942 Shop Manual some two months ago, many sharp-eyed Servicemen have been checking up on the editor and have discovered several items that require correction. Please mark these changes in your personal copy of the Shop Manual.

On page 11, the Series 67 gasoline tank capacity is incorrect. The correct capacity is 20 gallons, which is correctly given on page 141.

The body styles, as listed on page 18, are correct and complete, but some of the style numbers are incorrect. The correct style numbers appear in the 1942 Body Parts List, announced elsewhere in this issue.

The illustration of the disassembled front wheel mechanism on page 116 is incorrect in that it shows the type of brake seal that is used on 41-Series cars. The 42-Series brake seal is explained and illustrated on pages 39 and 40 of the October, 1941 "Serviceman".

Removing Oil Pan Sludge Is A Vital Preventive Service

PERHAPS THE MOST noticeable harmful effect that restricted, low-speed driving has had on cars is the increased tendency for sludge to form inside the engine.

Water vapor or steam is a normal by-product of gasoline combustion (each gallon of gasoline upon burning forms over one gallon of water). Under normal operating conditions, the engine temperatures become sufficiently high to drive this moisture out of the exhaust system and also to "dry up" moisture which may have entered the crankcase.

With the many short trips being made today, however, this moisture is not dried out completely. As it accumulates in the crankcase, it mixes with foreign substances and oil to form a sludge.

While a small amount of sludge formation in the crankcase is not harmful, this condition, if allowed to continue, may increase the amount of sludge to the point where it will interfere with proper lubrication of the engine.

For this reason it is strongly recommended that the engine oil pan be removed and cleaned at least once a year. Since sludge formation is accelerated by the colder winter weather, it is particularly important that the oil pan be cleaned at this season of the year.

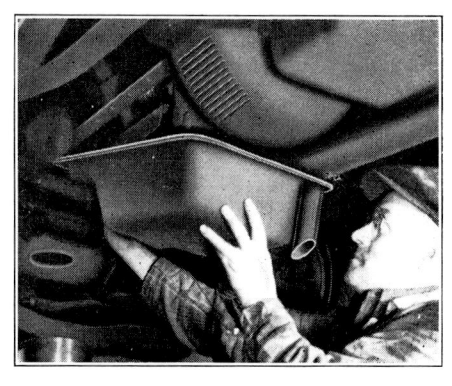

Removing and cleaning the oil pan should be recommended to every owner.

Whenever excessive sludge formation is found in an oil pan, it is well to clean the engine lubricating system and the valve chambers thoroughly.

When cleaning the oil pan, it is important to clean with kerosene or its equivalent the copper gauze in the crankcase ventilating breather cap and to re-oil this breather by dipping it in engine oil.

Service men would do well to recommend this engine oil pan cleaning operation to all owners who come in for their winter conditioning work. This "ounce of prevention" will do much to forestall engine failures in the future.

« »

Lacquer and Enamel Finishes Now Used Instead of Chrome

AS ALL SERVICEMEN probably know, car manufacturers have been restricted in the use of chrome for car part finishes in all cases with the exception of bumpers and bumper guards. To conform with these restrictions, Cadillac has produced an entirely new line of cars in which lacquer and enamel are used to finish parts that were previously chrome-plated.

Cadillac engineers and artists spent much time and effort in selecting the right finishes and the proper colors for the affected parts, with the result that the new cars not only present an appearance equal to the first 42-Series cars, but many believe that the present finishes add materially to the beauty and dignity of the new Cadillac cars.

No Mechanical Changes

Although the appearance of the new cars has been changed, no mechanical changes are incorporated.

To help Servicemen distinguish between the two series, all cars on which chrome was used extensively for finish on appearance parts will be referred to as the "42A" Series. All cars on which lacquer and enamel are used in place of chrome on appearance parts will be referred to as the "42B" Series.

A complete list of both the "42A" and the "42B" Series is shown below:

Series	Wheelbase	Starting Engine Number
42A-61	126"	5,380,001
42A-62	129"	8,380,001
42A-63	126"	7,380,001
42A-60S	133"	6,380,001
42A-67	139"	9,380,001
42A-75	136"	3,380,001
42B-61	126"	5,386,001
42B-62	129"	8,386,001
42B-63	126"	7,386,001
42B-60S	133"	6,386,001
42B-67	139"	9,386,001
42B-75	136"	3,386,001

Failures Of Starting Motor Traceable To Ground Strap

ONE OF THE first things to check when complaints are received regarding failure of the starter to turn the engine over easily is the engine ground strap.

There have been several cases in the field in which trouble of this nature has been traced directly to a worn or broken ground strap.

Ground straps usually break at the terminal, and the installation of a new one is therefore required. The ground strap must also be replaced if it shows signs of wear at some other point.

Many Factors Must Be Given Consideration When Diagnosing and Correcting Vapor Lock

IN RESPONSE TO several inquiries from Cadillac service men, the following article regarding the causes and the correction of vapor lock has been prepared.

Vapor lock is caused by boiling of the gasoline in the fuel supply system and many factors must be considered when attempting to correct this condition.

In any discussion regarding vapor lock it is important to remember that the nature of a fuel itself, as well as atmospheric pressure, can help to cause this condition.

Some fuels have lower boiling points than others, the boiling point being the temperature at which the fuel will vaporize. During the winter, fuels with a low boiling point are used to assure proper starting. These same fuels are sold in the spring season until the stocks are depleted, which explains why vapor lock is more prevalent during that time of the year.

Most of the fuels furnished today, however, have a relatively high boiling point, and no trouble should be experienced with fuel systems that are in proper operating condition.

Atmospheric pressure directly affects the boiling point of a fuel. The lower the atmospheric pressure the lower the boiling point. Thus in extremely high altitudes, where the atmospheric pressure is low, gasoline will boil at temperatures as low as 100°F.

How Vapor Lock Occurs

Vapor lock usually occurs in the fuel system between the fuel pump and the gasoline tank, or within the fuel pump itself. What happens is that the suction of the pump reduces the pressure on the gasoline, which in turn results in a reduction of the boiling point of the fuel.

The pump, instead of drawing gasoline only from the line, draws a combination of solid fuel and vapor. Then when the pump attempts to force the fuel to the carburetor it compresses the vapor and does not deliver a sufficient amount of fuel. On the next suction stroke the vapor expands, greatly reducing the efficiency of the pump.

The efficiency of the average fuel pump when pumping gasoline that vaporizes easily is none too good, but if the entire fuel system is at peak operating efficiency it will usually handle such vapor as is formed, plus a sufficient quantity of fuel to start and operate the engine.

Any factor which further contributes to the inefficiency of the pump, however, may cause vapor lock. Some of these factors, together with the proper corrective measures, are described in the balance of this article.

Inspect Connections and Lines

Any leakage or restrictions in the connections and fuel lines between the fuel tank and the pump may cause vapor lock and/or hard starting. The connections and lines should be inspected first in the event of hard starting or improper operation caused by vapor lock. The points to check are as follows:

Pick-up tube inside tank (rare)
Coupling at fuel tank
Coupling in middle of fuel line (some models)
Fuel line between tank and pump (cracks or dents)
Fittings at pump
Flexible connections (check for twisted, flattened or swollen connections)
Non-standard fuel filter or gascolator other than that on the pump (these should be removed)

Carburetor and Fuel Pump

The next things to check are the carburetor float valve and the fuel pump exhaust valve. The efficiency of these valves is determined by installing a pressure gauge, with absolutely air-tight connections between the pump and the carburetor.

Run the engine until the pump reaches its maximum operating pressure, which should be from 3½ pounds to 5½ pounds. When the engine is stopped the pump should maintain this pressure for several minutes. If it does not, gasoline is leaking either at the carburetor float valve or back through the fuel pump valves.

Leaks at the carburetor float valve will cause flooding, for there is always the possibility that the engine will stop at the extreme of the fuel pump stroke, with one entire pump stroke discharge being forced into the carburetor.

To determine whether the leak is in the pump or the carburetor, duplicate the above test with the gauge on the pump only, doing it so that there is no discharge of gasoline to the carburetor.

If the pressure is then held for several minutes, it indicates that the carburetor float valve is leaking. If the pump does not hold the pressure, the leak is in the pump valves or the diaphragm.

If the above inspections and tests reveal that the carburetor float valve, the lines and the fuel pump valves and diaphragm are satisfactory, the trouble may still be caused by inefficient operation of the pump.

Checking Capacity of Fuel Pump

In such cases, the capacity of the fuel pump must be checked. Make this test according to the procedure described on page 53 of the 1942 Shop Manual. Complete instructions for inspecting and servicing a pump that does not deliver the proper amount of gasoline were included in the March-April, 1944, issue of the Serviceman.

With these inspections made and any necessary corrective service performed, the fuel system should function properly, providing the engine is not overheating and that the vehicle is not being used for some unusual service, such as towing a heavy trailer.

1936 Through 1939 Series Cars

The fuel pump used on 1940 and later series cars is different in design from the pump used on 1936 through 1939 V-8 engines. The later pump has a higher output and better cooling and vapor handling characteristics, and in most cases can be installed on earlier series cars by making special lines. It is recommended that this be done when vapor lock cannot be corrected by using normal methods.

To install this pump on 1936 through 1939 V-8 engines, a special 30-inch piece of copper tubing should be used. This tubing must be bent as required, cut to length, the fittings installed and the ends flared. The tubing is supplied with the pump as an assembly, under Part No. 1097176.

This later pump is available on an exchange basis, as explained in General Service Letter No. GS-316, and is definitely an advantage in sections of the country where heat and elevation are extreme.

Under extreme conditions it may also be advisable to insulate the fuel lines to the pump. This is especially true of the line in the engine compartment on the intake side of the pump and that portion of the line that is near the muffler on those series cars in which the fuel line and muffler are on the same side of the car. Electrician's loom, known as Romax, is ideal insulating material for this purpose.

THE CADILLAC Serviceman

NOVEMBER 1945

VOLUME XIX NUMBER 10

ANNOUNCING THE NEW Cadillac For 1946

The new Cadillac cars for 1946 will be available in ten body styles, in the following four series:

Series	Wheelbase	Starting Engine Number
46-61	126″	5400001
46-62	129″	8400001
46-60S	133″	6400001
46-75	136″	3400001

The 1946 Cadillac car has many features that mark it as the most improved Cadillac ever built. Production has been started with the series 46-62 Four-Door Sedan, and at the start of production only this body style will be produced. Other body styles will be forthcoming soon.

The changes in the 1946 series Cadillac cars group themselves into appearance and mechanical items. Extensive changes have been made, although they require very few new servicing procedures. The changes are covered in detail in the following paragraphs:

Appearance

The radiator grille has been changed to accent horizontal lines, and create a lower car appearance; the front and rear bumpers are extended around the fen-

214

ders for added protection; new trim mouldings, new type Cadillac radiator and trunk emblem, and a lower, sleeker radiator ornament are other changes that head the list.

A very important service feature of the new bumpers is their three-piece construction. The center bumper bar or either of the ends of the bumper can now be replaced separately, in case of collision damage.

Numerous improvements increase body life and reduce the need for body service.

Body

A number of changes have been made in the Cadillac car bodies to increase body life and reduce the need for service. The interior sheet metal surface of all body panels, doors, and other parts below the body belt line are now painted to reduce the possibility of rusting through.

Areas where moisture might collect, such as rocker sills and bottoms of doors, have had ventilating louvres added or enlarged. Rear panels have been increased in metal thickness for rust and corrosion resistance. Water drain slots have been enlarged and all joints where water or road salts might collect are now sealed with caulking compound.

With the lifting of material restrictions, all mouldings have again been changed to either stainless steel or plated die castings. The chrome plating throughout the car has been increased in thickness to resist corrosion.

Other improvements include door lock striker plates with hardened surfaces and safety catches with double retention ears, added clamps for the door weatherstrips, and sturdier inside door lock controls. Rubber mounted bronze bushings in the windshield wiper pivots give longer life and quieter operation.

Brakes

A synthetic rubber bellows seals the joint between the cable and the sheath of the parking brake and prevents entry of water that, in freezing weather, would prevent the hand brake from being released after a short parking period. A waterproof lubricant is forced into this sheath to eliminate moisture collecting in the cable and to reduce friction drag.

Engine

Many new improvements have been incorporated in the 1946 Cadillac engine as a result of the application of the Cadillac V-8 engine to various types of military vehicles.

The main and connecting rod bearings are greatly improved by the use of Morraine Durex-300 type bearings. These are steel-backed shells with a matrix of copper-nickel alloy and a thin overlay of high quality babbitt. This process results in better bonding of the babbitt to the steel-back and increases the life expectancy of the bearings.

The new piston, of three-ring design, has greater resistance to fatigue. The rings are lowered on the piston to provide increased resistance to scuffing, and the oil ring has larger slots to obtain better oil control and economy than was possible with the prewar design that used two oil rings.

Valve guides are ferrox-treated for quieter operation and to prolong valve guide and stem life. The valve guide counterbore has been increased 3/16-inch in depth and 1/16-inch in diameter, to improve resistance to valve sticking.

The fan and generator belts are of a new type, heat and oil resisting, synthetic rubber. The new type synthetic rubber belts have been used on military equipment during the war and have demonstrated a greater durability than prewar belts.

A new Cadillac-designed inertia oil fitting provides cleaner oil for the valve lifters. Pressure from the high velocity oil stream forces oil to make a right angle turn into this fitting. The heavier dirt particles which sometimes cause trouble by lodging in the hydraulic valve lifters bypass the inertia fitting thus insuring a cleaner supply of oil to the valve lifters.

The carburetor has been improved in many respects to resist sticking of choke and throttle shafts due to gasoline with high gum content.

An improved accelerator pump provides more positive pump action, thus improving acceleration.

The choke mechanism is improved by using a chrome-plated shaft mounted in narrow support bearings, which reduces the sticking tendency when there is a slight gum deposit on the shaft. The choke heater stove on the exhaust manifold is of a new design and the position of the heater stove has been changed from the left to the right manifold. This change provides sufficient heat to assure constant choke control during the warm-up period, and insure no choke operation after the warm-up.

The throttle controls have been redesigned for cars with Hydra-Matic drive to provide a more simple and accurate linkage adjustment. The accelerator pedal and linkage have been changed on all models to reduce likelihood of pedal sticking and to make car operation smoother and easier. One type accelerator pedal is now used for all models.

Full details of the Hydra-Matic Drive improvements are described on page 41.

Engine water hoses are made from heat resisting rubber and incorporate an extra ply of fabric at the clamps on the outside diameter to prevent the hose clamp from embedding, causing leakage and loss of coolant.

The new labels quickly identify Blue Coral as part of the Cadillac line of cleaners and polishers.

Hydra-Matic Improvements

The Cadillac Hydra-Matic Drive on 1946 Cadillac cars has been greatly simplified and improved as a result of use in military vehicles.

One of the most important improvements is a hydraulic blocking valve on the reverse mechanism to keep the anchor from engaging while the reverse gear is turning. This eliminates the main cause of gear clashing when shifting into reverse. The new reverse anchor has also been redesigned to avoid butting of the anchor teeth on the reverse internal gear.

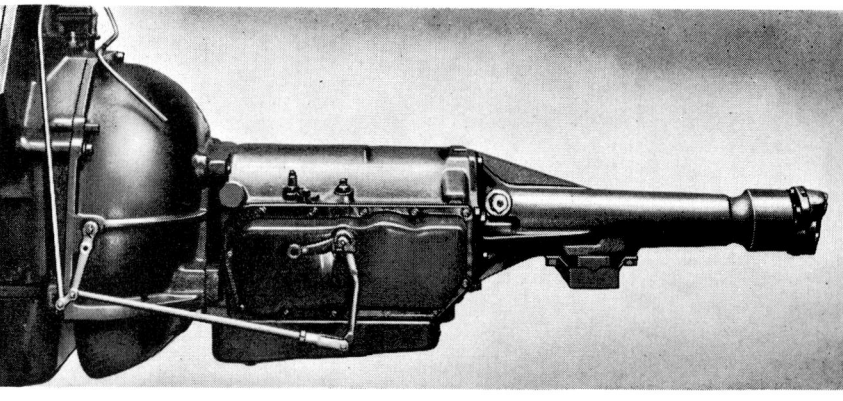

The rear planetary unit now has only a single reduction; the front and rear unit bands are larger for greater strength, and stronger anchors are used on both the front and rear bands. Front and rear bands are now ground to the proper shape and, therefore, should not be twisted out of shape when removing or installing.

Front oil pump noise has been overcome by the use of a newly designed internal-external type gear pump. The new oil pump has a greater capacity and maintains a more uniform control of the operating units. Longer life can be expected from the new oil pump, as the cross shaft and cross drive gears have been eliminated.

The slight whirr sometimes heard when starting previous Cadillac cars equipped with Hydra-Matic Drive has been eliminated in the 1946 series Cadillac cars by changing the fin spacing of the torus member from even to uneven.

The 1946-series Hydra-Matic Drive has been simplified and improved.

Another important improvement contributing to smoother Hydra-Matic operation is the single, hydraulically-operated piston in each clutch. One piston, measuring $5\frac{1}{8}''$ in diameter, is used in place of the six pistons of $1\frac{1}{2}''$ diameter used in previous models.

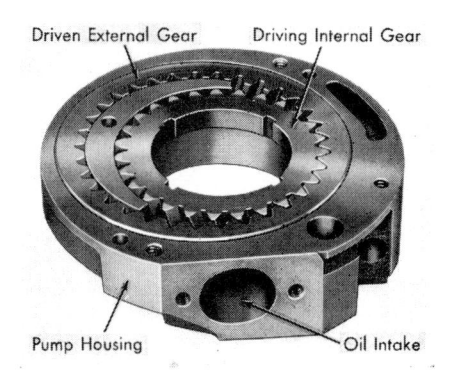

The internal-external gear front oil pump provides greater oil delivery with less wear and noise.

The use of non-metallic facings on the clutch drive plates permits a smoothing out of the shifts. Life of the plates is also increased.

Clutch and Standard Transmission
No changes have been made in the clutch or the standard Syncro-Mesh transmission.

Front Suspension and Steering
The steering gear and front end suspension of the 1946 Cadillac cars are the same as the 1942 series Cadillac cars.

Rear End Suspension
The rivets which attach the ring gear to the differential case have been increased in size. On commercial chassis, heavy duty bearings are used in the rear wheels.

Wheels and Tires
Tires of synthetic rubber will be used on all 1946 series Cadillac cars. No wheel change has been made.

The new reverse anchor incorporates a blocking valve to prevent clash when shifting into reverse.

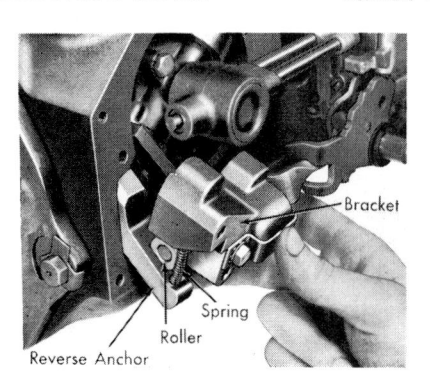

The Hydra-Matic bands must not be twisted out of shape when removing or installing them.

Parts Repair Kits Simplify Water Pump Overhaul

THE INTRODUCTION of spring-loaded, chevron-type water pump packings in the 1937 Cadillac and LaSalle cars was a major step forward in reducing leakage through the elimination of the troublesome job of adjusting water pump packings at frequent intervals. The spring-loaded water pump can run for thousands of miles before any attention other than lubrication is required.

When a water pump does require servicing, however, it is very important that servicemen inspect and repair the pump carefully in order to restore the new-car standards which originally existed.

When overhauling the spring-loaded type of water pump, used on all V-8 cars since 1937, first completely disassemble the pump. The pump body should be cleaned, and inspected for cracks or other damage. Machined surfaces, particularly bearing and bushing bores, should be inspected for nicks or burs.

The impeller and shaft should be inspected, and discarded if any of the following conditions are found to exist: 1) badly corroded impeller vanes, 2) impeller loose on shaft, 3) bent shaft, or 4) shaft badly scored, grooved from packing, or corroded.

If thorough inspection indicates that the impeller and shaft and the ball bearing are suitable for further use, the serviceman should then obtain and install all of the parts included in the Water Pump Packing Kit (Part No. 109 7122). If, however, the impeller and shaft require replacement, the serviceman should obtain and use all the parts included in the Water Pump Overhaul Repair Kit (Part No. 109 7413).

For ready reference, the contents of each of these kits is listed below:

WATER PUMP OVERHAUL REPAIR KIT (Part No. 109 7413)
1 106 749   Key
1 954 301   Ball Bearing
1 109 6696 Impeller with Shaft
3 140 3956 Packing
1 141 1203 Gasket
1 141 1243 Ring, outer
1 141 1244 Collar
1 141 1248 Spring, packing retaining
1 141 1982 Retainer, wire, inner bearing
1 143 4264 Retainer, wire, ball bearing
1 143 7012 Bearing, inner (rear)
2 144 1416 Ring, inner

WATER PUMP PACKING KIT (Part No. 109 7122)
1 106 749   Key
3 140 3956 Packing
1 141 1203 Gasket
1 141 1243 Ring, outer
1 141 1248 Spring, packing retaining
1 141 1982 Retainer, wire, inner bearing
1 143 4264 Retainer, wire, ball bearing
1 143 7012 Bearing, inner (rear)
2 144 1416 Ring, inner

Correct Number of Packings

Servicemen will note that only three packings are included in the two water pump kits. Only three should be installed when overhauling the water pump, regardless of the number found in the pump when it is disassembled.

Through early 1942-series and in early 1946-series Cadillac cars, four packings were used in the water pump. Late 1942-series and all future cars will have only three packings—sufficient to provide a tight seal, the spring satisfactorily taking up the difference in total thickness of the packings.

Correct Packing Installation

When assembling the water pump, extreme care should be taken to install the inner (rear) bearing assembly parts in the correct order. Parts are of the chevron type, and a water-tight fit is possible only if parts are in the correct order and if the chevrons face the right direction (see illustration).

When installing the impeller shaft, the special tapered pilot (Cadillac Tool No. J 831) should be fitted on the end of the shaft, and the locking ring slot in the pump shaft should be filled with tape, which can be smeared lightly with water pump grease, to prevent damage to the packings by the slot shoulders. String or a lead ring may also be used temporarily to fill the locking slot until the shaft has been installed.

After the pump has been fully assembled, it should be thoroughly lubricated with water pump lubricant and the impeller shaft rotated by hand to make sure the bearing is completely lubricated.

Servicemen who carefully follow the suggestions above in overhauling water pumps will save much time and reduce the possibility of comebacks.

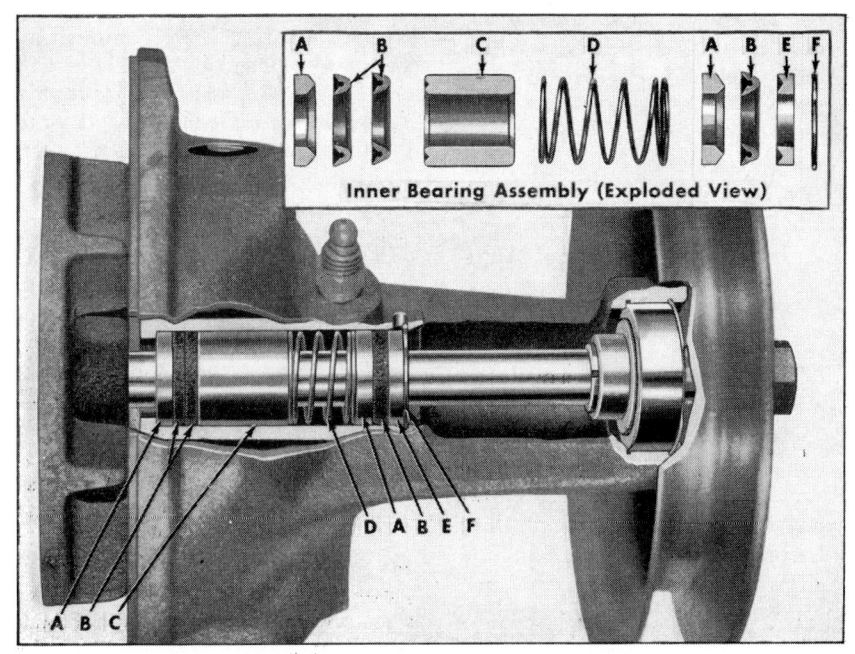

KEY: A—Inner Ring (2), B—Packing (3), C—Inner Bearing, D—Packing Retaining Spring, E—Outer Ring, and F—Wire Retainer.

ANNOUNCING THE 1947 Cadillac IMPROVEMENTS

Cadillac's line of quality cars for 1947 will soon be in Distributorships and Dealerships throughout the country. These cars will be known as the "47" Series, individually designated as follows:

Series	Wheelbase	Starting Engine No.
47-61	126″	5420001
47-62	129″	8420001
47-60S	133″	6420001
47-75	136″	3420001

The 1947 Cadillac car has many features that continue to mark it as the automobile industry's car of distinction. The improvements in the 1947 Series Cadillac cars group themselves mainly into appearance and mechanical items, and require very few new servicing procedures.

Servicemen know that the first requisite of a successful service business is to know the product. For this reason, the major improvements and developments in the 1947 Series Cadillac are presented here.

Appearance

The spacing between the horizontal grille bars has been increased and the number of bars reduced from six to five. The new horizontal bars are larger, huskier, longer, and give a much neater appearance to the grille. All of the horizontal bars, except the top header bar, are stampings, which means lower maintenance costs. Small extensions to the top header bar have been added on the front fenders. The vertical bars are the same, except that they will be made of stainless steel and chrome plated after approximately the first 2,000 1947 Series cars.

The 1947 Series Cadillac may be equipped with combination fog, parking and directional signal lamps. When no fog lamps are installed, a plate with a combination round parking and directional signal lamp in the center covers the fog lamp opening. The lamp itself is surrounded by a heavy die-cast ornament which harmonizes with the grille design. The plate, ornament, and round lamp make a very pleasing appearance on those cars so equipped.

The combination parking and directional signal lamps use the standard 21-3 double filament bulb. There are two bulbs in the fog lamps. One is a No. 55 parking bulb, and the other a 32-21 candlepower fog and directional signal bulb.

The rubber stone guards which were used on 1946 rear fenders have been discontinued in favor of stainless steel stone guards which are chrome plated to harmonize with the rest of the chrome parts. The rocker sill extensions are also chrome-plated stainless steel.

Appearance of the 1947 Series carpet has been considerably improved. Small, round grommets, edged with chrome mouldings, surround the steering column, clutch and brake pedals. This gives a very trim and neat appearance to the front compartment. New Car Conditioning men should be careful in engaging the carpet under the chrome mouldings so as to give a good, neat appearance. The improved carpet will be installed on all 1947 Series 60 Special, and after the first few hundred cars of all other Series.

A new hood emblem and a new rear deck lid emblem are used on the 1947 Cadillac. The new hood emblems tie in the "V" with the Cadillac crest. The deck lid emblems consists of a wing below a crest. The Cadillac name on the front fenders will be a one-piece unit written in script.

Brakes

An improved emergency brake cable conduit is used on the 1947 Series Cadillac cars. The brake cable and coil spring around the cable are tightly enclosed by a new synthetic rubber tube, thus eliminating any water leakage into the cable, and minimizing the possibility of freezing. The 1946-type rubber bellows is used on the front end of the tube.

Engine

One of the major improvements in the 1947 Series engine is the inclusion of hydraulic valve lifters which have hardened ball seats. This improvement was of such value that it was put into production in the late 1946 series cars.

This hardened seat, together with the hardened ball, decreases the possibility of dirt sticking between the ball and seat, thereby permitting better seating of the ball. The ball cage of the lifter is also hardened. Hardening the ball seat and the cage provides controlled ball travel.

The shape of the ball seat has also been changed. The 1946 Series seat had a concave surface contacted by the ball, with a seating width of about 1/32 inch

(Continued on page 219)

January, 1947 — The Cadillac Serviceman

CHANGES IN 1947 CADILLAC CARS

(Continued from page 218)

in some cases. The new seat has a convex radius at the ball contact area so that the seating width averages about 0.004 inch. The line contact, of course, has more ability to crush or move aside anything that resists seating of the ball.

A new oil filler tube is used which decreases the sharp bend of the oil level indicator. The oil level indicator and the filler cap remain the same.

Hydra-Matic Transmission

A new upper bearing retainer to eliminate wear on the selector lever stops in the retainer will be used on cars equipped with the Hydra-Matic Drive. The new retainer is still a die-casting, but incorporates a hardened steel pin which is used as a selector stop from Drive-to-Low step and the Low-to-Reverse step.

The early 1947 Series Hydra-Matics will be identical with the improved 1946 series Hydra-Matic transmissions. A constant product improvement and development program is being carried on in Cadillac Engineering and the Detroit Transmission Division on the Hydra-Matic, and changes will be made as approved. Any changes on 1947 Hydra-Matics will be announced in THE CADILLAC SERVICEMAN.

The new 1947 Series accessories will be announced in the next issue of THE CADILLAC ACCELERATOR.

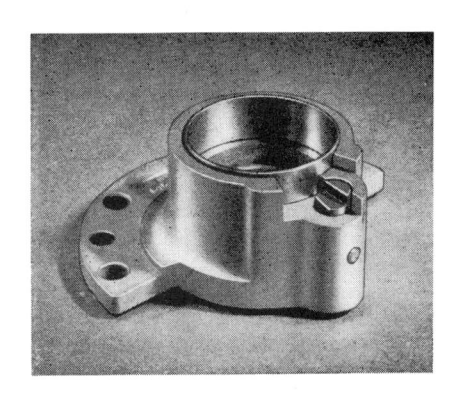

1947 Upper Bearing Retainer

LOCATING CAUSES OF OIL ON DISTRIBUTOR CONTACT POINTS

WHENEVER THE DISTRIBUTOR SUPPORT is removed from an engine for any reason, Servicemen should check to make sure that the oil drain-back hole in the support is not plugged. This hole extends from the chamber above the upper bearing in the distributor support to a cast relief in the mounting surface.

If Servicemen find oil on the distributor contact points, they should examine the oil drain-back hole to see if it is blocked.

A check should also be made of the crankcase ventilating system and on the clearance between the distributor drive shaft and the drive shaft bushings in the support. The maximum clearance between the drive shaft and the bushings in the support should not exceed 0.005 inch.

The crankcase air inlet in the engine oil dip stick cap and the crankcase air outlet at the rear of the crankcase and engine oil pan should be examined for any dirt or other foreign substances which might restrict the free circulation of air, causing a pressure, rather than the normal depression (partial vacuum), in the crankcase thus forcing oil past the distributor support bushings, as well as the piston rings, front cover oil seal, etc.

EFFECTIVE WITH THE 1947 SERIES 60 Special and 62 Engine Numbers listed below, the notch at the top of the steering tube which indicates the high spot of the steering gear was moved 180 degrees from its former location:

Series	Engine No.
62	8422446
60S	6420770

When the steering wheel is in the straight-ahead position, the notch is now on the *lower* side of the tube, as shown in the illustration, instead of the upper side, and should line-up with the middle steering wheel spoke to minimize the possibility of mispositioning the steering wheel with relation to the notch on the steering tube.

At the time this change becomes effective on the 1947 Series 61 and 75, it will be called to the Servicemen's attention.

REAR DOOR SAFETY LOCK NOW SET AT FACTORY FOR POSITIVE LOCKING ACTION

THE REAR DOOR LOCKS on 1940 through 1946 series 4-door sedans have a safety feature which permits locking the rear doors by means of the safety latch button so that the rear doors cannot be opened by either the inside or outside door handles until the safety latch button is raised.

This safety feature, covered in detail on page 31 of the August, 1946, SERVICEMAN, reduces the possibility of small children accidentally opening the doors either while the car is being driven, or when it is parked. Because of the popularity of this feature, it is now being used in all sedans in production.

Listed below are the first body numbers of the 1946 series sedans which had this safety feature on the rear door locks set at the factory. That is, the rear door handles on cars built after body numbers listed *will not* open the door when the safety latch button is depressed:

Body Style	After Body No.
6069	2786
6109	1913
6269	10853
7519	81
7523	71
7523L	9
7533	35
7533L	6

Owners should be advised of this change, and their preference for locking action learned. This information will forestall any difficulty which owners may experience in trying to open the rear doors when the safety latch button is depressed.

« »

Use of Bumper Jack

IN USING a bumper jack of any type on Cadillac cars, three precautions are advisable:

1.) Set the parking brakes and put the car in low gear.
2.) Block the car wheel diagonally opposite the one being changed.
3.) Position the jack just inside the bumper guard (or bracket) with the shaft of the jack slightly towards the center of the car.

When selling bumper jacks of any type or when advising on the use of these jacks, the above cautions should be outlined to aid in safe, quick use.

THE CADILLAC Serviceman

SEPTEMBER 1947

VOLUME XXI   NUMBER 9

NEW PROCEDURE FOR CLEANING CADILLAC CYLINDER BLOCKS

Cars that have been in use for a long period may accumulate a considerable amount of rust and scale deposit in the water passages of the cylinder block.

In most cases, ordinary reverse flushing of the cylinder block, as prescribed in the Cadillac Cooling System Cleaner (Part No. 143 5736) instructions, will correct this condition. If an inspection of the cylinder blocks reveals that deposits of rust and scale remain after the cooling system has been cleaned with Cadillac Cooling System Cleaner, Servicemen should use the following procedure to correct this condition:

1. Remove one or two lower rear cylinder head cap screws which are located between the cylinder bores on both of the cylinder blocks.
2. Insert a long rod or tube through the bolt holes to the bottom of the coolant or water passage.
3. Remove the rod or tube and note the presence of any sludge clinging to it.

If rust and scale deposits are found in the cylinder blocks, the blocks themselves must be given a thorough cleaning. A good cleaning procedure for restricted cylinder block passages is as follows:

1. Remove water pump. The right block can be further checked for rust and scale deposits through the water pump opening.
2. Connect water supply to left cylinder head outlet.
3. Starting from the rear of the left cylinder block, remove the bolts in the lower row, insert Cylinder Block Air Gun, Special Tool No. J-1543 (See illustration), and blast with air. NOTE: This operation should be performed one bolt at a time.

This operation should be performed on each bolt on the lower and center rows on the left bank before proceeding to the right bank. The same procedure

Cleaning a Cadillac cylinder block with Cylinder Block Air Gun, Special Tool No. J-1543.

should be followed on the right bank except for the front bolt in both the lower and center rows, which need not be removed.

After this operation is completed on both sides of the cylinder block, all excess water should be drained by removing the hex-head brass plugs on each side of the cylinder block. Using a flashlight, Servicemen should examine the water passages in the cylinder block to make certain that all deposits of rust and scale have been completely removed. If some deposits remain in the water passages, the operation should be repeated.

If the radiator was not reverse flushed before removing the water pump from the cylinder block for this cleaning operation, it should be reverse flushed before the water pump is installed in order to prevent rust and scale deposits in the radiator core from finding its way into the now clean cylinder block.

When this has been done, Servicemen should install the water pump, using a new water pump gasket, and also install the hose connections which were removed for the cleaning operation. The cooling system should then be filled, making sure that Cadillac Cooling System Inhibitor has been added to the new cooling fluid.

The engine should then be run until its operating temperature is reached, at which time the cylinder head bolts should be checked for their proper torque tightness.

The new trigger-equipped Cylinder Block Air Gun, J-1543, complete with the extension nozzle which is used in the cylinder block cleaning operation, is priced at $3.35 and may be ordered from the Kent-Moore Organization, Inc., 5-105 General Motors Building, Detroit 2, Mich.

CONVERTIBLE REAR CURTAIN GLASS CAN BE REPLACED WITHOUT REMOVING THE CURTAIN

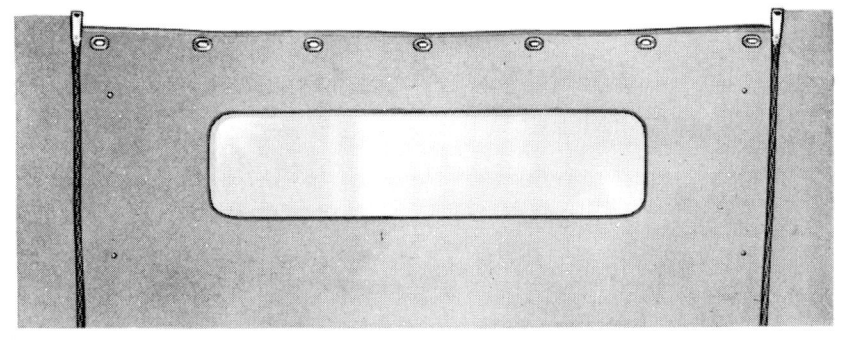

ORIGINAL APPEARANCE

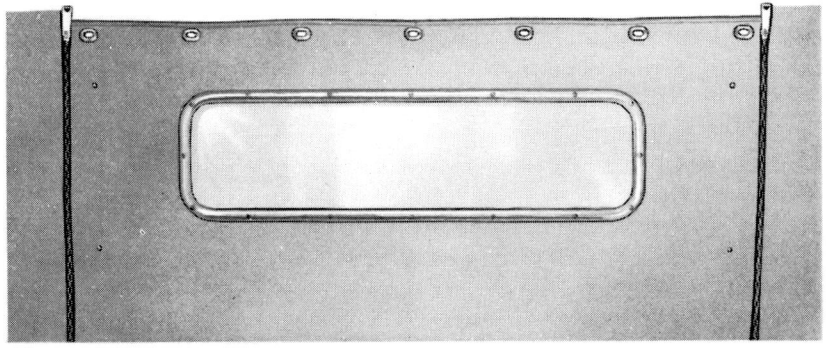

AFTER GLASS HAS BEEN REPLACED

IN ORDER TO PROVIDE Cadillac Servicemen with a method of replacing the glass in the rear curtain on a convertible coupe top without replacing the rear curtain, the factory Engineering Department has developed the following procedure:

1. Cut the rear curtain inner lining along the edge of the glass.
2. Remove Phillips Head Screws from inner glass molding.
3. Using a screwdriver as a guide, pry molding loose and remove.
4. Remove glass.
5. After the molding has been removed, it should be soaked in gasoline. This will remove excess lining and adhesive.
6. Install new glass.
7. Stretch inner lining evenly over the glass. Use small strips of masking tape to hold the lining in place and apply in such a way that the tape will not extend beyond the outside edge of the molding. Also, be careful not to cover screw holes with the tape.
8. Apply a thin layer of adhesive (3-M EC164) to the back side of the molding.
9. Install molding over the inside lining and glass.
10. Install Phillips Head Screws and tighten evenly.
11. Trim away inner lining, masking tape, and excess rubber molding.
12. Clean glass with white gasoline.

The illustration shows the inside of the rear curtain as it appears originally and also after the window glass has been replaced according to the procedure given above.

CHECKING THE HYDRAULIC BRAKE SYSTEM FOR LEAKS

A VITAL PART of a brake service job is checking the hydraulic system—inspecting all lines and seals for leaks and making sure the circuits and fluid are clean.

Whenever Servicemen find it necessary to overhaul the master brake cylinder and wheel cylinders on a Cadillac car, the hydraulic brake system should be flushed out with alcohol and the brake fluid renewed. Operation No. 5-67 covers this procedure.

In adding brake fluid or refilling the system, use only factory recommended Delco Super No. 9 Brake fluid, which may be ordered from the factory Parts Department in the one quart can size (Part No. 545 0285), one gallon can (Part No. 545 0286), or the five gallon can (Part No. 545 0288).

IGNITION COILS IDENTIFIED BY POSITION OF BOLT HOLES

1946-1947   1942 PREVIOUS

INCORRECT LOCATION OF WATER PASSAGES IN CYLINDER HEADS

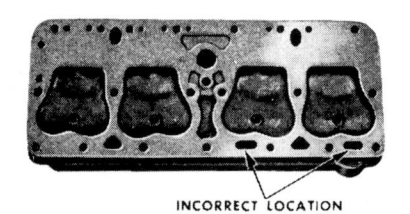

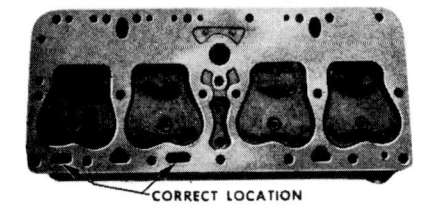

INCORRECT LOCATION

CORRECT LOCATION

IN CASE OF AN EXCESSIVE coolant loss and resulting overheating on early 1947 Series cars, the right hand cylinder head should be examined for proper location of the cored water passages in the mounting face. The illustration above shows both the correct and incorrect position of these passages. Right hand cylinder heads which have the water passages in the wrong location should be replaced.

A second cause of overheating may be traced to restricted water passages in the cylinder heads. It has been found that the cause of these restricted passages is due to core breakage during the casting process. When this condition is found by Servicemen, the cylinder head should be replaced.

Any cylinder heads replaced for the reasons above, should be returned to the factory on an AFA in the usual manner.

Cadillac

595-S Carter Carburetor

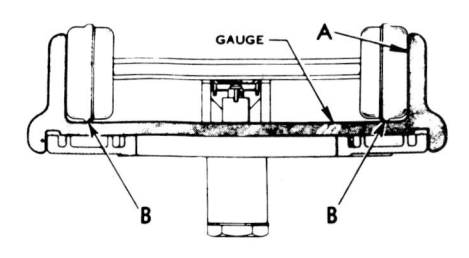

Float Adjustment

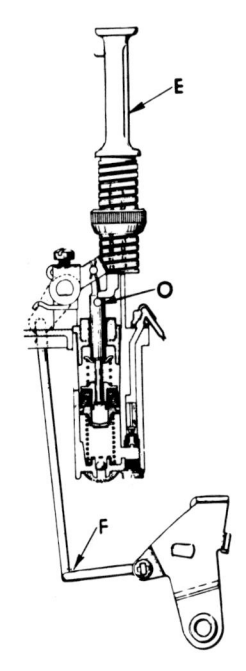

Accelerator Pump Adjustment

Illustrations by Courtesy of Carter Carburetor Corporation

IMPROVEMENTS IN CADILLAC CARBURETION AND MAJOR ADJUSTMENTS ON CARTER 595-S

DEVELOPMENT OF THE CARTER CARBURETOR for the 1946 and 1947 Series Cadillac cars has resulted in a number of changes in adjustments and specifications. As a help to Cadillac Servicemen, a summary of the improvements, major adjustments, and specifications of the Carter 595-S carburetor is here presented.

The Carter 595-S carburetor is of the dual, down-draft, climatic-control type—like all carburetors on Cadillac engines produced in recent years. Recalibration has materially increased the efficiency. The tendency toward off-idle leanness has been minimized by redesigning the idle port holes in the throttle body; too lean a mixture of gasoline and air could result in a loss of power.

The choke mechanism has been redesigned for consistent operation. A chrome-plated, under-cut choke shaft is used. The choke shaft support bearings have been narrowed to reduce the tendency to stick from dirt and gasoline deposits on the shaft. The choke heater stove was changed from the left to the right exhaust manifold, and redesigned to provide sufficient heat to assure consistent choke control during the warm-up period and to stop choking of the carburetor after the engine has reached operating temperature.

An improved accelerator pump affords more positive action and assures a constant fuel supply at all times.

Improvement of the carburetor has necessitated some changes in adjustments and in tools used in servicing it. The more common adjustments required to service the Carter 595-S carburetor are described below:

Float Adjustment

The float circuit maintains the correct fuel level in the fuel bowl, and thus controls the amount of fuel available to the other circuits of the carburetion system. Since proper operation of the carburetor cannot be had without an accurate float assembly adjustment, the following method of float adjustment is recommended:

Remove the bowl cover and gasket from the bowl, remove the gasket from the cover, and invert the bowl cover assembly with the float bracket resting on the seated needle. Place the Float Level Gauge, No. J-1884 (Carter No. T109-160), under the floats, with the short notched legs of the gauge fitted over the edge of the bowl cover, as illustrated. The gauge must be centered under the floats and seated firmly on the bowl cover at exact right angles with the machined surface of the bowl cover. The sides of the floats should just touch the vertical arms of the gauge at "A," and the floats should just clear the horizontal bar of the gauge at "B."

If it is necessary to adjust the floats vertically or horizontally, remove the gauge and bend the float arms, as required, with Bending Tool No. J-787. Regauge to determine if the adjustment is now correct, or if further bending of the arms is necessary.

The float assembly should have a free movement of ½ inch at the extreme free end of the floats. If it is necessary to reduce the free movement of the floats, bend the lip of the float bracket inward with a screwdriver. To increase the free movement of floats, first remove the float assembly and then bend the lip outward with Bending Tool No. J-787.

When floats have been properly adjusted, carefully remove the assembly, install a new bowl cover gasket, and replace the float assembly.

Accelerator Pump Adjustment

The total distance that the accelerator pump plunger (not the shaft) moves from the closed to the wide-open throttle position controls the amount of fuel discharged. Since the correct travel of the pump plunger is important to economical fuel consumption, this should be checked each time the carburetor is disassembled.

When the bowl cover assembly including the metering arm assembly, the throttle pump connector rod, the vacuum piston link, and the pump connector link have been installed, proceed to gauge the pump plunger travel. Back out the throttle lever set screw and the fast idle adjustment screw to allow the throttle valves to seat in the throttle body bores. Support the carburetor on a wood block, so that the throttle can be closed without the levers dragging on the bench top.

Place the Universal Pump Travel Gauge "E," Carter No. T109-117S, on the edge of the dust cover boss on the bowl cover, as illustrated. With the throttle valve closed, turn the knurled nut of the gauge until the finger just touches the pump connector link at "O" where it extends through the pump plunger shaft. Read the figure on the gauge at the inscribed line on the knurled nut.

Open the throttle slowly until the plunger bottoms in the pump cylinder bore. This occurs just beyond the point at which the throttle valves seem to be fully open. (Additional pressure on the throttle lever will be needed to compress the plunger spring.) Relocate the pump travel gauge and turn the knurled nut until the finger again touches the pump connector link where it extends through the pump plunger shaft. Read the figure on the gauge at the inscribed line on the knurled nut.

Carburetion

SPECIFICATIONS FOR CARTER 595-S

Float Level:
Distance from top center of seam on each float to lower edge of bowl cover, when needle is seated with or without gasket (Use Gauge No. J-1884, Carter No. T109-160) 9/64"

Vents in Air Horn:
Outside (2 holes).......No. 30 drill
Inside (2 holes).........No. 35 drill

Gasoline Intake: Square vertical needle
Needle seat........No. 38 drill

Low Speed Jet Tube:
Jet...................No. 70 drill
By-Pass..............No. 55 drill
Economizer..........No. 58 drill
Idle bleed...........No. 56 drill

Upper Idle Port:
Port opening (slot type): length 0.156", width 0.030", with 0.0635" diameter hole located 0.071" from top of port opening.
Port opening above upper edge of valve with valve closed tight ....0.100-0.106"

Lower Idle Port (For Idle Adjustment Screw):
Diameter..........0.0615-0.0655"

Idle Adjustment Screw:
Setting......... ½ to 1½ turns open
NOTE: For richer mixture, turn screw out. Do not attempt to idle engine below 375 R.P.M.

Metering Rod:
Jet......................0.089"
Setting (Use Gauge No. J-1883, Carter No. T109-163)......2.940"

Accelerator Pump:
Discharge jet (twin).....No. 70 drill
Intake ball check........No. 40 drill
Discharge (needle seat)..No. 53 drill
Plunger travel from closed to full open throttle position (Use Gauge Carter No. T109-117S)......27/64"

Choke:
Choke heat suction hole in bowl cover ....No. 42 drill

Vacuum Spark Port:
Diameter..........0.039-0.041"
Top of port above valve.0.033-0.037"

The difference in the two readings is the pump plunger travel, which is measured in 64ths of an inch. The correct pump plunger travel is 27/64 inch. If it is necessary to correct the travel of the pump plunger, bend the rod at the lower angle "F," as required, using Carter Tool No. T109-41B.

Metering Rod Adjustment

The metering rod position must be synchronized with the throttle valve position so that the proper ratio of air and gasoline for all speeds and driving conditions is delivered through the intake manifold to the combustion chambers. The setting of the metering rods should be checked each time the carburetor is disassembled, or whenever rods are replaced.

Install Metering Rod Gauge, No. J-1883 (Carter T109-163, 2.940"), in place of either metering rod, with the notch on the gauge under the upper cross-arm of the vacuum piston link and facing away from the accelerator pump. Be sure that the gauge seats properly in the metering jet. Check the throttle valves to make sure that they are fully closed, and press down on the vacuum piston link "A" until lip "D" just touches the metering rod arm "C." The bearing on the vacuum piston link cross-arm "B" should just touch the shoulder in the notch of gauge, or clear it by not more than 0.005 inch.

Metering rod adjustment can be corrected by bending the metering rod arm, using Bending Tool No. J-787.

Remove the gauge and install the two metering rods and discs. Hook the ends of the metering rod spring around the metering rods and lubricate the countershaft through the dust cover attaching-screw holes with "Lubriplate" or light graphite grease. Install the dust cover.

Unloader Adjustment

Install the air horn and climatic control assembly. Install the fast idle connector rod.

Two adjustments are necessary to insure the correct unloader or dechoking setting:

1. Loosen the choke lever and screw assembly "G" on the choke shaft. Insert a 0.010 inch flat feeler gauge, Carter No. T109-71, between the inward tongue on the fast idle cam and the boss on the flange casting "H." With the choke valve tightly closed, hold the cam snugly against the gauge and tighten the choke arm clamp screw "G."

2. With the throttle in wide open position, there should be 3/16" clearance between upper edge of the choke valve and the inner wall of the air horn "J". Check by inserting Unloader Gauge, Tool No. J-818-3 (Carter No. T109-28), between the upper edge of the choke valve and the inside wall of the air horn. To correct this clearance, adjust the unloader lip "K" on the throttle shaft lever, using Bending Tool, Carter No. T109-41.

Fast Idle Adjustment

Insert an 0.018" wire gauge, Carter Tool No. T109-44, between either throttle valve and the bore in the throttle body, on the side "M" opposite the idle adjusting screws. With the choke valve tightly closed, adjust the fast idle adjusting screw "L" against the high step on the fast idle cam "N" until the gauge just slides free. If necessary, change this setting slightly to satisfy a few car owners.

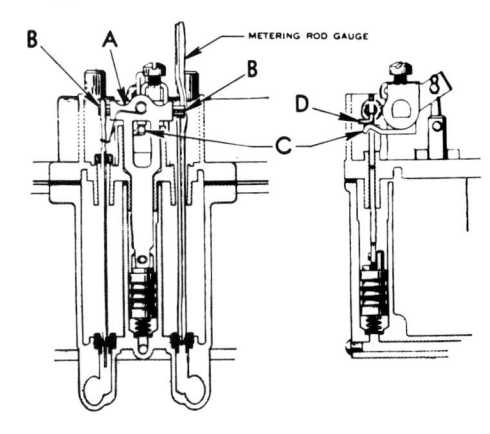

Metering Rod Adjustment

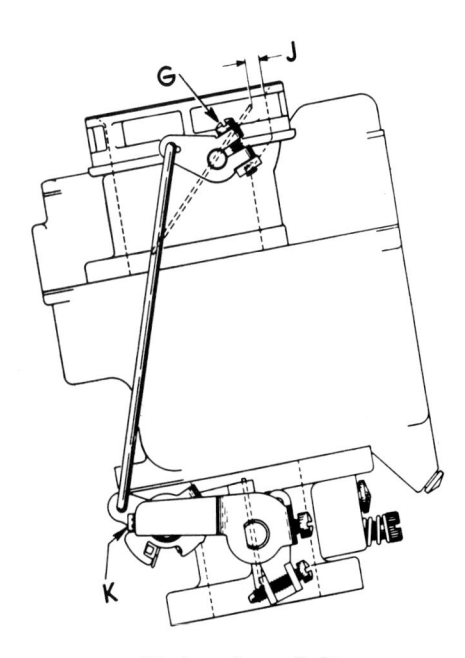

Unloader Adjustment

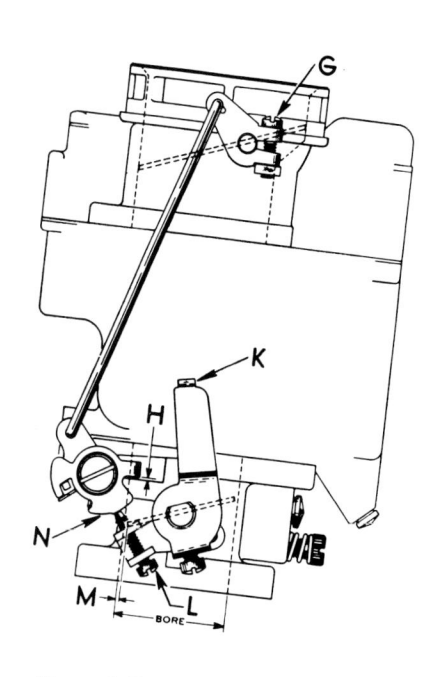

Fast Idle Adjustment

THE CADILLAC Serviceman

MARCH 1948

VOLUME XXII NUMBER 3

ANNOUNCING The 1948 Cadillac

Cadillac's 1948 program introduces a completely new line of luxurious automobiles, styled to post-war appearance. Rich in beauty of appointments and outstanding in mechanical excellence, Cadillac cars again reflect traditional engineering advancements.

Cadillac Servicemen will be primarily interested in the differences between the 1948 car and its predecessors. The important changes follow below so that Servicemen will be ready to do their part when these cars appear in their area.

The 1948 Series Cadillac cars are individually designated as follows:

Series	Wheelbase	Starting Engine No.
48-61	126"	486100000
48-62	126"	486200000
48-60S	133"	486000000
48-75	136"	487500000
48-76 (Comm. Chassis)	163"	487600000

Servicemen should note the change in engine numbers for 1948. The first two numbers of the engine number indicate the model year, while the next two numbers indicate the series. The last five numbers indicate the order in which the cars were built. This change in engine numbers will enable Servicemen to identify the model and series of the car without further reference.

The New Body

The new body has a completely restyled front end and a lower and wider radiator grille and hood. The front bumper style is changed to complement the body. The side view shows long, unbroken lines from front to rear bumper with the fenders blending into the extended sides of the body. At the rear end, there is a definite rise to the "rudder type" rear fenders. The windshield glass and the rear window glass are curved and, combined with narrow pillars, provide a greater range of vision.

Windshield Wiper

The windshield wiper motor now has more power. The wiper blades press harder against the windshield, resulting in a better cleaning job. The wipers are cable operated and are quiet when in operation. The wiper arm carries a flexible blade and therefore can follow the curved windshield glass closely. If a windshield washer is ordered as an accessory, its control button will be located in the center of the wiper control knob.

Trunk Hinges

The trunk hinges are counterbalanced so that the lid stays up without support, increasing useful trunk space. The trunk lid seal is on the lid, leaving the gutters open for better drainage. The two trunk latches swing across the car instead of fore and aft so luggage can be placed all the way back against the latches with no danger of operating interference.

(Continued on page 225)

224

The Cadillac Serviceman — *March, 1948*

CADILLAC PRESENTS THE NEW STANDARD OF THE WORLD

The 1948 Series Instrument Panel

Instrument Panel

The instrument panel has a completely new and distinctive styling, as shown in the illustration. All driving instruments are grouped into the compact cluster just ahead of the steering wheel for visibility. The balance of the instrument panel has been redesigned to provide a maximum of comfort and pleasing appearance by carrying down the lines of the instrument panel from the windshield to the floor.

The Chassis

Changes have also been incorporated on the chassis to improve its riding and driving characteristics. Caster and camber are set at zero for improved steering ability. Axle ratios for standard transmissions are 3.77:1 for 61, 62 and 60 Special, and 4.27:1 for Series 75 and 76. Axle ratios for Hydra-Matic equipped cars are 3.36:1 for Series 61, 62, and 60 Special, and 3.77:1 for Series 75 and 76.

Some changes were also made in the shock absorber mounting holes and in the shock absorber valves and springs.

Tires

Larger low pressure tires are standard equipment for all series except the 75 Series. The new tires are 8:20 x 15 on six inch wide rims and run on 24 pounds pressure as compared with the former 28 pounds.

This type of tire yields to both lateral and vertical shock and therefore flows easily over road irregularities. Considerably improved riding qualities can be easily noticed. Longer tire life can be expected because the lower air pressure and increased sidewall area have less tendency to build up high pressures during temperature variations. These low pressure tires are less likely to cut or bruise due to the sidewall flexibility. These larger section tires improve the entire appearance of the car and provide better riding and more directional stability.

Engine

The same popular V-8 type engine as was used on the 1947 models will be used in the 1948 Series cars. However, a change was made in the thermostat in order to provide a more positive closing pressure, thus reducing thermostat leakage and shortening the warm-up period.

Hydra-Matic Drive

The dependable Hydra-Matic Transmission has been continued in 1948. The rotating weight in the transmission has been lessened by using die cast aluminum front and rear clutch pistons.

Electrical System and Instruments

The instrument cluster is contained in a semi-circle of which the upper two-thirds consists of a half-moon speedometer. The lower third has the ammeter, gasoline, temperature, and oil gauges all plainly identified. The cluster face has a blue gun-metal overtone finish, with all white figures and graduations on clear lucite. All pointers are also white for easy visibility.

In all 1948 models, the speedometer case also functions as a mounting panel for the gauges. In order that the gauges may be mounted and the car operated whenever it is necessary to remove the speedometer for repairs, dummy panels will be furnished by the factory Parts Department under Part No. 145 4916. The net price is 60c each. The dummy panels are made of cardboard, but they can and should be used over and over again.

When removing the cluster from the instrument panel, Servicemen should first disconnect the battery and then remove the two chrome headed screws at the base of the instrument cluster. The cluster should then be lifted out and up in order to disengage it from the hook on top of the instrument panel. This will allow the cluster to be moved about two inches away from the panel, allowing space for Servicemen to insert a wrench for removing the oil pressure line and the speedometer cable. When this has been done, the cluster may be further removed from the instrument panel and placed on the front seat for servicing.

In order to remove the instrument assembly from the cluster case, Servicemen should remove the four Phillip head screws from the back of the cluster and then lift the assembly out. The lens retainer should then be uncrimped from the assembly case. After the lens and its retainer have been removed, the speedometer should be turned face down on the seat and the two fillister head screws removed from either side of the speedometer drive. When this has been done, the case may be lifted up and out and the dummy speedometer face installed. Servicemen can assemble the cluster by reversing the procedure given above.

Glove Compartment

A large cloth lined, bin-type glove compartment is built into the instrument panel just below the radio grille. A new and easy operating release handle and compartment lock are both finished in bright chrome. The map light on the radio grille operates as a glove compartment light automatically when the compartment door is opened.

Map and Courtesy Lights

The attractive and unique map light also operates as a courtesy light and glove compartment light. When either front door is opened on all coupes and sedans, the map light operates as a

March, 1948   The Cadillac Serviceman

ANNOUNCING THE 1948 CADILLAC

courtesy light. On the four door sedans, the rear doors operate the dome light.

The map light knob may be pulled out to maintain continuous illumination for map reading or auxiliary lighting.

Ignition Coil

A new and completely moisture proof, hermetically sealed, oil filled ignition coil is used for 1948. These features result in longer coil life and increased efficiency.

Owner Identification Card

Another change which will greatly aid the Serviceman is the shifting of the Owner Identification Card from the 1947 location on the cowl kick pad to the holder provided on the radiator air deflector under the hood. This new location makes readily accessible to Servicemen the owner's name, address, engine number, and the selling Distributor or Dealer.

Accessories

All accessories have been redesigned to complement the development of the 1948 Cadillacs. They not only match the new modern styling but are also designed for maximum performance, convenience, safety and motoring pleasures. The new 1948 Series accessories are announced in the current edition of THE CADILLAC ACCELERATOR.

Service Information

Detailed service information on 1948 Cadillac cars will be published in succeeding issues of THE CADILLAC SERVICEMAN and in the 1948 Shop Manual which will be released shortly.

TWO DRAIN HOLES DISTINGUISH 1948 SERIES WHEEL DISC FROM 1947 SERIES WHEEL DISC

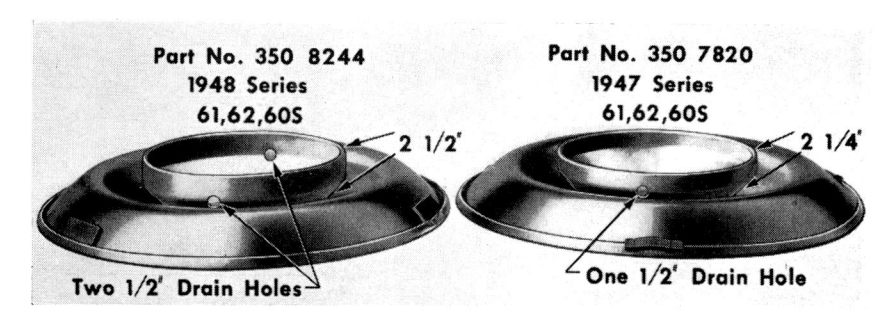

The illustration above will assist Servicemen in identifying the difference in Wheel Discs for 1947 and 1948 Series 61, 62, and 60S Cadillac Cars.

The 1948 Series Wheel Disc, Part No. 350 8244, has two ½" drain holes on the inside retainer while the 1947 Series Wheel Disc, Part No. 350 7820, has one ½" drain hole through its inside retainer.

The 1947 and 1948 Series Wheel Discs *are not interchangeable* because the inside retainer on the 1948 Series Wheel Disc is ¼" deeper than the 1947 Series Wheel Disc retainer to fit the increased wheel rim width which is used with the 8:20x15 low pressure tires on 1948 cars.

Removal Procedure For Glove Box Lock

SEVERAL INQUIRIES HAVE BEEN MADE recently concerning the removal of the lock from the glove compartment on the 1948 Series cars.

The glove box lock, located directly above the glove box opening lever, can be removed in six easy steps.

1. Remove knobs from defroster and heater levers.
2. Remove four screws holding grille to instrument panel.
3. Slide panel back far enough to work on lock.
4. Remove one of the two lock retainer screws from the lock retainer.
5. Loosen other lock retainer screw and swing retainer out of the way.
6. Slide lock cylinder out of the grille.

To reinstall glove box lock servicemen should reverse the above procedure.

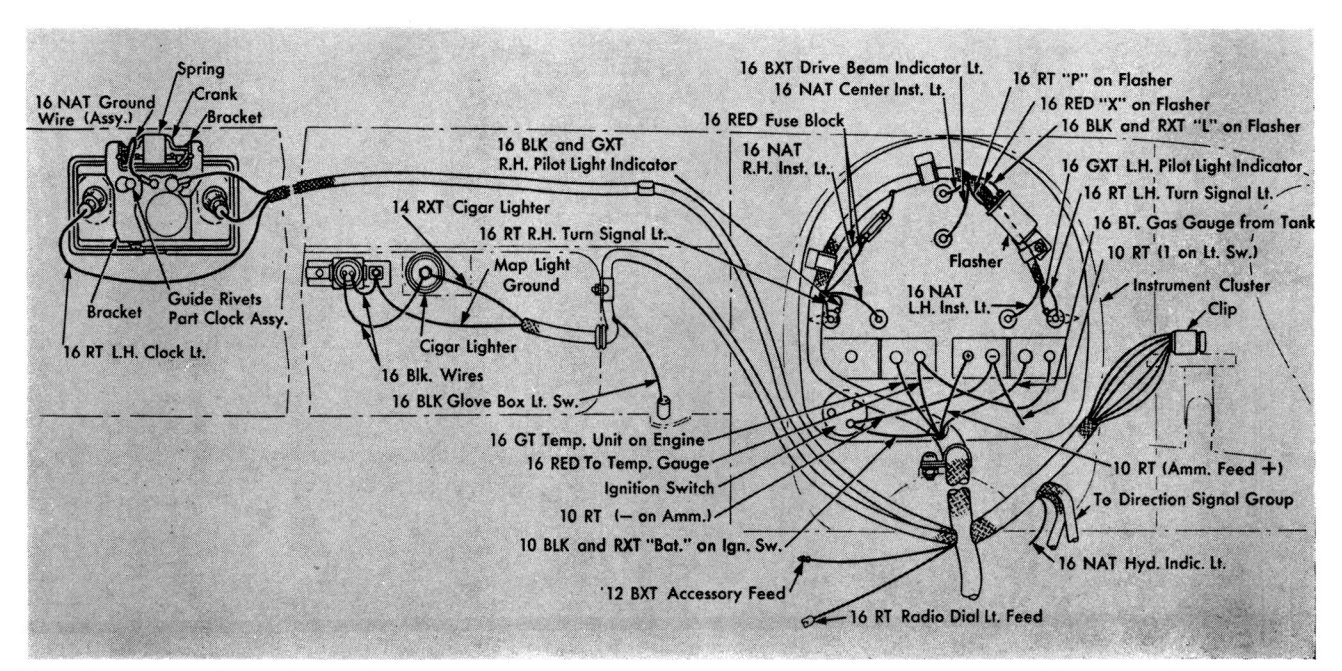

The illustration above shows the instrument panel connections for 1948 61, 62, 60S, and 75 series Cadillac cars.

BODY BY FISHER

Hydro-Lectric — Hydro-Lectric
Better By Far

THE HYDRO-LECTRIC POWER SYSTEM FOR "C" BODY CONVERTIBLE COUPE TOPS
(ALSO USED FOR FRONT SEATS, DOOR AND QUARTER WINDOWS)

1948 "C" style convertible coupes incorporate the use of a Hydro-Lectric power system to raise and lower the folding top. In addition, the windows and front seat adjuster mechanism are also hydraulically operated. This same power system for operation of the front seat and windows is also used on Cadillac and Oldsmobile 1948 "C" style closed bodies as optional equipment with the exception of Cadillac "60" Series on which it is standard. For lowering and raising the top on convertible coupes, the operation of a push-pull control knob located at the instrument panel, selects the port openings of an operating valve assembly, and energizes a solenoid operated switch on the hydraulic motor located on the dash panel underneath the hood of the car. This starts the hydraulic motor which pumps fluid under pressure through the operating valve and via metallic tubes to a pair of double-acting lift cylinders equipped with piston that raise and lower the folding top.

Each door window and quarter window is operated by a single-acting hydraulic lift cylinder mechanism. The piston pushes the window upward to a closed position, while spring tension lowers the window to an open position. The operation of the windows is controlled by electrical switches located on each door and also the quarter window area. The movement of the front seat backward or forward is controlled by a single-acting hydraulic seat adjuster regulator assembly located under the front seat. Its operation, which is similar to the door window hydraulic lift assembly, is controlled by an electrical switch located at the lower front corner of the seat ----drivers side. The illustration above shows the position of the various power units and hydraulic lines on a convertible coupe.

227

Hydro-Lectric

BODY BY FISHER — Better By Far

HYDRAULIC FLUID REPLACEMENT

CHECKING FLUID LEVEL

1. LOWER THE TOP. Operate front seat to maximum rearward position -- operate windows to fully lowered position.
2. Disconnect positive terminal of battery to prevent accidental pumping of fluid.
3. Move spring wire bail out of position and lower the reservoir from pump assembly so as to inspect the fluid level.
4. If necessary, add additional fluid to reservoir so that fluid level is within 1/2 inch of the top or to the fluid level marker as indicated on reservoir. Use Delco Super No. 9, or 11 Brake Fluid. Replace reservoir, spring wire bail and positive terminal of battery.

REMOVING FLUID FROM COMPLETE SYSTEM

1. Lower top and operate windows to maximum downward position and front seat to maximum rearward position.
2. Disconnect positive terminal of battery.
3. Remove and empty pump reservoir. With a receptacle held under the pump assembly to catch the fluid, move the top manually up and down, in conjunction with the operating valve, so as to drain the fluid from both ends of the top lift cylinders.

REPLACING FLUID IN COMPLETE SYSTEM

1. Fill reservoir to within 1/2 inch of top or to the fluid level marker and replace at pump assembly.
2. Connect battery terminal and operate top up and down so as to pump the fluid into top lift cylinders.
   Note: One filling of the reservoir may not be sufficient to completely raise the top, as the fluid capacity of the two (2) top lift cylinders is almost double that of the pump reservoir, therefore, it will be necessary to refill the reservoir as outlined in step 3.
3. With window still lowered and seat still in a rearward position, again remove reservoir -- refill to within 1/2 inch of the top as explained and replace. Operate top up and down 4 or 5 cycles until all air has left this part of the system.
4. Now operate windows and the seat a few times so as to expel air from this part of the system; once more check the fluid level.

FLUID LEVEL LINE

NOTE: Hydraulic fluid must be changed once a year, preferably in the Fall. The hydraulic pump is vented to atmosphere. With the seasonal use of the system a certain amount of air is drawn into or expelled out of the system through this vent hole. Intake air carries a certain amount of fine dust which accumulates as sludge in the bottom of the reservoir. Before replacing fluid, clean out this sludge from the bottom of the reservoir, also screen on the pump intake. After wiping reservoir clean and dry, fill with new hydraulic fluid as specified. Do not over-fill.

Hydro-Lectric

BODY BY FISHER — Better By Far

Hydro-Lectric

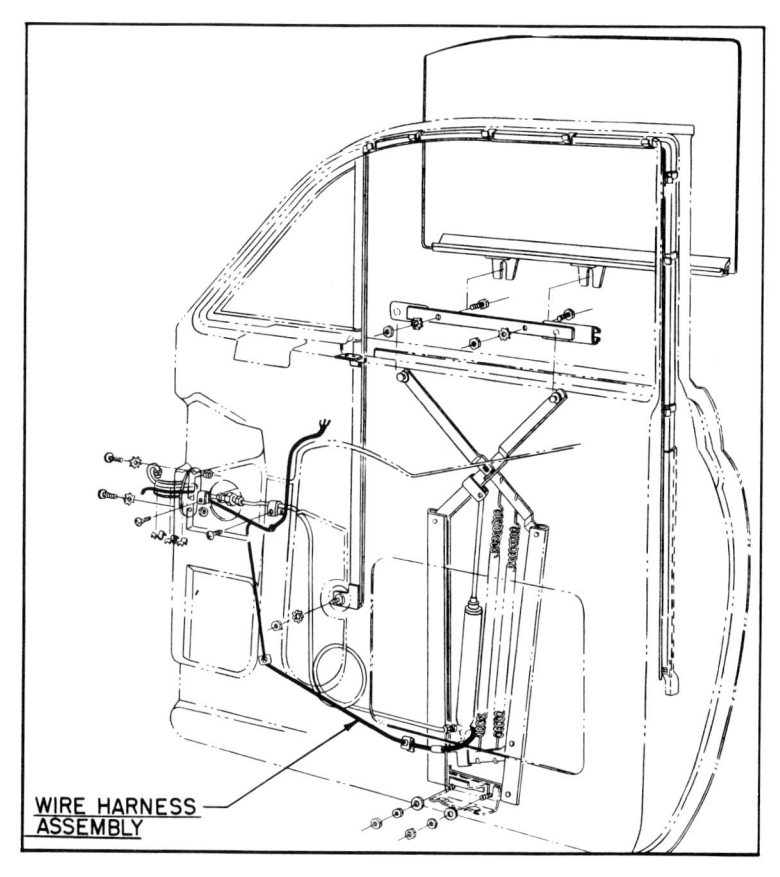

REMOVAL AND REPLACEMENT OF DOOR WINDOW HYDRAULIC LIFT ASSEMBLY

1. Lower the window to extreme open position and disconnect positive terminal of battery.
2. Remove door trim pad, (See Operation No. 18).
3. Disconnect solenoid wire at the bottom of the cylinder assembly and tape the lead wire.
4. Disconnect fluid line nut at connector on solenoid at the bottom of the cylinder assembly, capping the loose line to prevent loss of fluid.
5. Loosen the two attaching nuts at lower glass channel, and raise glass so as to disengage the lift assembly from the glass lower sash channel.
6. Disengage cam channel from cross arms of lift assembly by sliding cam sideways. (Illustration at left shows the components of the hydraulic lift, also the wiring harness on a closed body front door.)

7. Next, loosen the two attaching nuts holding the hydraulic unit to the support at bottom of door, lift hydraulic unit out of position and remove.

To replace: Reverse the order of the forgoing procedure. Important points to check are as follows:

A. Be sure the complete assembly is in proper alignment. The glass should move freely by hand until the hydraulic connections are made.
B. Be sure all connections are tight.
C. Place all windows in the maximum down position and move the hydraulic seat to the extreme rear position, then, check the level of the fluid in the pump reservoir. Illustration at right shows the hydraulic lift components, also wiring harness on rear doors. Return springs not shown. Procedure for removal of hydraulic lift on convertible doors is similar.

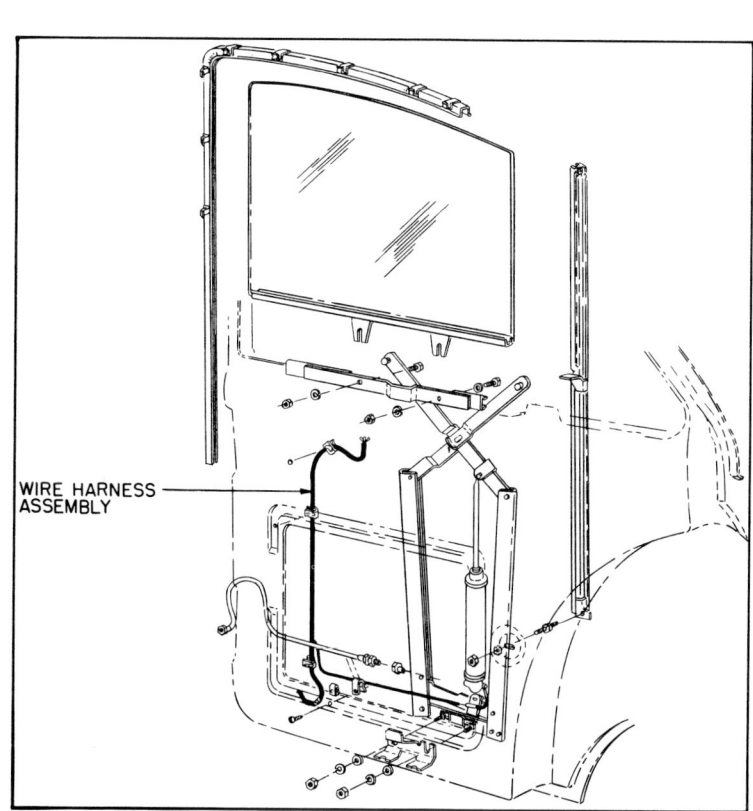

229

BODY BY FISHER
Hydro-Lectric — Better By Far — Hydro-Lectric

POSSIBLE CAUSES OF FAILURE OR FAULTY OPERATION OF THE HYDRO-LECTRIC SYSTEM

TYPE OF FAILURE

	MECHANICAL	ELECTRICAL	HYDRAULIC
1. Window Lift Inoperative.	a. Glass run channel misaligned. b. Glass guide misaligned. c. Interference from door arm rest screw. d. Window lift not connected to lower sash channel.	a. Battery too low. b. Motor ground loose. c. Motor solenoid inoperative. d. Motor inoperative. e. Circuit breaker inoperative. f. Short in BAT, MOT. or CYL. circuit. g. Cylinder solenoid inoperative.	a. Lack of fluid. b. Piston rod dismounted. c. Broken port plate. d. Pump pressure relief valve stuck. e. Fluid line crimped.
2. Seat Regulator Inoperative.	a. Seat adjuster mechanism misaligned. b. Hydraulic seat adjuster not attached to seat or floor support properly.	a. Same as above.	a. Same as above.
3. Two windows operate from one switch.		a. Switch CYL. terminals touching.	a. Pump pressure too high.
4. Window lifts operate slowly upward or seat regulator operates slowly forward.	a. Units may be binding. b. Window run channels may be excessively damp, wet.	a. Low battery.	a. Pump pressure relief valve stuck. b. Top control rod holding control valve partially open allowing fluid to enter top lines.
5. Window lifts operate slowly down or seat regulator operates slowly rearward.	a. Units may be binding. b. Window run channels may be excessively damp, wet. c. Window lift spring broken.		a. Pump pressure relief valve stuck. b. Fluid congealed, old.
6. One window will not quite close.	a. Run channel misaligned. b. Stops improperly adjusted. c. Glass misaligned.		a. Insufficient fluid.
7. One window raises when top or any other unit is operated.		a. Switch CYL. terminal in touch with BAT. terminal.	

POSSIBLE CAUSES OF FAILURE OR FAULTY OPERATION
OF THE HYDRO-LECTRIC SYSTEM
TYPE OF FAILURE

	MECHANICAL	ELECTRICAL	HYDRAULIC
8. Both windows raise when top or seat regulator is operated.		a. Switch CYL. terminal in touch with BAT. terminal.	a. Pump pressure too high.
9. All units operate slowly up and down.	a. Units possibly misaligned.	a. Low battery.	a. Pump pressure relief valve stuck. b. Crimped fluid lines.
10. Top will operate in one direction only.	a. Top control valve rod misaligned.	a. Top control valve switch contacts only at one point.	a. Top control valve shaft and rotor not assembled properly. b. Top lift cylinder rod and piston disassembled, retaining nut loose.
11. Top will not operate.		a. Battery low. b. Motor solenoid inoperative. c. Motor inoperative. d. Short in switch circuit. e. Switch connections loose.	a. Elbows or tees not drilled through. b. Foreign material in lines. c. Broken port plate.

SERVICE SUGGESTIONS FOR HYDRO-LECTRIC SYSTEM

To have satisfactory window or seat operation it is absolutely necessary that door glass and other parts be in proper alignment, and these conditions must be checked to assure free movement before the hydraulic system is connected.

For example, with hydraulic lift disconnected, should the door glass fail to move freely by hand, or should there be misalignment in the assembly of the regulator arm to the glass, or if the felt on the door garnish molding causes excessive friction, then unsatisfactory operation will result. Any of these should be corrected before connecting the hydraulic mechanism. This also applies to the seat mechanism as well.

Interference with the mechanical operation of the top, seat or windows, such as holding or retarding their operation in any way should be avoided. Do not try to force a window down. If the solenoid valve at the bottom of the hydraulic cylinder is closed, hydraulic fluid is trapped in the cylinder and no amount of manual pressure on the window will force it down. An occurrence of this kind may bend the window regulator arms and trouble will result.

Be careful when disconnecting hydraulic fluid lines. Make sure the electrical circuit is disconnected, otherwise, an accidental touch of a switch will cause the pressurized fluid to squirt out the end of the disconnected tubing causing serious damage.

In no case should mineral oil be used for priming purposes. To guard against contamination of the hydraulic fluid, which may be injurious to the system, hydraulic fluid should not be put into dirty containers or squirt cans containing mineral oil or oil residue.

Before working on the hydraulic system, make sure trim and parts adjacent to the working area are protected with a suitable cover. This applies particularly to front fenders. Hydraulic fluid is injurious to a car finish. Its damage to a car finish is almost instantaneous. Hydraulic fluid is also inflammable; be careful of fluid drippage on a hot manifold or exhaust pipe. Suitable cloths should be at hand to wipe up any slight drippage of fluid when lines are disconnected.

When connecting "Tees" or "Elbows" in the hydraulic tubing, make sure all connections are tight. The threads of male couplings before installation must be coated with AMBEROID cement or "3-M ADHESIVE, EC-847, to insure a leak-proof connection. In cases of chronic leaks install a new coupling.

In the electrical circuit, be sure and re-install the wiring to its proper terminal on the hydraulic unit, otherwise, in the case of switches, reverse operation may occur.

The Cadillac Serviceman

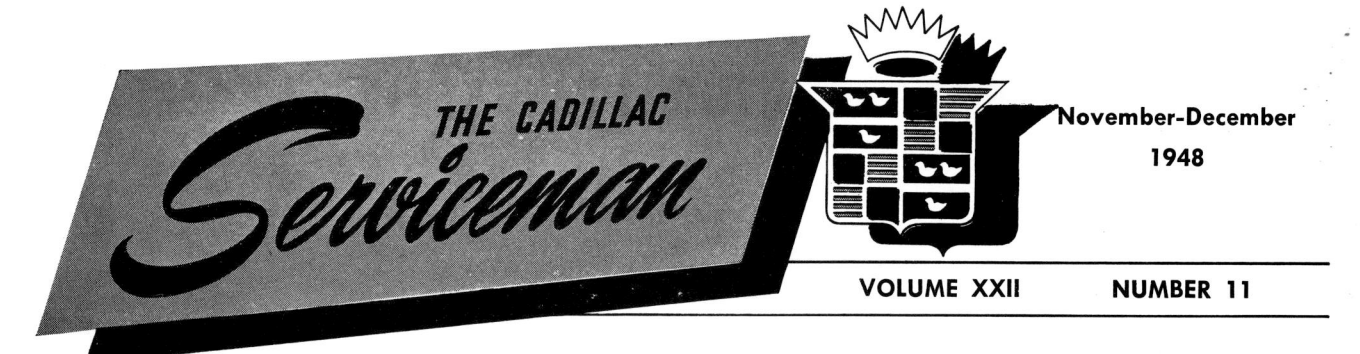

November-December 1948

VOLUME XXII NUMBER 11

SERVICE INFORMATION ON THE 1949 SERIES CADILLAC

THE 1949 CADILLAC SERIES 62 FOUR-DOOR SEDAN

THE CADILLAC PROGRAM FOR 1949 is a forward step in establishing Cadillac engineering supremacy at an even higher level than it has attained today. The enthusiastic acceptance of Cadillac is the greatest in Cadillac history.

Body Changes

Having again set a new "Standard of The World" in motor car beauty, it has not been necessary to make any major changes or improvements in the 1948 basic body designs in order to maintain a position of unquestionable leadership.

Minor body changes for 1949 include a longer hood line with the goddess ornament moved forward to increase the appearance of over-all length. A new grille extending across the fenders to the wheel openings adds to the low, broad appearance. The interior of the 1949 Cadillac is completely new, featuring a new instrument panel, new door mouldings, and trim.

Mechanical Changes

Mechanically, the 1949 Cadillac offers one of the greatest engineering advancements in 45 years of fine car building. This year Cadillac introduces the Cadillac Valve-In-Head V-8 Engine, a bold step forward. It is a bold step forward because it completely displaces the finest performing engine ever to power a motor car. Now at the height of its success, Cadillac offers an entirely new engine—smoother, quieter, better performing, more economical to operate and maintain—one of the greatest engineering advancements in Cadillac's entire history.

As Cadillac Servicemen, you will want to learn the facts about the 1949 Valve-In-Head V-8 Engine. In this respect Servicemen will be glad to know that copies of the 1949 Shop Manual will soon be available to you. In addition "Preliminary Engine Service Information" books as well as complete engine and car specifications are being distributed at the Engine Clinics now being held in the field.

The following information is divided into sections similar to the 1948 Shop Manual and will enable Servicemen to make necessary adjustments on the 1949 Cadillac cars until the 1949 Shop Manual is available with complete servicing information.

Lubrication

The lubrication schedule on the 1949 chassis is the same as that used in 1948 except that the engine will require only 5 QUARTS of engine oil as compared to 7 quarts in 1948, and the distributor is to be lubricated as outlined in the Engine Section.

Body

The door handle retaining screw on later 1949 series cars is now a ¼" hex head cap screw, and can only be removed with Special Tool J-3190, Door Handle Retaining Screw Remover and Replacer. This tool will be released to Servicemen in the near future with an explanation of its use. Some of the other 1949 body changes are: New "Snap On" type clips on the reveal moldings, windshield wiper cables equipped with new automatic windshield wiper cable tensioners, a newly designed instrument panel, crease lines that extend from rear

The Cadillac Serviceman — Nov.-Dec., 1948

SERVICE INFORMATION ON 1949 SERIES CADILLACS

door to rear door on 61 and 62 sedans and the top part of the deck lid weatherstrip being located in the gutter.

Frame

The frames used on the 49-Series Cadillac cars are of the familiar X-type construction used in previous models. The frames of all series are similar in design, although there are differences in dimensions and other details, due to varying wheelbases and other body requirements.

Commercial car frames are much the same as the passenger car frame, but with differences in length and heavier construction features. Servicemen should consult the 1948 Shop Manual for all service procedures on 1949 frames until the 1949 Shop Manual is available.

Chassis Suspension

Independent front wheel suspension is again used on all 1949 series cars. This type suspension permits either front wheel to follow the irregularities of the road without carrying that side of the car up or down with it and without transferring shocks to the other wheel. The servicing of the chassis suspension is the same as that in 1948 except for the removal and installation of the rear wheels and brake drums which is as follows: First, remove the five wheel nuts and remove the wheel, and second, remove the two 5/16" cap screws that hold the drum in place and remove the brake drum. Reverse the procedure for installation.

Rear Axle

The rear axle for 1949 is of the semi-floating design. Ball bearings are used in the rear wheels, and are permanently lubricated and sealed. A new type flanged axle shaft is used to simplify service operations which involve removal of rear brake drums. This operation is explained in detail for servicemen below and is the only different service procedure on rear axles for 1949. All other servicing information may be found in the 1948 Shop Manual. The differential carrier assembly for 1949 series cars is the same as that used on 1948 series cars.

1949 Distributor

1949 engines, Servicemen should be sure to use the correct terminal in the package, and to gap the plugs correctly before installing them.

Engine Fuel And Exhaust

The engine fuel and exhaust system for 1949 is somewhat different than in 1948. The Carter carburetor used in 1949 is of the dual down-draft climatic control type designed for greater fuel economy and better performance. The choke is moved on the right, and the throttle arm carries the linkage control which simplifies adjustment. The pump stroke has been reduced from 27/64" to 1/4" due to the heat control which speeds warm-up time. The method of adjustment is never the same. Another new feature on the 1949 engine fuel and exhaust is the cross-under pipe with heat control valve. The heat control valve is installed between the cross-under pipe and the left exhaust manifold. A thermostatic spring is used to control the action of the heater valve and hold it closed under pressure when the manifold is cold. When the manifold is cold the exhaust gases from the left manifold are forced back through the passage under the intake manifold and out through the right exhaust manifold to the muffler. This feature heats up the intake manifold for a quick warm-up period. As the exhaust manifold becomes hot, the heat control valve automatically opens and permits the exhaust from the left manifold to go through the cross-under pipe to the right manifold, then out directly to the exhaust pipe and muffler. A dampener spring on the heat control valve silences

Adjusting Ignition Timing

any flutter noise during the warm-up period.

To remove the cross-under pipe and heat control valve simply remove the four nuts holding the cross-under pipe to the right and left exhaust manifolds and remove cross-under pipe. Remove gaskets and heat control valve under left exhaust manifold. The heat control valve is installed on the left exhaust manifold above the cross-under pipe. The counterweight on the heat valve must be to the outside and to the rear of the engine. A gasket is installed on both sides of the heat valve. The heat valve should be worked a few times after final installation to make sure that it is free and not binding. One of the loose flanges on the cross-under pipes has an "R" stamped on it and must be assembled to the right hand manifold. To insure leak proof joints at the two flanges the four attaching nuts must first be run up finger tight then torqued to 30 to 35 foot pounds.

The overflow stack and tube connection have been eliminated. The only reason an overflow stack was used on previous models was due to the position of the generator and the exhaust manifold. Now with the generator mounted on the outside of the engine there is less chance of a fire due to the arching of the brushes and heat from the exhaust manifolds.

A hole has been added in the dust cover over the throttle pump and the two washers on the metering rods have been eliminated. This allows ventilation through the carburetor.

The spring on the throttle pump has been weakened to eliminate a sticking

SERVICE INFORMATION ON 1949 SERIES CADILLACS

spot in "feel" of accelerator pedal action, just before the 4-3 downshift.

The carburetor air cleaner has been redesigned. The new air cleaner reduces air restriction by approximately 50%.

Engine Cooling

Since the 1949 engine does not transmit as much heat to the cooling system as previous models it has been possible to decrease the radiator size and weight. The cooling capacity has been reduced from 25 quarts to 18 quarts in 1949.

The thermostat has an opening temperature of 162 to 168 degrees F. and opens fully over a 20 degree F. range. The pressure radiator cap does not affect the opening of this thermostat. The new thermostat, which is sensitive to temperature only, is installed with the element down, thus the vent rivet or "jiggle" pin in the thermostat will always hang downward, making the radiator easier to fill. The 1949 radiator cap has a pressure setting of 12 to 15 pounds, thus raising the boiling point up to 245 to 250 degrees.

The operation of the 1949 engine cooling system is shown in the illustration on next page. To clarify the illustration for Servicemen the operation of the cooling system is outlined below.

Engine Cooling System Operation

The water pump draws fluid from the bottom of the radiator into the chamber in the pump ahead of the impeller. Then it is forced through the impeller chamber and the two lower pump outlets and into both blocks simultaneously. The water circulates around the cylinders and up through drilled passages to the cylinder head. NOTE: Not all cored holes in the block go through to the cylinder head.

After the water circulates through the head, it passes out through outlets at the front of each head to the upper inlet passage of the water pump. If the thermostat is open the water will flow upward past the thermostat, out the top of the thermostat housing and to the upper tank of the radiator. There it is cooled as it is drawn to the lower end of the radiator to repeat the cycle. If the thermostat is closed, a drilled by-pass in the pump body allows the fluid to flow through the pump and back through the cylinder blocks again.

1949 ENGINE SPECIFICATIONS

Number of Cylinders	8
Cylinder Arrangement	90° V-type
Firing Order	1, 8, 4, 3, 6, 5, 7, 2
Piston Displacement	331 cu. in.
Taxable Horsepower	46.5
Maximum Brake Horsepower	160 at 3800 R.P.M.
Standard Compression Ratio	7.5 to 1
Bore and Stroke	3 13/16" x 3 5/8"
Crankshaft Bearings	5
Camshaft Bearings	5
Piston Material	Aluminum Alloy
Compression Rings per Piston	2
Oil Rings per Piston	1
OIL CAPACITY	5 QUARTS
Oil Pump, Type	Helical Gear
Normal Oil Pressure	36 lbs. at 30 M.P.H.
Engine Lubrication	Full Pressure
Crankcase Ventilation	Road Draft Type
COOLING SYSTEM CAPACITY	18 QUARTS (19 quarts when car is equipped with heater)
Accessory Drive Belt	Cog Type Vee
Carburetor	Dual Down-draft (Carter)
Automatic Choke	Thermostatic Type
Valve Arrangement	Valve-In-Head
Cylinder Head Material	Cast Iron
Cylinder Block Material	Cast Iron

Hydra-Matic Transmission

The Hydra-Matic transmission in 1949 series Cadillac cars operates essentially the same as those incorporated in previous models. Service Information outlined in the 1948 Shop Manual should be used for all adjustments, except the throttle linkage and manual control adjustments which are new and are explained below.

The 1949 transmission torus members contain vanes extending through the inner shell, which have increased the efficiency to such an extent as to allow a decrease in overall torus member diameter. This has resulted in reduced creeping.

A spring has been added behind the compensator valve, in the outer valve body, to keep it in a closed position. To maintain the same shift points, a change has been made in the throttle-valve spring (now copper plated) and the throttle valve. The outer valve body is not interchangeable with previous models.

The rotary inertia of the rear unit has been decreased by the elimination of one composition and one steel clutch disc. The discs are assembled alternately with a composition disc contacting the inside face of the drum and a steel disc contacting the annular piston.

The flywheel cover can only be mounted one way on the flywheel because of a 1/32 inch difference in pilot dowel diameters (see next page).

Steering Gear

A re-circulating ball-type steering gear is again used on all 1949 Series Cadillac cars. Servicemen should refer to the 1948 Shop Manual for all necessary adjustments on the steering gear until such time as the 1949 Shop Manual is available.

Brakes

The braking system on 1949 Series Cadillac cars includes brakes of the hydraulic type combined with a hand lever that operates the rear brakes through a mechanical linkage, of the same type used on 1948 Series cars. However, Servicemen will note that the brake linings, shoes, and drums on the rear brakes are

Nov.-Dec., 1948 — *The Cadillac Serviceman*

SERVICE INFORMATION ON 1949 SERIES CADILLACS

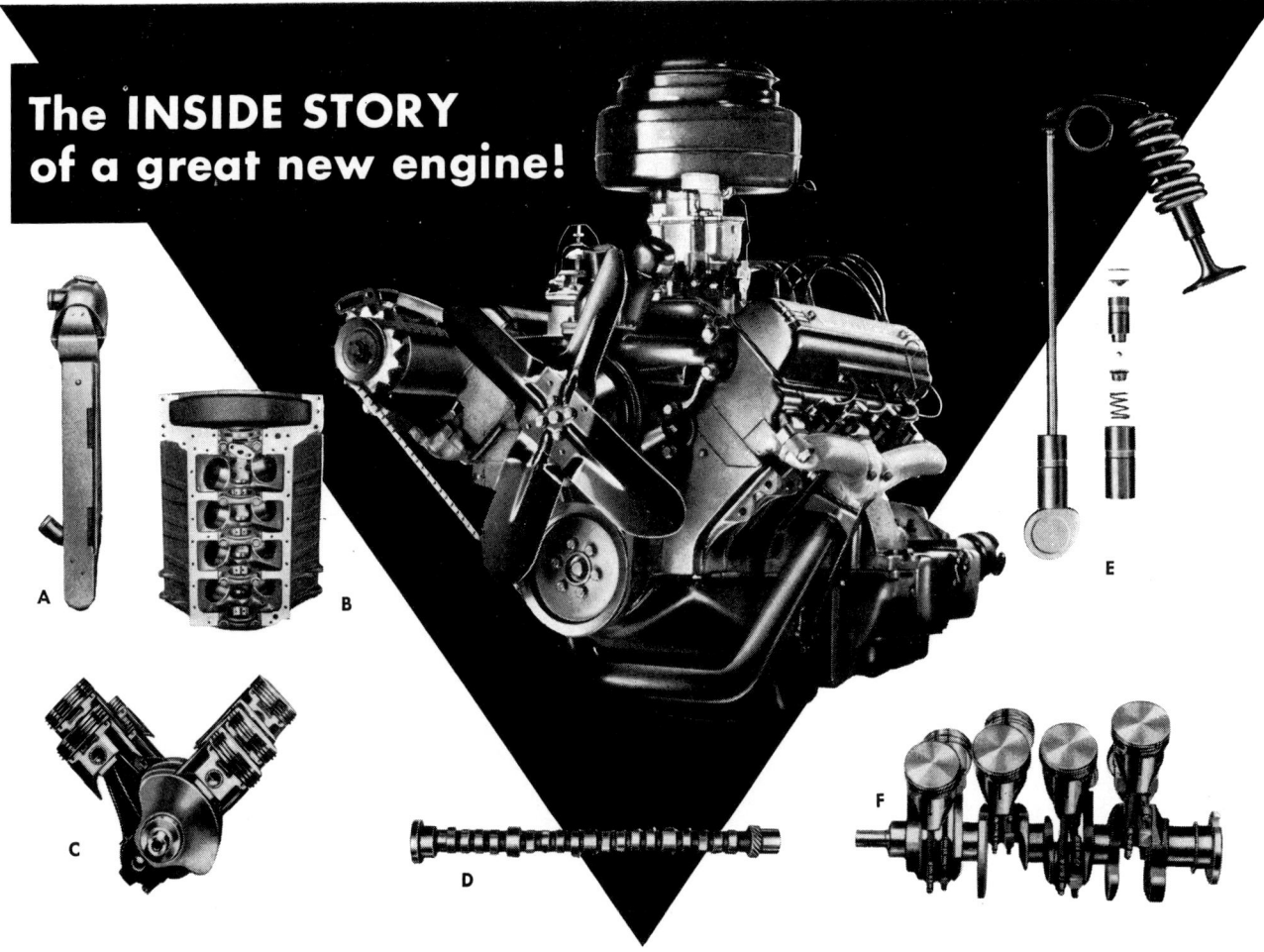

The INSIDE STORY of a great new engine!

A. A smaller, lighter radiator is possible with the new engine because friction and heat losses have been reduced. It requires only 18 quarts of coolant as compared to 25 quarts on previous models.

B. The 1949 cylinder block is of rigid, box-like construction, containing five main bearing bulkheads which distribute power stress evenly throughout the casting, thus reducing vibration.

C. A new design slipper-type piston allows the use of a shorter connecting rod. Pistons nest into the crankshaft counterweights. Reduction of weight and inertia means faster acceleration.

D. The new camshaft is shorter and lighter in weight, and is mounted in five bearings instead of three. These extra supports give added rigidity in operation, for smooth, quiet performance.

E. Lightweight, rigid overhead valve mechanism actuated by hydraulic valve lifters insures accurate timing and exceptionally quiet operation.

F. A well designed, piston-crankshaft assembly is vital to any engine. The 1949 Cadillac engine uses smaller, lighter parts. The new five bearing crankshaft has greater rigidity, greater torsional resistance for extra smoothness, quietness and power.

¼" wider in 1949 to increase braking action. This change has no effect on the servicing of brakes in 1949. Servicemen should refer to the 1948 Shop Manual for servicing information on all brake problems. Removal of 1949 brake drums is covered in the Chassis Suspension Section on page 46.

Engine Mechanical

The crankcase ventilating system provides positive air circulation through the crankcase whenever the car is moving.

With this system air enters the crankcase through the oil filler cap. This cap is fitted with a copper mesh air filter which filters dust out of the air entering the crankcase. (See illustration on next page.)

The air is drawn down through the timing gear compartment into the front of the crankcase. The air and any contaminating vapors then pass around the crankcase bulkheads and up into the valve gear compartment through an opening in the rear of the cylinder block between the crankshaft and valve gear compartments. The air then circulates toward the front of the valve compartment and is drawn up through a hole in the valve compartment cover baffle to the ventilating pipe at the rear of the cover. This pipe directs the air downward below the engine where vacuum caused by air flowing by the pipe when the car is in motion provides the motivating force for crankcase ventilation.

Engine Lubricating System

The engine lubricating system for 1949 is a much more effective system than in the previous engine because there are no external pipes, fittings, etc., to service.

235

APPENDIX IV
CLUBS

In 1970, when we began accumulating material for the first edition of *Cadillacs of the Forties* (published in 1976), most of the subject cars were orphans. Not one vintage car club in the United States recognized postwar Cadillacs. The Cadillac-LaSalle Club (CLC), among others, had an onerous 25-year rule and the Classic Car Club of America (CCCA) limited forties recognition to prewar 75s.

Now, 18 years later, this historic generation of Cadillacs has attained a revered position in the heirarchy of collectors cars. Today every passenger car manufactured by Cadillac from 1940 through 1947 has been designated *Full Classic* by the CCCA, excepting LaSalles and the B-bodied 61s. The owner or admirer of a sanctioned Cadillac can derive great enjoyment and comradeship from CCCA membership. The CCCA's 5,000 members enjoy a full spectrum of concours and touring events on the local and national level, plus the finest of club publications.

The marque club for the Cadillac enthusiast is the CLC. At this writing, the CLC has been around for 30 years. Its early history was beleaguered with a period of inept national management, but today it's dynamic 3,000 members enjoy regular publications, an annual convention, regional national meets, and many active regions.

Aside from the CCCA, three other national multi-marque clubs also have activities and publications that the owner of a Cadillac of the 1940s may find of interest. They are the 50,000 member Antique Automobile Club of America (AACA), the Contemporary Historical Vehicle Association (CHVA), and the Milestone Car Society.

The best source for the current addresses for any of these clubs is *Hemmings Vintage Auto Almanac;* published annually and available at many book stores and newsstands.

Hundreds of thousands of Americans have become involved in the burgeoning collector car hobby over the last 30 years. The changes have been mind boggling. The price spiral, the availability of replacement parts, the ever higher quality of restorations and the explosion of information, all have made the hobby more interesting than ever. Within the framework of the clubs, and with the advantage of hindsight, today's enthusiast can truly enjoy the world's greatest hobby.

Personally, I was lucky to have owned many fine Cadillacs of the 1940s. Like many readers of this volume, I wish I had done more preservation and perhaps kept one or two more good original cars. Nevertheless, logging half a million miles behind the wheels of flathead Cadillacs, many of them on club events, was, and still is, great fun. Through this hobby I have met legions of wonderful people, toured much of this beautiful land, and derived immeasureable pleasure from the esthetic perfection that can be found in the automotive art form. It is my sincere hope that through these pages the reader can also share in the great heritage of Cadillacs of the Forties.

Roy A. Schneider
February 22, 1988

INDEX

—A—
Accessories, 176, 180, 181, 182, 183, 192
Adams, Mrs. Morgan, 173, 175
Advertising, 32, 49, 75, 138
Ahrens, D. E., 95, 151*
Air conditioning, 88
Aleman, Miguel, 175
Allison engine, 78, 99
All-Weather ventilation, 77, 87
Andrade, Julio, 9
Antique Automobile Club of America, 236
Autorama, 152, 153, 166, 167, 168
Autry, Gene, 120

—B—
Barr, Harry, 144
Battery cables, 202, 212
Battery ground, 94
Blackouts, 78, 79, 212
Blue Coral, 215*
Body construction, 87
Bohman and Schwartz, 36, 37, 120
Brake system leak test, 221
Brunn and Company, 36, 69
Buick, 12*, 44, 94
Bumper jack use, 219

—C—
Cadillac - LaSalle Club, 236
Carburetors on 1941 models, 201
Carburetors on 1942 models, 210
Carburetors on 1946-1947 models, 222, 223
Carburetor float, 207
Caribbean (show car), 166
Catwalks, 15, 28

Chassis, 67*, 146*
Chrome plating, 150
Clark Avenue, 6, 94
Classic Car Club of America, 109, 237
Clubs for the enthusiast, 236
Coachcraft (coachbuilders), 68, 172, 173
Coil identification, 221
Cold test, 145
Cole, Edward N., 99*, 143, 144
Commercial chassis, 66, 67*, 120, 149
Contemporary Historical Vehicle Association, 236
Convertible rear window, 221
Cooling system, 18, 196, 203, 220
Cord automobile, 39
Coupe de Ville, 149, 162, 163, 168
Curtice, Harlow H., 44
Cylinder block cleaning, 196, 203, 220
Cylinder head position, 221

—D—
DeLuxe interior, 40, 77, 84
Derham Body Company (coachbuilders), 69, 118, 119, 161, 174
Detroit City Airport, 122*
Die cast, 28, 150
DiNoc transfers, 114, 131, 139, 148
Dip stick, 207
Directional signals, 28
Distributor testing specifications, 203
Division partition, 22*, 33, 44, 200*
Door lock safety setting, 205, 219
Dreystadt, Nicholas, 17, 44, 99*
Drop-out grill, 15
Duesenberg automobile, 39

—E—
Earl, Harley, 12*, 13, 39, 44, 71, 72, 73, 78, 109, 124, 148, 152, 163
El Dorado Brougham towncar, 65
El Rancho (show car), 170
Embassy (show car), 167
Emblem spring clamps, 202
Engine, 45, 66*, 70*, 94, 100*, 101*, 142*, 143, 145, 146, 147*

—F—
Fastback styling, 40, 62, 85, 87, 105, 112, 113, 135
Features of 1940-Series cars, 193, 194, 195, 196
Features of 1941-Series cars, 199, 200, 201
Features of 1942-Series cars, 204, 205, 206, 207, 208, 209
Features of 1946-Series cars, 214, 215
Features of 1947-Series cars, 218, 219
Features of 1948-Series cars, 224, 225, 226
Features of 1949-Series cars 232, 233, 234, 235
Fleetwood, 15, 16, 35, 43, 72, 126
Florentine curve, 164
Fog lights, 26, 28, 97
Fuel pump tests, 197

—G—
Gas cap vent, 202
General Motors Proving Grounds, 124, 144
Glove box removal (1948), 226
Gordon, John F., 99*, 123, 124, 151*

* Illustration

—H—
Hershey, Franklin Q., 123, 124*, 126, 148
High-performance, 112
Historical Milestones, 140, 141
Hood closing procedure, 197
Hood hinges (1941), 203
Hubcaps (wheel discs), 97, 226
Hydra-Matic Drive, 46, 78, 94, 127, 216
Hydro-Lectric System, 98, 133, 149, 227, 228, 229, 230, 231

—J—
Jones, Jennifer, 88
Jump seats, 22*, 164*

—K—
Karl, Harry, 120
Kettering, Charles F., 56
Knudsen, William S., 24

—L—
Lacquer, 103
LaSalle automobile, 8, 9, 15, 40, 41, 53*, 157
Liebendorfer Collection, 64
Livery trim, 149
Lockheed P-38, 78, 123, 125*

—M—
Mechanical Features of 1941 cars, 199-201
Milestones (Cadillac), 140, 141
Mitchell, William, 9, 11, 13*, 16, 39, 71, 78, 123
Mock-up, 16, 53, 73, 74, 81, 126, 144
Motorama, 65

—O—
Oil pan service, 212
Oldsmobile, 46, 105
Optional equipment, 176, 180, 181, 182, 183, 192
Overheating, 18

—P—
Percolating, 17, 213
Photo credits, 7
Plating (chrome), 150
Pontoon fenders, 72
Pot metal (see die cast)
Production line, 4*, 101*
Production statistics, 177-183

—R—
Radiator shutters, 77
Rear door safety lock, 205, 219
Retouching grained dash, 201
Rollson Company (coachbuilders), 69
Rollston Company (coachbuilders), 69
Ross, Arthur, 39
Running boards, 27*, 40, 95, 97, 109
Rust inhibitor, 209

—S—
Saoutchik, Jacques (coachbuilder), 171
Schwartz, Maurice (coachbuilder), 120, 175
Selfridge Field, 78, 123, 125
Selznick, David O., 88
Service information on 1942-Series, 204
Shock absorber service, 208
Shop manual corrections (1942), 212
Sidemount fenders, 26*, 30*
Sixteen Cylinder Motorcars, 16
Skirted fenders, 19*, 77, 203

Slipper piston, 143, 145
Sludge test on block, 203
Special Car Design Studio, 123, 124
Special Features, 44, 95, 184-191
Specifications (1942), 75
Specifications (1949), 234
Standard interior, 45*, 115*
Starrett, Charles, 68
Starting problems, 18
Steering wheel (plastic), 98, 127, 219
Stone guard, 97
Storage procedures, 211
Sunshine Turret Top, 16

—T—
Tail lamp jewels, 63
Tank engines, 78, 91*
Tanks (Cadillac-built), 78, 93
Tell, William J., 72
Torpedo body, 11, 17, 27, 40
Transfers (DiNoc), 114, 131, 139, 148
Trunk lid precaution, 205

—V—
Vacuum pump test, 197
Valve lifter cleaning, 196
Vapor lock, 17, 213

—W—
Waldorf-Astoria Hotel, 34, 152
Water pump, 18, 217
Wheel balance, 196
Wheel discs, 97, 226
Wilson, Charles E., 64, 99, 169
Window handle position, 202
Windsor, Duke and Duchess of, 56
Wood grain dash (see transfers), 20, 201

—Z—
Zumbach's Motor Repair, 161

LUBRICATION

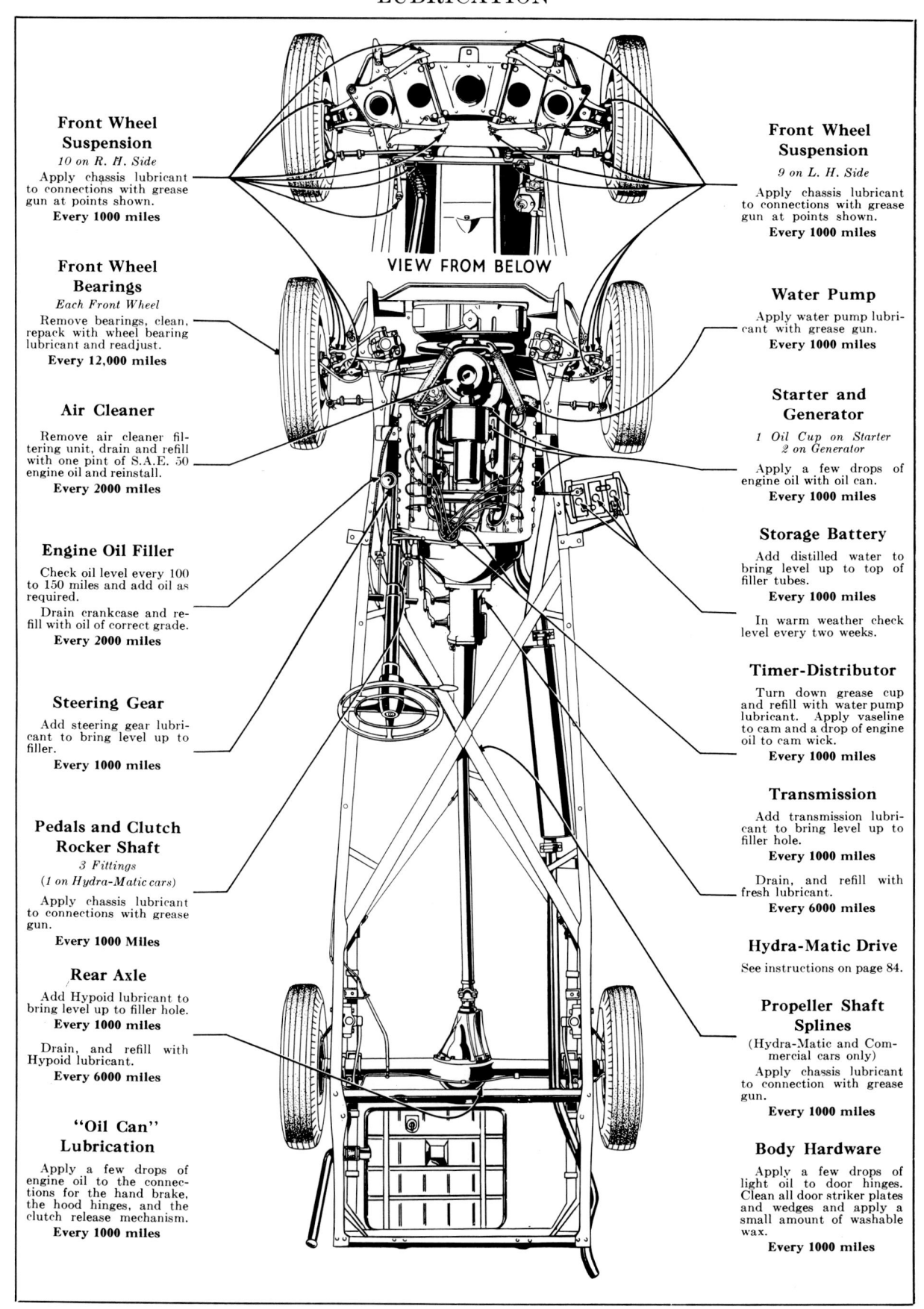

VIEW FROM BELOW

Front Wheel Suspension
10 on R. H. Side
Apply chassis lubricant to connections with grease gun at points shown.
Every 1000 miles

Front Wheel Bearings
Each Front Wheel
Remove bearings, clean, repack with wheel bearing lubricant and readjust.
Every 12,000 miles

Air Cleaner
Remove air cleaner filtering unit, drain and refill with one pint of S.A.E. 50 engine oil and reinstall.
Every 2000 miles

Engine Oil Filler
Check oil level every 100 to 150 miles and add oil as required.
Drain crankcase and refill with oil of correct grade.
Every 2000 miles

Steering Gear
Add steering gear lubricant to bring level up to filler.
Every 1000 miles

Pedals and Clutch Rocker Shaft
3 Fittings
(1 on Hydra-Matic cars)
Apply chassis lubricant to connections with grease gun.
Every 1000 Miles

Rear Axle
Add Hypoid lubricant to bring level up to filler hole.
Every 1000 miles

Drain, and refill with Hypoid lubricant.
Every 6000 miles

"Oil Can" Lubrication
Apply a few drops of engine oil to the connections for the hand brake, the hood hinges, and the clutch release mechanism.
Every 1000 miles

Front Wheel Suspension
9 on L. H. Side
Apply chassis lubricant to connections with grease gun at points shown.
Every 1000 miles

Water Pump
Apply water pump lubricant with grease gun.
Every 1000 miles

Starter and Generator
1 Oil Cup on Starter
2 on Generator
Apply a few drops of engine oil with oil can.
Every 1000 miles

Storage Battery
Add distilled water to bring level up to top of filler tubes.
Every 1000 miles

In warm weather check level every two weeks.

Timer-Distributor
Turn down grease cup and refill with water pump lubricant. Apply vaseline to cam and a drop of engine oil to cam wick.
Every 1000 miles

Transmission
Add transmission lubricant to bring level up to filler hole.
Every 1000 miles

Drain, and refill with fresh lubricant.
Every 6000 miles

Hydra-Matic Drive
See instructions on page 84.

Propeller Shaft Splines
(Hydra-Matic and Commercial cars only)
Apply chassis lubricant to connection with grease gun.
Every 1000 miles

Body Hardware
Apply a few drops of light oil to door hinges. Clean all door striker plates and wedges and apply a small amount of washable wax.
Every 1000 miles